Stanley Graham

NISEI

The Quiet Americans

NISEI

The Quiet Americans

BY BILL HOSOKAWA

William Morrow and Company, Inc.

NEW YORK   1969

Printed in the United States of America by
Quinn & Boden Company, Inc., Rahway, N.J.

Library of Congress Catalog Card Number 73-88356

To the *Issei*,
who made it all possible

CONTENTS

Preface   ix
Foreword   xi
Prologue   xiii

PART ONE   *The Early Years*

PART TWO *The Years of Travail*

PART THREE *The Years of Fulfillment*

PREFACE

THE JAPANESE AMERICANS are a small but not insignificant segment of the United States population. Their history is unique among the stories of American minorities. Yet because their numbers are so few, their story has been all but overlooked by other Americans and was in danger of being forgotten and lost forever.

Because they believed it was a story that deserved to be preserved, the Japanese American Citizens League, a nationwide organization of fewer than 25,000 members, launched in 1962 what was called the Japanese American Research Project. Funds were contributed by members and other interested persons and $100,000 presented to the University of California at Los Angeles. UCLA in turn undertook to seek out and preserve documentary materials and gather and analyze information relating to the Japanese Americans. Despite its modest scale this research project proved to be of sufficient academic and sociological interest that the Carnegie Corporation and the National Institute of Mental Health, a federal agency, provided grants for detailed studies into specific contributions by Japanese Americans to the American way of life.

It was anticipated that a number of independent papers, both popular and scholarly, would result from the Japanese American Research Project, and, in fact, several have. The Research Project's documents were made available to this writer and a great deal of valuable material was gleaned from them. Nonetheless, this volume in much more substantial part is the product of the author's individual research, contacts with *Issei* and *Nisei*, and his own experience as a *Nisei*. In this endeavor I am deeply indebted to the many persons who took time to correspond with and be interviewed by me.

In the final analysis, however, this volume was made possible by the *Issei* and *Nisei* themselves, for they created the history which I have recorded. That history is given a particular poignancy at this time, not only because of reawakened American awareness of its minorities, but also because 1969 has been designated as the centennial of Japanese immigration to the United States, marking one hundred years since the arrival of the Wakamatsu Colony in El Dorado County, California. That event is treated in detail in Chapter 4. On June 7, 1969, the site of the Wakamatsu Colony near Coloma was dedicated as a California Historical Landmark, constituting official recognition of the not unsubstantial role of Japanese immigrants in the nation's development.

This volume is an effort to provide, among all Americans, an understanding and appreciation of the Japanese American minority, but more particularly, among my children, Mike, Susan, Pete and Christie, and their offspring, present and future. They have much to be proud of in their heritage.

Bill Hosokawa
Denver, Colorado
July 4, 1969

FOREWORD

THE UNITED STATES has been called a nation of immigrants. This it certainly is, but some immigrants have found the doors to America less open than others and the path ahead strewn with more obstacles. Until recently, the great American ideal of justice and equality for all did not seem to apply to those who differed radically in race or in cultural background from our so-called founding fathers. This limitation, of course, has been a grave injustice to those excluded, but it also has been a limitation on all Americans, making the ideal on which the nation is based less valid for everyone.

No immigrant group encountered higher walls of prejudice and discrimination than did the Japanese—the denial on racist grounds of the right to naturalization, the denial in the areas where they largely lived of the right to own land or enter certain professions, and eventually complete exclusion. None experienced a more dramatic crisis than they did when, on the outbreak of war with Japan, one hundred thousand of them—aged immigrants and their assertively loyal American-born children alike—were herded from the West Coast into what amounted to concentration camps. None retained greater faith in the basic ideals of America or showed stronger determination to establish their rights to full equality and justice, even when their fellow Americans seemed determined to deny them both. None showed greater loyalty to the United States or greater willingness to make sacrifices on the battlefield or at home for their country.

The outcome, of course, has been the great American success story writ large—a Horatio Alger tale on an ethnic scale. No group has won greater respect or a position of more solid achievement in this country than have the Americans of Japanese origin. Constituting less than half of one percent of the population, they provide today one Senator and two Congressmen in Washington and distinguished representatives in almost every major field of endeavor in our national life.

This book recounts this dramatic story of adversity, challenge, and triumph. In particular it details the role of Nisei, the "second generation" Japanese born with the citizenship denied their parents, and the organization they created, the Japanese American Citizens League, to help them win their full rights and thus help all of us move another step toward the achievement of the great American ideal.

This is, of course, no isolated story, which concerns only one small ethnic group. It has much broader significance, particularly at this time when the gravest problems our nation faces revolve around the denial of full equality and justice to large segments of our population. It should give hope to those struggling for their rights. It should give faith to all Americans in the validity of the ideal and the possibility that we can achieve it more fully. It should show to others that, although we fall short of our perhaps too loudly vaunted ideals, we are moving steadily toward their achievement.

Edwin O. Reischauer

PROLOGUE

HER NAME WAS MISS BOHAN, and a barely perceptible brogue in her speech hinted of not distant Irish forebears. If she had a first name, none of her charges was aware of it. She was a lean, lank, red-haired maiden lady who had grown old in the thankless profession of civilizing children—other people's children—who had reached their sixth birthday and therefore were both required and privileged to enroll in first grade.

Miss Bohan enforced a strict discipline and whetted the children's native curiosity into a keen desire for learning. She taught them to recognize the letters of the alphabet, count to one hundred, wipe their noses with handkerchiefs (pinned by their mothers to blouses) rather than their sleeves, raise their hands when they wished to speak or go to the lavatory, and line up in a quiet, orderly column on command. She was a dedicated teacher of a type that has all but disappeared.

More than half of her pupils had pale white skins, brown curly hair, and on Saturdays they dressed in their best clothes and went to the synagogues with their parents. There were other children with German, Scandinavian, Polish, Italian and Russian names. And although some of them did weird things to the English language, scrambling syntax in their eagerness to express themselves, Miss Bohan, somehow, understood them all.

But one child, a shy, quietly alert boy with snapping black eyes, sat with his hands folded and spoke not a word. He knew no English at all.

This boy was different from the rest in other respects. He had straight black hair. His skin was a tawny tan, the color of pale honey. For want of a better description, the anthropologists called it yellow. Miss Bohan did not know the term, but he was a *Nisei*, which is neither a disease nor a tribal name.

Nisei is a Japanese word. It means "second generation." The boy was the American-born child of Japanese immigrant parents, the *Issei*, or first generation.

Today, the word *Nisei* is recognized widely. The *Nisei* as a group have registered enough of an impression on the American scene that most dictionaries list the word. In Miss Bohan's time, shortly after the end of World War I, few other than the Japanese knew it. Acceptance of the word into the English language parallels the acceptance of the *Nisei* themselves into the stream of American life.

This particular *Nisei's* father, a short, muscular man with a bristly mustache and glasses to correct severe myopia, had been apologetic when he registered his son at school. "My boy is not speak English," he had explained painfully. "We is not teach him because we is not want him learn bad accent from me."

Miss Bohan had nodded sympathetically, but she was not perturbed. She knew that small children in her classes managed to become Americans very quickly.

Miss Bohan has a place in this story because she was this *Nisei's* first significant contact with the great, wide, wonder-filled world of America outside his family and the family's immediate circle of friends. But with that, she drops out of sight and will be heard of no more, leaving only a faint memory of patience, kindness and warm understanding, the first person among many outside his family to help shape the course of his life.

Even as he struggled with his English lessons, memorized the Pledge of Allegiance and learned the legend of George Washington and the cherry tree, the boy was vaguely aware of the Japanese heritage that made him a bit different from his classmates. But of Japan he knew next to nothing. Japan was a distant place, somewhere beyond a vast ocean, where his grandparents lived. It was also something of a fearful place. His mother told him sometimes, particularly when he toyed with his food, of the hunger that often stalked that land. From this, he learned frugality.

Sometimes when his father was angered by the lad's indolence or disobedience, he was threatened with the punishment of being sent "back to Japan" to live with the grandparents he had never met. He assumed his grandparents were kindly people; nonetheless, the threat of being shipped off to Japan was frightening enough to cause him to improve his behavior, at least for a little while.

Two other guidelines, held up frequently by his parents, helped govern his deportment. One was *Hito ni warawareru*—you will be laughed at by others. The other, *Sonna koto wo shitara haji wo kaku*—such actions will cause disgrace. This deference to the opinions of his peers led to a certain conformity of behavior until one day he staged a quiet personal teen-age rebellion and said: "To hell with what others think of me; I'll live my own life." Perhaps that was the day that completed his Americanization.

That process was started with birth when, by the act of being born on American soil, he became a citizen of the United States. The process was advanced significantly a few days before he started school when he was given an American first name, an action which in his father's eyes was both fitting and proper. (For the first few weeks the boy was dismayed to find times when he couldn't remember his new name. Later, when he was old enough, he had the name formally entered on his birth certificate.)

His progress in school was rapid. The boy who could speak no English as a first-grader was, by the time he reached sixth grade, enough of a student and class leader to be assigned the role of George Washington in a patriotic play about the travail at Valley Forge. This caused quite a stir in the community, some members of which were not ready to have a "Jap" boy take the role of Washington, no matter how deserving he might be. The boy did not learn of the furor until many years later. It is to the school principal's credit that he stood by the teacher's choice, and together they shielded the boy from this exhibition of petty bigotry. Later, he would have to fend for himself, but that was in the uncertain future.

Still, despite the shelter of school life, he was not unaware of pressures based on racial differences. He heard his parents talking about *haiseki*—social and economic discrimination and rejection because they were Japanese. He heard them discussing the Ku Klux Klan which then was experiencing a revival and terrorizing Negroes in the Deep South and threatening Catholics in many parts of the country. In immature fashion he felt compassion for the Negroes and wondered if the Japanese someday would be made a target of the Klan's hate. Once, when he went to a privately operated pool to take a Boy Scout swimming test, he was turned away by an excuse that even he recognized as lame. But the YMCA allowed him to use its pool, and he all but forgot the rebuff.

At home he learned the virtues of hard work, honesty, humility, obedience, loyalty, respect for parents and love of learning. These were attributes highly thought of by his elders, and their values became his. By the time he entered high school, the boy had developed a fierce love for the United States, its history and traditions and all it stood for. Despite the differences between him and his classmates, he shared the American dream. And he came to feel, in a way that he seldom articulated, that to be a 100 percent, red-blooded American like his heroes, he had to reject his Japanese background. This is not to say he resented his Japanese blood. He accepted that as fact, and with not a little pride while, simultaneously, he nursed a feeling that his ancestral heritage was inferior.

And yet, because he respected his parents, the rejection was neither violent nor total. It might be more accurate to say he ignored rather than rejected the old-world portion of his heritage.

The *Nisei* was shaped in thought and action, far more thoroughly than others realized, by the American school system. He was, in fact, a tribute to its capacity for molding the offspring of immigrants, whatever their port of embarkation, to the American image. There were many who doubted the ability of the schools to accomplish so much, and in the case of the *Nisei* as a group, the doubt was magnified by the matter of race. For no matter what the *Nisei* felt and how he reacted, genetically—the contours of his face, the length of his legs, the texture of his hair and the color of his skin—he was the product of centuries of breeding in Japan.

He was, thus, a creature of two worlds. He approached manhood with an American heart and mind and a Japanese face. He was steeped in the American culture but cognizant of an alien heritage as well. It was a situation fraught with complications in a society which was not quite ready for him. And so there were times, following particularly abrasive experiences, when he asked himself difficult questions: *What am I? Where am I going? What is my destiny? What can I do to claim my rightful place in this, my beloved native land?*

But before he could find answers to these and many equally provocative questions, he was engulfed in a cataclysmic war that, as surely as the nuclear bombs that ended it, destroyed the comfortable, frustrating, secure, shaky, promising, dead-end world in which he had grown up.

The end came with the violent abruptness of the Sunday morning attack on Pearl Harbor. One day he was an American—a proud, native-born United States citizen—with a Japanese face. The next, he found himself with fewer rights than enemy alien Germans and Italians. He found himself discriminated against as no other American citizens had been discriminated against before and learned to his bewildered chagrin that the highest tribunal in the land approved such extraordinary treatment. He was called on to endure what no other Americans had endured.

This was his trial by fire, and like fine steel, he emerged from the ordeal tempered, tough, resilient. Out of the bitterness and triumph of the trial came both answers and assurances. And new questions, questions only a secure person could ask:

What are my origins? What is there about my cultural heritage that sustained me in the time of trial? What have I and my people contributed to this, my country?

PART ONE

---

the early years

1

THE ORIGINS

THE ROOTS OF JAPAN are lost in the mists of antiquity. There was in the beginning, the legends say, a formless, swirling chaos. Like most myths, those of Japan are confused, complex, gory, filled with unexplainable phenomena. In some mysterious manner, the god Izanagi and the goddess Izanami emerged. Being gods, they could travel freely between heaven and terrestrial regions and accomplish other supernatural things.

This celestial couple gave birth to, among other things, the land of Yamato—the Japanese islands, the mountains on them and the seas that surround them. They must have loved these islands, for they shaped them of rare wooded loveliness, misty and craggy, green and tranquil, circled by restless blue waters. It was a land of cameo beauty—an infinite variety of mountains and hills and narrow valleys, of pine and bamboo groves, of swift-racing rivers and sandy coves—crowded into a limited space like the gardens the Japanese learned to build and love.

When the land was ready, Izanagi and Izanami produced Amaterasu, the Sun Goddess, mythical progenitor of all Japanese.

Jimmu, one of Amaterasu's descendants, was ordered by the gods to Kyushu, southernmost of the four main Japanese islands. There he conquered assorted semi-civilized tribes and laid the foundations of the Japanese Empire. The date of his coronation is set at February 11, 660 B.C., which is probably no more inaccurate than some milestone dates in the ancient history of Western civilization.

Jimmu is considered the founder of a dynasty which has extended unbroken through 135 reigns to the present emperor, Hirohito, a gently human man who in the transformation of Japan following defeat in World War II, disclaimed all pretensions to divinity.

Fundamentalists among the Japanese believed implicitly these legends of Japan's origins. Even in fairly recent times it was sacrilege as well as treason to doubt them. It is likely, however, that most *Issei*, even though they had been deeply indoctrinated as children and continued to pay lip service to the myths as adults, had their private reservations.

Scientists tell a story somewhat different from the legends. Sir George Sansom, the distinguished historian, sets the first settlement of the Japanese islands in the late Stone Age, about 5000 B.C. These were an aboriginal people, and they left little record of their life and times.

The first written records, compiled in the seventh century, Sansom writes in his *A History of Japan*, "ascribe the foundation of the Empire to . . . Jimmu who is said to have set forth from Hyuga in Kyushu in 667 B.C., and to have reached Yamato some years later. The legend as it stands is quite impossible to accept, though it certainly echoes well-based traditions of an eastward expedition of people from western Japan under a chosen leader supported by an armed force.

"It tells how they embarked in ships and went by easy stages and a roundabout route into the Inland Sea. Then, either on land or by water, they continued eastward until they reached a point near the site of the present city of Okayama, where they stayed for three years collecting provisions and preparing their ships and weapons. In the spring of 663 B.C., the record says, they reached Naniwa, at the mouth of the Yodo River, near the site of the present Osaka. There they began to meet resistance from local warriors. It was not until three years later that, with some divine assistance, opposition was overcome and the emperor was enthroned at a place called Kashiwabara . . .

"There is nothing to indicate the true date of these events, but it is hard to believe that they took place before the Kyushu leaders had been under the influence of an advanced iron culture (from the mainland) long enough to allow them to form a combination of clans and to equip a considerable fighting force with superior weapons. A likely date for the eastward migration appears to be about A.D. 350, or perhaps a generation sooner."

If this is so, it would eliminate about 1,000 years from the traditional version of Japanese history.

Professor Edwin O. Reischauer of Harvard, former ambassador to Japan, suggests the imperial family stemmed from the priest-chiefs of the Yamato clan who overwhelmed other priest-chiefs during the third or fourth century. In his *Japan Past and Present*, Reischauer notes: "This was not so spectacular an origin as the direct descent from a Sun Goddess claimed in Japanese tradition. Nevertheless, it was an origin of great antiquity when compared with the origins of other ruling families of the world."

The first residents of the Japanese islands probably were the ancestors of the present-day Ainu, classified by anthropologists as proto-Caucasoid (*proto*, first in time; *Caucasoid*, of or relating to the white race), who probably migrated from the continent. A few full-blooded Ainu still survive, mainly in villages in northern Japan. Their position is roughly comparable to the role of the Indian in American society. The typical Ainu is short and powerfully built, with heavy facial and body hair and frequently, light-colored eyes.

"The Japanese," say Alfred Crofts and Percy Buchanan in *A History of the Far East*, "form in many ways a racial enigma." They show Mongolian as well as Malay-Polynesian characteristics as many *Nisei* have discovered in examining each other. Sansom suggests the Japanese are the product of an intermingling of people who came from the South Seas by way of Formosa, and those who migrated from China through Korea, plus the aboriginal Ainu. But, he adds, "the truth is that we have not enough evidence to form a valid opinion about the origins and composition of the Japanese people."

Reischauer, noting the relative hairiness of the Japanese compared to other Mongoloid peoples, says their bristling mustaches may well be their Ainu legacy.

The first reliable records of Japanese history go back only to about the third century A.D., a comparatively recent period when compared to China's well-documented Hsia dynasty, somewhere around 2000 B.C., and the Egyptian Empire which goes back to about 3000 B.C.

In the third century of the Christian era what is now Japan was divided into a large number of small tribal units among which feminine rule was not uncommon. At the same time, the mighty Roman Empire, having spread its borders to include the barbaric tribesmen of the British Isles, had begun to decline. Greek civilization had bloomed and faded centuries earlier.

Japan, however, under the influence of the flourishing Chinese civilization and protected by the relative isolation of the islands, made rapid cultural progress. The records show that Chinese and Korean arts and handicrafts began to reach Japan about the fifth century. Scribes using Chinese script appeared in the Japanese imperial court about this time. Buddhism arrived in Japan from Korea in 552, launching a wave of temple-building (paid for by heavy taxes) and helping to shape the basis of much of Japanese philosophy. Clans rose, ruled for a period and were overthrown. Centuries slipped by, and the distinctive Japanese culture evolved. In 1004 a court lady named Murasaki Shikibu wrote *The Tales of Genji,* the world's first novel. This was nearly four hundred years before Geoffrey Chaucer, first great literary artist to write in English.

An aristocracy developed, often living in debauchery while serfs toiled to keep them in food and luxuries. While the aristocrats practiced effete arts, military families created the *samurai* or warrior caste which glorified honor and fidelity and professed a contempt of death. The literature of Japan is rich in tales of *samurai* derring-do, men of courage and dedication and fabulous skills with the long sword. These swords, creations of master craftsmen whose spiritual descendants run Japan's booming steel industry today, were surrounded by a reverence and mysticism comparable to that accorded King Arthur's Excalibur.

Professor Claude A. Buss of Stanford University writes in his book, *The Far East:* "In spite of individual variations, the Japanese displayed from earliest times characteristics which stamped them apart from the rest of the world . . . Spartan virtues were cultivated as a means of strengthening character. The Japanese made life hard for themselves by cultivating the pleasures of the flesh and then sacrificing them to duty. The strong were those who disregarded personal happiness and conformed to the rigors of prescribed conduct."

Wars, famine, pestilence came and went along with periods of social reform and a flourishing of the arts. Ambitious warlords crossed the 90-mile-wide Straits of Tsushima to invade and occupy portions of Korea in at least three periods of history. But Japan was also endangered from abroad. In 1274 and 1281, Mongol legions under Kublai Khan assembled ships for an invasion of Japan. What the Mongols lacked was a reliable weather forecaster. Both times typhoons swept up from the south and scattered the Mongol fleet before it could land troops in Japan. These were the original *Kamikaze*, the "divine winds" that saved the nation. Young pilots who plunged their bomb-laden aircraft into American warships were a latter-day *Kamikaze*. They wreaked ghastly damage but failed to halt the Allied advance on the Japanese islands in the final phases of World War II.

The peasants grew rice, paid taxes and clung stubbornly to their generally miserable lives. Their lot was little different from that of serfs in medieval Europe. And much as they did in Europe, legends grew around warrior heroes—the kind, fearless men who by amazing feats of swordsmanship and valor vanquished bandits, evil warlords and others who preyed on the poor and meek.

Oddly enough, among commoners the peasants ranked at the top of the status ladder. At the very summit were the aristocracy, or *kizoku*. Next came the *samurai* warriors, the *shizoku*. Then followed the commoners, or *heimin*, who were divided into three classes. The farmers (*nomin*) had the highest status "for one who owns the rice fields holds the life of the nation in his hands." Next were the artisans (*konin*), and at the bottom were the traders and merchants (*shonin*), the nonproductive money grubbers. Still, money talks. Merchants lent money to impoverished *samurai* and to the farmers when crops were bad or at tax-paying time. Whatever their social standing, the influence of the merchant class was considerable.

Periodic civil wars wracked the country as rival clans vied for territory and influence or sought to avenge affronts, real and imagined. The Onin War, which broke out between rival lords in 1467, launched nearly a century of civil strife. This was the situation when the first Europeans reached Japan.

The date was 1543, just fifty-one years after the first voyage of Columbus. Portuguese merchant captains, pushing ever eastward in their search for silk, gold and spices, skirted the southeast coast of Asia. Three seamen on one of these expeditions staged an un-successful mutiny off Thailand and escaped to a Chinese pirate junk. The junk in turn was wrecked near Japan. The three Portu-guese made their way ashore on Tanegashima, an island off the southern coast of Kyushu. What happened to them is not clear; it is likely they were looked upon as uncouth barbarians and de-ported to China.

This was a momentous time in history. Henry VIII, he of the many marriages, was on the throne of England. Only twenty-two years earlier, Magellan's tiny fleet had circumnavigated the globe for the first time, missing Japan but establishing that the world was indeed round. It was to be thirty more years before Sir Francis Drake would cruise up the west coast of the Americas.

The first Portuguese visitors to Japan were quickly followed by others, primarily merchants in search of peaceful trade. But close behind them were the indefatigable missionaries. The famous Jesuit priest, St. Francis Xavier, arrived in Japan in 1549 and re-mained two years during which he gained a number of converts. He was quick to note the combativeness of the people, writing: "The Japanese have a high opinion of themselves because they think that no other nation can compare with them as regards weapons and valor, and so they look down on all foreigners. They greatly prize and value their arms, and prefer to have good weap-ons, decorated with gold and silver, more than anything else in the world . . . They are very warlike and are always involved in wars, and thus the ablest man becomes the greatest lord."

By the time Sir Walter Raleigh established the first Roanoke Colony in Virginia in 1584—it was quickly abandoned—Christianity was so strongly established in Japan that the brilliant warlord Toyotomi Hideyoshi was preparing to banish Portuguese mission-aries as a potential political danger to his regime. Hideyoshi died without enforcing his deportation order. In 1600 Ieyasu, the first of the remarkable Tokugawa clan, defeated a coalition of his rivals in the battle of Sekigahara and took over as ruler of all the land. The imperial family was pushed into the background, and the Tokugawas were to run the country as *shogun* (regents) until the restoration of the emperor in 1868.

Meanwhile, early in the Tokugawa era, a most significant series of events took place. A Spanish galleon bound from Manila across the Pacific to Mexico was wrecked in Japanese waters. The survivors, including the Spanish governor, Don Rodrigo de Vevero, were entertained by Japanese officials who undertook to build another ship for the Spaniards. Properly supplied and outfitted, this ship set sail for the New World with twenty-three Japanese merchants and two noblemen among those aboard.

Zelia Nutthall in her scholarly paper, *The Earliest Historical Relations Between Mexico and Japan*, tells us the ship reached Acapulco sometime in August of 1610—a decade before the *Mayflower* landed the Pilgrims at Plymouth Rock. Some of the Japanese made the overland trip to Mexico City before sailing home again. Three years later, Miss Nutthall reports, a larger party of Japanese sailed to Acapulco. Some crossed Mexico and journeyed on to Spain. A dozen Japanese Christians remained in Mexico when their ship returned home. They apparently were the first Japanese immigrants in North America, although there is no record of what happened to them.

At this dramatic point in history, Japan was in position to establish colonies on the west coast of North America, just as England, France and Spain were busily colonizing the east coast. One can only guess at what might have happened if the Tokugawas had directed their energies and ambitions across the Pacific rather than to internal matters—perhaps we might be viewing television dramas of painted Indians stalking eastbound wagon trains of *samurai* and their families.

But this was not to be. The Pacific was a vast ocean, Mexico held little of interest to the Japanese leaders, and there were pressing domestic problems. In 1617, four years after the second expedition to Mexico, Tokugawa Hidetada took the initial steps to sever all intercourse with the West. Disillusioned by quarreling among the various European national groups and religious sects in Japan, he intensified the persecution of missionaries and the estimated 300,000 Japanese Christians. By 1623, British traders left Japan, and a year later all Spaniards were driven out. In 1636—just ten years after Peter Minuit bought Manhattan Island from the Indians for twenty-four dollars—Japanese were forbidden to go abroad. Those abroad were not allowed to return, and all ocean-going junks were destroyed.

In the next few years all Portuguese merchants were expelled, and Dutch traders were confined to Deshima, a tiny island in the harbor of Nagasaki. For more than two centuries this was to be Japan's only window to the outside world. (In one of those strange repetitions of history, China went into a somewhat comparable self-imposed isolation after the Communist takeover in 1949, with the British Crown Colony of Hongkong serving as its window.)

But even though Japan was sealed off from the world, she was like a chrysalis undergoing many basic changes that prepared her to make her own great leap forward once the doors were reopened.

An Encyclopedia of World History, edited by William L. Langer of Harvard University, has this to say of the years of isolation:

"The peace and prosperity of the early Tokugawa period brought a gradual rise in the standard of living and an increase in the population as well as in the national wealth. With the growth of industry and commerce, a powerful merchant class grew up in the larger cities, and a gradual transition from a rice economy to a money economy commenced. This transition, together with the rise in living standards and the increase in population tended to make production inadequate and brought about great economic ills during much of the period.

"Political conservatism and isolation from the rest of the world made the Tokugawa period outwardly stagnant, but it was inwardly a time of great intellectual development. Buddhism was in decline and Christianity was early stamped out, but there was a great revival of lay learning, the old feudal code of conduct received definite formulation under the name of *Bushido*, Confucian philosophy enjoyed a protracted period of unparalleled growth and popularity, philosophers and teachers of ethics abounded, there was a revival of interest in Japanese antiquity, *Shinto* developed new life both as a nationalistic philosophy and as a popular religion, and the newly arisen merchant class contributed greatly to the intellectual and cultural growth of the land."

Nor were the Japanese unaware of what was going on in the rest of the world. In 1720, Yoshimune, one of the ablest of the Tokugawa rulers, removed the ban on the study of Europe and the importation of European books. In Nagasaki, students of Dutch probed into the Occident's store of scientific knowledge—medicine, chemistry, cartography, military tactics, shipbuilding, and the like.

They studied all they could about the West—its history and geography, government, industry and way of life. Later, American seamen shipwrecked on the shores of Japan were questioned exhaustively about their country.

One account reports that as early as 1708 a book that dealt in part with North America, titled *A Study of the Commerce of Chinese and Other Barbarians*, was published in Japan. The United States was described as "a country cold and large . . . the natives are pugnacious and love to fight."

There seems to be no simple explanation for the interest of the isolated Japanese in the West. Foster Rhea Dulles in his very readable book, *Yankees and Samurai*, observes that "there was always among the Japanese, in spite of their seclusion, a natural curiosity and thirst for knowledge." Apart from their interest in Europe, they were anxious to discover what they could of the new country which the Dutch told them had been established in the Western Hemisphere—"those onetime English colonies that had become the United States."

It is likely that the information filtering through the Deshima window impressed on Japanese scholars the fact that outside, while Japan was enjoying her isolation, strange and wonderful things were happening. And having seen a little, they were anxious to learn more. Perhaps the Japanese also were aware of the economic and political foothold European powers were carving out in other parts of Asia; they were astute enough to realize the walls of isolationism would not protect them forever, and it was only prudent to be prepared to meet the West on its own terms, "with respect but not fear."

At any rate, when Commodore Matthew Calbraith Perry first dropped anchor in the Bay of Yedo (now Tokyo) in 1853, his officers were greatly surprised at how much the Japanese knew about the U.S. Dulles writes:

"They knew all about steamships, although those in Perry's squadron were the first that had ever visited their shores; they even knew the make of the guns with which the vessels were armed. When they asked their visitors where they came from and were somewhat superciliously answered the United States, they quickly made it clear that they meant what city: New York, Philadelphia, Washington? 'There can be no doubt,' the official report of the expedition compiled by Francis L. Hawks states, 'that however backward the Japanese themselves may be in practical science, the best educated among them are tolerably well informed of its progress among more civilized or rather cultivated nations.' . . .

"When the members of Perry's squadron celebrated Washington's birthday at Uraga, on February 22, 1854, it was remarked that the 'Japanese seemed perfectly acquainted with the name of the great father of our country.' Because of their own mistrust of the British, Washington had become something of a hero to the Japanese."

What the visitors did not realize at the time was that American histories of the United States, translated and published in China, had reached Japan. Translated once more into Japanese—and no doubt embellished with information from other sources—these books had enjoyed a wide circulation in that country. In fact, says Dulles, the Dutch had told them a year before he arrived that "a person named Perry" was expected to lead an armed American expedition to Japan.

2

MEETING OF TWO NATIONS

THE RECORDS SHOW that relations between the United States and Japan were formalized for the first time on March 31, 1854, with the signing of the Treaty of Kanagawa. While it was something of a shotgun wedding performed under the muzzles of Commodore Perry's guns, the intent was noble. Article One of the Treaty reads:

"There shall be a perfect, permanent and universal peace, and a sincere and cordial amity, between the United States of America on the one part, and the Empire of Japan on the other, and between their people, respectively, without exception of persons or places."

No one can quarrel with this lofty ideal, but it proved to be less than durable, and as it so often does among nations, "permanent" turned out to be only a relatively few years.

Actually, Perry was something of a late-comer. As William Harlan Hale has written, "There had been prior contact of a sort; in fact, over a hundred American ships, curious, had at various times dared the approach to the forbidden islands, but usually they were just driven off."

The first American ships to call in Japan were received without open hostility. The *Lady Washington*, commanded by Capt. John Kendrick, and the *Grace*, Capt. James Douglas, dropped anchor in the port of Kashinoura, on the Kii Peninsula not far from Osaka, one day in the spring of 1791. The two ships were homeward bound after a trading voyage to Canton, China. Apparently the visit was brief and uneventful.

Between 1797 and 1807, Dulles says, eight different American ships called at Nagasaki. However, they were under charter to the Dutch East Indies Company and flew the Dutch flag when they entered port. American seamen were permitted ashore. They traded for lacquerware, silks and porcelains and took them home to New England.

By 1820, an ever-increasing number of American whaling ships prowled northern Japanese waters in the worldwide hunt for oil. Some of these ships tried to put into Japanese ports for provisions and water, and usually were ordered away. Inevitably, some ships foundered in the stormy waters. Seamen who managed to make shore were usually imprisoned as spies. Some were executed. Others were taken in time to Deshima to be repatriated by the Dutch.

This was the background for a rising tide of sentiment in the United States that something ought to be done to bring Japan out of her seclusion. First, of course, there was a demand for an understanding that would guarantee more humane treatment for shipwrecked American seamen. But there were other important pressures at work.

The prospect of trade with Japan was inviting, and American merchants were anxious to get their foot into the door before their European competitors. There was also a sense of "Manifest Destiny," the feeling that now the American continent was spanned from ocean to ocean, it was the nation's responsibility to press on, awaken Asia and bring Japan into the family of nations. "It is our Manifest Destiny to implant ourselves in Asia," the New York *Herald* editorialized.

It was under these circumstances that President Millard Fillmore authorized Commodore Perry to lead an expedition to Japan. His mission was to "persuade" the Japanese to change their ancient anti-foreign laws in the interests of "friendship, commerce, a supply of coal and provisions, and protection for our shipwrecked people."

The decision as to whether force should be used in the process of persuasion was left to Perry. It was to be a peaceful mission, but Perry's fleet was heavily armed, and he had instructions to use his guns if attacked. Today, if an American military commander were given such blank check authority, there would be an enormous public and congressional outcry. In Perry's time it took months to get word halfway around the world, and the man on the spot had to have the authority to make decisions. Fortunately,

Perry found cannons talked loudly even when they were silent.

Perry set out with a squadron of four ships. Two were the first coal-burning paddlewheelers in U.S. naval history, the U.S.S. *Mississippi* and the *Susquehanna*. After a stop in Hongkong, the squadron headed for Japan with Perry, being a prudent man, preparing for the worst. Daily, he oversaw battle drills in which the crews practiced repelling imaginary boarders, and the bands played "Yankee Doodle" after each simulated victory.

On July 8, 1853, Perry's ships sailed cautiously into the Bay of Yedo and anchored off the village of Uraga. To the men aboard the flotilla of small boats that came to greet them, Perry made known his wish to deliver a letter from President Fillmore to the Japanese Emperor.

Perry did not know that the Emperor was merely a figurehead in a government run by the *shogun*. American diplomatic intelligence even then had its shortcomings. Nonetheless, Perry met with Japanese emissaries on July 14, delivered the letter, and left three days later for South China waters after promising he would return in the spring—with a larger naval force, he pointed out. The American commander must have presented an impressive sight— powerfully built despite his sixty years, haughty, formal, unmistakably firm. Dulles observes:

"There was something in the nature of this naval commander that foreshadowed the character of another American military figure who nearly a century later steamed into this same Bay of Yedo . . . aboard the U.S.S. *Missouri* to make far more drastic demands upon Japan. For Commodore Perry had much the same personal arrogance and much the same sense of destiny that would stamp General MacArthur."

Hale advances another view of the Perry mission: "A fact our schoolbooks sometimes neglect to teach is that Perry's expedition, undertaken by special decision of President and Cabinet, was at bottom an act of aggression and a virtual challenge to war. Perry's genius, for all his bluster and his pivot guns, lay in his preventing an actual war and in achieving a peaceable agreement that surmounted immense barriers of language, culture, suspicion and ignorance and afforded satisfaction and respect all around."

By fortunate coincidence for all concerned, Perry arrived at a time when Japan was in political ferment. A demand was growing for restoration of the Emperor to the throne. The shogunate realized that to give in to the foreigners weakened their position, yet they knew they were in no shape to repel an armed invasion. Many of the provincial lords urged resistance to the death. But Japan had little with which to turn back warships of the U.S. Navy. The reluctant decision was to negotiate when Perry returned—to make the fewest possible concessions but also to avoid war. No doubt it was the lesson of this experience—of having to negotiate from a position of weakness—that spurred Japan to adopt Western technology and build up her army and navy with frantic haste once she opened her doors.

In March of 1854 Perry returned as he had promised, this time with a fleet of ten of the great "black ships."

The Americans were welcomed with much pageantry and fanfare, and Perry, no mean showman himself, responded in kind. The bay seemed to be filled with black ships when Perry came ashore on March 8, accompanied by an honor guard of U.S. Marines with bayonet-tipped rifles. *Samurai* warriors with topknots, armed with swords and halberds, stared in both wonder and disdain as Perry's men marched smartly to the specially prepared Treaty House in Yokohama. As Perry entered, his ships fired a 21-gun salute with their deck cannon in honor of the Emperor, and 17 guns for the Japanese commissioner to the meeting, filling the scene with thunder and smoke, startling the *samurai* and sending small children scurrying for cover. Toasts and gifts were exchanged. (Among the American gifts presented later were a tiny steam locomotive and cars, the first the Japanese had seen, and 100 gallons of Kentucky bourbon. History does not record which was the more appreciated.) Entertainment was part of the occasion. American Negroes put on a minstrel show while Japanese sumo wrestlers astounded the Yankees with their size.

In the course of the ceremonies the Japanese handed Perry a scroll which he interpreted as an answer to President Fillmore's letter. The answer was, in a way, reminiscent of other meetings between American military men and Indian tribal leaders yielding to the inevitability of progress. The Japanese note restated the importance of "the laws of our imperial ancestors" but acknowledged that times had changed, making it essential to consider favorably President Fillmore's proposal for opening friendly relations. "We are governed now by imperative necessity," the Japanese note admitted somewhat sadly.

It is something of a wonder that anything as complicated as a treaty changing the entire course of a nation—and the world, for that matter—should be negotiated by parties which could scarcely understand each other. On one side were Perry and his interpreter, S. Wells Williams, a onetime missionary to China. On the other, Hayashi Daigaku-no-Kami, rector of the University of Yedo who had been upgraded in rank and hurriedly drafted as negotiator, and his interpreter, Moriyama Einosuke. Moriyama had learned something of English from the Dutch at Deshima and through contacts with American sailors who passed through the port while being deported. In view of Japanese difficulties with the English language in later years, it does not seem probable that Moriyama was well-qualified. He also quickly disgusted the Americans by scuttling between one party and the other on his knees. This may have been quite proper from the Japanese understanding of etiquette, but it did nothing to strengthen American confidence in him. Nonetheless, with generous amounts of good will being demonstrated by both sides, a basic agreement—the Treaty of Kanagawa—was signed March 31, 1854.

Reischauer writes: "Once the door had been pushed open a crack, there was no closing it. Within two years Yedo had signed treaties with England, Russia and Holland, and in 1856 Townsend Harris, the first American consul general, arrived in Japan to negotiate a full commercial treaty. This he concluded two years later, and the European powers soon made similar treaties with Japan. The door was now wide open."

3

THE FIRST ISSEI

LONG BEFORE COMMODORE PERRY knocked on the gates of Japan there had been contact of sorts between that nation and the New World. As we have seen, at least two Japanese ships voyaged to Mexico in 1610 and 1613. But there is reason to believe that even prior to this time there must have been unplanned traffic from the Japanese islands to North America, carried there on the ocean tides which the Japanese call Kuroshiwo—the Black Current. It swings northward through the Pacific past the Japanese islands, looping toward the east in a great semicircle past the Aleutians, and southward again along the West Coast of the United States. This is the mysterious ocean stream, traveling at only a few miles an hour, that is responsible for the temperate winters of the Pacific Northwest States.

The early Japanese had no idea, of course, that a continent lay to the east on the other side of the ocean, although they knew something of navigation and their pirates and traders ventured deep into Southeast Asia. Yet, who is to deny that in the distant past a hardy fisherman or two or three, cast adrift by a storm, did not survive the long, slow journey with this current and make landfall on the North American continent? Even today the flotsam and jetsam tossed on Pacific beaches after a storm often include timbers with Japanese markings and buoyant glass balls that Japanese fishermen use to keep their nets afloat.

There is record of several such incredible voyages in more modern times. One source reports that in 1814 the British ship *Forrester* rescued the three survivors of a crew of seventeen on a junk drifting off what is now Santa Barbara, California. The men were nursed back to health, placed aboard a ship for Kamchatka, and presumably sent home by the Russians.

Greater detail is available about a Japanese rice-carrying sampan which was swept adrift by a storm in 1833 and made its way across the North Pacific. It is not known how many men were aboard, but three survived the trip, probably due in no small part to the nature of their cargo. The boat was washed ashore near Queen Charlotte Island, in the northern part of what is now British Columbia. Indians held them prisoner for a year when they were rescued by a Hudson's Bay Company ship and taken to London. An American ship transported them by way of the Cape of Good Hope to Macao where they were placed aboard another American vessel, the *Morrison*, along with four Japanese fishermen ship-wrecked in the Philippines. S. Wells Williams, the missionary who was to interpret for Perry, was also on the ship. The *Morrison's* mission was twofold: to seek trade with Japan, and to introduce Christianity. The Americans hoped to win Japanese favor by returning the seven castaways.

Alas, their hopes were in vain. The *Morrison* was fired on in the Bay of Yedo and at Kagoshima on Kyushu. The ship returned to Macao with the Japanese still aboard, and there is no record as to what happened to them. Only the hostility of their own people prevented the three sailors from being the first Japanese to circle the globe.

The first Japanese to live in the United States for any length of time was Manjiro Nakahama. He might be called the first *Issei*. His remarkable life story is told in considerable detail by Hisakazu Kaneko in a book titled, appropriately enough, *Manjiro, the Man Who Discovered America*.

Manjiro also was a fisherman, born in 1827 in the village of Nakanohama in Tosa Province, on the Pacific Ocean side of Shikoku, smallest of the four main Japanese islands. In January of 1841, when Manjiro was fourteen years old, he and four other villagers set out on a fishing expedition. A storm came up, and they drifted for thirteen days before reaching a small, uninhabited island. Five months later, ragged, unkempt and hungry, they were rescued by the whaler *John Howland* from New Bedford, Massachusetts, whose captain was William H. Whitfield.

Manjiro was an unusually alert lad and Captain Whitfield took a liking to him. Four of the castaways were left at Honolulu in the Hawaiian islands, but Manjiro accepted Whitfield's invitation to visit the United States.

Like so many others, Captain Whitfield had trouble with Japanese names. So he changed Manjiro to John Mung. During the long voyage around Cape Horn and northward along the coasts of two continents, Manjiro picked up a good deal of English and learned the duties of a seaman. He was a sturdy, broad-shouldered young man of sixteen when the *John Howland* reached its home port of New Bedford on May 7, 1843.

Author Kaneko, perhaps with some poetic license, has Whitfield saying: "We've at last come home, John Mung!" And Manjiro replies: "I can't believe my eyes, Captain. It's like a dream."

Since Whitfield was a widower, he asked a friend named Eben Akin to take Manjiro into his home. Manjiro thus became the first Japanese schoolboy. He did chores around the house for his room and board while attending a private school to learn to read and write English. Meanwhile, Whitfield remarried and bought a farm near Fairhaven with the profits of his whaling expedition, and Manjiro went to live with him while continuing his education.

And like those Japanese who were to come later, Manjiro ran into discrimination. One Sunday Manjiro went to church with the Whitfields. Kaneko reports:

"One of the deacons of the church, who had been horrified, came to see Captain Whitfield after a few weeks and told him that the Japanese boy would have to sit in the pew for Negroes, because some of the members had objected to having Manjiro sit in the captain's pew. Captain Whitfield bowed politely and made no reply . . . Immediately he took a pew in another church but soon met the same result. Before long the captain found that a Unitarian Church was willing to admit John Mung into the fold."

Whitfield joined the church, one of whose more prominent members was Warren Delano, a part-owner of the *John Howland*. In time, Warren Delano was to have a great-grandson named Franklin Delano Roosevelt who became the thirty-second President of the United States, and who was to have a peculiar role in the history of the Japanese in the U.S.

In school Manjiro proved to be an apt student. He excelled in mathematics and learned surveying and navigation. When Captain

Whitfield went to sea again, Manjiro became an apprentice cooper and learned to make the barrels used to store whale oil.

Three years after he reached New Bedford, Manjiro was offered a berth on a ship called the *Franklin* being outfitted for a whaling cruise. Manjiro had experienced pangs of homesickness and although he mentioned it to no one, he saw the voyage as a chance to return to Japan. With Mrs. Whitfield's blessing, he signed aboard and on May 15, 1846, he set sail across the Atlantic.

Manjiro's knowledge of navigation and seamanship made him a valuable member of the crew as the *Franklin* touched at the Azores, skirted the Cape of Good Hope and slowly made her way into the Southwest Pacific. In March, 1847, the ship dropped anchor at Guam, then sailed along the coast of Taiwan and the Ryuku Islands in search of whales. By August, the ship was 150 miles off northern Japan. Once the Americans encountered a fleet of Japanese fishing boats, but Manjiro could not understand the men's dialect and found no opportunity to go ashore with them.

In October, the *Franklin* put in at Honolulu. Seven years had passed since Manjiro had left his Japanese friends there. The one called Jusuke, he found, was dead. Denzo and his brother Goemon had been granted land by Queen Kakaluohi and had made their living as fishermen, but only a year earlier had boarded a whaler to return to Japan. Only Toraemon remained, working as a carpenter. Manjiro located him and they had a happy reunion. A few weeks later Denzo and Goemon returned to Honolulu. The captain had refused to put them ashore on an uninhabited island off Japan where they had first stopped, and stormy weather had prevented another try.

After a month in Hawaii the *Franklin* put to sea again. When the captain fell ill, he was left in Manila and Manjiro was named the ship's second officer. In August, 1849, after a voyage of more than three years, the *Franklin* returned to its home port with several thousand barrels of oil in her holds. Manjiro's share of the profits was $350. Captain Whitfield had come home only a short time earlier, and he welcomed Manjiro warmly.

Manjiro was happy with the Whitfields and well treated in Fairhaven, but he still wanted to get back to Japan. For one thing, he wished to see his mother. But, says author Kaneko, he wanted to go back "to tell his countrymen that Japan could no longer remain isolated from the rest of the world."

News of the California gold rush helped Manjiro make up his mind. For fear of offending the Whitfields with his concern for Japan, he said only that he wished to go to the gold fields. In October, 1849, Manjiro and a friend remembered only as Tilley signed as deckhands aboard a lumber ship bound for California by way of Cape Horn. The following May they arrived in San Francisco, took a paddlewheeler to Sacramento, and proceeded by foot and horseback into the mining country. They worked as mine laborers for a month, just long enough to save money to buy equipment, then staked out a claim of their own. Their luck was good. In two months Manjiro had found enough gold to exchange for "600 pieces of silver." He gave his share of the claim and tools to Tilley and quickly arranged to work for his passage to Honolulu.

Once more he looked up Toraemon, Denzo and Goemon. Toraemon by this time had determined to remain in Hawaii. Since no American ships would agree to take him all the way to Japan, the ingenious Manjiro bought a whaleboat, which he named the *Adventure*, and arranged for the clipper ship *Sarah Boyd*, bound for Shanghai, to drop him off the Japanese coast together with Denzo and Goemon.

On January 2, 1851, the *Sarah Boyd* stopped four miles off the southern tip of Okinawa. The *Adventure*, heavily loaded with food, gifts, books and Manjiro's personal effects, was lowered over the side. Manjiro waved farewell to his benefactors, and the three Japanese set out for the shore they had departed unwillingly so long ago. But the welcome home, after ten long years, was anything but warm. The Okinawan villagers could not understand Manjiro and he had no idea what they were saying. Petty officials took charge of the three. Once the officials were convinced the strangers were Japanese (their ability to eat rice with chopsticks was evidence in their favor), they were not mistreated, but were kept under virtual house arrest and questioned almost daily about their experiences, apparently more as a matter of curiosity than for security reasons. The party was held six months in Okinawa, two months at Satsuma and ten months at Nagasaki—a delay of a year and a half in all—before they were cleared to go home to Tosa.

Word of Manjiro's return preceded him to the village of Nakanohama. Manjiro had a tearful reunion on October 5, 1852, with his widowed mother. But there was no rest for this Japanese who knew more than any of his countrymen about faraway lands.

Within three days the lord of Tosa summoned him to teach a class of young men about the wonders of the civilized world outside Japan. Not long afterward Manjiro was called to Yedo. Officials there had been forewarned by the Dutch of Perry's impending arrival, and they were anxious to learn about the United States and how to deal with the American emissaries.

U.S. Captain John Mercer Brooke, who helped the Japanese to make their first modern transpacific voyage with the *Kanrin Maru* in 1860, noted of Manjiro in his report: "I am satisfied that he had more to do with the opening of Japan than any man living."

Dulles says in his book: "While this may have been an extreme judgment, hardly warranted by the known facts, this first Japanese to know the United States at first hand was certainly highly influential in persuading the officials of the *Bakufu* (feudal government) that the objectives of the Perry expedition were wholly peaceful."

Manjiro quickly learned to be diplomatic in his conversations with Japanese officialdom. Some were extremely eager to learn about America. But others resented being told the Western world was superior. Once, when he remarked that American horses were bigger and more powerful than Japanese horses, he found himself being accused of disrespect for his country. He realized how insular his countrymen had become when he was asked questions like: "How is it possible for Americans to live without rice?"

Some of his observations about the New World were quaint and touching. For example:

"Refined Americans generally do not touch liquor. Even if they do so they drink only a little, because they think that liquor makes men either lazy or quarrelsome. Vulgar Americans, however, drink just like Japanese."

"American men, even officials, do not carry swords as the *samurai* do. But when they go on a journey, even common men usually carry with them two or three pistols; their pistol is somewhat equivalent to the sword of the *samurai*."

"American women have quaint customs; for instance, some of them make a hole through the lobes of their ears and run a gold or silver ring through this hole as an ornament."

"For their wedding ceremony, the Americans merely make a proclamation to the gods, and become married, after which they usually go on a sightseeing trip to the mountains. They are lewd by nature, but otherwise well-behaved."

(The first Americans to visit Japan were convinced that the Japanese were a lewd people because of their custom of mixed bathing.)

"When a mother happens to have very little milk in her breasts to give her child, she gives of all things a cow's milk as a substitute. But it is true that no ill effect of this strange habit has been reported."

"Toilets are placed over holes in the ground. It is customary to read books in them."

Manjiro had been summoned to Yedo to serve as an interpreter when Perry arrived, but Kaneko reports isolationist elements in the government opposed his employment because he advocated "progressive ideas in favor of the opening of the country" and they feared he "might reveal some of the secrets of the country to the Americans and conclude the negotiations on their own terms."

Japan, however, could ill afford to ignore a man of Manjiro's experiences and abilities. Manjiro later was commissioned to translate into Japanese a book on navigation, and he taught navigation and engineering at the newly established Naval Training School. He taught Japanese fishermen American whaling techniques, and he was the official interpreter and navigation instructor when Japan sent the *Kanrin Maru* to the United States.

She was a sailing vessel with a small steam engine, purchased from the Dutch and outfitted as a warship. A party of about a hundred Japanese was aboard, including several lords and Shimmi Buzen-no-Kami, the first ambassador to the United States. Captain Brooke, mentioned earlier, was on the ship as an adviser when it set sail for San Francisco accompanied by the U.S. warship *Powhatan*. The *Kanrin Maru* entered the Golden Gate and tied up in San Francisco on March 17, 1860, the first of thousands of Japanese flag vessels that were to bring passengers and cargo into this great port.

It had been ten years since Manjiro had passed through San Francisco on his way home. In 1850 it had been a rough frontier town, burning with gold fever. Now Manjiro saw an orderly community with wide streets and handsome buildings. The Japanese were escorted to the International Hotel and met Governor John

At the White House on May 17, 1860, Japanese envoys wearing *eboshi* headgear and silken sandals presented a state letter from the Shogun to President James Buchanan. (Engraving from *Frank Leslie's Illustrated.*)

G. Downey. Manjiro performed efficiently as interpreter at the many official functions where the Japanese were warmly received. One typically superficial newspaper account noted that the Japanese "seemed to be far better-mannered than the Chinese" who already were in California in substantial numbers as laborers.

Most of the Japanese party boarded the *Powhatan* in San Francisco and sailed for Panama. They crossed the isthmus by train, then took another U.S. warship, the *Roanoke*, for Washington where they were received by President James Buchanan.

A diary kept by Norimasa Muragaki, second in command of the Japanese mission, provides some interesting insights. He was surprised to find Buchanan "wore a simple black costume of coat and trousers in the same fashion as any merchant, and had no decoration or sword on him."

At a ball in honor of the Japanese, Muragaki noted the dancing couples "went 'round and 'round as nimbly as so many white mice on the monotonous walk, without even making fluttering gestures with their hands." This last, no doubt, was in reference to Japanese dances in which hand gestures are as important as foot movements.

And of American women: "Ladies of this country are all fair-complexioned and beautiful, always dressed handsomely, wearing gold and silver ornaments. Although we are getting accustomed to their appearance, we find their reddish hair uninteresting as it reminds us of canine eyes. We have come across, less frequently, ladies with dark hair and dark eyes. They must have been descended from some Oriental races. Naturally, they appeared to be more beautiful."

When Helen Lane, the President's niece, asked Muragaki whether American or Japanese women were "superior," he replied diplomatically:

"American ladies are the more beautiful of the two with their fair complexions." But he noted in his diary: "She and her companions looked well-pleased. They must be of a very believing nature."

After triumphant tours of Philadelphia and New York, the Japanese left on the U.S. ship *Niagara* for home by way of the Cape of Good Hope. Manjiro helped sail the *Kanrin Maru* back across the Pacific, taking with him dictionaries, a sewing machine and photographic equipment. He well might be considered the father of Japan's now-thriving camera industry.

Ten years later, in 1870, Manjiro accompanied another Japanese mission to Europe by way of the United States. The party landed in San Francisco, then proceeded across the United States by rail. While in New York Manjiro took time to hurry up to Fairhaven to see his old benefactor, Captain Whitfield, and revisit the scenes of his youth. Manjiro suffered a light stroke soon after his return to Japan and was never very active again. He died in 1898 and is buried in Tokyo.

While Manjiro was the first and most notable of the early Japanese to spend time in the United States, he had a number of lesser known contemporaries. Some time after Manjiro was taken to Massachusetts another fisherman, Senpachi, was rescued under now-forgotten circumstances and spent some time in Hamilton, New York. Senpachi, whose name was Americanized to Sam Patch, returned to Japan as a common seaman aboard the *Susquehanna* which was part of Commodore Perry's fleet. (One account suggests

Principal members of Japan's first diplomatic mission to the United States in 1860, wearing formal *hakama* costumes and swords.

that Senpachi had a habit of muttering *shinpai, shinpai*—worry, worry—which led to his being named Sam Patch.) He made his way ashore and apparently did no more for Japanese-American relations than to become a cook for an American teacher.

A second Japanese linked with the Perry mission is one Iwakichi who became known as Dan Ketch. Somehow, in a way that is not clear, he reached the United States aboard the *Mississippi* on its return voyage. Iwakichi returned to Japan in 1859, Dulles reports, wearing Western clothes and carrying a Colt pistol "to swagger and defy his countrymen." Japanese toughs did the predictable. Within a year they killed him.

Perhaps the first Japanese to become an American citizen was Hikozaemon, better known as Joseph Heco. His story is much like that of Manjiro. Heco was fourteen years old in 1850 when the junk he was sailing on was severely damaged by a storm. The American sailing ship *Auckland* rescued the survivors and took them to San Francisco. Heco went to school, got a job with the collector of customs, eventually went to Baltimore where he attended a Catholic school, and became a naturalized citizen. In 1859 he sailed back to Yokohama and was hired as an interpreter in the U.S. consulate. Heco applied for an assignment with the *Kanrin Maru* mission in 1860 but he was not accepted. He then went into business with American merchants. Several years later he returned to the United States, and according to his account, saw President Lincoln in hopes of being appointed U.S. naval storekeeper in Yokohama. But Lincoln had other things on his mind and again Heco was disappointed. He returned to Japan where he worked on the fringes of the government and eventually wrote a book about his life.

Until the *Kanrin Maru* made its memorable voyage, Japanese had reached the United States only by accident. But even after that milestone event the Japanese were reluctant to open the gates to citizens wishing to go abroad. In a very few cases, adventurous young *samurai* stowed away aboard American vessels. The most notable of the stowaways was Niijima Jo, who became known to Americans as Joseph Hardy Neesima. He reached the United States in 1864, was graduated from Amherst College and ordained as a Christian minister after studying at Andover Theological Seminary. With financial support from Americans, Niijima founded the school that was to become Doshisha University in Kyoto.

Japanese leaders realized, however, that if they were to catch up with the West, their brightest young men should be sent abroad to study. Founding of the official Office for Study of Barbarian Books (*Bansho Torishirabesho*) in 1856, only two years after the signing of the Treaty of Kanagawa with Perry, was the first step in this direction. By 1866 two *samurai* were sent to study at Rutgers University, and they were soon followed by several others. Still, the number of students was quite limited. Dulles estimates that "no more than 200 Japanese students came to the United States under the original government program." Official U.S. statistics show the overall total for the entire twenty-year period between 1865 and 1885 was only 446. Harvard, Yale, Cornell and Princeton received many of these students, while several Japanese naval cadets attended Annapolis.

Meanwhile, new turmoil in Japan was to have far-reaching results. Clan leaders in distant fiefs agitated for an end to the shogunate and restoration of the Emperor, and the Tokugawas lacked the vitality to resist. In 1867 Yoshinobu resigned, bringing an end to 700 years of feudal military government. Mutsuhito, then only fifteen years old (later to be known as Emperor Meiji), destined to guide Japan's momentous emergence from feudalism, ascended the throne in January, 1868. The imperial capital was moved from Kyoto to Yedo, which was renamed Tokyo.

The lords and their young *samurai* warriors who had supported the restoration were bitterly anti-foreign at first, largely because it had been the hated Tokugawas who had opened the nation to the United States and European powers. Reischauer notes that until the Tokugawa collapse the loyalists "echoed the popular cry, 'honor the Emperor—expel the barbarians.' But long before they came to power in the final months of 1867, they had come to realize that it was impossible to 'expel the barbarians.' "

The restoration created a renewed interest in the outside world for two conflicting reasons.

First, government grants were made available to the sons of *samurai* to study abroad and help shape a new Japan.

And second, nobles and their *samurai* who had been on the losing side, sensing that important positions in the new government would be barred to them—or even fearing for their lives—looked to the United States as a political and economic refuge. Thus for the first time some Japanese considered the United States a place in which to make permanent homes.

4

THE VANGUARD ARRIVES

STAINED from her long voyage across the Pacific, the sidewheeler *S.S. China* of the Pacific Mail Co. steamed through the Golden Gate into San Francisco Bay on May 27, 1869. On her decks stood a handful of Japanese, weary from the ordeal of the crossing, fearful of the unknown that lay ahead, yet looking forward with hope and excitement to new experiences. This was probably the first immigrant party from Japan to arrive in the United States, the vanguard of thousands who would follow in the next half century.

Yet this pioneer contingent differed in several significant respects from those who were to come later. It consisted of venturesome persons from the vicinity of Aizu Wakamatsu, now a pleasant, modern city about 200 miles northeast of Tokyo. While most Japanese immigrants came to the United States for economic reasons, this first group was in effect made up of political refugees. Matsudaira Katamori, feudal lord of Aizu Wakamatsu, had sided with the Tokugawa shogunate in opposing the restoration to power of the imperial family. When the Tokugawas finally lost the struggle, their allies were stripped of wealth and influence, their retinue of warriors cast adrift as *ronin* (masterless *samurai*). One of Matsudaira's advisers was a Dutchman (some say German), John Henry Schnell, who was married to a Japanese and had adopted a Japanese name, Hiramatsu Buhei. Schnell suggested that Matsudaira do what many European political leaders had done in similar circumstances—seek refuge in the vast and under-populated United States. Schnell was commissioned to lead an advance party which would pave the way for later groups. Apparently the project had special approval, for general emigration was still prohibited.

The records of the time are incomplete, but Mrs. Fern Sayre and Soichi Nakatani of Sacramento through painstaking research have uncovered considerable information about this project, called the Wakamatsu Tea and Silk Farm Colony. Henry Taketa of Sacramento, in an article based on this research, has written in *The Pacific Citizen:*

"Much of the group was made up of farmers and those in the trades, but several were *samurai* followers of Lord Matsudaira. Four women, including teen-age nursemaid Ito Okei of the Schnell family, were with the pioneer party.

"The settlers, arriving in San Francisco, proceeded to Sacramento by riverboat and wagontrained to Placerville and nearby Gold Hill, where Schnell had arranged to purchase 600 acres for the farm colony. With them came 50,000 three-year-old mulberry trees for silk farming, a large quantity of bamboo shoots for food and craft industry, tea seeds, grape seedlings and other varieties of plants and seeds of their native land."

The colony was short-lived. The plants from Japan, weakened from the long voyage, failed to thrive in the dry soil, and water for irrigation was scarce. Financial aid expected from Japan failed to materialize. Schnell left with his wife and two daughters, promising to return with money, but he did not come back. The colony lasted less than two years. Some of the Japanese are believed to have returned to their homeland. Others drifted away and left no trace of their passage.

There is reliable record of only three. One was Okei, the second a *samurai* and carpenter named Sakurai Matsunosuke, the third Masumizu Kuninosuke. Within two years Okei died of a fever that periodically swept the West and was buried atop Gold Hill. One can imagine this girl, hardly more than a child, climbing the hill at sunset, gazing with longing westward across the slopes so reminiscent of her home country, and yet so different. The indications are that Sakurai collected funds from remaining members of the immigrant party and erected a marker. Her grave was forgotten until the 1930's when members of the Placer County chapter of the Japanese American Citizens League, investigating the Okei legend, discovered and restored it. The original stone over her grave bears this stark epitaph: "In memory of Okei, died 1871, age 19 years, a Japanese girl."

Sakurai, who was befriended by a pioneer farmer named Francis
Veerkamp, lived another thirty years. He is buried in Vineyard
Cemetery at Coloma, not far from Gold Hill. Veerkamp's son
Henry, eighty-two years old when he was interviewed in 1930,
said he had known Okei personally and remembered her as a bright,
perceptive girl.

Masumizu reportedly married a Negro woman and operated a
fish store in Sacramento for many years. A writer who researched
the life of John Henry Schnell says Masumizu had three daughters
and a son, George, who ran a barber shop in Sacramento. Masumizu died in 1915 and is buried at Colusa, California.

The state of California in 1966 recognized the arrival of the
Wakamatsu colony as an "historic event" and the Japanese American Citizens League designated 1969 as the centennial of Japanese
immigration to the United States. On June 7, 1969, a State Historical Plaque, telling the story of the Wakamatsu Colony, was
placed on the grounds of Gold Trail School in El Dorado County
some one hundred yards from the Okei grave.

There are, however, indications that Japanese settlers were in
California prior to the Wakamatsu Colony. The San Francisco
Chronicle under date of June 17, 1869, mentions the arrival of
Japanese "upwards to a year ago." They were described as "gentlemen of refinement and influence in their country, from which
they were compelled to flee, almost destitute, because their travel
in civilized countries had made them too liberal in their ideas to
suit the Mikado." The report goes on to say the Japanese spoke
English and French, and on the advice of a Mr. Van Reed, "father
of the United States consul at Jedo [sic]," leased a farm in Alameda County. Nothing further is heard of these gentlemen.

Eugene M. Van Reed was Hawaiian consul general in Yedo,
the original name of Tokyo, and he had a principal role in sending
the first contingent of Japanese to Hawaii almost exactly one year
before the Wakamatsu group. Strictly speaking, they were not
immigrants. They were contract laborers, most of whom expected
to return home after completing their work agreements.

Hawaii at the time was suffering from a shortage of cheap labor
for the sugar plantations. The first Hawaiian census in 1832 showed
a native population of 130,313. By 1860, the population was down
to 69,000. Diseases brought to the islands by the white man swept

in cruel epidemics through the natives who had no built-in immunity and who, besides, took poorly to the semi-slavery of plantation labor.

Roger Daniels, in his *The Politics of Prejudice*, says:

"The American planters who dominated Hawaii knew that they would have to import labor. They would have preferred white labor, but, as a committee ruefully reported, such labor could only be had under 'onerous conditions that would result in the complete demoralization of labor in these islands.' "

In other words, they would have had to pay more than they wished to in wages.

"Forced to make a choice between maintaining a low wage scale and their desire to make Hawaii a white man's country, the planters chose the former. In 1851 they began to import Chinese laborers under five-year contracts."

After their contracts were up, many of the Chinese chose to remain in Hawaii and go into business for themselves. This was an eventuality the planters had not counted on. Before long the Chinese were an economic power, and the planters were seeking others to do the heavy, unpleasant work in the cane fields.

In 1865, R. C. Wyllie, minister of foreign affairs in the reign of Kamehameha V, wrote to Van Reed, inquiring about the possibility of recruiting plantation hands. "I myself could take 500 for my own estates," he wrote. "Could any good agricultural laborers be obtained from Japan or its dependencies, to serve like the Chinese under a contract for six or eight years? They would be treated well, enjoy all the rights of freemen, and in our fine islands, under our beautiful and salubrious climate, they would be better off, as permanent settlers, than in their own country."

Japanese laws prohibited labor emigration because, as Daniels observes, the government rightly concluded that permitting contract laborers to go abroad "would, in the long run, lower the prestige of Japan as a nation." However, the country was in political turmoil, and after three years Van Reed persuaded Japan to permit 180 laborers to go abroad. His request for 350 men was turned down.

Contracts were for thirty-six months. The men were to be paid four dollars per month—half of this sum to be withheld until the contract was completed—with food, lodging such as it was, and passage provided. There were two headmen for each group of twenty-five, and they were to be paid one dollar a month extra.

At the last moment a hitch developed, and it appeared the project might be cancelled. Van Reed chartered a British ship, the *Scioto*, and placed 149 Japanese aboard, including six women and two children. The ship sailed without official clearance of Japanese authorities, and its passengers had no proper passports. Nonetheless, they arrived in Honolulu on May 17, 1868, after a 23-day voyage.

Japanese officials protested violation of their laws to American Minister Van Valkenburgh on the grounds that Van Reed was an American citizen. Van Valkenburgh did the only thing he could do. He said Van Reed was acting in this instance as the consul general of the kingdom of Hawaii, and therefore the United States had no jurisdiction.

Van Reed, meanwhile, wrote jubilantly to the plantation owners in Hawaii: "No better class of people for laborers could be found than the Japanese race, so accustomed to raising sugar, rice and cotton, nor one so easily governed, they being peaceable, quiet and of a pleasant disposition."

But Van Reed made one grievous error which was to be repeated time and again by other Americans. He assumed that all Japanese were alike. He saw the well-kept fields of Japan and assumed all Japanese were skillful farmers. But those he had recruited for plantation labor were city people, fresh off the streets and sordid back alleys of the tough port of Yokohama. It would have made as much sense to take a native of New York's Lower East Side and try to make a Wyoming cowboy of him. And while the Japanese laborers stuck it out, the experiment was less than a rousing success.

But the virtual shanghaiing of Japanese citizens had two significant long-range results.

First, Japan refused to permit further emigration of laborers until internal conditions forced her to change the law in 1886.

Second, by the time labor emigration was finally legalized, recruiters had learned to look for farm workers in rural areas. Professor Hilary Conroy reports that Robert W. Irwin, representing the Hawaiian Board of Immigration, sought a location "about 1,000 miles from Tokyo" which at the time seemed like a safe distance from the metropolis. But since this would have put him in the ocean somewhere south of Okinawa, he settled on an area about

Matsudaira Tadaatsu came to the United States in 1872 at age 17. He earned a degree in civil engineering at Rutgers University, became an assistant to Colorado's inspector of mines in 1886.

half that distance away—the southern portion of Honshu Island around Hiroshima. Thus it was that young men from the green valleys of Hiroshima and Okayama prefectures were most numerous among those who first came to the United States. And it was only natural that later, in the periods of heaviest Japanese migration to the U.S., the largest number should come from areas with earlier emigration experience and contacts, thus accounting for the abundance of *Issei* from Hiroshima, Okayama and Yamaguchi prefectures.

Oddly enough, while later immigrants tended to concentrate on the Pacific Coast, many of the early arrivals quickly headed east. Take the case of Matsudaira Tadaatsu, a seventeen-year-old lad who set out for the United States in 1872, three years after the Wakamatsu expedition left for California. He was a blood relative of the Tokugawa clan, but his relationship to Matsudaira Katamori, lord of Aizu Wakamatsu, is not known. Somehow, young Matsudaira made his way to Rutgers University in New Brunswick, N.J., and earned a degree in civil engineering. Common labor was not for him. In 1879 he worked for a time as an engineer with the Union Pacific in Wyoming, then attended the Colorado School of Mines in Golden. In 1886 he was appointed assistant to Colorado's inspector of mines, and although the record is murky, he apparently worked as an engineer for a coal mining firm and enjoyed a measure of social status since he married the daughter of General Archibald Sampson, retired U.S. Army officer. Matsudaira died in 1888 when he was but thirty-three years old. His grave in Denver's Riverside Cemetery was forgotten until 1952 when some *Issei* erected a tombstone in memory of the "first Japanese resident of Colorado."

A somewhat happier story is told by Etsu Inagaki Sugimoto in her autobiography, *A Daughter of the Samurai*. Although she mentions no dates, she grew up during the early post-Restoration period in Nagaoka in northern Japan and came to the United States to marry Matsuo Sugimoto, who had established an art goods business in Cincinnati, Ohio. Although there were few Japanese with whom to socialize, the Sugimotos led a not unenjoyable existence until his death caused her to return to Japan with her children.

Still, prior to repeal of the law prohibiting laborers from going abroad, most of the Japanese in the United States were students.

Dr. Inazo Nitobe reports that in 1887 there were only 1,275 Japanese men and 77 women in the U.S., of whom more than half were students. He classified them into three categories—those sent by the government; sons of the wealthy, many of whom were interested primarily in having a good time; and ambitious youths of scanty means with wild hopes of gaining an education or making a fortune, a not unfamiliar pattern in the history of U.S. immigration.

Rapidly changing conditions in Japan were responsible for altering the emigration picture. The Japan of this period was a nation in ferment. Remaining vestiges of feudalism were being thrown off with great vigor. In 1876 the pensions granted the *samurai*, who were no longer needed as retainers and warriors, were cut off. They were denied the privilege of wearing swords and suddenly they were faced with the necessity of earning livings like ordinary people. Only six years earlier, commoners had been extended the right to take surnames. (Until then, ordinary people had only one name. Dr. Robert Wilson notes that since the masses were poorly educated, they tended to adopt names easily written in simple ideographs, accounting for the large number of names like Ota, Yamada, Tanaka, Yamamoto, Ogawa, Kimura, Murata and the like.)

Japan's population was increasing swiftly without a corresponding rise in food production. Business and industrial cartels were taking shape, but the lot of peasants who had drifted to the cities in search of work was a miserable one. Government officials began to look abroad for relief. They saw the plantations in Hawaii pleading for labor. In the United States, railroads were recruiting European immigrants by the tens of thousands to settle the vast, undeveloped West. Liberalization of the Japanese emigration law was inevitable. It came in 1886, the same year a number of labor unions united to organize the American Federation of Labor. In due time the immigrants and the A.F. of L. would meet head-on.

Despite the new law, there was no sudden rise in the number of Japanese immigrants. U.S. figures show that in 1886, only 194 Japanese immigrants arrived. In 1887 the number had crept up to 229; in 1888, 404; in 1889, 640; in 1890, 691.

The number of Japanese immigrants topped a thousand for the first time in 1891 when it reached 1,136. It did not reach the two thousand mark until 1898, when 2,230 entered the U.S. The vast majority were male, unmarried, too young to be burdened with family responsibilities, and extraordinarily venturesome. Leaving hearth and home to make one's life in a foreign land was a wrenching experience, particularly for a people whose family ties were strong. Nitobe quotes a moving admonition written by a father to his son who was about to embark for the United States:

"Above all, take it close to thy heart to live worthy of thy country. Remember that thou wilt be thrown amongst strangers of different ideas and customs. With a standard different from that to which thou hast been accustomed, and with a harsher measure, will they meet thee. Every word thou utterest falls not upon indifferent ears; every act of thy hand somebody watches. Should any action of thine dim in the least the lustre of thy country's glory or stain the brightness of thy family's records, then father me no longer father, I will no more son thee my son."

5

THE SIGN OF THE DOLLAR

"Give me your tired, your poor,
  Your huddled masses yearning to breathe free,
  The wretched refuse of your teeming shore,
  Send these, the homeless, tempest-tossed, to me:
  I lift my lamp beside the golden door."

NO SUCH NOBLE MESSAGE of welcome, which appears at the foot of the Statue of Liberty in New York harbor, greeted the tired, poor, yearning, wretched, tempest-tossed immigrants from Japan. There wasn't even a Statue of Liberty—nor has anyone ever seriously suggested there ought to be one—to hold aloft a lamp of hope for the benefit of Asian immigrants beside the Golden Gate or any other Pacific portal.

Japanese immigrants, as distinguished from the students mentioned in previous chapters, were recruited by American employers for only one reason. They were needed to replenish the supply of reliable, energetic labor on farms, the railroads, the mines and canneries, which began to dwindle with passage of the Chinese Exclusion Act in 1882.

Chinese immigration to the United States began a generation earlier than the Japanese movement. As early as 1848, there were 54 Chinese known to be in California. By 1849, there were 737, and in 1850 the number had jumped to 3,227. A comparison of Chinese and Japanese populations in the United States follows:

Year	Chinese	Japanese
1850	3,227	—
1860	34,933	—
1870	63,199	55
1880	105,465	148
1890	107,488	2,039
1900	89,863	24,327
1910	71,531	72,157
1920	61,639	110,010
1930	74,954	138,834
1940	77,504	126,947

The Chinese were imported to assume the menial, unpleasant kind of work that white Americans shunned. There was plenty of it in the frontier West where the ethic demanded that men act like men. But as the Chinese gained knowledge about the peculiarities of the New World and socked away a little money, they were emboldened to leave the semi-slavery of their jobs and strike out as independent businessmen, running restaurants, laundries and small retail shops. This was in the best American tradition, but the whites didn't like it. Frugal and industrious, the Chinese proved to be tough competitors. The whites hated competing with coolies. Regarded as something a bit less than human, the Chinese were a ready-made whipping boy for demagogues. In some areas killing a Chinese was no more a crime than killing a dog. The slayers were safe; the testimony of a Chinese carried no weight in court. By 1882 Congress was persuaded to pass the Chinese Exclusion Act that barred further Chinese immigration for ten years. The Act was extended another ten years in 1892, and in 1902 it was extended again for an indefinite period.

Murray Morgan in his book *Skid Row* gives us an insight into the nature of the Chinese issue:

"When the Chinese arrived the Western people had looked on them as the genii who would bring from the East on their narrow backs the much desired (railroad) tracks. The Chinese, one and all, were called 'John,' and the stories of John's prowess as a construction worker almost reached the status of folk legend. John could work 12 hours on a handful of rice; impassive John could handle blasting jobs that other men were too nervous to carry out; brave John would work all day at the end of a hundred-foot rope, chiseling notches for trestle supports; inscrutable John had the best poker-face in a poker-loving nation. Good old John.

"And then the final sections of track were laid, the golden spikes were driven, and the construction workers poured into the Western cities, into Tacoma and Portland, San Francisco and Seattle. The streets teemed with restless men, men with money to burn; restless men, soon broke, the Chinese among them. The fact that the Chinese were accustomed to receiving less than the white men no longer seemed laughable to the white workers; with the construction boom over and business slow, there was competition for every job—and fear of economic competition always increases prejudice. The hard-working, industrious Chinese who were willing to take any job, to accept any wage, became symbols of discontent to the unemployed. 'Go home, John,' the slogans said, 'Go, John.' "

And when John refused to take the hint, he was thrown out. At Rock Springs, Wyoming Territory, a mob of unemployed miners burned the shacks of Chinatown, killing nine men and two women, and driving the rest out of the area. In the fall of 1885 a committee in Tacoma, Washington, headed by the German-born mayor, gave Chinese residents a month to get out of town. When hundreds refused to leave because they were too poor to buy tickets, vigilantes swept through Chinatown and escorted the residents to the railroad tracks and herded them into boxcars. They were taken off to Portland, Oregon. The following January, Washington Territory passed a law prohibiting Chinese from owning real property, and other laws barring Orientals from *public or private* employment were narrowly defeated. On February 7, 1886, after weeks of tension, a mob led by labor leaders rounded up most of Seattle's 350 Chinese and marched them to the foot of Main Street with the intention of shipping them out aboard the *Queen of the Pacific*. But the captain wanted $7 each to take the Chinese to San Francisco. The hat was passed among the vigilantes and $600 collected. Eventually 196 Chinese sailed on the *Queen*, all that could be accommodated. When home guard troops escorted the remainder back to their shanties to await the next boat, shooting started and a logger was killed. That was enough for the Chinese. Most of them were glad to board the next ship for the relative safety of San Francisco, which also was known for its intemperate outbreaks against the Chinese. As someone observed: "The Chinamen, who had done the hardest and dirtiest part of the work in the West, were driven out as soon as the work had been completed, simply because it was the will of the whites."

This was not quite accurate. There was plenty of work to be done, and the Japanese were the logical successors to the Chinese in many fields. Unfortunately the Japanese inherited the hostility faced by the Chinese as well as their jobs. They were of the same race, came from the mysterious Orient, demonstrated fairly similar work habits, spoke an alien language. But there were important differences, too. The Chinese wore queues and preferred their own dress. The Japanese did not. The Chinese were inclined to be servile—it was safer that way. As one observer put it, "The Chinese was a good loser." The Japanese were better educated, proud of their native country, more inclined to resist exploitation and fight back against personal affronts. They refused to honor what they considered to be unfair labor agreements and quickly gained the reputation of being unreliable.

In her book, *Mountain of Gold*, Betty Lee Sung writes: "The Japanese differed little from the Chinese in physical characteristics. They supplanted the Chinese in the farms and homes, and for the same reason that the Californians objected to the Chinese, they objected to the Japanese—only more so. The Japanese were not as docile as the Chinese. They took exception to the discrimination against them, and they made themselves heard through a strong militaristic government in Japan."

At one time the Japanese caused the San Francisco *Chronicle* to have second thoughts about Chinese exclusion. Commenting editorially on the labor problems faced by big ranchers, the *Chronicle* said:

"The Japs are utterly undependable and the Hindoos are worse. If we are going to have Oriental labor at all the only proper course would be to repeal the Chinese Exclusion Act, and exclude the Japanese and Hindoos. We should then, at least, have Oriental labor which would keep its contracts. But we want no Oriental labor."

The various aspects of Japanese labor in America will be treated at greater length in other chapters. It is sufficient at this point to quote an implacable, sincere and effective foe of Japanese immigration, V. S. McClatchy, a leader of a small group of political and economic nabobs who made a career of defending California against the "yellow peril." McClatchy withdrew from the newspaper publishing business to form and spend his time directing the California Joint Immigration Committee, leading what Carey McWilliams describes as "a holy crusade against the resident Japanese." Appearing before a U.S. Senate committee, he revealed the economic basis of his bias when he declared:

"They have greater energy, greater determination, and greater ambition than the other yellow and brown races ineligible to citizenship, and with the same low standards of living, hours of labor, use of women and child labor, they naturally make more dangerous competitors in an economic way."

At any rate, no high-held torch of liberty or flaming political or religious causes attended the departure of the bulk of Japanese immigrants from their native villages. Nor, except in rare instances, were they driven to the U.S. by extreme poverty or hunger. The majority were, to put it crassly, looking for a fast buck to be made working at jobs where, in the beginning at least, their labor was solicited.

When they first arrived, few had thoughts of remaining permanently in the United States. The majority saw America as a land of economic opportunity which would provide them the means of gaining the security of land ownership when they returned home, a measure of status, and freedom from predatory moneylenders. In his autobiography, *Journey to Washington*, U.S. Senator Daniel K. Inouye says his grandfather migrated to Hawaii in hopes of making enough money to pay off a family debt of honor. (And he did pay the debt, after nearly thirty years of unremitting effort, although by then he considered Hawaii his home.) The dollar sign was stamped on every shipload of immigrants.

Professor Yamato Ichihashi, for many years in the department of Japanese history and government at Stanford University, in his book *Japanese in the United States*, puts the immigration picture in perspective—and introduces still another factor—with this observation:

". . . Japanese labor emigration to this country and Hawaii was impelled by desire for improvement rather than by the necessity of escaping misery at home; this was the fundamental, positive cause of Japanese emigration. But coupled with this there was a powerful negative cause: the military conscription law. Neither religion nor politics constituted a cause for Japanese emigration."

Contrary to widespread belief, the Japanese government did not encourage emigration. She was not trying to export immigrants. We have seen that emigration was not legalized until 1886. Even after that, Japan erected formidable barriers to indiscriminate emigration. W. M. Rice, U.S. Commissioner of Immigration, who went to Japan in 1899 on an official fact-finding tour and filed a series of lengthy reports with Congress, was quite impressed by the government's attitude. Among other things, he found that procuring a passport to leave Japan was no simple matter. He wrote:

"It is a feature of the construction of the Japanese law regulating emigration that . . . the government has acted upon the theory that the character of the Japanese abroad will be taken as an index of the character of the nation at home. Hence these regulations provide for the careful inquiry into the character of those going abroad and also require that provision shall be made for the return of the emigrant, in the event that he becomes sick or a public charge in a foreign country, before the passports are granted."

As early as 1891 Japanese Consul Sutemi Chinda in San Francisco was warning his government about the need for carefully screening applicants for passports to the United States. He urged Tokyo to "try to prevent such undesirable applicants as prostitutes, contract-laborers, men of no means, and unhealthy persons" from obtaining passports. He stressed the need for having "at least 15 yen" ($7.50 at the then rate of exchange) on arrival. And he wrote prophetically: "Even if all the Japanese passengers arriving at this port do in fact possess the required amount of money, the continuation of the mass migration of lower class Japanese in the future will undoubtedly create a grave situation in the relationship between Japanese and Americans in this country which, sooner or later, will adversely affect the honor and reputation not only of the Japanese in this country but of those in Japan."

Although the prospective emigrant was not specifically required to return to Japan, he had to show he was capable of paying his way back. If he did not have the means, he needed a guarantor. This person who signed as a surety was held responsible for aiding the emigrant, and had to prove he was qualified by showing he had a certain amount of land, or paid a certain amount of taxes over a period of years.

When a situation becomes excessively complicated, it is axiomatic that experts will step in (for a fee) to help the poor befuddled citizen cope with his problems, as witness the abundance of income tax consultants in the United States today. It was natural that "emigration companies" and agents (*Imin Toriatsukainin*) should appear in Japan.

For a price, they helped prospective emigrants to apply for passports, arranged passage, and made sure the client would be met in America and helped to find work. Because few emigrants knew anyone affluent enough to qualify as guarantors, the companies posted security insuring return passage. The larger companies had agents in the U.S. to look after matters.

Back in 1855, however, even though slavery was still condoned, Congress had enacted a law prohibiting the importation of foreigners under contract to perform labor. Over the years this law was enforced unevenly and uneventfully. Partly as a result of the agitation over Chinese labor, the law was amended and made more stringent in 1885, just about the time Japan first legalized emigration. It was inevitable that the Japanese emigration companies should be regarded as labor contracting organizations and come under hard scrutiny.

These businesses were not without opportunity for substantial profit. First, they collected fees from clients for their services. Then they were in position to seek, and get, a commission from the shipping companies which were competing for steerage passengers, for booking their clients. And finally, they or more often their agents received a fee from the employers for delivering laborers.

The steamship lines were no small factor in stimulating emigration. Since there was no common schedule of fares for steerage passengers, established lines and owners of tramp ships competed vigorously for the business. Ship owners published advertisements promising well-paying jobs in the United States and hired Japanese agents to recruit men for work that often did not exist.

A Japanese government report of the time tells how one Sato Eishiro was hired by the owners of a small fleet of ships to drum up business. He visited a number of towns in Okayama and Wakayama prefectures. "At each stop," the report reads, "he told an interested audience that an American railroad company in Portland, Oregon, was urgently in need of 1,000 workers. He then mentioned that any healthy men who would apply for the job could go to the United States, that the job did not require any special skill . . . that the job would pay a wage of $30 a month." The fare was 45 yen ($22.50) usually payable in advance, but the agent offered a special arrangement whereby the passengers could pay 25 yen before boarding, and the balance plus a carrying charge after they had started to work in the United States.

Transporting steerage passengers was a lucrative business. They were jammed into holds and provided a minimum of care and food. One *Issei* recalls: "We were packed into the ship in one big room, men and women together. There was no privacy, no comforts, no nothing. We were like silkworms on a tray, eating and sleeping and wondering what the future held for us. The fortunate ones found jobs."

One gets a vivid idea of what steerage passage across the Pacific was like in the earliest days in this observation from the autobiography of Takahashi Korekiyo, later a Japanese cabinet officer, who sailed aboard the 700-ton American paddlewheeler *Colorado* in 1867:

"There was a conspicuous difference when one compared the treatment of and services for cabin passengers and those for steerage passengers. The steerage was dark and filled with a foul odor. A large number of us were crowded into it, and each slept in one of the hammocks tied to four poles in three tiers. . . . About at 8 each morning, we were all chased out of it. While on deck, the steerage was cleaned and fumigated by smoking peppers for sanitary reasons. We had to eat our meals out of a large tin can together with Chinese laborers. And steerage passengers were provided with three or four large barrels which were placed on the deck where the paddlewheel was, for their need to ease nature. Straddling over two wooden boards placed on top of these barrels, one had to obey the calls of nature. When I went out there on the first day of the voyage, the barrels were surrounded by many Chinese, both men and women, waiting for their turn to go to stool. Since then, I dared not go near that place. Instead, I managed to sneak into the toilet for cabin passengers whenever they had all gone to the dining salon."

Commissioner Rice, on his fact-finding tour of Japan, found nine emigration offices in Hiroshima and an association of emigration companies in the Kyobashi district of Tokyo. "The offices of these companies are well equipped for business," he wrote, "and have the appearance of being well supplied with employees and clerks. The managers and stockholders are among the leading businessmen and politicians of Japan . . . Among the capitalists and politicians thus interested is Den Sugawara, who is a member of the lower house of Parliament and editor of the *Jinmin*, the leading vernacular newspaper of Japan, published at Tokyo. Mr. Sugawara spent several years in Idaho, where he had extensive connections with railway contractors, and presumably laid the foundation of his fortune . . ."

In short, these emigration companies were brokers of manpower, a business open to many abuses. Still, it can be argued that they were filling a need, for men were being sought to take on the back-breaking work of an expanding America, and young Japanese were anxious for the opportunity of doing it. In 1903 there were 36 agents handling emigrants, and one source says the emigration companies had a part in recruiting and sending along anywhere from 30 up to as many as 89 percent of Japanese emigrants in the early years of the century. The service provided by these companies sometimes included Western clothing, a satchel, and even coaching as to what to tell immigration inspectors. Little wonder, when platoons of Japanese immigrants appeared uniformly clothed and equipped, and with standard replies to questions, that Americans suspected a contractual system.

Professor Ichihashi says the movement of Japanese laborers was "greatly facilitated and stimulated" by emigration agents between 1894 and 1907, but generally the agents played a more important role in emigration to Hawaii than to the mainland. Contract labor, based on the indentured servant system of colonial America, was legal in Hawaii. Organized labor on the mainland was particularly hostile to contract labor, and a study of a "Memorandum of Agreement" used by the Honolulu Sugar Co. in 1899 in employing Japanese laborers substantiates the unions' fears that the system led to exploitation.

This contract was for three years, and pay by this time had increased to "$15 U.S. gold coin per month." If the laborer had a wife and she worked, her pay was $10 per month. The company withheld $2.50 each month to be applied to the laborer's return passage. Twenty-six days of 10 hours each actual work in the fields, or 12 hours in the sugar mill, constituted a month's service. Overtime work was paid for at the rate of 10 cents per hour for men, 7 cents for women. The laborer was provided free fuel, unfurnished lodgings, domestic water and medical attention.

Organized labor on the mainland argued that workingmen who knew nothing about conditions in the United States were by signing contracts obligating themselves for years in the future, thus hurting themselves while depressing the labor market. However, because Japanese immigrants were so unfamiliar with American ways, it was inevitable that some acceptable institution should succeed to the role of the emigration companies. What was "acceptable" was a moot point.

Before the turn of the century, the San Francisco *Bulletin* cried in outrage:

"The United States contract labor laws are being violated every two or three weeks by the Japanese. The country is being flooded with cheap Japanese labor; the little brown men are pouring in upon us in greater numbers than did the Chinese before the Restriction Act was passed by Congress, and the state of California is threatened with an epidemic of cheap labor and hard times in farming and commercial circles. It is time to sound the warning and to expose the ways and means by which certain rural citizens have provided their orchards with fruit pickers and packers from the ranks of the Japanese unemployed, while white American workingmen stand idly by and watch the harvest of the Golden State being reaped by the alien hordes of Asia. To all appearances the United States immigration officers have been neglectful of duty, and what is worse, alleged American citizens have contracted for cheap Japanese laborers who agree to receive per capita 40 cents and 50 cents per day for 12 or 14 hours work.

"Within the past year, about 10,000 Japanese have found employment on farms in the San Joaquin Valley, Napa Valley, Livermore Valley, and the fertile valley of the San Gabriel. Especially in the Livermore Valley have the busy little followers of the Mikado worked their way into every farming industry . . ."

(The Japanese consul's figures at that time showed there were 5,861 Japanese in all of California—5,620 male, 241 female.)

Investigators tried to show that laborers were being recruited in Japan and consigned to labor brokers through Japanese hotel operators in San Francisco and other port cities. The innkeepers maintained this was an innocent relationship, that they simply were doing business with people they knew and trusted. At a hearing held in San Francisco, a K. Shiono, who ran a lodging house at 529½ Geary Street, was asked:

"Is it not a fact that they (immigrants) come consigned to your place?"

Shiono replied: "There is one hotel in Japan where they know me and they may send my countrymen to me, but I never write asking them to send anyone to me."

Shiono admitted receiving a letter from a Yokohama hotel keeper which was translated in part as saying: "On this date the steamer *China* will sail. I wish to let you know the following persons (names given) will sail on her. Please meet them as I am sending them to you."

Was such a letter to be construed as a consignment of contract labor? Or was it an innocent notice that some travelers were en route, and a request that they be looked after? As such hearings and investigations progressed, Japanese witnesses became frightened and uncooperative, often refusing to answer questions, saying they didn't know or had forgotten details. Undoubtedly, the Japanese were in fear and resented what they considered to be harassment. In addition, they understood little English, and the interpreters who translated both questions and answers were usually less than adequate. The result was far from satisfactory, and investigators and press considered the Japanese to be intentionally evasive.

From the Japanese point of view, the hotels and boarding houses were a necessary convenience as well as a profitable business for entrepreneurs. The Fujii family's efforts in this field in Seattle provide an interesting insight. Their story starts with Kojuro Fujii, a native of Yasu village in Hiroshima who came to the United States in 1894. Kojuro was then a mature man. He was accompanied by his second son, sixteen-year-old Chojiro. Kojuro remained in the Pacific Northwest for two years, apparently survey-

Rose Hotel in Los Angeles, about 1950. Sanjuro Mizuno opened it
boarding house for Japanese railroad workers in 1898. (Miyatake
lection)

ing job and business prospects. Then he went home. In the dec
that followed, he was responsible for encouraging some 500 yo
men from his district to emigrate to Seattle.

Chojiro remained in Washington after his father returnec
Japan. He worked as a farm laborer until he had saved eno
money to lease a small hotel in 1899 at the corner of 5th Ave
and Jackson streets. He promptly changed its name from Rai
to Fujii Hotel. When Kojuro counseled young men about g
to the United States, he would say: "Incidentally, my son h
lodging house in Seattle. He will be able to help you. You
find no difficulty." And Chojiro prospered.

Eventually Chojiro persuaded a younger brother, Yoshito
join him in Seattle. Yoshito helped at the Fujii Hotel, which

moved to roomier quarters at the edge of Seattle's Chinatown, while attending the University of Washington. After Chojiro's death Yoshito also went into the hotel business.

Yoshito contends his father was not a labor contractor. He says Kojuro encouraged young Japanese to go to the United States because he felt there was economic opportunity waiting. But the profit motive was not entirely lacking. A steady stream of patrons helped his son's hotel to do very well. And in Japan, Kojuro was the recipient of *orei*, gifts from the families of persons he had assisted.

By 1900 there were six Japanese-operated hotels in Seattle. Most of them provided only dormitory-style rooms in basement quarters for 15 cents a night. The Fujii boasted it had eighteen upstairs rooms which rented for 25 cents a night. By 1905 there were some sixty-five small Japanese-operated hotels and rooming houses in Seattle. They and their counterparts in other Pacific ports, notably San Francisco, provided not only shelter and a touch of home for newcomers, but also served as job clearinghouses. Railroad, farm and cannery labor recruiters and others seeking Japanese workmen made their needs known to agents covering the hotels. The Japanese contractors were known as *keiyaku-nin*, and they maintained a working relationship with laborer-immigrants familiar in American immigration history.

The *keiyaku-nin* were the ones who knew the ropes. They could provide jobs or withhold them. They arranged the terms of employment and transportation to places where jobs were available. They provided room and board and working tools. They served as the buffer between the immigrants and the white employers, thus both protecting them from the white man's abuse and retarding the immigrant's efforts to learn English and become acquainted with American ways. The *keiyaku-nin* held a position comparable to the ethnic bosses among immigrant colonies on the East Coast, and in fact the *Issei* called them *bosu*.

All things considered, it was a practical and workable system. No one was hurt except the immigrants, and it took them quite some time to realize they were being exploited. In fact, they were happy to get work, work that they would have found difficult to locate without the help of the bosses, and so perhaps the system was inevitable.

Human nature being what it is, perhaps it was also inevitable that the *keiyaku-nin* let greed get away with them, for there were many ways to squeeze out a profit. The employers paid the Japanese contractors so much per head for the men they provided. (During much of the period the going rate was one dollar per man per month.) In addition, the employer provided the contractor a food and housing allowance; by spending less than he was allowed, the contractor could pocket the difference with no one being the wiser. In isolated areas the contractor was the only source of supply for clothing, tobacco, and other material needs, and here again he could see that there was a handsome markup. If the men gambled, as they often did in the absence of other recreation, the contractor's representatives played the "house" and took a cut. In the hearings referred to above, a witness charged that labor contractors pocketed from 20 to 40 cents from the one dollar a day wages then prevalent. But even 60 to 80 cents a day was about double what a man could earn in Japan and few workers were inclined to complain.

The Japanese American Research Project at UCLA turned up one *Issei* who reported his best earning year was 1906 when he made $25,000. He turned out to have been a labor contractor for an Alaskan salmon cannery. The men he employed were paid from $160 to $225 for a five-month season extending from May through September. During the height of the salmon run, when highly perishable fish was brought to the cannery by the tens of thousands, the *Issei* worked as long as twenty hours a day. There was seldom any provision for overtime pay, but the contractor was paid a bonus for each case his men packed. So the harder they worked, the more money the contractor made. Since salmon was plentiful, it was served three meals a day, and the contractor had to provide little outside of rice, soy sauce and bean paste (*miso*) for soup. The men themselves grew vegetables which seemed to leap out of the ground during the long hours of Alaskan sunshine.

(One *Nisei* cannery hand remembers that as late as 1936 he watched a shipload of provisions being unloaded with ten sides of beef being delivered to the Caucasian mess hall, only one to the Japanese kitchen even though the two crews were made up of approximately the same number of men. Beef had to be shipped up from Seattle at considerable cost; the Japanese ate salmon which was free for the taking.)

It is impossible to describe the typical Japanese immigrant because there was no such person. Despite the stereotypes, the immigrants did not fall into a mold. Each man and each woman was an individual with characteristics and motivations not easily explainable in terms of averages. Moreover, when one studies the writings of experts in an effort to draw a consensus, he finds they are far from agreement.

Take, for example, what would seem to be the simple matter of determining the principal occupation of the immigrants before they left Japan. Immigration Commissioner Rice wrote: "The great mass of emigrants, say 95 per cent of the whole, are coolie laborers and small farmers, who class as coolies."

But Professor Ichihashi, citing U.S. Department of Commerce and Labor figures, says that in the early years (1886 to 1908), laborers, farmers, fishermen and artisans formed only 39.3 percent of Japanese immigrants. After the Gentlemen's Agreement cut off the flow of the unskilled, immigrants classified as laboring men dropped to 35.4 percent. The others were listed as merchants, students, professionals, bankers, manufacturers, traders and the like. Perhaps the truth lies somewhere between the two figures, for obviously records were poorly kept.

The Japanese American Research Project has come up with a third estimate. Interviews with 1,047 *Issei* showed 52 percent indicating their principal occupation in Japan was in some field of agriculture. Only 3 percent admitted to having been laborers, while 16 percent said they had been craftsmen, foremen and operatives, and 11 percent said they were clerical and sales workers. Because of the nature of the survey—interviewing survivors of immigrants who had come to the United States forty and more years earlier—these findings hardly deserve to be considered conclusive.

Ichihashi, again quoting reports of the U.S. Commissioner-General of Immigration, says that in the 1896–1907 decade, Japanese arrivals had more money with them and a considerably lower illiteracy rate than the average European immigrant. For instance, 24.6 percent of Japanese were listed as illiterates compared to 68 percent among Portuguese and 59 percent among Turks. However, in view of Japan's system of compulsory education, Ichihashi expresses "shock" at the illiteracy figures and challenges their accuracy. He suspects that many Japanese might have answered "No" when asked whether they could read or write, assuming the reference was to English. "Moreover," he observes, "it should be noted that the Japanese have the habit of answering what seems to be wanted—'No,' when 'Yes' is meant."

But getting back to the "typical" *Issei*, chances are that he was quite young when he arrived. If Immigration Commission figures are to be believed, 22.6 percent were under twenty years of age when they arrived in the U.S., and 53 percent under twenty-five.

As Ichihashi has observed, he had very little money, for aside from being young, he and his family worked for appallingly low wages. A skilled craftsman might make one yen (worth 50 American cents at the time) a day, and because living costs were relatively high, it might take as much as five years to save 200 yen. In some instances, young immigrants or their families sold or mortgaged everything they owned to raise money for fares. Others were financed as a family or clan project, with relatives contributing whatever they could to send a strong-armed young man to the New World. Another UCLA survey discovered that the eldest son was somewhat more likely than his younger brothers to emigrate. Professor John Modell observes: "The high proportion of eldest sons—the guardians in Japan of the family line and the family traditions—indicates that in a very deep sense the parents of the *Issei*, too, were involved in immigration . . . On the conscious level the *Issei* did not feel driven *out*, but lured *towards* something . . ."

In the preponderance of instances it would seem the dollar sign was the *Issei's* lodestar.

Yet, ties with the homeland were never really severed. Quoting again from Modell: "For virtually no *Issei* was the trip to America a declared, open, intentional break with his family. Only 3 per cent of the *Issei* never maintained any contact with relatives in Japan after emigrating . . . Fewer than a quarter of the *Issei* have never been back to Japan since they left."

UCLA-JACL interviewers, talking to the *Issei* in the 1960's, found only one in four saying that they had intended to stay permanently in the United States when they first arrived. However, the years have a way of changing opinions and altering recollections, and this figure is at considerable variance from the findings of a Japanese Association survey in 1925. Two thousand families in Seattle were surveyed as to their intentions of returning to Japan, with the following results:

	No. of Replies	Percent
Definitely will *not* go back	0	0
Would like to return, but no present prospect	258	12.9
Will return to Japan	471	23.6
Undecided	1,271	63.5
Total	2,000	100.

Professor Shotaro Frank Miyamoto, University of Washington sociologist, in a paper published in 1939, quotes an *Issei* community leader:

"All of them came over here with the idea that they would stay for about three years, and then go back to Japan to set up their own businesses. Among all whom I know, I can say that not one in a hundred stayed here all the time. The rest of them went back to Japan after a few years, and they came to America again only after they failed in their native land, and found that life in Japan was harder than life over here. But even then, I think in the bottom of their hearts they wanted to go back to Japan to live."

Miyamoto points out that the Japanese Association survey was taken only a year or so after passage of the Immigration Act of 1924 and adoption of anti-alien land laws in many Western states, resulting in widespread uncertainty and resentment against the United States. Obviously a number of factors helped to change the minds of many of the "will returns," and caused the "undecideds" to decide in favor of permanent residence in the United States. They will be treated at length in subsequent chapters.

6

WORK FOR WILLING HANDS

IN 1910, some years before most *Nisei* were born, there were 72,157 Japanese in the United States, of whom only some 9,000 were women. The previous year the United States Immigration Commission had undertaken an extensive study of the Japanese and published a series of reports, no doubt over the protests of Congressmen who could see no possible value in such an expenditure. We are, however, indebted to these reports for an insight into what these immigrants were doing to support themselves.

The Commission estimated that in the summer of 1909 there were some 39,000 Japanese working in some phase of farming—which would account for more than half of all the Japanese in the United States. Possibly no more than 6,000 were independent farmers, with most of the rest working as hired hands. By states they were distributed as follows:

California		30,000
Washington		3,000
Colorado		3,000
Utah		1,025
Oregon		1,000
Idaho		800
Montana		700
	Total	39,525

The fact that the figures are rounded off would indicate that the survey was only a rough estimate. Many farm workers were migrants, traveling wherever jobs could be found, while others were seasonal employees. Thus, it is likely that the "permanent" farm population was considerably fewer than the Immigration Commission indicated. Contributing to the unreliability of these figures is the difficulty Caucasians had in distinguishing Japanese from Chinese, no small factor in a survey such as this. However, these figures and those that follow are interesting as indicators.

The leading occupations listed by the Commission appear this way in tabular form:

Farming and allied agricultural work	39,525
Domestics, including "schoolboys," hotel and restaurant workers	12,000
Small business establishments	10,000
Railroads	10,000
Salmon canneries	3,300
Lumber mills	2,200
Mining and smeltering	2,000
Total	79,025

Since the number of employed is some 7,000 greater than the total number of Japanese in the United States at that time, many obviously were counted more than once. This is understandable since a dishwasher classified as a "domestic" might well have worked on a farm and as a railroad section hand within the same year; a man might be a domestic in the winter, a cannery hand during the summer and a fruit picker in the fall. Nor is there any provision made for juveniles and nonworking housewives. It is distressing to contemplate that many of the campaigns against Japanese immigration were based on similarly unreliable figures about the number of jobs "cheap Japanese labor" was taking away from the white man.

Let us examine each of these fields of employment in turn. The Commission reported as follows that some of the earliest Japanese immigrants were farm laborers:

"One of the first districts entered by the Japanese was Vaca Valley, where several members of that race came in the winter of 1887–88. In 1890 eight Japanese came to Fresno, but left because of the hostile attitude of white men. The following year, however, about thirty Japanese entered the vineyards of that locality. They entered the Newcastle district in 1891. In 1893 twelve Japanese were employed as hop pickers in the Sacramento and San Joaquin

country and the Marysville and Suisun districts. Within the next
three or four years they made their appearance as beetfield laborers
and as fruit pickers in the Santa Clara and other valleys."

From these humble beginnings came the multimillion-dollar
Japanese-operated agricultural industry that, depending on one's
viewpoint, could be damned as a seizure of American jobs and land,
or praised as an important contribution to American wealth and
food needs. In California alone, production of Japanese farmers
rose from 6 million dollars in 1909 to 67 million dollars in one
decade—one-tenth of California's output. Most of the gain, it should
be noted, was in stoop labor crops which Caucasians disliked, and
in areas where poor soil or other conditions made farming unattractive.

The hostility against Japanese laborers was bad enough; it became considerably more intense when the immigrants stepped out
of the role of the exploited and became competitors of the white
man as farm operators and businessmen. That was a dangerous
position for an Asian immigrant group to assume in the West of
that time. Like the Negroes of the South, the Japanese were accepted without rancor only so long as they remained in their place.

In a rare (for that time), objective survey, Colonel John P. Irish,
president of the California Delta Association, reported to Governor
William B. Stevens in 1921:

". . . They (the Californians) had seen the Japanese convert
the barren land like that at Florin and Livingston into productive
and profitable fields, orchards and vineyards, by the persistence
and intelligence of their industry. They had seen the hardpan and
goose lands in the Sacramento Valley, gray and black with our
two destructive alkalis, cursed with barrenness like the fig tree of
Bethany, and not worth paying taxes on, until Ikuta, the Japanese,
decided that those lands would raise rice. After years of persistent
toil, enduring heartbreaking losses and disappointments, he conquered that rebellious soil and raised the first commercial crop of
rice in California. Due to the work of this great Japanese pioneer,
this State now has a rice crop worth 60 million dollars (in 1921),
and the land that he found worthless now sells for $200 per acre.

". . . (these Californians) had seen the repulsive 'hog wallow'
in the thermal belt of the west slope of the Sierra, avoided by white
men, so unproductive and forbidding that they defaced the scenery,

reclaimed by the genius and toil of the Japanese Sakamoto, and now transformed into beautiful vineyards and citrus orchards from Seville to Lemon Cove. They had seen that 70 per cent of the total 74,000 acres owned by Japanese were these lands that disfigured the State until they had been reclaimed by Japanese genius and industry. . . ."

The Ikuta named above (his initial was K.) was associated with the Maxwell and California Rice Companies in the Sacramento Valley. He perfected the technique of controlling water grass, which plagued the rice growers, by irrigation. Between 1910 and 1920 increasing numbers of corporations and partnerships were organized in Colusa County for farming rice. *Issei* who had been accustomed to growing rice on an acre or two of land in the old country were excited by the prospect of farming hundreds of acres in California, and they plunged heavily. But their bubble burst in November of 1920 when, just at harvest time, the rains came. The rains continued for weeks, followed by a dense fog that blanketed the Sacramento Valley. The mature rice could not be harvested. The banks foreclosed on loans and most of the *Issei*, after salvaging what they could, returned to the San Francisco Bay area and other employment. Thanks to their pioneer efforts, however, land once considered useless is valued at around $500 an acre today and Colusa County is one of the nation's most important rice-producing areas. Ironically, only one of the rice growers is a *Nisei*.

How were the Japanese farmers able to make the wasteland bloom? With unusual candor, the Immigration Commission noted: "The Japanese commonly work longer hours than either the East Indians or the Mexicans. The Japanese, moreover, are quicker workmen and capable of closer and more continuous application than the other races. Their greater desire to adopt American standards of life and especially their greater eagerness to become independent farmers and business men go far toward explaining their greater industry."

Yet, Americans who had taken pride in creating a nation out of the wilderness through ambition, industry, hard work, sacrifice and other traditional virtues, began to complain about these very same characteristics in the Japanese immigrants. The following remarkable passage appears in an official *Report on the Japanese Situation in Oregon* published by the state in 1920:

"Americans cannot possibly compete with Japanese in agricultural production. The activity of the Japs, their willingness to work long hours and to assume tiresome postures, their general standard of living and the fact that men, women and children work in the fields, all combine to give them a decided advantage over an American family."

While this may have been true in many cases, it was hardly the reason for the extraordinary success enjoyed by George Ushijima (which he shortened to Shima) in the delta country where the Sacramento and San Joaquin Rivers meet. Born in Fukuoka prefecture in 1863, Shima came to California in 1889. He worked as a laborer, then as a labor contractor. Meanwhile, he saw the potential in low-lying islands in the river channel. When the water was high, the islands were submerged. In summer, the area was a swamp swarming with mosquitoes, but the soil had been enriched by centuries of flooding by silt-laden waters. Shima and a group of associates built dikes around the islands and drained excess water. They deepened natural channels to lower the water table and planted potatoes, onions and other crops. The potatoes were most successful. By 1913 he reportedly was harvesting potatoes from more than 28,000 acres—the great bulk of it leased—employing some 500 men, both Caucasian and *Issei*. He reached as far north as Central Oregon, near the town of Bend, to grow potatoes for seed. When he died in 1926, his estate was estimated at 15 million dollars, an impressive sum in those days when many *Issei* were still working for a few dollars a day.

Another large agricultural operator was Harry Yaemon Minami, who helped introduce production of garden vegetables near Santa Maria in the early 1900's. His profits were plowed back into the land while Caucasian neighbors wondered aloud where he was going to market all his crops. Before World War II he was shipping vegetables from his 4,000 acres of farmland and his own packing sheds to all parts of the nation.

But these were the exceptions. The majority of *Issei* farmers struggled to make their way, succeeding by hard work and ingenuity, often, as Colonel Irish observed, on land that no one else wanted. In the Pacific Northwest, Japanese farmers cut the timber, dynamited the stumps, and cleared the land for strawberry farms. Professor John A. Rademaker learned in one of his studies that in a boggy valley of Western Washington, Japanese farmers dug by hand a ditch five feet wide, six feet deep and more than a mile long to drain the soil. In the Hood River valley of Oregon, Japanese were brought in to clear the hillsides of timber. Many stayed to plant apple and pear orchards on land they themselves developed. The Chinese and others discovered the shallow hardpan land around Florin, not far from Sacramento, would grow strawberries and grapes. The Japanese took over from them, raised excellent crops, but came in such numbers into this particular area—a 1923 survey showed seven-eighths of the population was Japanese—that it became a notorious hotbed of anti-Japanese agitation.

Winifred Raushenbush wrote in *Survey of Race Relations:* "Ever since 1905, when the Japanese question first began to trouble the dreams of the native son, investigators have poured into Florin. They arrive every other season, and when they come, the only white storekeeper in town takes a day off to show them the sights. Mostly it is the anti-Orientalists who go to Florin . . . For the unforgettable fact about Florin to the Californian mind is that in this town only one-eighth of the people are white."

By contrast, Raushenbush found nearly ideal race relations in Livingston, a few counties south of Florin, where the Japanese helped conquer the sandy desert. She found, in the mid-twenties, that seven-eighths of the population was white, one-eighth Japanese, and that "the Japanese have not made themselves offensive by being different." For whatever it may be worth, she wrote: "It should be the first rule in the book of etiquette on race relations that the foreigner should never become the major element in the population, unless he is a slave; in fact, unless the foreigner remains a very small element in the population there is inevitable friction and alarm."

We are indebted to the late Larry Tajiri, perhaps the most knowledgeable of reporters of the *Nisei* scene, for the next few paragraphs about farm development in California:

"The first Japanese in San Fernando Valley (where now live refugees from Los Angeles' smog and congestion) brought their families on horse-drawn carriages into a village which boasted two buildings on a dusty wagon road. They lived and worked at the San Fernando Mission, historic home of the padres. They were able to purchase farmland now in the center of the fabulously wealthy

San Fernando Valley at ridiculously low prices. They planted many of the oldest citrus groves in the area, and it has been said that every foot of the valley was at one time or another farmed by Japanese pioneers. (Tajiri's grandfather once owned a farm in what is now the Sunset Strip in Los Angeles.)

"The first Japanese in Lodi, seven in number, arrived in the 1890's, growing sugar beets and grain, but the first large-scale entry was in 1900, when some one hundred came to the country. Shortly after their arrival they began to purchase and rent farmland, setting in vineyards and laying the foundation for the large grape industry, now the economic mainstay of the area. Between 1910 and 1915 the bulk of the orchard planting and cultivation was done by the *Issei*.

"In Reedley, farmers from Japan studied the grapevines which were planted on hilly ground. They noticed that while the high areas dried out, the lower spots remained muddy. They leveled the ground and planted trees and vines planned for irrigation, and they produced lush and heavy crops.

"In the San Gabriel district they converted rock-strewn hillsides and sandy areas both into flourishing farms. The alkali regions of South El Monte were turned into one of the richest celery and bunch vegetable areas of Southern California. Among the crops they introduced were strawberries in 1904, blackberries, loganberries and raspberries in 1912, and cauliflower in 1917.

"In Contra Costa county they pioneered in the development of fruit crops, strawberries, tomatoes and peas. In Orange county, now one of the richest agricultural counties in the whole of the United States, *Issei* converted areas of boggy bottom lands bordering the Santa Ana River, and followed up by introducing a number of unique crops for which this area is now famous.

"The Japanese developed the garlic industry in San Juan Valley and opened the first lettuce shed in Hollister; they introduced peas to Visalia; they developed watermelon culture in the Dinuba area and pioneered truck gardening in the Delano region. Many of the garden and orchard products begun as experiments by *Issei* flourished into million-dollar industries. The small plots of barren ground reclaimed for production opened the way to full-scale land development of vast acreages deemed unfit for use. Always, with the *Issei*, there was this love of the land, a turning of the soil."

Japanese farmer and his wife in Gardena, Calif., about 1910. They were probably dressed for a visit to Los Angeles. (Kishima Collection)

No complete listing of the *Issei's* pioneering efforts in California agriculture is possible, but it would be a gross oversight not to mention the introduction of rice culture in the area around Marysville, bush peas on the hillsides of Pismo Beach, and strawberry culture in the Watsonville area. By 1910 Japanese were producing about 70 percent of California's strawberries although overall they cultivated less than one percent of the state's total farm acreage. Unfortunately, that one percent was concentrated in a relatively few areas. This concentration, plus the Japanese farmer's ability to make a living by intensive cultivation of a few acres of land (a type of farming with which they were familiar) led in substantial part to the eventual passage of anti-alien land laws which prohibited land ownership by aliens, meaning the Japanese.

It is impossible at this point to check the accuracy of the figures (which appear to be grossly inflated) quoted in the letter reproduced below, but it is typical of the fears, real or inspired, that led eventually to passage of California's alien land law. The letter, signed by "Raisin Grower," was published in the *Fowler* (California) *Ensign* in 1920. It said in part:

"Self preservation is nature's first law, and when any class of people, no matter from what country on earth they come, threatens to undermine us and become the landlords of our state and drive us out, we would not have the sense of dumb brutes if we did not adopt measures to protect ourselves and posterity from disaster.

"The Japanese not only threaten to do this, but they have done it to the point of already controlling nearly one-sixth of the irrigated lands of California and are going ahead in the same direction by leaps and bounds . . . In Placer County, for instance, there are 20,000 acres of land under irrigation that can be farmed, and the Asiatics own or control 17,000 of those acres, and in some other counties the situation is nearly as bad. Suppose that was the situation in every county in California! . . .

"Personally I like the Japanese . . ."

The Japanese immigrant arriving in the United States in the earliest years of the century had an important alternative if he did not want to go into agricultural labor. The railroad tracks that the Irish and the Chinese had helped to lay across the vast distances of the West needed maintenance, and as the number of Chinese laborers available diminished, the Japanese stepped in. H. A. Millis in his book, *The Japanese Problem in the United States*, published in 1915, reports the Japanese labor contractor system was a larger factor than the willingness of the immigrants to work cheaply in opening up these jobs. He writes:

"This method of securing laborers was the greatest factor in creating an effective demand for Japanese section hands. But once employed, another factor entered the situation. The Japanese found favor with the roadmasters and foremen because of their efficiency, and their good behavior in camp. On the whole they proved to be better workmen than any of the immigrant races, the Mexican excepted, and the absence of brawls in camp set them in strong contrast to certain other competing races. So it is found that with the shrewd bargaining ability of the contractor as an active factor, the rate of wages of Japanese advanced more rapidly than that of other races . . ."

In 1906, just before the Gentlemen's Agreement halted the influx of unskilled labor, there were an estimated 13,000 *Issei*—perhaps as many as one in every three *Issei* in the United States—working on the railroads. Responding to the demand for labor and

The first job that many Japanese immigrants found was on railroad section gangs. At one time 13,000 Japanese worked on railroads.

the urging of the bosses, the newcomers headed eastward into the hinterland almost directly off the ships. According to Immigration Commission reports, the Oriental Trading Co. of Seattle alone supplied 15,000 Japanese laborers during the decade between 1898 and 1908. Few had any opportunity to see or learn anything of America before they were rushed off to join section gangs made up entirely of Japanese. With others of their kind, they spoke Japanese, ate Japanese food, shared quarters only with other Japanese in the bunkcars. Although long trains laden with freight and passengers raced by them many times a day, that was about as close as most of them got to white Americans.

In the north, immigrants followed the Great Northern and Northern Pacific tracks over the Cascade Mountains onto the high eastern Washington plateau, into the forests of Idaho and Montana and the endless plains of the Dakotas. As early as 1898, 380 Japanese were employed by the Northern Pacific on the stretch between Tacoma and Billings, Montana. Their pay was 95 cents to one dollar a day. Paralyzing cold swept down on them in winter, and sometimes these men from the mild Japanese islands suffered painful frostbite as they struggled to keep the tracks open. At one time hundreds of Japanese worked for the Oregon Short Line. In the midlands the Central Pacific climbed the High Sierras, wound through historic Donner Pass and stretched out across the desolate Nevada desert into Utah. The sun beat down fiercely on section hands stamping ballast and replacing ties for the Union Pacific in parched Wyoming and Nebraska where the coyote's song was a nightly serenade. In the far south, the Santa Fe and Southern Pacific tracks snaked through a treeless land of mesquite and sagebrush where the sun seared a man's eyes. As many as 400 Japanese worked at one time in Colorado where the Rio Grande and the Colorado and Southern had to maintain rails through the Rockies. It was a vast and hostile country, but the *Issei* were equal to the challenge.

From the peak in 1906 the number of *Issei* railroad workers dropped to 10,000 in 1909, 4,553 in 1913, and 4,300 in 1920. Some who remained in the industry left the section gangs and became skilled roundhouse mechanics. Others rose to foremanships and often were put in charge of non-Japanese crews. Most of the section hands drifted back to the Pacific Coast, but some remained inland to open restaurants, laundries and barber shops, to farm, mine coal and copper ore, butcher cattle in slaughterhouses, find employment in steel mills and lumber camps, and eventually to marry and start families. These hardy laborers with a strong spirit of adventure account for the fact that small clusters of Japanese families are to be found in places like Billings and Havre, Montana; Rock Springs and Cheyenne, Wyoming; Pocatello, Idaho; Scottsbluff, North Platte and Omaha, Nebraska; in the valleys of the Arkansas and South Platte rivers in Colorado; places like Winslow, Arizona, and Gallup, New Mexico; towns with names reminiscent of the lonely wail of locomotive whistles, of the smell of desert dust and greasewood.

Nor were the *Issei* all as docile as Millis seemed to think. Setsugo Hosokawa, later a businessman in Seattle, liked to recall how, as a sixteen-year-old immigrant, he was sent off to join a section gang in northern Montana almost as soon as he landed in Tacoma in 1899. One day he and another section hand neglected their work as they argued, boyishly, over whether the white streak on a distant peak was snow or a salt deposit. When the foreman reprimanded him, Hosokawa in a fit of temper quit his job, collected his pay and set out on foot for California. He knew no English and almost nothing of American geography. Following the tracks, sleeping under bridges, sneaking rides on freight cars, he turned up months later in Sacramento. The experience taught him that he needed to know English. He got a job as a houseboy, learned something about cooking American dishes, and went to grade school.

One of those who remained to farm was Manyumon Fujita who married in 1906 and became a sharecropper near Billings, Montana. His son, Frank, recalls that the lease contract always called for Fujita to improve a certain amount of land, and he remembers hauling away rocks, dynamiting stumps and burning sagebrush.

"My Dad grew dryland beans and sugar beets, mostly," he says. "It wasn't easy. I remember him walking through the dirt behind a two-horse plow, wearing 'shoes' of canvas bean sacks which were white with blue and red stripes. Almost every spring he had to auction his implements—plow, horses, wagon—to pay his debts. Then he would sign another mortgage at the bank to buy new implements and seed to farm another crop. A good part of the time all we had to eat was fried potatoes and something we called *bottera*—fried batter, like pancakes, stuffed with mashed, sweetened beans. Wherever we lived, it was a two-day wagon trip to town. When Dad took us, he'd head for his favorite saloon and we would go along and fill our bellies with the free lunch that was always available—cold meats, rye bread, hardboiled eggs, pickles. We were poor, but all the farmers in the area were in the same fix. We were the only Japanese family, and were completely accepted by our neighbors. I didn't know the meaning of discrimination until we quit farming and moved to Seattle."

A somewhat different railroad story was told by Mrs. Shizuko Iwa Mashino when interviewed in her Oklahoma City home in 1967. She was then ninety-one years old. She came to the United States in 1903 at the urging of an older brother, hoping to continue her study of midwifery. Without money, with no knowledge of English, schooling was hard to come by. She went to work picking fruit in an orchard. The standard wage was $1.25 a day for ten hours. She chose piecework, and her nimble fingers earned her as much as $10 a day, a small fortune at that time. She married another Japanese immigrant in 1906 and moved with him to Kansas City to work in a Harvey House restaurant. When oil was discovered in Oklahoma the family followed the boomers from one town to another, opening and closing a series of restaurants. "I knew I was Japanese, but I was never around other Japanese people," said Opal Mashino Baker, one of Mrs. Mashino's three children and herself the mother of three.

If a Japanese immigrant did not go directly from his ship to a farm labor crew or to a railroad section gang, chances are he became a "schoolboy." American housewives who could not afford full-time domestics opened their homes to Japanese who were interested in working a few hours a day for room, board and a dollar or two per week while attending school—usually grade school. The difficulties of learning English were too much for many of the schoolboys; it seems safe to say the largest part of the education they acquired in that role was in the training they received in their employers' homes—learning to set the table, polish silver, clean house, wash windows and serve the food that an Irish or Chinese cook prepared. This, in most cases, was their first introduction to some of the niceties—and complexities—of the American way of life. After weeks or months of this training they drifted on. Many went into hotel and restaurant work, starting as bellboys and dishwashers. The more observant learned to cook, a skill that was salable almost anywhere. (Years later, it was not uncommon in *Issei* homes for the man to take over the kitchen and cook festive Sunday or Thanksgiving dinners even though he may not have worked professionally as a chef for twenty or thirty years.) The schoolboy experience also led to the development of a group of *Issei* known as "day workers." They hired out by the hour or day to do the heavier cleaning work around a house—washing windows, mopping and waxing floors, moving furniture, beating rugs. Such day workers, usually bachelors, waited at Japanese employment offices for jobs to be telephoned in, and were common well into the 1920's.

Meanwhile, other Japanese were making their way in the cities. The Immigration Commission in 1909 estimated there were between 3,000 and 3,500 separate Japanese-owned establishments employing some 10,000 individuals. Thus it can be seen that on the whole these were modest businesses run usually by the proprietor and his wife, if he had one. Six out of ten of these businesses were capitalized at less than $1,000. Ichihashi explains this situation:

"The Japanese found no opportunity to rise in the occupations in which they were engaged, such as railway construction, mining, lumbering, and agricultural labor. This situation greatly stimulated their general desire to escape from the ranks of wage earners, affecting in particular those who had been in business or reared in cities of their native country. There were two possible avenues of escape from the dependent position of wage earners, namely independent farming and shopkeeping. Then there was the fact that Japanese were invariably discriminated against in American boarding houses, restaurants, barber shops, places of amusements, etc., necessitating the creation of these facilities themselves. Finally, as Japanese became familiar with American life, some of them entered the general competitive field of trades."

The business experience of Kikumatsu Togasaki, pioneer San Francisco merchant and sire of an illustrious family, is not untypical. Togasaki came to the United States in 1887 after graduating from a Japanese government school of jurisprudence. He intended to make only a short visit, but decided to remain in the United States after his marriage. He operated a small rooming house, but as his family grew he sold out and opened a gift and art goods shop. When anti-Japanese pressure forced wholesale houses to cut off supplies for Japanese laundries, Togasaki organized a cooperative and purchased machinery and other needs from Eastern firms, thus enabling the operators to ride out the boycott. This effort resulted in Togasaki forming the Mutual Supply Co., which his son, Susumu, continues to operate as an importing firm.

The Japanese found a place in the salmon canning industry when the Chinese labor supply began to dwindle. A special report issued by the Washington State Bureau of Labor in 1915 reports that one Chinese contractor was employing a large number of Japanese because of the shortage of Chinese workmen. He paid Japanese laborers $40 to $45 a month while he was paying his Chinese up to $70 because "they were better workers and more efficient." This same report has this to say:

"It is almost invariably the rule that Japanese are filling the places thus vacated by the Chinamen, and this intensified the problem rather than offering a solution, for the people in general have a greater antipathy toward the Japs. The Japs are not nearly as trustworthy and reliable as the brown-hued brother of the Celestial race. Moreover they are not as amenable to the requirements of the employer, are quarrelsome among themselves, as well as less efficient in their work. As a matter of fact, the Jap laborer is loom-

ing up much stronger now than the Chinese and is causing much
irritation in the communities of the state where his labor, for certain reasons, is sought in preference to that of the white workman."

The Chinese were hired at first to do the most unpleasant kind
of work. Most of them were fish butchers, cutting off the head,
tail and fins of the salmon, slitting open the bellies, removing the
entrails and washing out the cavities under cold running water.
In later years a machine was invented to do this work, and it was
nicknamed the "Iron Chink." Since the machine failed to completely eviscerate the fish, a certain amount of Chinese and Japanese hand labor was still required at the washing troughs.

Because of the nature of the work, long hours during the rush
season, reports of poor food, unpleasant voyages in ancient freight-
ers to Alaskan canneries, harsh bosses and long months of isolation,
many Japanese scorned this kind of work and the regular "cannery
boys" came to be regarded as roughnecks. It is difficult to tell at
this point in history how much general Caucasian resentment
against Japanese cannery hands was due to the fact that they were
a tough group, and how much could be laid to the fact—as other
employers discovered—that the Japanese were independent, proud
and often outspoken in comparison to the Chinese.

Beginning in the twenties, *Nisei* began to join the cannery crews
and many of them financed a large part of their college educations
with summer jobs in Washington, Oregon and Alaska salmon proc-
essing plants. How the Japanese lost these jobs is another story.

It was a shortage of labor, rather than the exit of the Chinese
from the manpower market, that provided Japanese immigrants an
entree into the lumber industry of the Pacific Northwest. At the
turn of the century the manufacture of lumber and timber products
provided employment for 75,000 persons in Washington and Oregon. By 1907, the Immigration Commission found 2,685 Japanese
were working in Washington sawmills and lumber camps. The
Commission reported:

"Where the Japanese have been employed, they have, without
exception, been paid lower wages than men of other races engaged
in the same occupations. In the one mill investigated they were
employed in skilled and semiskilled positions . . . While the Japanese were employed as trimmers, edgermen, planing-mill feeders,
lumber graders, lathe mill men, and carpenters at wages varying

from $1.65 to $2 per day, at other mills white men engaged in these occupations were paid from $2.75 to $3.50 per day."

This kind of work must have offered a certain satisfaction, however, for the men in the Japanese crew at Port Blakely, Washington, were among the first *Issei* to start families. Many of the older *Nisei* of the Seattle community, now in their sixties and early seventies, were born at Port Blakely. And like *Issei* who remained with the railroads until the outbreak of war in 1941, there were other *Issei* who were employed in supervisory positions at sawmills in places like Eatonville and Enumclaw, Washington, until evacuation forced them out.

Professor Frank Miyamoto of the University of Washington observes that characteristically, "the Japanese accepted work at the mills in groups rather than individually, and wherever they worked, a colony tended to develop that was separated from the rest of the mill town. In fact, employers often assumed the expense of building a separate cluster of longhouses to quarter Japanese workers, which may have reflected the value placed on them as laborers."

When the men married and established families, the bunkhouses were partitioned into apartments and, Miyamoto says, there were created villages where "often appeared incomplete but colorful reconstructions of life in Japan, for example, the public bathhouse, the confectionery store, performances of Japanese drama and art, and the like."

Mining provides a somewhat similar story, although in different areas of the West. Like other immigrants, the *Issei* mined copper in Utah and Nevada, coal in Wyoming, Colorado and New Mexico. They worked in the smelters of Garfield, Tooele and Magna, Utah, and the steel mill at Pueblo, Colorado. Joe Grant Masaoka remembers that he used to deliver fish from his father's Salt Lake City market to the bunkhouses in nearby Bingham Canyon where some 800 *Issei* worked in the world's largest open cut copper mine. These men, mostly bachelors, like the sawmill workers, were supervised by Japanese bosses and housed in their own quarters. In central Utah, centered around the town of Helper, approximately a thousand *Issei* mined coal in the early 1920's.

In Colorado, *Issei* both mined coal and helped make steel. As many as 500 *Issei* worked in the C.F. & I. steel plant at Pueblo shortly after the turn of the century, getting $2.50 a ten-hour day for blast furnace work, $1.90 for lesser jobs, while others were employed in the shallow coal mines north of Denver.

A simple listing of places where the Japanese worked, and their numbers, fails to capture the bitterness, the conflict and tragedy that marked the mining industry in that period, and of which certainly the Japanese were a part. Unfortunately the record is not complete. The United Mine Workers were trying to organize the pits of the West at the time, asking for recognition of the union as bargaining agent, better wages, payment in cash rather than scrip, the right to trade at stores other than the one the company ran, and honest weight for the coal they mined. (The miners charged they had to produce 2,600 to 2,800 pounds of coal to get credit for a ton.)

Judging from their record elsewhere, it seems likely that some Japanese either through ignorance or simple acceptance of whatever their bosses told them, worked in the mines for less money than Caucasians. Other Japanese were employed as strikebreakers in the series of disputes that wracked the industry. In his authoritative book, *Out of the Depths*, which is the story of the infamous events that led to the so-called Ludlow Massacre in the coal fields of southern Colorado in 1914, Barron B. Beshoar writes:

"Hatred and despair gripped the polyglot peoples of the Colorado coal district as the violent winter of 1907 gave way to a mountain excuse for spring. Far underground, in labyrinths of gaseous shafts, thousands of men toiled long hours each day with a sullenness matched only in the squatty mules that tugged at overladen coal cars . . . The Scotch, the Welsh and the Irish miners, who had seen thousands of their blood brothers driven from the coal fields after the strike of 1903, loathed the hordes of foreigners gathered by enterprising labor agents of the coal barons from the Mediterranean countries and the far corners of Europe and Asia to take the places of the rebels of 1903. The newcomers, in turn, despised each other, according to race. The Italians looked down on the Greeks, the Greeks scorned the Poles as social inferiors, and the latter had only contempt for the skinny-armed Mexicans. They were united only in their hatred for their employers and their belief that Japanese were scum of the worst sort . . ."

Beshoar writes that striking miners, goaded beyond endurance by brutal mine guards, attacked the mine at Forbes with cries of

"Remember Ludlow!" He goes on: "A number of Japanese ran into the boarding house and barricaded the doors. 'Come out and surrender,' a miner yelled. The answer was a shot. A torch was applied to the building and the miners waited grimly for the Japanese to come out. They never did. Eleven guards were dead in the street . . ."

But there was at least one Japanese, and probably many more, on the side of the union. Beshoar mentions a K. Uyada (probably Uyeda) who was one of three strikers charged with killing a Major Lester in a battle between militiamen and miners. The judge who had ordered the three held for trial was ousted by the Colorado Supreme Court as too biased and prejudiced to render justice, and there is no record that Uyada went to trial.

In relation to other occupations, however, the Japanese did not play a large part in the mining industry. Few had either mining experience or came from a mining background, and many were not physically rugged enough to stand up under back-breaking mine and mill work.

Still, many adapted to the needs of the burgeoning frontier. Harry Hokasono saw the West's need for skilled construction laborers. He organized a crew of more than 500 Japanese, and with them he built irrigation systems, laid rails deep into the Rockies, cleared the way for power lines, graded highway routes. It is said that at one time he owned more than a thousand horses and mules which were used to haul earth-moving scoops. Although he is scarcely remembered, Harry Hokasono deserves a place among Colorado's builders.

Life was hard for the young, vigorous, unattached immigrants, but it was not always grim. Despite legal and social discrimination, economic hardships, unfamiliarity with language and customs, and strong ties of kinship and sentiment that linked them with the homeland, most of the young *Issei* found life in America interesting and not entirely unpleasant. Although they were aliens, they found their labor had a value. And in settlements of their own people, they found they could observe old country customs as they desired, for America was a wondrously free land. In later years, the *Issei* loved to reminisce about their early-day experiences. This speaker remembers the swift passage of time:

"There was always plenty of work. Two days after I came to

this country, I had a job on the railroad. I could have worked on the railroad as long as I wanted. But I wanted to learn something besides railroad work. I wanted to learn English. So I quit and went to the city and got a job as a schoolboy. Any Japanese could work as a schoolboy. We made room and board and a dollar a month wages and went to grade school. We learned housework, cooking, and American customs. On Sundays we would get together with other Japanese schoolboys and talk about the Mrs. who was our boss and wish we had more money to spend. It was a very pleasant time. At first we thought we would go home to Japan, rich and famous, in two or three years. But ten years later we were still here with no money to go home."

Of fun times: "Near the town of Thermopolis, Wyoming, are some fine hot springs. They reminded us of hot springs resorts which are highly treasured back home in Japan. One Sunday several of us *Issei* went to the springs and found a cave filled with steam. We took off our clothes, walked into the cave and relaxed. We got to feeling good and we sang Japanese folk songs which to Americans sound like people moaning and groaning in great pain. Some boys walking by heard us. They saw our clothes and thought somebody was being killed, so they ran to get the police. How embarrassing!"

And of unfamiliarity with American food: "I was very hungry for rice, but the family did not serve rice. I liked meat, too, but meat was expensive. The Mrs. always said, 'Eat potato, Roy, eat potato. Potato is good for you.' "

Of the first encounter with a tomato: "I never had seen tomatoes in Japan. The first one I saw in America was beautiful. I bit into it, expecting a wonderful fruit taste, like an apple. I spit it out right away."

And pumpkin pie: "The Mrs. said pumpkin pie was a great delicacy and I expected something wonderful. Then I found out pumpkin pies are made from *kabocha* (squash, a humble vegetable eaten by the poor in Japan). I was disappointed in *kabocha* pie. Then the Mrs. showed me how to make it, and I tried it, but the pumpkin filling cracked on top, like an earthquake cracks the earth, so my first experience as a pie-maker was a failure."

On language difficulties: "First English words we learned were useful words like 'hot' and 'work' and 'drink water.' We learned 'go home,' too. When the boss said 'go home,' that meant we were fired. 'Go home *kutta*' (roughly translated to 'got stuck with go home') became a familiar expression. One time a friend of mine borrowed a rowboat from an American farmer and tipped it over accidentally. He wanted to apologize, but didn't know how. Finally he said: 'Boat-oh, up-down, *gomen nasai*.' The farmer understood, mainly because of the gestures. There are many stories of Japanese railroad section hands who went to a farmhouse to buy eggs to supplement their skimpy meals. When they couldn't make themselves understood, they would squat, cackle like a hen and drop a rock. Japanese hens acted exactly like American hens."

But these were carefree times that could not last.

7

NEITHER WHITE NOR AFRICAN

ABOUT THE TIME Puerto Rican immigrants were moving into large sections of Manhattan and Chicago, block by block—and causing long-time residents to flee to the suburbs—there was circulated a story that was told only half in jest. It seems that in the year 1492 some Indians were lurking in the bushes when a small boat set out for shore from a fleet of three sailing vessels anchored offshore. As they watched, Columbus stepped on land and planted the Spanish flag. At that moment one Indian turned to another and remarked: "Well, there goes the old neighborhood."

There is nothing to tell us when signs reading, "No Japs Wanted," or some similarly endearing phrase, first appeared. The first true immigrants, arriving in the decade after 1880, encountered little personal hostility. They did, however, walk right into a hornet's nest of anti-Chinese feeling which had come to a climax with the Chinese Exclusion Act of 1882.

If a date has to be set for the start of serious hostility against the Chinese, it would be 1869 when the Central Pacific railroad was completed, throwing more than 10,000 men out of work. Back East, economic depressions were blamed on Wall Street manipulators; in the West of that time, it was "cheap Asiatic labor." An Irish immigrant labor leader, Dennis Kearney, is credited with popularizing the slogan, "The Chinese must go," with labor unions, politicians and the press vying to see who could be most violently anti-Chinese.

Actually, discrimination against late-comers was nothing new in the history of American immigration. During the waves of migration following the Irish potato famine, proper Bostonians became accustomed to seeing the letters "NINA" in front of shops and employment agencies. They stood for "No Irish Need Apply." Professor Robert Wilson remembers that his father, a carpenter from the British Isles, was bitter that Swedish immigrant contractors would hire only other Swedes, and if there were none, they hired Norwegians. "It's getting so that a white man can't make a living any more," he complained.

The history of California—where one in ten residents in 1870 was Chinese—is replete with stories of Chinese being stoned, robbed, assaulted and murdered. They were a fair target for hoodlums, for only occasionally were whites punished for outrages against Chinese.

Largely under pressure from the West Coast, Congress in 1879 passed a law prohibiting further immigration of Chinese laborers. President Rutherford Hayes vetoed it because the law violated the Burlingame Treaty of 1868 with China which recognized "the inherent and inalienable right of man to change his home and allegiance and also the mutual advantage of free migration and emigration of their citizens and subjects respectively, from one country to the other, for the purpose of curiosity, or trade or as permanent residents."

But, says Betty Lee Sung, "an election was coming up and the West had to be placated."

A commission was sent to Peking in 1880 to negotiate a revision of the Burlingame Treaty. China recognized the right of the United States to regulate immigration of laborers, but noted that "Chinese subjects, whether proceeding to the United States as teachers, students, merchants, or from curiosity, together with their body and household servants" would be free to come and go. The Chinese government understood this enumeration represented examples of the various categories. But the United States promptly interpreted this as meaning *only* Chinese in the five listed categories could migrate to the U.S. The Chinese Exclusion Act in 1882 effectively sealed out the Chinese until World War II.

It did not take long for "The Chinese must go" to be modified to "The Japs must go." Ichihashi reports the revised cry was heard as early as 1887, just five years after the Chinese Exclusion Act. At that time there were all of 400 Japanese in the entire state of California, most of them employed as domestics and hardly calculated to pose a danger to the American workingman. Most Californians at that time had never even seen a Japanese. The instigator was one Dr. O'Donnell of San Francisco, a person of somewhat clouded reputation, and he succeeded in stirring up little support.

Later agitators were much more successful. By 1890, members of a shoemakers' union forced a white man to get rid of fifteen Japanese working in his factory, presumably for less money than he was paying his white help. (In retrospect, it seems reasonable to assume that the Japanese would have been happy to work for the same pay as whites, if it had been offered.) Boycotts, intimidation and violence were employed to discourage employers of Japanese labor and Japanese businessmen who had gone into competition with whites. When one George Sugihara opened a restaurant in San Francisco, pickets in front of the establishment passed out matchboxes on which was printed: "White men and women, patronize your own race."

Until after 1900, however, most of the organized hostility against the Japanese was what Roger Daniels calls "a tail to the anti-Chinese kite." As each ten-year period of the Chinese Exclusion Act neared an end, agitation would be stirred anew in California to insure an extension of the law. It is interesting to note that some *Issei* failed to see in this period that, like it or not, their welfare was linked closely to that of the Chinese. At a meeting of the so-called Chinese Exclusion Convention in San Francisco in 1901, attended by some 800 unionists and 200 politicians, a small group of Japanese stood at the entrance and passed out leaflets saying in effect that it was all right to exclude Chinese but leave the Japanese alone.

(The Chinese were to have their day some forty years later. After Pearl Harbor, when Japanese Americans were the targets of a misplaced hate campaign, some Chinese made sure their origins were known by wearing buttons that proclaimed "I am Chinese." In fact, both were Americans.)

In 1900, two events focused American attention on "the Japanese problem." First, annexation of Hawaii to the United States had the effect of freeing thousands of Japanese contract laborers on Hawaiian sugar plantations. Many of them made their way to the mainland, packed like cattle in the holds of ships. In 1899, 2,844 Japanese had entered the United States. The next year the number quadrupled to 12,635, alarming the West. Their arrival coincided with a report that a Chinese victim of bubonic plague had been discovered in San Francisco. In an action reminiscent of Europe in the Dark Ages, Mayor James D. Phelan quarantined the Chinese and Japanese sections of the city and ordered mass inoculation of Orientals. He did not explain why it was not necessary for Caucasians to be inoculated. Japanese community leaders protested the action was political and intended to put them out of business. As one result, the Japanese realized the need of organization to protect their interests, and the Japanese Association of America was born. Later, when San Francisco businessmen protested that the plague scare would hurt commerce in the entire city, Phelan decided there had been no outbreak after all.

The Japanese government was not insensitive to American reaction to the flow of immigrants to the mainland from Hawaii. It clamped down on the number of passports issued to laborers the following year, and only 5,269 entered the United States.

As for the Japanese Association, Daniels says "it seems quite clear that this organization did in fact have very close ties with the Japanese government and should properly be designated as semi-official." But, he adds, "there was nothing sinister or improper in its connection with Tokyo; after all, the *Issei* were, because of their status as 'alien ineligible to citizenship,' still Japanese nationals despite their permanent residence here. They were, therefore, to a certain extent, the responsibility of the home country—a responsibility that, through its consuls, Japan shouldered. Had she not done so, the *Issei* would have passed into the legal limbo of stateless persons . . ."

Following extension of the Chinese Exclusion Act in 1902, there was a three-year period of relative quiet on the West Coast's racial front. Then the first big guns in what Carey McWilliams calls "The California-Japanese War" were fired in a series of inflammatory articles in the San Francisco *Chronicle*, at that time perhaps the most influential West Coast newspaper. On February 23, 1905, the *Chronicle* carried a front page headline: "THE JAPANESE INVASION, THE PROBLEM OF THE HOUR." On subsequent days the *Chronicle* published stories under headlines such as these: "JAPANESE A MENACE TO AMERICAN WOMEN, BROWN MEN AN EVIL IN THE PUBLIC SCHOOLS, BROWN ARTISANS STEAL BRAINS OF WHITES, CRIME

AND POVERTY GO HAND IN HAND WITH ASIATIC LABOR."

We quote from McWilliams:

"Just why the *Chronicle* should have launched this attack has never been determined. But the owner of the *Chronicle*, M. H. DeYoung, had been a candidate for the United States Senate a few years previously and some observers construed these vicious articles as a renewal of his candidacy."

DeYoung did not run again, but the articles helped to focus attention on the Japanese military successes in the war against Russia, a white country, and touched off a wave of apprehension that Japan would become "a serious menace, not only to California, but the nation." Shortly after the *Chronicle* series began, both houses of the California legislature voted unanimously a resolution asking Congress to "limit and diminish the further immigration of Japanese." Shortly after that the Asiatic Exclusion League was formed in San Francisco and within a year it boasted a membership of more than 75,000.

The resolution charged the Japanese were undesirable, could not be assimilated, and expressed fear that after the war with Russia thousands of discharged soldiers would flood the state—"immoral, intemperate, quarrelsome men, bound to labor for a pittance, and to subsist on a supply with which a white man can hardly sustain life." The resolution also termed the Japanese immigrants "mere transients" who do not buy land or build houses and who "contribute nothing to the growth of the state."

Daniels comments: "The resolution was not only insulting; it demonstrated that the legislators did not know what was happening in their own state . . . The *Issei* were buying land and building houses, and later legislatures would spend much time and energy trying to stop them . . . For the next four decades, without exception, anti-Japanese bills were introduced in every biennial session . . . From the day of the League's formation, May 14, 1905, until after the end of the Second World War, there was in California an organized anti-Japanese movement that would eventually draw support from all segments of the state's population."

The basis of this hostility was both racial and economic. Virtually all the arguments against the Japanese stressed the contention that the Japanese could not be assimilated. By their definition, as-

similation meant biological absorption—the melting pot concept—
and they contended assimilation could not leap over the color line.
Apparently the possibility of cultural assimilation did not cross
their minds. As a matter of fact, the Japanese were much more
ready to be assimilated culturally than biologically; intermarriage
was relatively rare. The propaganda also was replete with charges
that the white man could not compete with the Japanese' willingness to work for coolie wages. The Asiatic Exclusion League was
to prove relatively ineffective and its leadership was soon discred-
ited. But, says Daniels, "Its constant propaganda helped distort
further the already twisted image of the *Issei;* its very existence
set the pattern for more efficient successors. While the League
lasted, the flames of prejudice were never allowed to go completely
out."

Far more significant than the emotional rabble-rousers of the
League were the various elements that employed legal means to
harass the Japanese immigrants, harassment based on denial of citizenship. They pointed out that the law did not permit Orientals
to become American citizens, and because they were ineligible to
citizenship, they were entitled to fewer rights than other immigrants.

The fault, then, was in the law that set up two classes of immigrants—one desirable enough to be granted American citizenship,
the other undesirable.

(American-born offspring of Japanese immigrants were citizens
by birth. In the hysteria of World War II, a few members of Congress sought to strip the *Nisei* of their American citizenship and
send them "back to Japan." Cooler heads prevailed.)

As late as 1950 there were more than 500 federal, state and local
laws and ordinances aimed directly or indirectly against resident
Japanese. Most of these restrictions had as their basis the phrase,
"ineligible to citizenship." Persons ineligible to citizenship, meaning the Japanese and prior to 1943 the Chinese, were denied the
right to own land or buy homes. Other barriers were erected to
prevent them from engaging in a variety of businesses and professions, ranging from hairdressing to the law, and having thus built
up obstacles against their integration, people of McClatchy's ilk
later were to protest that the Japanese were extremely clannish and
totally unassimilable.

If the Japanese immigrants had any doubt about what it meant to be denied citizenship, they were told frequently, as in this editorial published in a San Francisco newspaper:

"The Board of Education made a serious mistake last night, but one that we think it will correct when the members have thought the matter over. The Board decided to allow Japanese to attend the public schools on equal terms with American children. The Japanese are ineligible to citizenship, and, as such, are not fit to associate and be classed with American children. The American government has declared them an inferior race, and such they are in the eyes of all true Americans. To endeavor to force them upon Americans as equals is therefore an insult . . ."

The tortured line of logic went like this: The law says Japanese are ineligible for citizenship. This means they are inferior. Because they are inferior they should not be permitted to attend public schools. Since they cannot go to school, they cannot be assimilated culturally. Because they cannot be assimilated, they are undesirable!

The first reference to segregating Japanese school children appears in the San Francisco *Chronicle* of June 15, 1893. At the end of a ten-paragraph story on a meeting of the Board of Education, it reported simply: "Director Burke introduced a resolution providing that hereafter all persons of the Japanese race seeking entrance to the public schools must attend what is known as the Chinese school. It was adopted."

A few days later the Japanese consul, Chinda, protested the board's action. Chinda said there were between forty and fifty Japanese in the public schools and described them as "respectable and well behaved and fully cognizant of the privileges extended to them." He argued that the school board's resolution was "unjust" and caused Japanese residents "mortification."

The California political code at the time contained this provision: "Every school, unless otherwise provided by law, must be opened for the admission of all children between 6 and 21 years of age . . . Trustees shall have the power to exclude children of filthy or vicious habits, or children suffering from contagious or infectious diseases, and also to establish separate schools for children of Mongolian or Chinese descent. When such separate schools are established, Chinese or Mongolian children must not be admitted into any other school."

At this point it is not clear whether Consul Chinda was protesting segregation or the indignity of having the Japanese lumped together with Chinese and Mongolians. However, after receiving the protest, the president of the board ruled it had no right to compel Japanese to attend a school set apart for Chinese because there was no separate school for the Japanese. This would indicate that he favored a separate school for the Japanese. But in an apparent contradiction, the president went on to say that to exclude Japanese children from public schools was an "unjustifiable and unwarranted insult" to the Japanese race. The board voted 7 to 2 to rescind the resolution.

The next major attempt to segregate Japanese children attracted national and international attention. On May 6, 1905, the San Francisco school board announced it would send Japanese pupils to an enlarged Oriental school to save white children from being "affected by association with pupils of the Mongolian race."

No date was set for the action. On April 18, 1906, San Francisco was rocked by a violent earthquake, and a large part of the city was swept by fire. On the pretext that the surviving schools were overcrowded, the Board of Education on October 11, 1906, passed a resolution which directed principals "to send all Chinese, Japanese and Korean children to the Oriental School, situated on the south side of Clay Street, between Powell and Mason Streets, on and after Monday, October 15, 1906."

Historians have pointed out that two leading San Francisco political figures were about to be indicted on graft charges and suggest that the school segregation order was an effort to draw attention away from their plight. If so, they were successful. The Board of Education's order was quickly noted in both Tokyo and Washington. Japan was riding high after humbling Russia in the war that had ended only thirteen months earlier and was touchy about her national honor. President Theodore Roosevelt, who had a healthy respect for power, had been impressed by Japanese military success and felt that her immigrants deserved better than to be discriminated against by a municipal school board. Late in 1906 he sent Victor H. Metcalf, a Californian who was his Secretary of Commerce and Labor, to see what could be done to protect the rights of the Japanese. Metcalf found the issue involved all of 93 Japanese pupils—25 of whom were American-born—and they were distributed among 23 schools.

But if the number was insignificant, the principle involved was monumental. It would have been easy enough for the *Issei* to bow to the injustice—as the Chinese had done and as some persons of faint heart had advocated—and accept the board's resolution. To their credit, the *Issei* decided to fight discrimination against the children, arguing that the *Nisei* never could be expected to become good Americans if they were not permitted to associate freely with Americans of other racial and ethnic backgrounds, and if they were to be segregated on the basis of race. One suspects that a strong element of racial pride was present; discriminate against the Chinese if you must, but not the Japanese. At any rate, they protested mightily, even though their numbers and resources were limited. What would the historical outcome have been if they had accepted the principle of segregation and permitted San Francisco to establish a precedent? Would the thousands of *Nisei* who came later have been confined, like the Negroes in the South, to "separate but equal" educational facilities? San Francisco-born George Kiyoshi Togasaki, who was one of the twenty-five little *Nisei* caught up in the struggle, and who in 1968–69 served as president of Rotary International, says: "I am confident that the decision to fight was a very large factor in the subsequent integration of the *Nisei*, and the respected position they hold today, in the greater American community."

Dr. Thomas T. Yatabe of Chicago, one of the founding fathers of the Japanese American Citizens League which was to play such a large role in the history of the Japanese in the United States, recalls vividly the day he was told of the segregation order. Born in San Francisco in 1897, he lived outside the Japanese community and was the only Oriental child in his school. One day the principal called him into her office, put her arms around him, and with tears in her eyes she said: "Tom, I am going to have to transfer you to the Oriental school."

Tom was only eight years old, and the racial implications escaped him at the moment. He knew only that he would be separated from his friends, that he alone would have to take a horse-drawn street-car and ride across town to go to school. He angrily tore up the transfer. While his educational future was being discussed in Washington and Tokyo and the Board of Education offices, Tom and many other Japanese children went to a special school organized by the *Issei* with private tutors.

This was the period when he heard the bitter boyhood taunt aimed at Orientals: "Hey, skibbee, yellow-belly green-guts!" Its precise meaning, if there ever was one, has been lost over the years. "Skibbee," of course, comes from *sukebei* which is the Japanese word for a lewd and lascivious person. (At eight years of age?) And during certain periods in certain circles "yellow-belly" was an adjective that preceded "Jap" as inevitably as "damn" was linked to "Yankee" in the South. As for "green-guts," it is probably an epithet whose full horror was comprehensible only to small boys of the day.

Five months later when the Japanese were integrated back into the school system, Tom's parents had moved into another part of the city. When he reported to the office for enrollment, the principal in Tom's presence telephoned the superintendent's office to ask: "We have a Jap child here. Can we let him in?"

As for Secretary Metcalf, he found both the school board and the resident Japanese had points in their favor. School authorities pointed out that many of the aliens were teen-agers—43 were fifteen years old or older—who, because of an inadequate command of English, were in classes with much younger children and presumably had an unhealthy interest in little girls. Ultimately, San Francisco authorities were invited to Washington where a compromise was worked out: All overage alien pupils were to be placed in separate schools where they could be given special help with English; all other Japanese children could continue in the regular schools. Even though the *Issei* in San Francisco claimed and deserved much of the credit for the settlement, it must be added that this was a case where the influence of "the strong militaristic government in Japan" noted by Betty Lee Sung had made itself felt.

More significant was the fact that a relatively minor local issue had forced the President of the United States to take notice and act. Thirty-five years later West Coast pressure was to force another Roosevelt, Franklin Delano, to approve the unprecedented removal of 110,000 Japanese, citizens and aliens alike, from their homes to inland camps.

Theodore Roosevelt was astute enough to realize that the San Francisco school issue was only the surface eruption of a deep-seated California infection. He figured that continued immigration of Japanese would only lead to greater trouble so he set out to try and stem the flow. And he made at least a gesture to open up naturalization to the Japanese. In successive annual messages to Congress in 1905 and 1906 he proposed changing the naturalization laws. Assailing discrimination against immigrants "who desire to come here as a citizen," Roosevelt in the 1905 message said: "We cannot afford to consider whether he is Catholic or Protestant, Jew or Gentile; whether he is English or Irish, Frenchman or German, Japanese, Italian, Scandinavian, Slav, or Magyar." But he made it a point to exclude "the entire Chinese coolie class" from the list of desirables. The next year he recommended to Congress an act "specifically providing for the naturalization of Japanese who come here intending to become American citizens." His sincerity in these proposals is a matter of doubt. Some historians suggest Roosevelt was interested primarily in barring all Japanese labor and was offering naturalization for resident Japanese in return for a commitment from Tokyo.

Daniels observes: "Roosevelt never again publicly proposed naturalization for the Japanese . . . Since there is no evidence that he ever made the slightest effort to have this proposal implemented . . . it is reasonable to assume that Roosevelt made it chiefly for Japanese consumption and in order to have an advanced position from which to retreat in his dealings with California."

It may not have been apparent to the *Issei* at that time, but they were being victimized from two directions. On the one hand, Roosevelt was not entirely innocent of the charge that he was playing politics, knowing that he needed the support of the West while aware that a coalition of the West and the racist Deep South could block pet projects of his not related to Japan. He had to tread softly. On the other, Tokyo found California's anti-Japanese attitude a useful bogeyman to be dusted off and displayed whenever it was necessary to distract the people's attention from domestic ills, new taxes, or troubles elsewhere. Racial discrimination was particularly galling to an emerging nation seeking equality.

The Japanese classification as "aliens ineligible to citizenship" goes back to an interpretation of naturalization laws which held that no provisions had been made for persons who were neither black nor white. Naturalization procedures were established for "free white persons"—some whites were not free—in the earliest days of the nation when, of course, there were no Orientals on the scene. From time to time the law was amended as circumstances required. As an aftermath of the Civil War, citizenship was extended to Negroes in 1870. In 1887 Indians were given the right provided they voluntarily left their tribes and took up homesteads. On the other hand, naturalization of Chinese was expressly prohibited as part of the exclusion act of 1882. This slur was not remedied until 1943 when Congress recognized the injustice of discriminating against the Chinese while embracing China as an ally fighting for a common cause in World War II.

Over the years various Japanese had sought naturalization, and since interpretation of the law was in the hands of local officials, a few were granted citizenship, usually in the East. One source estimates that as many as 460 *Issei* were naturalized. The earliest on record in California is Iwao Yoshikawa, a native of Osaka, who arrived in the United States about 1887. He had been a clerk in a court of law in Japan. On his arrival in San Francisco he worked as a schoolboy and studied American law in his spare time. He quickly learned enough English to get along, and because he was familiar with legal proceedings he frequently served as an interpreter in court. In 1889 he filed application for naturalization in San Francisco and was granted his first papers, and although the record does not show whether he was granted citizenship five years later when he would have fulfilled the residency requirement, the presumption is that his naturalization was completed. Yoshikawa's story has been recorded because the Japanese government was curious as to whether his naturalization automatically would mean renunciation of his Japanese citizenship. The Foreign Office found that there was no law providing for such renunciation—a situation later remedied—and ruled that if Yoshikawa became an American, he would still be considered a citizen by Japan. Generally in California, however, it was assumed that Japanese were ineligible for citizenship, and this assumption was given legal standing by a Supreme Court decision in 1922.

The decision involved Takao Ozawa, born in Japan but a graduate of high school in Berkeley, California, and for several years a student at the University of California. He brought suit seeking American citizenship, partly to test the legality of California's Alien Land Act which prohibited "aliens ineligible to citizenship" from owning land. The Supreme Court ruled that the law limited naturalization to "free white persons and to aliens of African nativity and to persons of African descent." Obviously Ozawa was neither white nor African. Thus, U.S. policy left Ozawa and immigrants like him in limbo.

At the same time, the Supreme Court in the Yamashita and Kono cases cancelled certificates of naturalization which had been issued to these two Japanese by a superior court in the state of Washington. The Supreme Court held that the superior court had been in error when it extended citizenship to persons who were ineligible.

There was one last hope. Congress had passed a law offering citizenship to "any person of foreign birth who served in the military or naval forces of the United States" during World War I. Many Japanese aliens saw duty with U.S. forces. One of them, named Toyota, had been issued a certificate of naturalization in Massachusetts in 1921 under this law. The action was challenged, and in 1925 the Supreme Court returned a decision which said in part:

"It has been the settled policy of the United States since the beginning not to allow the naturalization of any person unless he was a free white person. An exception was made to this in 1870 when persons of African nativity or African descent were admitted to the list of eligibles. There is no question that a Japanese who has not served in the Army or Navy of the United States cannot be admitted for naturalization . . . It is contended, however, that a different rule applies to persons who have been in the United States military and naval service . . . This is denied."

The law did not specifically bar the Japanese as it did the Chinese. But the effect was the same. From time to time it had been urged that education and good character standards be substituted for racism in the naturalization laws. But racial barriers were not eliminated until passage of the Walter-McCarran Immigration and Nationality Act in 1952, a measure strongly supported despite a number of shortcomings by the Japanese American Citizens League.

The effort to reduce the flow of immigration following the San Francisco school trouble took two directions. First, President Roose-

velt by executive order in 1907 barred entry into the United States
of Japanese from Hawaii, Mexico and Canada. There is no record
of how many Japanese who legally had entered Mexico and Canada
slipped across the casually guarded borders into the United States,
or how many made legal entry, but it is likely they numbered in
the hundreds rather than the thousands. The executive order was
directed primarily at Japanese seeking entry from Hawaii.

Second, a series of conversations were started in Washington
between Secretary of State Elihu Root and Ambassador Kogoro
Takahira. After many months of negotiations the Japanese government agreed not to issue passports to the United States for either
skilled or unskilled laborers. Exceptions were made for laborers
who had been in the United States previously and their blood relatives. This was the so-called Gentlemen's Agreement, the precise
text of which was not divulged. However, the effect was that Japan
voluntarily undertook to restrict emigration. Although the agreement was hailed as a diplomatic triumph in the United States, it
was criticized in Japan and vigorously condemned by the *Nichi Bei*
of San Francisco, then the most influential Japanese language newspaper in the United States.

Soon, however, the Gentlemen's Agreement was found to be not
nearly so effective in excluding the Japanese as Americans had been
led to believe. Perhaps the fault was in the expectation. There were
two primary points of friction. First was lack of agreement on
what constituted a laborer. The Japanese government felt it was
right in classifying a prospective immigrant as a farmer because he
had indeed operated a farm. But when the man came to the United
States he had neither the knowledge nor the resources to become
an independent farmer. So he became a laborer, sometimes on a
farm, sometimes elsewhere. Californians charged Japan was trying
to evade the spirit of the Gentlemen's Agreement.

The second point of friction was more far-reaching. In the 1900–
08 period, men immigrants had outnumbered women 6 to 1. As we
have seen, most of the men intended to remain in this country only
temporarily. But as their stays became extended, they sought wives.
Those who could afford it returned to Japan to marry and brought
their brides back to America. Others sent for mail order brides, the
match being made by friends or relatives in the old tradition and
approved by the principals after an exchange of photographs, a
familiar practice among some groups of European immigrants. Such

marriages were usually solemnized by proxy. Under Japanese law a woman was considered married when her name was entered on her husband's family record, strictly a bookkeeping process. The Japanese government contended it was only reasonable and humane that such couples be permitted to be united. But many Californians demanded that Japan abide by the letter of the agreement which permitted entry of non-laborers or "laborers, who, in coming to the continent, seek to resume a formerly acquired domicile, *to join a parent, wife or children* residing therein." They complained, correctly, that the agreement said nothing about wives from Japan joining a husband in the United States.

Aside from the legal aspects, the picture bride system provides intensely interesting human studies. Both parties to a proxy marriage were anxious, of course, to put on the best face possible both before and at the time of meeting. Men and girls from the same village who were matched were likely to know at least something about each other. But often brides and grooms, seeing each other for the first time at dockside, discovered that the marriage partner looked nothing like the photograph submitted for examination. A bald or gray-haired man was likely to be photographed with his hat on. Men who did not have a decent suit to their names were photographed in borrowed or rented outfits. A butler or a janitor might be photographed in front of the mansion or factory building where he worked, and if he neglected to provide the details, it was easy for the bride to assume that in the wonderful land of America where everyone was wealthy, her husband owned the building. It was not unusual for brides to learn the husband was a virtually penniless laborer, an itinerant farmhand or a coarse, uncultured misfit. On the other hand, many was the man who dreamed of a tender, gentle mate and found he had drawn a shrew. One *Issei* woman recalls that her husband met her in San Francisco and took her home to a sod house on the Nebraska prairie. She could not understand that many Caucasian farmers in the Midwest of that time were living in soddies because of the shortage of lumber, and that the soddies were comfortably cool in summer and warm in winter. "You made me come all the way across the Pacific to live in a hole in the ground like a wild animal?" she raged. Some of the women never got over their disappointments—"I wept for ten years, and then I gave up," said one—but a surprising number quickly made adjustments as pioneer women from other lands had done before them. The development of genuine love matches was not at all unusual.

Yoshito Fujii, the Seattle hotel operator mentioned earlier, recalls that the innkeepers had a busy time of it during the picture bride period. Days before a ship was due, the bridegrooms would come into the city from farms and sawmill camps and engage a room. They would be waiting anxiously at dockside when the ship approached, some duded up with derbies and walking sticks, searching the girls lined along the rail for a face they could recognize. Usually it took several days for the brides to clear immigration, and each day the men would congregate outside the immigration station hoping for a glimpse of their brides.

Chojiro Fujii, who was an old hand and well-known to the immigration authorities, would be showered with questions each time he emerged from the building with a bride who had been cleared. She and her husband, shy and awkward in each other's presence, would be whisked to the Fujii Hotel. There she was quickly taken to an outfitter in the same building and provided with a complete set of American clothing and her feet, broadened by a lifetime of freedom in sandals, were jammed into the narrow, high-laced shoes that were the fashion of the day. Stripped of the familiar kimono, trussed into a corset, the bride's severance from all that she had known was quick and complete.

With marriage it was natural that children should be born. The arrival of these offspring, Americans by birth, marked a new era in the history of the Japanese in America. Through marriage the Japanese in America were in position to increase their numbers without immigration although, as we shall see, this did not necessarily happen.

At this point a review of Japanese immigration statistics may be appropriate.

The Gentlemen's Agreement failed to seal off immigration, but it did reduce the flow. The most amazing thing about this immigration, in view of the long history of agitation, is that such a relatively insignificant number of individuals was involved. Between 1900 and 1924, when the Immigration Act effectively barred the gates, fewer than a quarter million Japanese immigrants came to the United States. In that period the influx from Europe had been approximately 15 million.

Japanese women arrived in the United States in kimono (below) but were quickly outfitted in American clothing. In these photos taken about 1907, the same women appear but in different positions. (Akita Collection)

The great preponderance of Japanese immigration took place in less than a decade—in the nine years between 1900 and 1908.

During the century's last decade, 15,572 Japanese entered the country, an average of just over 1,550 annually.

Following the annexation of Hawaii, the number in 1900 jumped to 12,635 for reasons explained earlier.

A voluntary clamp-down by Japan followed in 1901, but the flow was resumed after that until 1907 when the pending Gentlemen's Agreement caused a major rush to get in under the wire. The Gentlemen's Agreement took effect in 1908, and the number of Japanese coming to the U.S. dropped sharply from 16,418 that year to only 3,275 in 1909. In tabular form, immigration from Japan in that nine-year period looks like this:

Year	Total	Male	Female
1900	12,635	12,265	370
1901	5,269	4,902	367
1902	14,270	10,414	3,856
1903	20,041	15,990	4,051
1904	14,382	12,729	1,653
1905	11,021	9,810	1,211
1906	14,243	12,756	1,487
1907	30,824	27,845	2,979
1908	16,418	12,256	4,162
Nine-year total	139,103	118,967	20,136

The nine-year total was just over 139,000. During that same period nearly 10 million European immigrants entered the United States.

After 1908 Japanese immigration exceeded 10,000 in only two years—1918 and 1919—and in every year without exception women outnumbered male immigrants, often by a more than 2 to 1 margin.

Professor Ichihashi clarifies in these words why women came in such numbers: "In 1900 there were only 410 married women in a (Japanese) population of 24,326; in 1910 there were 5,581 married women in a population of 72,157, and in 1920 there were 22,193 married women in a population of 111,010. Thus males were predominant in the sex composition of the Japanese population, and the majority of those males belonged to the marriageable age-group. In 1920, of the adult males, 42.5 per cent were single. In addition, intermarriage between Japanese and members of the Caucasian races is legally prohibited, for instance, in the state of California, where the majority of Japanese are found. These facts alone ought to make it tolerably clear why women came; Japanese are human, and their attitude toward marriage is not different from that of other human beings . . . But in 1921 Japanese men were deprived of the right of marrying when the Japanese government stopped female emigration because of the American hostility to their coming, and 42.5 per cent of adult males, leading the life of bachelors, have been compelled to remain single . . ."

Limited as Japanese immigration was, it should be noted that traffic across the Pacific was a two-way affair, with westbound ships in some years more heavily laden than on their eastbound voyages. Between 1909 and 1924, the period in which the Gentlemen's Agreement was in effect, some 118,000 Japanese entered the United States as immigrants—an average of 7,375 a year. In the same period nearly 40,000 Japanese—one in three of those who had entered—left the United States. In fact, during the four years preceding the halt of immigration in 1924, and each year after that landmark date, more Japanese aliens left the United States than entered. Those who departed were men who had made their fortunes and their families, individuals who had wearied of harassment and decided their futures lay in their native land, and others who for one reason or another preferred Japan to the United States. It is with those who remained that this book is primarily concerned.

Attrition from outflow and deaths subtracted from the total so that the number of Japanese immigrants and their American-born offspring listed in the decennial federal census up to 1940 never exceeded the 139,103 who arrived in the 1900–08 period. The 1930 census shows a prewar peak of 138,834 "Japanese" in the United States. By 1940 this number had dropped by nearly 12,000 to only 126,947.

If this phenomenon was noted by California agitators who complained, among other matters, that the Japanese "breed like rabbits," there is no record that they offered an explanation. The truth is that demographic studies have shown the birth rate among Japanese in the United States is comparable to that of the general population. Since there was no large exodus of Japanese during the Depression years, the logical conclusion is that the population drop between 1930 and 1940 reflects a fall in the birth rate as *Issei* passed out of the child-bearing years whereas substantial numbers of *Nisei* had not reached that period.

(At the outbreak of war in 1941, the average age of *Issei* men was about sixty, the women about ten years younger. The majority of *Nisei* were in their early twenties. "It became apparent," says Roger Daniels, "that there was a 'missing generation' of Japanese, i.e., the generation which under conditions of normal population-sex ratio, would have been born in the years 1905–1915 had there been the normal number of marriages.")

The following table is revealing:

Year	Japanese in the U.S.	Total U.S. Population	Percentage of Japanese
1870	55	38,558,371	0.000014
1880	148	50,155,783	0.003
1890	2,039	62,947,714	0.003
1900	24,326	75,994,575	0.03
1910	72,157	91,972,266	0.08
1920	111,010	105,710,620	0.10
1930	138,834	122,775,046	0.11
1940	126,947	131,669,275	0.09

These, in Roger Daniels' words, "are what the agitation was about."

＊

In 1950, the first official postwar census showed 141,244 persons of Japanese extraction in the United States. There were an additional 184,611 persons of Japanese extraction in the Hawaiian Islands. In 1960, after Hawaii and Alaska joined the Union, the population of these two states was added to U.S. census figures for the first time. The number of Japanese in the U.S. was further augmented by the influx of several thousand Japanese war brides.

Year	Japanese in the U.S.	Total U.S. Population	Percentage of Japanese
1950	141,244	150,697,361	0.09
1960	464,342 *	179,323,175	0.25
1970	591,290 **	203,211,926	0.29

* Includes 203,455 in Hawaii.
** Includes 217,307 in Hawaii.

8

NO LAND, NO IMMIGRATION

FOR THE WORLD, the eleven years between 1913 and 1924 were momentous ones. A bloody war, reaching for the first time simultaneously into the farthest reaches, rocked the globe. Men fanatically dedicated to the Marxist-Leninist philosophy seized control of Russia and unleashed worldwide forces of unrest that have yet to be quieted. New standards of morality took over to the beat of jazz. For the Japanese in the United States, those years were memorable in a peculiarly frustrating way. The two most telling victories—until 1942—in what Carey McWilliams calls the California-Japanese war were scored by the forces of reaction that controlled California in that period. Both victories were achieved through legislation, indicating popular support for the legalization of discrimination. And the Japanese could not fight back because they had no political power.

Although the euphemism "aliens ineligible to citizenship" was employed in both measures, no effort was made to conceal the fact that the target was the Japanese. The first was the California Alien Land Law of 1913. Its intent, in the unembellished words of the State Board of Control, was "to prevent aliens who are ineligible to citizenship from owning land in California."

The second was the Immigration Act of 1924, originally designed to maintain the Anglo-Saxon character of the nation by drastically curtailing immigration from nations other than those of northern Europe. But before it was passed, the bill was amended to provide for total exclusion of "all aliens ineligible to citizenship." While it was a federal act of discrimination against the Japanese, the inspiration and thrust came from California.

Southern California Japanese businessmen's picnic in 1907. Men heavily outnumber women. (Inose Collection)

Since both acts had their emotional roots in California's long history of anti-Orientalism, it is necessary to go back a few years before the actual events to trace the buildup of hostile sentiment. A logical starting point is 1908 when the Democratic party of California, which had experienced many lean years, picked up the Japanese issue as a device for stirring up popular support. The rallying cry was: "Keep California white." So we see that once again the Japanese in the United States found themselves the innocent bystander who is victimized, the convenient whipping boy who is lashed because he happens to be there.

Included in the California Democratic platform for 1908 was an attack on President Theodore Roosevelt for proposing naturalization for Japanese. We have seen in the previous chapter that Roosevelt didn't really mean to do anything about changing the naturalization laws, but the very fact that he noticed the issue constituted a threat of sorts to California's legal basis for discrimination. While this plank had no effect on the election in which Roosevelt's heir, William Howard Taft, thrashed the shopworn Democratic nominee, William Jennings Bryan, California politicians quickly demonstrated they were in dead earnest about the Japanese issue. When the state legislature convened in 1909, a number of extraordinary and unabashedly racist measures were introduced. One proposed a law to prohibit aliens from owning land. A second sought to set up segregated schools for Japanese children. A third would have authorized municipalities to establish ordinances confining Orientals to ghettos!

Throughout the history of the Japanese in America, we have seen how their welfare, whether they liked it or not, has been closely linked to Japan itself. In forthcoming chapters we shall see even more impressive instances of this relationship. In 1909 Washington became alarmed about possible reaction in Tokyo to West Coast agitation and successfully put pressure on California officials to prevent passage of the anti-Japanese measures. The Democrats were only warming up to their crusade. In 1910 they introduced twenty-seven anti-Japanese proposals. But Governor-elect Hiram Johnson, at the urging of political friends in the White House, once again succeeded in keeping them bottled up. Then, help for resident Japanese arrived from an improbable direction. San Francisco and New Orleans at the time were competing for the Panama-Pacific International Exposition, scheduled for 1915, to celebrate the opening of the Panama Canal. San Francisco business leaders solicited Washington's support for their bid, pledging in return to keep anti-Japanese legislation at a minimum. The businessmen astutely realized that the exposition would not be successful (nor profitable) unless Japan supported it enthusiastically. Among those most anxious to get the exposition was San Francisco Mayor Patrick Henry McCarthy who had served his apprenticeship in rabble-rousing as a pillar of the Asiatic Exclusion League. In the end the hope of profits from the exposition overcame his exclusionist principles. He silenced the League. It never recovered from the shock of its abrupt reversal of policy, and shortly it dropped from sight as an effective organization.

But that was only postponing the inevitable. In 1913 an anti-alien land measure passed the state senate 35 to 2, the assembly 72 to 3. ("The exposition will be in California only a year, while the white race, I hope, will be here forever," one impassioned orator declared in the legislature. "Japan may not exhibit at our fair, but we cannot sell our birthright for a tea garden.") Pressure from Washington, including a visit from William Jennings Bryan who was now Secretary of State (which some observers suggest was a sham intended only to placate the Japanese ambassador) succeeded only in making a meaningless change in the wording of the law.

The offensive phrase "aliens ineligible to citizenship," who were denied the right to own land, was eliminated. Substituted for it in a barefaced act of sophistry were the phrases "all aliens eligible to citizenship" and "all aliens other than those mentioned." The meaning and the insult were not obscured.

Governor Hiram Johnson, who took credit for passage of the law now that his friend Roosevelt was no longer in the White House, sanctimoniously defended his position: "By the law adopted we offer no offense; we made no discrimination . . . We do not mention the Japanese or any other race . . . If invidious discriminations were made in this regard, the United States made them when the United States declared who were and who were not eligible for citizenship."

Hiram Johnson was both wrong and right when he wrote Roosevelt in defense of his action: "I think we have laid the ghost. I know that never again in California can the Japanese question be a political question, except as we shall want it to be." The ghost refused to be laid away; the "Japanese question" remained a lively issue for more than three decades.

The law that the legislature approved so overwhelmingly, and which Johnson signed, prohibited further purchases of agricultural land by Japanese aliens. It permitted them to lease farmland, but only for not more than three-year periods, thus discouraging them from investing in long-term improvements. The obvious implication was that Japanese were welcome as laborers on California's huge corporate farms or sharecroppers on white-owned lands, but not as independent farmers; the intention was to maintain the living standards of Japanese farmers at the low level for which they were criticized.

However, the law did not have the effect sought by its sponsors. One of the first to notice a basic flaw was Kyutaro Abiko, banker, publisher of the newspaper *Nichi Bei*, and sponsor of the highly successful Yamato Colony land development project near Livingston in central California. Abiko and his attorneys, Albert Elliott and Guy C. Calden, saw that there was nothing to prevent an alien Japanese from buying farmland in the name of his American-born offspring. Shortly, children in diapers were being listed as legal owners of property which was managed and operated on their behalf by their parents in their role as legal guardians. The *Issei*

1920 election poster for U.S. Senator James D. Phelan depicts an American restraining a clutching Japanese hand. The message reads: "Re-elect James D. Phelan U.S. Senator and let him finish the work he now has under way to stop the Silent Invasion."

also formed land-holding corporations with 51 percent of the stock held by American citizens, usually their attorneys, and breached the spirit if not the letter of the law. When such schemes were challenged in the courts, Elliott and Calden successfully defended the Japanese. (The State Board of Control complained plaintively: "It is a source of deep regret that there are attorneys in the state who despite their oath to support the constitution and the laws of the state, nevertheless sell their legal talent in aiding this breach of the spirit and purpose of the Alien Land Law.")

In 1920 the Alien Land Law became a raging political issue again. Ostensibly, political leaders brought up the matter in an effort to close the loopholes in the 1913 law. Carey McWilliams sees more sinister motives:

"United States Senator James D. Phelan, a Democrat seeking re-election when every sign pointed to a Republican landslide, premised his entire campaign upon the issue of white supremacy . . . To aid the sorely pressed senator, his colleagues arranged for the Committee on Immigration and Naturalization to hold hearings in

California during the summer of 1920. The hearings were opened on July 12, 1920, by Senator Phelan himself. He testified that the 'Japanese are an immoral people'; proceeded to confuse Buddhism and Shintoism; charged that California was headed toward 'mongrelization and degeneracy'; claimed that mysterious threats had been made upon his life; and urged that the Japanese be ousted to save the state from the threat of Bolshevism!"

V. S. McClatchy was not far behind. He told the committee that effective assimilation depended on intermarriage, but that intermarriage was undesirable because union of "races widely different in characteristics does not perpetuate the good qualities of either race." He charged that the Japanese "cannot assimilate and make good citizens because their racial characteristics, heredity, and religion prevent . . ."

Yet these considerations did not prevent McClatchy from maintaining a not unfriendly personal relationship with a number of Japanese. He met occasionally for lunch with Abiko. Kyutaro Abiko, his wife and son Yas were dinner guests at McClatchy's apartment on Nob Hill, as were attorney Saburo Kido and other *Nisei* leaders. Some of McClatchy's domestic servants also were Japanese. One can only observe that they were more broad-minded than their employer; they did not criticize him in public.

While echoes of the congressional hearing were still reverberating, a revised Alien Land Act was presented to the people as an initiated measure and was adopted by a vote of 668,483 to 222,086. Although the measure was approved in every county, the vote fell somewhat short of the 10 to 1 margin that had been predicted. Few audible voices had been raised in opposition to the measure, yet the affirmative vote was less than half the number of registered voters. It was in this period that alien land laws similar to California's were adopted, or ancient laws revised to conform in Washington, Oregon, Idaho, Nevada, Arizona, New Mexico, Texas, Nebraska and even Delaware.

Unfortunately, even at this late date it is impossible to find statistics about the effect of the alien land law that are beyond question. As in so many previous instances where feeling ran high, totally reliable statistics are lacking, and published information varies widely. Even figures used by Japanese groups are not consistent. However, Ichihashi provides the following table of land ownership and use by Japanese farmers in California, and we present it as probably reasonably reliable:

Year	Acreage Owned	Acreage Leased	Total
1910	17,035	177,762	194,799
1913	26,707	254,980	281,687
1914	31,828	268,646	300,474
1920	74,769	383,287	458,056
1922	50,542	279,511	330,653
1925	41,898	263,058	304,966

Since California has approximately 28 million acres of agricultural land including 11 million acres of improved farmland, simple arithmetic shows the Japanese never operated, by ownership and lease, more than 4 percent of improved crop land and 1.6 percent of the total. Ichihashi explains the Japanese stepped up purchase and lease of land between 1910 and 1914 because of the legislation then being debated, hoping to establish themselves before the barrier was raised. "The outbreak of the World War brought a boom to farmers the world over," Ichihashi notes, "and the Japanese farmers in California, like all other farmers, made money. They were tempted to buy land and they did, and landlords sold their lands because they received good prices for them. The expansion in leasing was affected for similar reasons." Mostly, California officials looked the other way. But when the boom days ended and prices fell, the Japanese could not keep up payments on their land and had to cut back acreage.

The fuss about Japanese land ownership was more a result of the kind of land they occupied, and their success in operating it, than the total acreage that they controlled. Accustomed to intensive farming practices in the old country, and limited by lack of capital in the size of farms they could operate, the Japanese looked for opportunities to grow truck crops near urban markets.

In later years, their persistence bore unexpected fruit. The urban centers, notably the area around Los Angeles and the San Francisco Bay areas, spread ever farther into the countryside, engulfing Japanese-owned farmland which became highly desirable for housing developments and shopping centers, and families that had been struggling to make a living off their land found themselves entertaining fabulous offers for it. For the first time many of these families required the services of attorneys and tax specialists.

In 1918 California's agricultural income was set at 523 million dollars, of which 53 million dollars, just a bit more than one-tenth, was produced by the Japanese. Toyoji Chiba, managing director of the Japanese Agricultural Association of California, observed: "Of this 10 per cent of farm products, those with which Japanese have most to do are truck crops such as strawberries, asparagus, celery, and tomatoes, of which 80 per cent to 90 per cent of the entire output in the state is produced by Japanese. But these crops all require a stooping posture, great manual dexterity and painstaking methods of work which other laborers with long legs unsuitable for stooping can not endure. Not only this, but this is a kind of farming which Americans and immigrants from Europe dislike to follow."

Ironically, when rumors spread that the alien land law would dispossess Japanese of the farms and prices of vegetables would soar, Californians seriously discussed the possibility of importing Mexicans or Chinese "under bond so they could be sent back at the end of five years" to cultivate the green produce which they had become accustomed to having on their tables. As a matter of fact, the position of Japanese in California agriculture did not change substantially in the two decades following the post-World War I shakedown period. However, the average size of Japanese-operated farms dropped from about 80 acres to 40—as a result of concentrating on truck crops. In 1941 they cultivated only 3.9 percent of California's farmland, but harvested anywhere from 50 to 90 percent of the state's tomatoes, celery, strawberries, green peppers, cucumbers, cauliflower, spinach and artichokes. Most of this produce was marketed in nearby urban centers.

The passage of the 1913 alien land law, with Governor Johnson's assurances that the "Japanese issue" had been laid to rest, was followed closely by the outbreak of war in Europe. Anti-Japanese agitation died down, particularly after Japan entered the war on the side of the Allies against Germany. Scores of *Issei* served in the United States Army, many of them in hopes of gaining the citizenship that had been promised aliens in American uniform. Later, as we have found, they learned it was a promise that applied to everyone except "aliens ineligible to citizenship."

Meanwhile, the forces that ultimately would create the Immigration Act of 1924 were bubbling in bitter ferment. Perhaps it was a symptom of basic insecurity that America, a nation of immigrants and their descendants, should experience a virulent, recurring fear of foreigners. Each succeeding wave of European immigrants was subjected to discrimination by those who had arrived earlier. With Europeans, a generation or two was all that was needed for immigrants to be absorbed into the American scene. With Asiatics, however, the racial difference was obvious, and the fear and dislike of foreigners flourished on fertile racist soil. Thus, an American only briefly removed from northern Europe might resent the influx of Italians, Armenians or Russians, but he didn't have nightmares about Italy, Armenia or Russia invading and taking over the United States. On the other hand, even though Asia lagged far behind the West in technology, many Americans found it easy to believe that teeming hordes of savage yellow heathens would, some day, engulf North America unless something were done about it, and in fact, were spending all their time plotting such an invasion.

The swift progress of Japan from feudalism to a world power—hadn't she, an Asian nation, humbled mighty Russia?—added basis to the fear. As early as 1905 the Hearst newspapers published a cartoon which showed a Japanese soldier casting a long shadow across the Pacific and over California. Nor did the fact that Japan seized German concessions in China and German islands in the Pacific during World War I sit well with some Americans who, somehow, felt uneasy about having Orientals on our side. No doubt some of this feeling can be traced to German sources which, since 1907, had been trying to convince Washington of the danger of Japanese aggression. In fact, it was Kaiser Wilhelm II who has been credited with coining the phrase *gelbe gefahr* (yellow peril) although he was referring to a possible Chinese invasion of Europe. The congressional hearings into German propaganda after World War I revealed substantial German efforts on the West Coast to stir up feelings against Japan, obviously an attempt to divert attention away from Europe. After the war Japan contributed to American concern. Its repressive occupation of Korea, the 21 Demands which compromised Chinese independence, and the morally correct but alarming demand for racial equality at Versailles fanned American fears.

It was also about this time that movies and books appeared to make the yellow peril seem more real. In another era they might have been considered fantasies. All were patterned after the first of the genre, *The Valor of Ignorance* by Homer Lea, published in 1909. Lea had been in China in the early years of the century and his book was a fanciful account of how Japan in a coming war would seize the Philippines, land on the Pacific Coast and bring the United States to its knees. It was a warning that America must arm and prepare for coming racial wars. One movie, *Patria*, was a ten-part serial produced in 1917 by William Randolph Hearst's International Film Service Corp., and purported to show how Japanese troops could conquer the United States by invasion through Mexico with the cooperation of Mexican villains. Another, titled *Shadows of the West*, was circulated by the recently formed American Legion which from the very beginning had joined the anti-Japanese forces. It was a parody of all the charges ever made against the Japanese in America, with a fiendish master spy keeping vegetable prices high to the despair of American housewives and white girls who had been abducted by Japanese sex fiends being rescued by Legionnaires. As improbable as such movies may seem, they were viewed by vast numbers of Americans and no doubt colored their thinking.

Two novels appeared in 1920, written by authors of considerable stature, and thus commanding a good deal of notice. Peter B. Kyne's *The Pride of Palomar* was serialized in *Cosmopolitan*, a Hearst magazine. Wallace Irwin's *Seed of the Sun*, which Carey McWilliams says was "prepared at the instigation of V. S. McClatchy," was published serially in the *Saturday Evening Post*. Both were issued as books a year later. In both, the Japanese were depicted as sly, deceitful villains with designs on California. The heroes were Anglo-Saxons who foiled Oriental skulduggery and upheld the contention that a good white man is worth a dozen nasty Asians any day. In these times it is inconceivable that a responsible editor would publish such patently false and derogatory material, but such was the atmosphere in the early twenties that the books were widely circulated, read, discussed and accepted as a warning against the yellow peril.

It was in this environment that the Japanese Exclusion League of California was organized. Denial of land ownership had not satisfied the members. They wanted the Japanese excluded, just as the Chinese had been excluded forty years earlier. In fact, one of the predecessor organizations went further and had stated that it wanted to change the United States Constitution so that no child born in the United States would be a citizen unless both parents were of a race eligible to citizenship. The Exclusion League was formed on September 2, 1920, in Native Sons Hall in San Francisco. Member organizations included the Native Sons of the Golden West, the American Legion, California State Federation of Labor, California Federation of Women's Clubs, California State Grange, Farm Bureau and Loyal Order of the Moose. The power behind the Exclusion League was McClatchy, who volunteered full time to it, and his powerful voice was to be heard for many years, even after the League vanished as an effective organization. The League, or rather McClatchy, promptly set out to make its wishes known in Washington.

A survey of American immigration laws shows that for the first century of its history the United States encouraged foreigners—Europeans—to migrate to the United States and help settle the ever-expanding border. The first act to restrict immigration was passed in 1875, barring criminals and prostitutes. The Chinese Exclusion Act came seven years later when, by the very fact of being Chinese, they were put in the same class as criminals and prostitutes so far as the immigration laws were concerned. Periodically thereafter barriers were raised against "undesirables"—idiots, the insane, paupers or persons likely to become public charges, persons with contagious diseases, polygamists, those convicted of moral turpitude, anarchists and those who advocate the overthrow of government by force, the illiterate, and in 1917, all Asians except Japanese. It was evident that after World War I, when European refugees clamored for admission, further restrictions would be adopted.

Early in 1921 Hiram Johnson, by then United States Senator, assembled the California delegation to hear McClatchy expound on the need for a Japanese exclusion law. Senator Johnson then organized an Executive Committee of Western States, made up of one senator and one congressman from each of the eleven Western states, to work with the California delegation in seeking an exclusion law.

In 1923 Congressman Albert Johnson of Washington introduced an immigration bill calling for reduced quotas that favored north

European countries and prohibiting admission of aliens ineligible to citizenship. The House offered little opposition to the measure, and the exclusionists focused their efforts on the Senate where the outcome was more doubtful. At committee hearings, California was represented by a formidable triumvirate: McClatchy, the now ex-Senator James D. Phelan who had been a foe of the Japanese for two decades, and Ulysses S. Webb, state attorney general. Their arguments were undisguisedly racist. McClatchy told the committee:

"Of all the races ineligible to citizenship, the Japanese are the least assimilable and the most dangerous to this country . . . With great pride of race, they have no idea of assimilating in the sense of amalgamation. They do not come to this country with any desire or any intent to lose their racial or national identity. They come here specifically and professedly for the purpose of colonizing and establishing here permanently the proud Yamato race. They never cease to be Japanese . . . In pursuit of their intent to colonize this country with that race they seek to secure land and to found large families . . . They have greater energy, greater determination, and greater ambition than the other yellow and brown races ineligible to citizenship, and with the same low standards of living, hours of labor, use of women and child labor, they naturally make more dangerous competitors in an economic way . . ."

Webb remarked: "It is not that we regard the Japanese as an inferior race or an inferior people. We are not concerned with that question. It is, however, because long experience and close touch with existing conditions have shown us that it is a question of race desirability."

Phelan was even more frank: "The people of California object to the Japanese—and I say it involves the whole question—because of racial and economic reasons . . ."

But some of the senators were unconvinced. Many expressed willingness to grant Japan a quota, an inoffensive gesture that would have permitted the entry of 146 immigrants per year. Secretary of State Charles Evans Hughes also endorsed a quota for Japan together with continuation of the 1907 Gentlemen's Agreement which, he said, would provide "double control" of immigration from Japan. As it turned out, his insistence on retaining the Gentlemen's Agreement was an error. Some Congressmen charged that the Agreement was a secret document whose terms were unknown. In an effort to dispel the uncertainty, Hughes asked the Japanese ambassador, Masanao Hanihara, to write a letter summarizing the Agreement and Japan's position on the immigration issue.

Hanihara wrote a detailed, straightforward and accurate letter covering the substance of the Agreement. He also protested the exclusion proposal in, considering the circumstances, remarkably moderate terms, saying in part:

". . . It is indeed difficult to believe that it can be the intention of the people of your great country, who always stand for principles of justice and fair play in the intercourse of nations, to resort—in order to secure the annual exclusion of 146 Japanese—to a measure which would not only seriously offend the pride of a friendly nation, that has always been earnest and diligent in its efforts to preserve the friendship of your people, but would also seem to involve the question of good faith and therefore the honor of their government, or at least of its executive branch.

"Relying on the confidence you have been good enough to show me at all times, I have stated or rather repeated all this to you very candidly and in a most friendly spirit, for I realize, as I believe you do, the grave consequences which the enactment of the measure retaining that particular provision would inevitably bring upon the otherwise happy and mutually advantageous relations between our two countries."

Senator Henry Cabot Lodge, the Massachusetts Republican, who had remained out of the fight over Japanese exclusion, suddenly stepped in and in an astonishing performance seized on two words in the Hanihara letter—"grave consequences"—to charge that it contained an improper "veiled threat" against the United States. "The United States cannot legislate by the exercise by any other country of veiled threats," he protested.

Ambassador Hanihara was astounded. "I am unable to understand how the two words read in their context could be construed as meaning anything like a threat," he wrote Hughes. "In using these words, I had no thought of being in any way disagreeable or discourteous and still less of conveying a 'veiled threat.' "

But it was too late. As so often happens in Congress, a stampede had been started. Lodge's outraged interpretation led to a 76 to 2 vote against continuation of the Gentlemen's Agreement, and Japanese exclusion became reality a short time later. The House passed the new immigration bill 308 to 62, the Senate 69 to 9. President Coolidge signed the measure on May 26, 1924, regretting "the impossibility of severing from it the exclusion provision which in the light of existing law affects especially the Japanese . . . If the exclusion provision stood alone, I would disapprove it without hesitation . . ."

Of Lodge, who had led the successful fight to keep the United States out of the League of Nations, Daniels observes:

"Lodge's action—and the action of the Senate in following him—can only be described as wanton. As an act of studied international insolence it makes the rejection of the Versailles Treaty seem a veritable judgment of Solomon. As we know, Lodge had helped Roosevelt arrange the preconditions for the Gentlemen's Agreement. Roosevelt himself, in a state paper Lodge helped to prepare, had used the superlative of Hanihara's phrase—'gravest consequences'—in referring to the possible consequences of discrimination against the Japanese. Why then did Lodge wreck an understanding he had helped establish? It is impossible to say; it is also impossible to take his statements at face value. He was far too sophisticated not to realize that Hanihara and Hughes were acting in concert, although this fact may have escaped some of his more rustic colleagues. Lodge may well have wanted to embarrass the Coolidge Administration—there was no love lost between Lodge and Coolidge and his Secretary of State—or he may have wanted merely to demonstrate that his talent for wrecking international agreements was still unimpaired. At any rate, his 'veiled threat' speech was the last major act of a long career. He died on November 9, 1924."

The exclusion portion of the new immigration law went into effect March 1, 1925, but not before displays of uninhibited gloating on the West Coast and bitter editorials in Japanese newspapers.

American Ambassador C. E. Woods in Tokyo resigned in protest against the law: "Japan does not want to force emigrants upon the United States if we do not wish to receive them," he said. "The Japanese government, I believe, would be willing to agree to almost any form of restrictive treaty, but the exclusion provision of the immigration bill has struck a blow to their natural pride . . ."

Ichihashi explains Nippon's angry reaction in this manner: "Japan's desire to enjoy equal privileges in respect to emigration in her relations with other powers has been misinterpreted and misunderstood as a desire to send large numbers of Japanese wherever Japan pleases. The fact of the matter is that Japan's stand on racial equality in her international relationships does not primarily concern itself with emigration as such; its underlying principle is political justice. No self-respecting nation can afford to be discriminated against on account of race."

Historians have observed that the Exclusion Act sounded the death knell for the liberal pro-Western civilian political leadership that was struggling against militarism for control of Japan. They see this as the turning point on a national course that led Japan inevitably to military aggression in Asia, and ultimately to war against the United States.

The Japanese in America in 1924 could not, of course, peer that far into the future. The immediate effect was to ruin the business of those who depended heavily on immigration for their livelihood—the innkeepers, those who provided clothing, bedding, furniture, kitchen utensils and all the rest of the things that the newcomers needed. Of necessity these entrepreneurs had to expand into the white community or go out of business. It was during this period that many Japanese innkeepers exchanged names like *Yamamoto-ya* for Crown Hotel and invited Caucasian clientele to their skid row establishments. More basically, however, the *Issei* had hanging over their heads the knowledge that they could not own land in the United States, that they could not become citizens, and now their countrymen, like the Chinese, were no longer permitted to enter this nation as immigrants. Even as they were forced to look outside their communities for a livelihood, their future in America seemed to be up against a blank wall. Yet most of them lacked the money to go back to Japan. Which way were they to turn? What were they to do? Their only hope seemed to be their American-born children.

9

WRETCHES, RASCALS AND CHURCHES

JUDGING FROM the bitterness and persistence of the campaign to harass the Japanese in America, one might conclude that the immigrants were complete rascals, moral degenerates, criminals, despoilers of virtue as well as farmland, carriers of typhoid and plague germs, and otherwise offensive to the frontier ethic.

This was hardly the case, although certainly not all were upstanding types one would be proud to have for a neighbor. Not all were meek and servile to the demands of the white majority, not all were totally dedicated to industrious labor, and not all saw themselves as pioneers breaking the sod, penetrating the wilderness and upholding the honor of Japan. The truth is that even though all Japanese may have looked alike to the undiscerning Caucasian glance, each was an individual; some were leaders and some were parasites and hoodlums. Virtually all were vigorous young men in the physical prime of life with normal appetites. It was natural that they should react in individual ways to the absence of the inhibiting influence of family. Professor Robert Wilson observes that most of the *Issei* were drifters and migrant workers with no particular aim or ambition until Japanese women began to arrive in the United States. The responsibilities of family life forced them to settle down which, in essence, is the history of civilization. If their detractors had taken the long view, they would have welcomed the influx of picture brides who transformed their husbands from footloose, relatively unstable bachelors into solid family men. However, the antagonism was such that fine nuances were lost on the white supremacists. Stability was what they did not want. In fact, they saw the founding of families as a fresh danger in that a new generation of "Japs," equipped with American citizenship, would spring from these unions.

Perhaps it is a commentary on the moral climate of the times that the attacks on the Japanese were based largely on economic fears, real or imagined, sincere or inspired—fears that large numbers of immigrants would inundate the country, that industrious Japanese would seize the best farmland, that whites would lose their jobs to the Japanese, that in some vaguely understood fashion the Japanese would harm America because they were an unassimilable ingredient in the American melting pot. Had their antagonists chosen to assail the Japanese for reasons of moral turpitude—at least in the earliest immigration period—they would have been on firmer ground. This aspect of the history of the Japanese in the United States is uncovered in a remarkable document in the files of the Japanese Foreign Office. It was written by Fujita Yoshiro, secretary in the consulate of Japan in San Francisco, forwarded to the Foreign Office by Consul Chinda Sutemi in 1891, and translated by Yasuo Sakata of the Japanese American Research Project at the University of California at Los Angeles.

On July 1, 1891, Fujita set out for Seattle under instructions "to make inquiries" about resident Japanese. It must be kept in mind that in 1891 there were only a handful more than 2,000 Japanese in the entire United States; the period of heaviest emigration was a decade in the future. Fujita learned that a large percentage of resident Japanese were seamen who had jumped ship and who therefore had no legal right to be in the United States.

In Seattle he encountered approximately 250 Japanese. About 40 owned or were employed by the one grocery store and ten restaurants in the community. The rest he found to be gamblers, pimps, prostitutes or proprietors of brothels. Furthermore, he found five or six of the restaurants were "connected, in one way or another, with prostitution in this city." Thus, he concluded sadly, "I can name only ten individuals who have absolutely nothing to do with prostitution or gambling and are indeed engaged in legitimate business or occupations in a strict sense."

Fujita assembled the respectable members of Seattle's Japanese community and urged them to "take some vigorous actions in cooperation with American authorities and try to expel these undesirable Japanese from this city." He got little encouragement. The law-abiding Japanese were badly outnumbered and feared reprisals from the gamblers. Fujita then went to see the city officials. He reported the mayor and president of the city council sympathetic but reluctant to act because of the "complexity of the problem." When he went to see the police chief, Fujita was told flatly that not only Japanese but Irish, Swedes and other nationalities were engaged in prostitution, and it was impossible to crack down on the Japanese alone.

Next, Fujita took a boat for Port Blakely on Bainbridge Island, across Puget Sound from Seattle, where he had heard 80 Japanese were among the 500 men employed at a sawmill. He arrived at 10 A.M. and found that 50 of the Japanese had gone to work, but about 30 were in the bunkhouse "in the midst of gambling even in that early hour." Fujita was told that about 20 of the men were habitual gamblers, working only when they had lost all their money, and only 10 of the Japanese worked regularly.

If Fujita was disheartened by what he learned in Seattle and Port Blakely, he found much to cheer him in Tacoma where there were no prostitutes or gamblers among the 90 Japanese residents. He was told that a man named Hishiya was the first Japanese resident, opening a grocery store in 1888. A short while later a Yukino started a restaurant, and at the time of Fujita's visit Japanese residents were operating two groceries, six restaurants and two laundries. In 1890, Fujita was told, several brothel operators from Seattle came to Tacoma "armed with a letter of introduction" from the police chief in Seattle requesting Tacoma officials to help them set up business. The Tacoma Japanese, with cooperation from their own city officials, refused to let the Seattle men stay. It is noteworthy that during the hysterical agitation for evacuation of Japanese Americans from the West Coast in 1942, Tacoma's Mayor Harry Cain was one of the few public officials to speak out for the *Nisei* in defiance of the tide.

Fujita next moved on to Spokane, Washington, where he found 12 Japanese employed at two restaurants, 17 Japanese prostitutes and 30 pimps or gamblers. A few months earlier, he was told, there had been 50 to 60 Japanese prostitutes in the city taking advantage of the patronage of construction workers who had poured into

Spokane after a devastating fire. But when the workers left, about 40 of the women moved on to Butte, Montana and Salt Lake City, Utah.

Fujita found similarly deplorable conditions in Portland where approximately 130 Japanese lived. "There are seven restaurants which altogether employ about 60 Japanese," he wrote. "The remaining 60-odd Japanese are prostitutes, their employers, gamblers or sailors. As in the cases in Seattle and Spokane, these restaurants in general cater to low class laborers and serve a 15-cent meal. Of these seven restaurants, only one or two are owned by respectable Japanese and operated with sufficient capital. Another two or three are run by a group of *shosei* (those who came originally as students) in partnership, and the rest all seem to be owned or financed by either the proprietors of houses of pleasure or gamblers."

Curious about the number of restaurants operated by Japanese, Fujita asked some questions and learned that a restaurant could be opened with initial capital of four to five hundred dollars. Restaurants had proven profitable even though the proprietors had little experience. In many instances three or four friends pooled their funds and went into business.

Fujita completed his report on this dolorous note: "On my way back to San Francisco, I have made inquiries as to the presence of Japanese at every train stop. As a result of these inquiries, I have learned that there is a group of Japanese in almost all of these places. These Japanese were, however, either prostitutes or their employers; none of them were engaged in legitimate business or occupations."

Consul Chinda, a dedicated civil servant, transmitted Fujita's report without comment to Tokyo. While Fujita's findings are well nigh incredible in these times, there is no reason to believe he distorted his report.

Chinda himself had submitted a somewhat similar document relating to San Francisco only a few months earlier. He noted that ten houses were in operation with "over 50 women of ill fame . . . almost openly" pursuing their profession. Chinda expressed concern that unless something was done, the number of Japanese prostitutes would increase rapidly, and Japanese-operated brothels would "soon be established all over the United States as in the case with Hongkong, Shanghai or Singapore." Chinda also noted that the traffic prospered only when local authorities tolerated it, and added: "Both the Society for Prevention of Vice and the police department in this city do not intend, it seems, to take any positive action against these prostitutes unless their conduct becomes the object of an excessive public scandal. They seem to feel it impossible to eradicate this evil entirely . . ." Chinda's report urged authorities in Japan to tighten control over stowaways in the port of Yokohama (presumably referring to women smuggled aboard ship by Japanese seamen) and sought the cooperation of U.S. authorities in curbing illegal entry of Japanese from Hawaii and Canada.

In this connection, Immigration Commissioner W. M. Rice in a report dated 1899 had this to say: "It is a fact, believed by all the immigration officers with whom I have talked, that at least 75 per cent of the (Japanese) women who come to the United States are lewd, or at least of such a low quality of virtue that they are easily overcome by the conditions which they find in this country."

Although this evaluation appears harsh, it is not inconceivable that such a situation existed prior to 1899 when the ratio of Japanese men to women was grossly abnormal. The 1900 census shows that out of a total population of 24,326 Japanese in the United States, 23,341 were males and only 985 were females—a ratio of one woman for every 24 men—and not all the females were adults. Only 855 of the women were fifteen years of age or older. Of these, 410 listed themselves as married; 445 were not married. However, a judgment of the character of early Japanese women immigrants such as Commissioner Rice has made is misleading without making it clear that a different type of immigrant began to arrive after 1900—the picture brides, the girls the men married on visits home, the women who bore the children, helped in the fields, and brought stability and permanence to the endeavors of their men. And in the 25 percent that Rice absolves—although the figure seems disproportionately low—were women of the mettle of Shige Kushida, daughter of the co-founder of the Japanese Women's Christian Temperance Union. Defying the tradition of female subservience, she came to the United States as a 23-year-old in 1892 to study on a W.C.T.U. scholarship. When the money that had been promised failed to materialize, she took a job as a domestic in San Francisco. There she met Kikumatsu Togasaki who had come to San Francisco six years earlier. She helped convert him to Christianity and they returned to Japan to be married, then sailed back to the United States where their first child, George Kiyoshi, mentioned earlier, was born in 1895. In the years that followed, the Togasakis and their growing brood of children were at dockside to greet each shipload of immigrants. They soothed the fears of the homesick, guided them through the red tape that barred their way to shore, took the immigrants to temporary quarters (often in their own home), helped the young couples buy clothing, bedding and housekeeping items, and kept a stern eye peeled for the welfare of the apparently unattached. Shige was a compassionate woman, but she lived by stern Christian principles which had no room for toleration of immorality. In time the prostitutes mentioned in Secretary Fujita's report disappeared from the scene, but women like Shige remained to write an indelible page in American history.

The Los Angeles area, because of its later development, missed out on most of the activity reported earlier in this chapter. The records show that there were perhaps 25 Japanese in Los Angeles as early as 1884. But in 1890, about the time Consul Chinda had first become aware of the problem of Japanese gamblers and prostitutes in San Francisco, Oregon and Washington, there were no more than 40 Japanese in all the sprawling City of the Angels. A decade later, in 1900, there were still only 150. Jinnosuke Kobata is credited with fathering the now extensive Japanese nursery business; he began operations in 1893. The Los Angeles City Directory of 1898 lists twelve Japanese-owned restaurants, four shops selling bamboo and wicker furniture which was enjoying a great vogue, a grocery store, an art shop and a nursery. These accounted for a surprisingly high ratio of one business enterprise for every eight Japanese. At the corner of Fifth and Broadway, Sanshichi Akita operated a shop that manufactured bamboo furniture. The shop gained a measure of immortality when President William McKinley was photographed in front of it while riding in a parade in his honor. The first Japanese boarding house in Los Angeles was the Rose Hotel at 112 Rose Street, opened by Sanjuro Mizuno on March 3, 1898, to house Japanese railroad laborers. Although it was an aged building even then, it was not torn down until the

Japanese entered the Southern California nursery business about 1896. This photo was probably taken about 1910. (Los Angeles County Museum of Natural History)

1950's. By 1904, however, some 2,800 Japanese—fewer than 200 of them women and children—were settled in the East First Street area where hotels housed them and restaurants and bars sprang up to serve Japanese food and drink. It was about the same time that the first Japanese farmers moved into the rich Gardena area and a few railroad workers, discovering abalone while on a beach outing, promptly quit their jobs and went into the abalone drying and shipping business. The Los Angeles Japanese population took another spurt in 1906 when the San Francisco earthquake and fire forced many residents to look for opportunities elsewhere.

Southern California's famed climate continued to attract hundreds of thousands of Americans and offered fabulous job opportunities, and the Japanese were not immune. Within two and a half

One of the earlier Japanese-owned businesses in Los Angeles was the White Star Soda Works. Photo taken about 1915. (Miyatake Collection)

decades, the corner of East First and San Pedro Streets became known as the Japanese crossroads in Li'l Tokyo, U.S.A. It was said that if one stood on this corner long enough, he would see every *Issei* and *Nisei* in America. In the early 1930's the Miyako Hotel, since replaced by the Sumitomo Bank, stood proud and austere on the southwest corner. On the southeast corner was the Tomio Building, headquarters for *Issei* and *Nisei* professional men, with the bustling Iwaki Drug Store on the ground floor doing a land-office business in coffee, Cokes and blueplate lunches. On the northwest corner, where the Los Angeles Police Department building now stands, was the Asia Company department store with a Japanese restaurant occupying the second floor. And on the northeast corner, where Ben Murayama had his insurance and real estate office, was Kataoka Jewelers.

With such a concentration of Japanese, it was inevitable that the kind of vice that disturbed Consul Chinda should make a comeback. A gambling house called the Tokyo Club was organized in Los Angeles in 1919, about the same time as, but with no visible con-

nections with, a somewhat similar group called the Toyo Club in
Seattle. An interesting rationale was employed in both cases: Since
the Japanese were gambling at, and losing heavily in, Chinese-
operated clubs, it made sense to provide them with their own
gambling clubs so the money could be kept in the community.
These clubs were set up as business enterprises with elected officers
as well as the usual strong-arm boys and bodyguards, all of whom
drew salaries. Chojiro Itami headed the Tokyo Club from 1919
until 1927, building up a surplus of a reported $250,000, an impres-
sive sum in those days. Yasutaro Yasuda succeeded him and was
president until 1931 when he died violently under mysterious
circumstances said to be connected with a power struggle within
the club. It was during this period that the Tokyo Club built up a
reputation for benevolence as well as ruthlessness. This was the
era of Prohibition, bootleggers and Chicago gangsters, and Little
Tokyo had its own version. But the Tokyo Club was also credited
with feeding and sheltering countless *Issei* bachelors down on their
luck, lending money to businessmen, merchants and farmers whose
bank credit was dubious, supporting Japanese cultural programs,
underwriting American tours by Japanese entertainers, and even
helping Japanese students in American universities with their
expenses. The Tokyo Club had 20 to 30 employees and had third
floor quarters in a building on Jackson Street. There was only one
public entrance—up three flights topped by a barred door with
peephole.

The principal game played was fan-tan, a Chinese invention. It
is played on a table marked off with four sides numbered in order,
1, 2, 3 and 4. A handful of metal checks, or in some cases beans, is
dumped on the table and quickly covered while the players wager
on the number that will be left when the checks are removed four
at a time. If you bet a dollar on, let's say, number 2, and two beans
remain, you win. The house pays you four dollars. You can also
hedge your bets by playing the corners, for example the corner
between number 1 and number 2. You win if either one or two
checks remain when the pile in the middle has been reduced four
checks at a time. But since your odds for winning are better, you
win a smaller amount—two dollars back for the dollar you wagered.
And if you pick the wrong corner, or the wrong number, you lose
everything you wager. The house took 10 percent of each pot as its

share, which added up to a tidy sum at the end of a long night of gambling, and as the night wore on the players were gambling with less and less of their own money. Traditionally, the Chinese were said to favor betting their entire bankroll—perhaps saved painfully over a period of months—in one heroic, desperate gamble, all or nothing. The Japanese were more conservative, betting a little at a time to drag out the thrill and agony of their wagers—and yielded up more of their money to the house.

Seattle's gambling boss for many years during this period was Sasaki Takeyuki, better known by his nickname Tosayama. He was a big, florid, soft-spoken man. He and his bodyguard, Yamamoto Kimpachi, a short, squat individual with long simian arms, pig eyes, undershot jaw and crude manners, were familiar sights around Seattle in the 1930's. Although there is no way to measure such matters, it was said the gambling clubs wielded more influence among the *Issei* than the Japanese consulate, exerting that influence by a strange combination of benevolent spending of money and intimidation through the threat of violence. Thugs employed by the clubs saw to it that there was no surreptitious gambling in the back rooms of Li'l Tokyo shops; if you wanted to gamble, you went to the clubs.

An informal truce existed between local police officials and the Japanese gambling clubs. The officials did not interfere with the clubs so long as they operated quietly among Orientals. As a matter of fact, the relationship was so cozy one must assume the Japanese gamblers invested considerable money for the privilege of conducting their business without official interference. The last of the big-time gambling bosses in Los Angeles was Hideichi Yamatoda who not only was widely disliked, but managed to bungle things more than somewhat. Some of his predecessors, notably Chojiro Itami and Yasutaro Yasuda, were regarded with affection. Not so with Yamatoda. Soon after he seized control of the Tokyo Club in 1938, he was kidnapped and showed up sometime later in Mexico. The story that came out was that certain officials in the Imperial Valley felt they were entitled to a larger share of Yamatoda's profits than he was willing to give up. When Yamatoda proved more stubborn than discreet, some armed men seized him and dumped him across the border, just to show they meant business.

Not many months later, Yamatoda became embroiled with the

law again. There are two versions to this deplorable incident. One
has it that one Namba, a farmer from Lodi, encountered a phe-
nomenal streak of luck and won enough to break the club. He
promptly vanished. The other is that Namba felt he had been
cheated at the Tokyo Club and complained vigorously. Either
way, he disappeared. The district attorney indicted Yamatoda and
several of his colleagues on a charge of doing away with Namba.
Apparently, Yamatoda was worried by the charge because he felt
it necessary to engage Jerry Giesler, a very expensive attorney who
had made a specialty of defending Hollywood motion picture personalities. Testimony was heard to the effect that Namba had been
slugged over the head with a billiard cue, and his limp body
dragged out of the club. Yamatoda and several of his lieutenants
were convicted of manslaughter. At this point Giesler earned his
retainer by getting the conviction reversed. He tells about it in his
book, *The Jerry Giesler Story:*

"To me, the case of Yamatoda was not so much a matter of
whether Namba's body was ever found or not, but the far more
important issue of whether he had actually died. I obtained a
reversal in Yamatoda's case by making an issue of that question.
There was clearly a reasonable doubt of Namba's demise. I don't
know whether that would have been enough to obtain a reversal
in itself or not, but it was never put to the test because, in the
original trial, in two of the instructions which the court had given
the jury the judge had referred to Namba as 'the deceased.'

"Because he had disappeared completely, the police assumed that
Namba was dead. That wasn't enough for me. I didn't insist that
anyone produce Namba's body, but I did insist that somebody
prove that the body was dead before it disappeared. Understandably the jury was immediately persuaded that the judge believed
Namba was dead or he wouldn't have used the word 'deceased.'
In the brief which I prepared arguing for a reversal of Yamatoda's
conviction, I said that the fact of Namba's death had been an issue
for the jury to determine, not the judge, and that by assuming out
loud in court that a missing man was dead the judge had committed
judicial error.

"It proved a judicial error big enough to set Yamatoda free, for
the higher court agreed with me. Yamatoda was not retried. World
War II stepped in and scattered all of the people involved in the

trial like chaff. Yamatoda himself went back to Japan and was killed there during the war."

The Evacuation in 1942 effectively closed the clubs, and like so many other aspects of life in the Japanese communities of the West Coast, they never came back. Even before the war, however, the clubs were an ailing institution. The *Issei*, particularly the unattached old bachelors who were the chief patrons of the clubs, were disappearing. The *Nisei* with an itch to try their luck preferred the horses, dice or games of blackjack and poker. The clubs had not kept up with the changing times.

It would not be fair to close this chapter without mention of the influences that were working to provide the young *Issei* immigrants with spiritual guidance. Virtually all of them came to the United States as Buddhists, although the depth of their piety varied widely. Almost from the day of their arrival, they were exposed to the missionary zeal of Christianity. And because the Methodists were particularly aggressive in this field, it was natural that they should encounter the Japanese immigrants first and shepherd the greatest number into their fold.

The records of the Pacific Japanese Provisional Conference of the Methodist Church show that three immigrants from Japan were converted in 1877—eleven years before Japan made it legal to leave the country as emigrants. Their names were Kanichi Miyama, Etsu Miyata and T. Saito. They heard Dr. Thomas Guard preach at the Howard Street Church in San Francisco and were impressed enough to want to know more. Dr. Guard did not know what to do with them, so he referred the Japanese to the Chinese Mission. There the three were baptized and received into the Chinese Methodist Episcopal Church. Thus was the pattern set for segregated churches: The Japanese, of course, understood no Chinese, but they were Orientals. And so they were sent to an Oriental church instead of being accepted into a white congregation where the language spoken would have been no more incomprehensible than Chinese.

In 1879, a Japanese Gospel Society was organized in San Francisco, sponsored by the Chinese Mission and headed by Kanichi Miyama. The Society met in the Chinese Mission until 1886 when it was strong enough to rent a small building of its own, and the Reverend M. C. Harris was recalled from Japan to work with the

Members of the Japanese Sunday School at Bethlehem School on Vignes Street, Los Angeles, about 1911. American-born Japanese (Nisei) were first beginning to appear in numbers about this time. (Akita Collection)

growing number of *Issei* adopting Methodism. Japanese Methodist churches were founded in Oakland in 1889, Sacramento in 1891, Fresno in 1893, and Vacaville in 1896. In the next few years Japanese Christian missions were set up in Alameda, Riverside, Spokane, Seattle, Selma and Oxnard; Bakersfield, Fresno, Pueblo in Colorado and Tacoma in Washington in 1907, and Denver in 1908.

Many of these churches had their beginnings as a night school to teach English to the young immigrants, or to provide them a place for gathering socially. The Japanese Baptist Church in Seattle, for example, opened an English night school in 1892. The beginnings usually were most humble. In 1904, Japanese immigrants in the Bakersfield area gathered at the Chinese Mission on O Street to hear the Reverend Herbert B. Johnson, another missionary recalled after service in Japan. He must have made a considerable impression, for the nucleus of a church was formed and the next year a house was leased for three dollars a month. In Buena Vista, evangelical services were included in the program of a night school for Japanese immigrants started in 1898, and five years later a church was formed. A social need also led to the formation of a church in Oxnard where, in 1903, between 900 and 1,000 Japanese farm laborers struck and won a wage increase. This victory gave the laborers what has been described as "an undue sense of superiority resulting in intemperate practices," resulting in community ill-feeling toward the Japanese. At this point Kusaburo Baba, a militant labor leader, sought the help of Christians to repair the situation. The result was an English language class with religious instruction. A year later a Christian church was organized.

A somewhat similar story is told in Fresno, where hundreds of Japanese laborers congregated during the grape harvest. Sanitary conditions were deplorable in the labor camps, and gamblers and prostitutes flocked to Fresno itself to greet the influx of laborers. The pioneer Japanese minister, Zenro Hirota, was named to found a church in Fresno in 1893. His first congregation, made up of immigrants who were scarcely more than teen-agers, met in a rented house on Inyo Street. The Reverend K. Imai was another early clergyman who led the fight against gambling and prostitution in central California.

While this report has been confined largely to Methodism, which today claims the largest numbers of followers among Japanese Americans, several other denominations, notably the Presbyterians, Baptists, Congregationalists, Episcopalians as well as the Catholics, yielded nothing in the way of zeal and interest in their work among the Japanese. The physical convenience of the church, the attractiveness of the minister and the program the church offered, and the desire to be with one's friends seem to have been more important than theological differences in drawing *Issei* to the various churches. For most of them, a Christian church was a Christian church, and never mind the fine nuances of theology. (In later years many a *Nisei* or Caucasian guest at an *Issei* party, after turning down the offer of a drink, was startled to hear: "Oh, you not drink? You are Christian?")

No recent figures are available regarding the religious preference of Japanese Americans. However, in 1936, just before the war years, Professor Frank Miyamoto made a survey in Seattle and found 1,200 Japanese members of the various Christian churches, 800 in two Buddhist sects, and less than 200 in other Japanese religious groups. Explaining why Christians outnumbered those adhering to native Japanese religions, Miyamoto wrote:

"The principal interest of the Japanese immigrants was, of course, to make a quick 'clean-up' in America and then return to Japan. In accomplishing this purpose the Christian churches served extremely important functions. The first necessity was that of getting jobs, and in this the church served as an employment agency, especially sending out a large number of houseboys known in those days as 'mission-boys.' There was, too, the immediate necessity of becoming acquainted with the American ways of behavior, speaking, and understanding, and in consequence the churches became centers in which the young immigrants, ambitious to learn the language and thus to rise in the American economic scale, crowded in with hopes of improving themselves.

"The significance of this social welfare work launched by the Christian missions lies in the fact that by this work they were playing directly upon the most deeply laid collectivistic sentiments of the Japanese people, and it is little wonder that these immigrants formed favorable attitudes toward Christianity. Nothing in Japan is more sacred than the helpfulness of one member of society towards another, and the Christian missionaries with their practice of benevolent aid to the young immigrants arriving on these shores must have endeared themselves to these people. Many, too, were Christians before they reached these shores, for it was those first Christians of the Meiji era who were most struck by the spirit of adventuring across the seas, influenced as they had been by the tales of wonder told them by the early Christian missionaries."

Oddly enough, organized Buddhist efforts were relatively tardy and in fact there was some official Japanese opposition to the introduction of Buddhist missionary activity in the United States. The first mention of Japanese Buddhist priests arriving in the United States appears in 1893 when four of them attended what was called the World Parliament of Religions in Chicago and lectured on their faith. Apparently they returned home soon after that with only limited contact with the Japanese immigrants. It was a Methodist minister, Yasuzo Shimizu, who was indirectly responsible for the Buddhists being aroused to action. The Reverend Mr. Shimizu conducted English language classes in San Francisco in 1897 and was winning many converts. One of his students, Nisaburo Hirano, appreciated the instruction but declined to become a Christian. The following year he returned to Japan, made his way to Kyoto, and urged leaders of the Nishi Hongwanji sect of the Jodo Shinshu denomination to do something about setting up Buddhist churches in the United States. Two priests, Eryu Honda and Ejun Miyamoto, were dispatched to San Francisco shortly to investigate the situation. On July 14, 1898, they met with thirty-two immigrants in the home of Dr. Katsugoro Haida, and it was agreed that a Buddhist church was a desirable institution. The two priests returned to Japan to make their report. Opposition then arose from an unexpected quarter. A Japanese consular representative pointed out that the United States was a Christian nation, and even though the laws provided for freedom of religion, he expressed fear that any vigorous introduction of Buddhism might jeopardize U.S.-Japanese relations.

The Nishi Hongwanji leader, Kenjyo Akamatsu, came up with a typically Japanese compromise. He would send two Buddhist missionaries, not to the United States, for this might be regarded as an unfriendly act, but to San Francisco where some residents had expressed a desire for spiritual guidance. The two ministers were Shuyei Sonoda and Kukuryo Nishijima. Their arrival on September 2, 1899, is regarded as the founding date for the Buddhist Churches of America.

The missionaries founded Buddhist churches in San Francisco and Sacramento in 1899. Other churches sprang up quickly—Fresno in 1900, Seattle in 1901, San Jose in 1902, Oakland and Portland in 1903, Kingsburg and Los Angeles in 1905, Watsonville in 1906, Stockton in 1907, Guadalupe, Bakersfield and Vacaville in 1909.

As the years went by, it became inevitable that the Buddhist churches should make adaptations to meet the requirements of life in America. Caucasian converts to Buddhism in Hawaii had been the first to translate chants and ritual into English. Although most Japanese weddings were solemnized by Shinto rites, the Buddhists developed their own marriage ceremony, not unlike the Protestant ritual, for use in the U.S. Sunday school and the singing of hymns were also American adaptations. One of the earlier efforts in this direction was borrowed from the Christian children's hymn, *Jesus Loves Me*. Little Buddhist children sang: "Buddha loves me this I know, for the Sutra tells me so."

Some observers have contended that the Buddhist churches, because of their naturally close affiliation to Japan and the Japanese language, retarded the Americanization of the *Issei* and particularly the *Nisei*. As a matter of fact, the Young Men's Buddhist Associations even in the 1930's sponsored oratorical contests for *Nisei* with separate Japanese and English language divisions. And it was not entirely unknown that some *Nisei* would enter both contests.

While Jodo Shinshu is by far the strongest Buddhist denomination in the United States, Zen, Nichiren and Shingon sects are represented in various localities. Jodo Shinshu is organized under the banner of the Buddhist Churches of America with headquarters in San Francisco. In 1968 the B.C.A. named a *Nisei* as its bishop for the first time. He is the Reverend Kenryu T. Tsuji, Canada-born and Canadian-educated, and it is noteworthy that he took his oath of office in English. The B.C.A. has a membership of fifty-seven churches, mostly on the West Coast, with some eighty ministers, a fourth of whom are *Nisei*.

"The Buddhist churches," says the Reverend Noboru Tsunoda of Denver, "are facing the same problems with the young people as the Christian churches. They are drifting away from their religion; there are many devout Buddhists among the *Nisei* and *Sansei*, but also many nominal Buddhists who are not active in the churches." Nonetheless, the *Issei* built many handsome Buddhist church buildings and created a strong foundation for religious organizations that played a major role in the development of community life and a practice of Buddhist ethics.

By the same token, whatever the reason the *Issei* were attracted to Christianity, many of them became faithful and devout church-goers, working for and sacrificing for their churches with the same dedication that they showed their families.

However, since the institution of the Christian church played such a large part in the lives of the *Issei*, one is led to wonder what their future in America would have been like, what their social adaptation to American ways would have been, if the churches had not segregated them from the very beginning into Japanese congregations. If, everyone being the child of God, they had been encouraged to become fully integrated members of Caucasian churches, would the integration of *Issei* into American society have been hastened and made more complete? And what would have been the result if Caucasians assigned to work in *Issei* churches had placed as much emphasis on the social education of their members as on the philosophy and ritual of worship? These are difficult and perhaps unfair questions, for it is only lately that the church has come to place heavy emphasis on social concerns. Yet, it is fascinating to ponder whether the fact that segregated churches were formed delayed or perhaps even blocked the Americanization of the Japanese immigrants. Or, on the other hand, would the inability to understand English and the discomfort of being "different" in white congregations have driven the *Issei* from Christianity? There are no incontrovertible answers to these questions, but they provoke thought. In times of need and crisis, Christian leaders were in the forefront of those rushing to the aid of the Japanese. Sidney L. Gulick, a former missionary in Japan, argued as forcefully and energetically (and sometimes as inaccurately) for the Japanese in the United States as men like McClatchy campaigned against them. During the tense pre-Evacuation weeks, Christian leaders were among the few Americans who dared speak up for the *Issei* and *Nisei*. And during the relocation period, other Americans moved by a sense of Christian brotherhood opened their homes, their hearts and the doors to jobs to the refugees from the West Coast's hysteria.

10

THE MINIATURE GIANTS

HISTORIAN BRADFORD SMITH has observed: "The *Issei* contribution to America was not in great men, but in the anonymous little men who made the desert spaces green with the labor of their hands, who kept the track even so that Americans could ride comfortably across the land, who tended the comfort of the well-to-do, and grew vegetables the poor could afford to buy, who sacrificed for the welfare of their children."

This was largely, but not entirely, so. There were no Japan-born Andrew Carnegies in the steel business, no A. P. Gianninis in banking and finance, no Japanese Joseph Pulitzers to set standards of excellence in publishing, it is true. But there were Japanese immigrants who in their own way left a mark in the story of America that is not covered in Bradford Smith's paragraph.

We have mentioned George Shima, who demonstrated that the Sacramento delta lands could be reclaimed and made to yield bountiful crops of potatoes, and grew wealthy in the process. We have also mentioned Harry Yaemon Minami who planted thousands of central California acres and grew "vegetables the poor could afford to buy." Certainly deserving listing along with them are two *Issei* who coaxed from the soil with uncommon success not crops to feed the physical man, but beauty to gladden the senses and enrich the esthetic side of all who beheld their efforts. One was Kosaku Sawada whose search for his personal destiny took him from his native Osaka to the humid latitudes of Mobile, Alabama. There he lived more than a half century, gaining quiet renown as a grower and hybridizer of camellias. Before his death in 1968 at age eighty-five, he had developed thousands of new varieties.

The other was Kotaro Suto, credited with helping to transform a swampy, sandy strand into the lush green showplace that now is Miami Beach, Florida. Suto was thirty-two years old when, during World War I, he left San Francisco for Miami Beach to work as a gardener for a pioneer Florida land developer, Carl Fisher. The vision that motivated Fisher captured Suto's imagination, and soon they were working as partners rather than boss and hired man to create beauty where none had existed. Grass, shrubs, trees took root, flower beds flourished, walks wound through banks of greenery under Suto's loving hands. In time he set up his own nursery, but his service to the community did not cease. When there was a corner of a park, land around a municipal building, a section of parkway that needed landscaping, Suto showed up unbidden with plants from his nursery and created new beauty. When Suto and his wife, Masa, decided to go back to Japan in 1953, a farewell ceremony was held at City Hall. But a man who had poured so much of himself into his community could not leave it forever. In a short while the gentle, stocky, white-haired Suto was back in Miami Beach, the city he had helped to build.

Kyutaro Abiko has been mentioned earlier as a newspaper publisher. It is possible his greater fame lies in his efforts with the Central California Land Company, also known as the Yamato Colony. Abiko was born in 1865 in the village of Suibara in Niigata prefecture, on the Japan Sea side of the main island of Honshu. His mother died at his birth, and Kyutaro was turned over to his maternal grandparents. At fourteen he ran away to Tokyo where he came under the influence of Christianity. In 1885, when he was twenty years old, Abiko landed in San Francisco with only a dollar in his pockets. Abiko was unusual in that he had made up his mind to remain in the United States. He found a job as a schoolboy and went to grade school to learn English with children ten years younger than he. At one time he operated a hand laundry and a restaurant that served 10-cent meals. The restaurant never succeeded, he said in later years, because penniless friends came to eat bread, which was served free, sprinkling it with sugar if butter was lacking. By 1898, when he was thirty-four, Abiko and four friends bought two Japanese language newspapers and merged them under the name *Nichi Bei* (Japanese American). The *Nichi Bei* proved to be an influential voice in encouraging *Issei* to take the long view of their stay in the United States, to buy land and settle down, to use the picture bride system to find wives if they could not afford to go home for a visit.

To implement his editorial position, Abiko organized the Central California Land Company and bought unimproved tracts near Livingston, "good only for hay and jackrabbits," on the edge of the Central California desert. Abiko came in for much ridicule. Dust swirled upward at the slightest breeze; winds whipped the sand into violent storms. Summer's oppressive heat seemed to suck the moisture right out of the ground. Abiko persuaded stout-hearted young immigrants, almost all of them Christians, to buy land on liberal terms financed by the *Nichi Bei* bank which he operated, and they embarked on the heartbreaking task of building farms out of wasteland. It was a revolutionary move, for most of the Japanese had been content to move into areas already opened up for agriculture. Now they were pioneering, a pattern that was to become familiar in later years as good land became too expensive for immigrant purses. The first project encompassed 2,000 acres, and he settled one hundred Japanese on it. As more and more Japanese moved into the area, Abiko optioned and bought additional land, eastward into the Cressy area, north toward Cortez, and parceled it out to immigrant farmers.

Abiko was acutely aware of what had happened in the Florin area, near Sacramento, where seven out of eight residents were Japanese. In self-defense the whites practiced segregation, just as they did in the South where they encountered large numbers of Negroes. Japanese customs flourished in the segregated community. There was little mixing between the Japanese and the whites; when they were not in conflict they ignored each other. Abiko insisted that his settlers remain on the farm; they did not compete with white storekeepers. Locally available labor was used on the farms when extra help was needed. Abiko's precautions proved wise. In the twenties, long after Abiko had left the scene, Winifred Raushenbush wrote:

"In Livingston almost everything that the anti-Orientalist would consider impossible has occurred. The Japanese and the Americans are living in the same town, and instead of slipping past each other like oil and water, they have mixed . . . While in Florin the Japanese have been excluded from the Fruit Growers' Association, in Livingston the secretary of the cooperative marketing association to which both races belong is a Japanese. In Florin the children do not share the same class rooms; in Livingston grown boys and girls go on camping trips together with American chaperons. The Japanese hold 20 per cent of the stock in the local bank, they are asked to address meetings of the Merchants Association and the Boosters Club, and they play in the town band . . . Livingston is really a laboratory experiment in race relations: as intelligent an experiment as has been made anywhere in the world, and comparatively speaking, a very successful one . . ."

Yas Abiko, Kyutaro's son and a long-time San Francisco newspaper publisher writes: "In Livingston during the anti-Japanese agitation in the 'Twenties, someone put up a sign along the highway just outside of which read: 'No More Japs Wanted Here.' Gordon Winton, Jr., Merced lawyer and former state assemblyman, likes to tell about the time when as a young boy he went out with his father on a dark night and painted out the first word on the sign. Several years ago the *Issei-Nisei* Grace Methodist Church merged with the First Methodist Church of Livingston. The Florin Methodist Church stood in segregated glory right across the road from the Japanese Methodist Church, which ultimately merged with the Japanese Methodist Church of Sacramento."

Kyutaro Abiko pumped profits from his newspaper into the land project and tied up more funds on land loans than prudent banking procedure called for. In the depression of 1913, when a number of banks failed, Abiko did not have enough ready cash to meet the demands of depositors and his *Nichi Bei* bank went under. The *Issei* who survived continued to build on the foundation that Abiko had laid for them. Today the Livingston Farmers Association, a cooperative, is managed by a Cortez-born *Nisei*, Buddy T. Iwata.

Abiko's newspaper continued to prosper until a costly labor strike during the depths of the Depression forced the newspaper into bankruptcy and it was published under a receivership. Kyutaro Abiko died in 1936. If there were no giants among the Japanese, he qualifies at least as a miniature giant.

Two other Japanese, although not giants by Abiko's or anyone else's standards, deserve mention here because they demonstrated the same kind of foresight and drive and influenced the lives of their fellow immigrants much as Abiko did, although on a somewhat smaller scale.

The first was Masuo Yasui, who came to the United States in 1901 as a sixteen-year-old youngster to join his father who was working as a railroad hand. After a period as a schoolboy to learn English, Masuo set out to see a bit of America. His immediate goal was Cincinnati, Ohio. As he told the story in later years, he was fascinated by the name. The Japanese pronounced it *Shin-shin-na-chi*, which means "New, new land." So he boarded a train in Portland, and it headed eastward up the magnificent Columbia River gorge. The train had traveled only about an hour when it stopped at Hood River. Yasui stepped out on the platform and was fascinated by the sight of the broad river and the wooded hills rising above its waters, the crystal-like air and the fresh smell of growing things. He got his suitcase and left the train. He had found his new, new land in Hood River. Yasui located work with gangs of Japanese clearing the hillsides of pine and fir and replacing them with apple and pear seedlings. Soon he opened a small shop which other *Issei* used as headquarters on their visits to town.

Yasui urged them to buy land and settle down in Hood River. When they lacked money for a down payment, he loaned them the necessary funds for a share of the land that they would buy and clear. He was doing what other American entrepreneurs had done in a somewhat earlier time—grubstaking men with much ambition but little money. In time, because of his land holdings, he had an interest in one out of every ten boxes of the apples and pears shipped out of Hood River. Yasui reared seven children, including two sons who became doctors of medicine, a son Minoru who is an attorney, and a son Ray who is a member of Oregon's State Board of Higher Education. Among them, the seven have completed fifty-six years of education beyond high school. Minoru Yasui is director of Denver's Commission on Community Relations and more will be heard of him in a later chapter. Kumeo Yoshinari, a native of the Hood River area and later a national president of the Japanese American Citizens League, credits Masuo Yasui with laying the foundation for the sound economic position of *Issei*, and later the *Nisei*, in that part of Oregon.

Yoshinari says: "He urged our parents to sink their roots into the American soil. And when we *Nisei* came along, he admonished us to become good Americans. 'You are American citizens,' he used to tell us. 'You have an opportunity your parents never had. Go to school and study. Don't miss that opportunity when it comes.'"

The other foresighted Japanese was Yoshie Inouye. He was chairman of the Japanese Association of Stockton, California in 1924 when his opportunity arrived in the person of Roy Shahan, manager of the Gibson Land Company which had purchased a major portion of a 548,000-acre estate in the high, dry San Luis Valley of south-central Colorado. Shahan and two real estate developers, Richard Blakey and C. B. West, were in California looking for land-buyers. Apparently they learned of California's recently tightened alien land law and the pressure being put on Japanese farmers.

A handful of Japanese railroad workers had been in the San Luis Valley a decade or more earlier but most of them had disappeared when the work was completed. Shahan had nothing against the Japanese and saw them as potential land-buyers. He invited Inouye to visit the San Luis Valley, which he did. Inouye found a vast, largely undeveloped valley surrounded by snowcapped peaks, with plentiful supplies of water a short distance below the light, sandy soil. He carried a favorable report back to Stockton, and in the next few years some twenty-five Japanese families, including Inouye's, moved to Colorado. Some, like Jintaro Katsumoto, arrived by train with all their farming equipment, much of it strange and unknown to residents of the valley. Others, like Toyosuke Ogura, drove. Ogura loaded his family and their possessions in a rickety touring car and with total resources of one hundred dollars cash, courageously drove over the then primitive highways. One of his sons, Dr. George Ogura, is now the highly respected pathologist in the Denver coroner's office. Inouye made the move in 1926, renting 160 acres near the town of La Jara. Yoshie Inouye's son, Roy, who now farms in the same area, recalls that he showed up at school in knickers and felt completely out of place, not because he was Japanese, but because all the other boys wore bib overalls.

Shahan, and C. T. McPherson who succeeded him, were extremely helpful in getting the Japanese settled. They arranged for credit with the merchants, helped with land leases and purchases, counseled the Japanese on farming problems, and even arranged for a bus to take the Japanese children to school at a time when school buses were not common. As in Livingston, California, the Japanese were welcomed to the San Luis Valley as hard-working, productive additions to a frontier-type community where there was no competition for land and good neighbors were to be cherished. In 1923, only 600 acres were in crops. By 1925, 4,000 acres of vegetables were grown, and two years later this total had been nearly doubled to 7,500 acres, largely due to the efforts of the Japanese newcomers.

If there was any doubt about the valley's high regard for the Japanese, it was dispelled in 1936 when a drive was started to build a Buddhist temple. The estimated cost was only $4,000, but still a sizable amount in view of the depressed price of vegetables. Whites donated the not inconsiderable legal work and a site across the street from the high school in La Jara. Gifts ranging from 25 cents to 50 dollars, including a quarter ton of coal, were contributed by 133 non-Japanese individuals and business firms. The friendship between the Japanese and whites (the hostile ones were mostly late-comers to the valley) suffered somewhat during the early years of World War II, but today the *Nisei* are considered among the most substantial members of the community. Roy Inouye, Republican county chairman, Rotarian, Farm Bureau Federation leader, has headed a number of committees seeking means of revitalizing the area's economy.

Cast more in the traditional giant mold were two Northwesterners, Masajiro Furuya, banker, merchant and manufacturer, and Harry Sotaro Kawabe whose activities in Alaska cover two eras. Furuya was born in 1862, five years before the Meiji Restoration, in Yamanashi Prefecture southwest of Tokyo. During military service he became fascinated with the idea of going to the United States, but the life of a common laborer had no appeal for him. He realized he must have some skill to take to the New World and spent two years learning the tailoring trade. In 1890, at age twenty-eight, he landed in Seattle and opened a tailor shop, specializing in women's suits. Two years later he launched a general mercantile business that in time occupied a six-story building in downtown Seattle, had wholesale and retail import and export divisions, provided a large percentage of the Japanese provisions consumed in the Northwest, and opened branches in Portland (1895), Yokohama (1898), Tacoma (1900), Kobe (1903) and Vancouver, B.C. (1904). In 1907 Furuya organized the Japanese Commercial Bank, and six years later he purchased control of the Oriental American Bank. In later years he combined the two banks and ultimately they were to prove his downfall. During World War I he organized the Gudewere Manufacturing Company to manufacture women's suits and coats. While a man of frugal habits, he enjoyed the luxury of a summer home on the seashore and his daughters, Masa and Kimi, became accomplished musicians under private tutelage. No estimate is available of his private fortune. His bank collapsed during the Depression, a time of widespread bank failures throughout the United States, which led ultimately to reforms in federal banking laws. Furuya lost control of his other businesses in the aftermath and died in California in obscurity. After his death, his widow Hatsu found fifteen shares of Marconi Radio stock, purchased fifty years earlier when most *Issei* didn't know what stock was, among his papers. It was convertible into highly valuable Radio Corporation of America stock.

While Furuya built his fortune largely doing business with other Japanese, Kawabe like many another young man of his time headed for the Alaskan frontier. He arrived in Seattle in 1906, when he was sixteen years old, and went to work as a houseboy to learn English. Two years later, at eighteen, he audaciously took over operation of a small hotel and restaurant and promptly went broke. Cooks were needed in Alaska. Harry went to a place called Port Graham in southwestern Alaska, cooking for sixty dollars a month until he learned that white dishwashers were being paid twice as much. He moved to Cordova to cook for the Copper River Railroad, saving his money, taking part unsuccessfully in a gold rush, and in 1916 he moved to Seward and bought a steam laundry. It proved to be the cornerstone for the Kawabe enterprises that came to include an Alaskan fur store, gift shop, hardware store, hotel, restaurant, bar and liquor store, a gold mining operation and investment firm. *Nisei* who passed through Seward on their way to and from the fish canneries were amazed to find Kawabe's name on many of that port's business enterprises. With many other *Issei* (although his laundry held long-term contracts with the Army and Navy), Kawabe was evacuated from Alaska during World War II and interned at Crystal City, Texas. After the war Kawabe moved to Seattle where he invested in real estate, opened an import and export firm, became an American citizen and plunged into the middle of the booming trade between Alaska and Japan. Childless himself, Kawabe and his wife raised and educated some fifteen boys —Indian, Eskimo and white. Kawabe went to Alaska when it was a raw frontier, grew with it, played a not inconsequential role in its development into thriving statehood.

An *Issei* Alaskan of an altogether different stripe was Jujiro Wada, dog-team driver and mail carrier who had a reputation for being so tough he could survive in a pinch by chewing on leather harness. Little is known of him other than that he delivered the mail in the frozen interior of Alaska for several years before bush pilots took over that hazardous duty, winning a niche in frontier history with astonishing feats of endurance in a land where only the hardiest survived.

Imbued with the same adventurous spirit, but gifted with talent of another sort, Yosuke W. (Nick) Nakano was a giant in his own right on the East Coast. Nakano was born in Yamaguchi Prefecture in 1887 and came to the United States when he was nineteen years old. His father had given him his inheritance before he left Japan, but the bank where he had deposited the money failed before it could be transferred to the U.S. Nakano went through high school in California to brush up on his English, then worked his way through the University of California. After graduation, he enrolled in the school of architecture at the University of Pennsylvania. It was a happy choice. A noted Japanese biologist, Shinkichi Hatai, was teaching at Penn. His secretary was Teru Yamamoto, a graduate of Tsuda College in Japan who had astounded her friends and family by going off to the United States alone in search of a career. Nakano soon courted and married her. Upon receiving his master's degree, Nakano joined the Philadelphia architectural firm of Wark and Company, and eventually became the firm's chief engineer. Nakano came to be recognized as an expert in the use of reinforced concrete and helped develop a now widely used process for pumping concrete into forms in the construction of large buildings. In all, he had a part in the erecting of more than 200 major buildings on the East Coast, including the Architect's Building, Bell Telephone Building, Gulf Oil and Sun Oil buildings, and the Presbyterian Hospital in Philadelphia. In 1942, when Nakano was deeply depressed by the war, an old friend, Edward G. Budd Sr., the Philadelphia industrialist, specified that Nakano be placed in charge of construction for his 11-million-dollar Red Lion plant in Bustleton, Pennsylvania. Although subjected to numerous government security checks, Nakano supervised many more millions of dollars'

worth of construction during the war, including the vast Quartermaster's Depot in Philadelphia. Nakano and his wife took out
American citizenship in 1952 after passage of the Walter-McCarran Law. Two years later, sixty of Philadelphia's leading engineers
and builders attended a surprise testimonial banquet for Nakano.
He was presented with a citation lauding him for having contributed to the construction of more than fifty major buildings on the
Philadelphia skyline. Nakano died in 1961 in Japan while on a trip
around the world. A grove of trees stands in Nick Nakano's memory outside the Nakano ancestral home in Japan. It was planted
by his father at the time young Nakano left to seek his destiny in
the New World.

Perhaps the most fabulous of *Issei* careers was that of a man who,
at least in his most active years, had little to do with other *Issei*.
Fantastic as his story seems, it is well-documented. His name was
Hachiro Onuki, quickly corrupted in the United States to Hutchlon Ohnick. He was five years old when Commodore Perry arrived
in 1854. The sight of Americans must have fascinated him, for
when he was twenty-seven he came upon a group of visiting American naval cadets trying unsuccessfully to make some purchases in
Yokohama and was moved to try to aid them with what little English he knew. One account has it that the Americans were so grate-
ful they persuaded Onuki to return to the United States with them
as their guest. A more likely possibility is that the cadets smuggled
him aboard their ship with Onuki a willing conspirator. He landed
in Boston in 1876, saw the Philadelphia Centennial Exposition, visited New York and Washington, then headed for San Francisco to
catch a ship for home. En route, he heard about the silver strike at
Tombstone, Arizona and quickly forgot about Japan.

What happened during the next decade is unclear, but his name
was Anglicized and in 1886 Ohnick and two associates, W. C. Par-
sons and Josiah White, applied for and were granted a franchise by
the then infant city of Phoenix "to supply said city of Phoenix
and its citizens and residents with illuminating gas or electric light
or both." What Ohnick understood about the utilities business is
not known; he must have had a great natural business ability and
the confidence of his partners, for they named him builder and
superintendent of the Phoenix Illuminating Gas and Electric Company.

Hachiro Onuki, whose name was Anglicized to Hutchlon Ohnick, was one of three men granted a franchise to supply Phoenix, Ariz., with gas and electricity in 1886.

Ohnick bought some land downtown for $1,200, then hurried to St. Louis to buy gas generating equipment, mains and fixtures. "It won't be long now before Phoenix will have illumined streets and Phoenix will commence putting on the airs of a city in good earnest," a local editor wrote. Two days before Christmas, 1886, Phoenix business houses lit gas lamps and were delighted by their brilliance compared to the coal oil lamps. Several years later the Phoenix Electric Light Company went into business and soon coaxed Ohnick to go to work for it as secretary and superintendent. Ohnick had been drawing a salary of $90 a month at the gas works, a handsome rate of pay in those days, but he did not hesitate to spend $25,000 for a new generator to provide the power that he knew Phoenix would soon be demanding. In 1894 he resigned from what was then the Phoenix Light and Power Company to run an 80-acre ranch just outside the city.

Ohnick married Catherine Shannon in 1888. Shortly before the turn of the century he visited Japan, then returned in 1901 to

Seattle where with two other *Issei* he opened the Oriental American Bank, the same bank purchased later by Masajiro Furuya. Ohnick died in California in 1921, in his seventy-second year, and the tiny utility he launched to serve a frontier town became in time the huge Central Arizona Light and Power Company.

The story of Japanese immigrants in Texas differs in several respects from that in other parts of the nation. The Houston Chamber of Commerce was looking for settlers at the same time that Japan was seeking new sources of rice. Saito Saibara, a member of parliament, was studying theology in Hartford, Conn., in 1902 when he was asked by the Japanese government to look into the rice-growing potential of the Houston area. Saibara liked what he saw, settled near the town of Webster, and sent for his family, including his son Kiyoaki. Their first crop, harvested in 1904 from Japanese seed, yielded nearly twice the local average. The Saibara family is still in the rice business and their name is recognized in the Saibara-Asahi strain of rice.

A second rice-growing colony was started near Houston by Shinpei Mykawa in 1903. The Santa Fe Railroad has a station called Mykawa and a road of that name leads from Houston to the farm. Unlike the penniless immigrants who came to the West Coast, many of the Japanese who settled in Texas were men of means planning to stay permanently. Saburo Arai of the Mitsui family came to Alvin in 1906 and invested $250,000 in orchards to raise oranges. When he was frozen out three years later he moved southeast of Houston and established a nursery. About the same time Kichimatsu Kishi and some friends invested $300,000 in land near Beaumont and grew rice, cabbage, figs and strawberries. Nancy Montgomery of the Institute of Texas Cultures in San Antonio reports that Kishi built a Protestant church for his colony, introduced contour levee rice farming, and started the Orange Petroleum Company which he later sold. A number of other Japanese became truck farmers in the lower Rio Grande Valley, but in 1940 there were less than 500 Japanese in all of Texas.

Space does not permit more than a mention of some other notable *Issei*. There was, for example, Masaharu Kondo regarded as the father of the Southern California fishing industry. Dr. Hideo Noguchi, conqueror of yellow fever, and Dr. Jokichi Takamine, who discovered adrenalin, can hardly be called true *Issei;* they were well-qualified scientists who left Japan to pursue their studies in the United States. Those who have been mentioned, while only a handful, are sufficient to disprove the stereotyped belief that the *Issei* were an entirely undistinguished and largely untalented and unimaginative group that made their way by sheer brute persistence.

As a matter of fact, *Issei* played a substantial role in the development of the motion picture industry, certainly a calling that required sensitivity, imagination and flair. The drama had an important role in the development of Japanese culture over the centuries, and it was a sorry group of *Issei* who, on occasion, failed to stage theatricals for their own pleasure. Early American visitors to Japan, starting with Commodore Perry, were fascinated by Japanese performers. As early as 1883, one Phillip H. Kilby imported a troupe of six men and four women, including wrestlers, tightrope walkers and foot-jugglers for an American tour, and a troupe of Japanese jugglers was reported in the Colusa (Calif.) *Sun-Herald* in 1868.

The most famous of Japanese actors on the American scene was, of course, Sessue Hayakawa, whose career spanned more than a half century. For details of the remarkable Hayakawa's life, we are indebted to Bob Okazaki, *Nisei* chronicler of the Hollywood scene, himself a motion picture and television actor, onetime labor organizer, son of a Baptist minister, dialogue coach and the stuff of which legends are made.

Hayakawa, born in Chiba Province, was nineteen years old when he came to the United States to enter the University of Chicago. One summer vacation he went to Los Angeles and joined an *Issei* amateur group staging *The Typhoon*. Okazaki says: "Film producer Thomas Ince saw the play, made a motion picture of it, with most of the original cast. It turned out to be, and is still regarded as, a history-making film. Hayakawa asked for, and got, $500 a week. Within a year Hayakawa's salary skyrocketed to $3,500 a week when he appeared in Cecil B. DeMille's *The Cheat* in 1915. This was the story in which a 'butterfly wife' is branded by a wealthy Nipponese (Hayakawa) for not living up to her agreement to become his mistress after he has loaned her a considerable sum of money. It was the first of the domestic dramas of the well-to-do in their own surroundings and with their own problems, presented without moralizing and from their point of view. Audiences were entranced and producers thunderstruck. It seemed to make everything that preceded it meaningless. In it, Sessue and his leading lady, Fanny Ward, displayed a new, restrained, oddly eloquent, and indirect style of acting, absolutely unlike anything to be seen on the stage at that time . . . That film, odd though it may seem, gave the cinema a new sense of proportion. And it was this Japanese, this Sessue, who made this contribution to motion pictures. Hayakawa zoomed to fame, and a $5,000 a week salary."

Hayakawa built a 100,000-dollar home called the Gray Castle at the corner of Franklin Avenue and Argyle Street in Hollywood and hosted lavish parties there. Advancing freeways destroyed the house in 1955, just as Hayakawa was staging a screen comeback.

Hayakawa played a series of romantic leads with leading American actresses between 1918 and 1924, even as the forces that led to the Exclusion Act were building up. Later he formed his own movie company, Imperial Picture Productions, played the lead on an Orpheum circuit tour of a play he wrote called *The Bandit Prince*, and in 1926 starred in the Broadway production of *Love City*. Bob Okazaki observes: "At a time when there were no income taxes, steaks were 25 cents a pound, and Nipponese gardeners, hoses coiled about their shoulders and tools strapped to the handle bars, pedalled their rounds from house to house on bikes, Sessue rode to the studios in a chauffeur-driven town car behind a sliding glass partition, while a retinue of servants ran his errands." Legend has it that Hayakawa lost $60,000 in one session at Monte Carlo, and another $90,000 two years later.

But the roulette wheel spun out the right numbers for Hayakawa in the end. "Discovered" in Paris after World War II, Hollywood found some minor roles for him. Then along came *Bridge Over the River Kwai*, and Hayakawa gave a memorable performance as the commander of the Japanese prison camp. No *Nisei* actor has been able to approach the heights Hayakawa attained, although James Shigeta, a Hawaiian *Nisei* has been featured in a number of leads.

Hayakawa's wife during the early years of stardom, Tsuru Aoki, was an actress in her own right. Bob Okazaki says that in 1901 a group known as the Kawakami Dramatists came to the United States with a repertoire of classic Japanese drama as well as Shakespeare in Japanese. In the troupe was Tsuru, who played child roles, accompanied by her father, the stage manager. The tour was far

Showing of Sessue Hayakawa films was occasion enough for staging "Japanese Nights" in downtown Los Angeles theaters. Nisei girls were decked out in *kimono* for this event in 1930. (Los Angeles County Museum of Natural History)

from sensational and was waiting for a ship home from San Francisco when a group of Seattle businessmen agreed to underwrite a visit to the Northwest. Among the businessmen, Okazaki reports, were Ototaka Yamaoka (father of George, now an attorney in New York City; Iris, who went on to a brief acting career in Hollywood; and Otto, who played countless Japanese butler roles in the movies); and Tetsuo Takahashi (father of C. T. Takahashi, prominent Seattle businessman). Tsuru, with her father, moved down to Pasadena instead of returning home, learned to dance with the Ruth St. Denis Company, appeared in some Keystone Comedy films, and went on to several leading roles. She played opposite Hayakawa in *Wrath of the Gods*, married Hayakawa and dropped out of films. Nonetheless, she paved the way for such *Nisei* actresses of the late thirties as Iris Yamaoka, Yoshiwara Tamaki, Miki Morita, Pearl Suyetomi, Toshia Mori, and more lately, Miiko Taka and Michi Kobi.

Among other Hollywood personalities of note, Okazaki lists Henry Kotani, who was graduated from Lowell High School in San Francisco in 1906, acted briefly before becoming a top camera-man whose assistant at one time was James Wong Howe, left for Japan in 1920; Yutaka Jack Abe, actor, director and writer of such scenarios as *Lotus Land* and *Tale of Two Countries* which starred Hayakawa, became a movie producer in Japan; Henry Okawa, onetime houseboy for General John J. Pershing, who was a class-mate of Gary Cooper at Paramount's Institute of Drama, stunt flier in several of the Howard Hawks epics, returned to Japan in 1932 to take a leading role in more than fifty pictures before he became a director; Sadakichi Hartman, son of a Japanese mother and Ger-man father, once called the "King of Bohemia" in Greenwich Vil-lage, a nonconformist who walked out on Douglas Fairbanks after filming some scenes as the Court Magician in *The Thief of Bagdad*, making it necessary for Fairbanks to reshoot the picture at a cost of $250,000; and the great Kamiyama Sojin who played Shylock, Hamlet, Macbeth and Othello in Japan before he came to the United States for a seven-year career in Hollywood, largely in roles that called for a mysterious, sinister Oriental, but also as the first Charlie Chan, returned to Japan in the mid-twenties.

One who did not return was Eddie Imazu who came to the United States with his family as a toddler, went to work for the old Metro Studio in 1920 as a scene-shifter, became a scene-painter when the studio became Metro-Goldwyn-Mayer, and for a third of a century has been one of Hollywood's leading art directors.

Parenthetically, it should be noted here that Okazaki calls Benji Okubo the first *Nisei* child actor. He is the brother of Mine Okubo who wrote and illustrated *Citizen 13660*, a poignant report on her evacuation experiences. Benji played the role of a six-year-old half-caste in a silent movie based on the Madame Butterfly theme. An-other *Nisei* child actor was Arthur Kaihatsu who appeared in the Hal Roach Our Gang comedies. Arthur's father, incidentally, has a rightful place in this chapter. His name was Masajiro Kaihatsu, but as Yukio Aoyama (often called the Japanese Ibsen) he ap-peared in some sixty Hollywood pictures including a number of

Among early Hollywood actors was Yukio Aoyama, stage name of Masajiro Kaihatsu. He appeared in some 60 films including a number of cliff-hanging serials.

cliff-hanging serials in the silent days, starred opposite some of the leading ladies of the World War I era, and worked as an assistant director at the Vitagraph studio.

Although the mark most of these men and women left was no more permanent than a fleeting shadow on a screen, they played no small role in the development of the vast motion picture industry, helping to bring thrills, excitement, drama and the stuff of dreams to a nation that craved to be entertained by a medium that had been its own invention. For this reason, if no other, they deserve to be listed in this chapter along with Kyutaro Abiko who envisioned green fields where there was only dust, George Shima who grew potatoes where once mosquitoes had bred, Nick Nakano who helped shape the skyline of a great American city, Hutchlon Ohnick who brought power and light to frontier Arizona, and a handful of others like them who were able to make the most of the happy combination of ability and opportunity.

11

THE NISEI ARRIVE

BY 1930 there were 138,836 Japanese in the United States. They represented just a fraction more than 0.1 percent of the total population. Less than half the Japanese—68,357, according to the 1930 census—were American-born, the *Nisei*, heirs to the rights and responsibilities of the American heritage.

Their average age was ten years. More than half of them had been born only in the preceding decade. The earliest *Nisei* arrived on the scene in the 1890's, as we have seen, but their numbers did not grow in proportion to the increase in the total number of Japanese in the United States because of the absence of family life. By 1910 there were only 4,502 *Nisei*. But with more and more families being established, the number of *Nisei* rose to 29,672 in 1920. Their number more than doubled in the next ten years to 68,357, alarming Californians who charged the Japanese multiplied like rabbits and would soon overrun the state.

Such fears were groundless; the total number of Japanese did not rise proportionately after immigration was halted in 1924. In fact the number of *Issei*, the foreign-born, decreased at a progressively faster rate as shown by the following table, based on federal census figures:

Year	Nisei	Issei	Total	U.S. Population
1900	269	24,057	24,326	75,994,575
1910	4,502	67,655	72,157	91,972,266
1920	29,672	81,338	111,010	105,710,620
1930	68,357	70,477	138,836	122,775,046
1940	79,642	47,305	126,947	131,669,275

In 1930 the average age of the *Issei* male was nearly forty-two; the average *Issei* woman was thirty-five. The end of their child-bearing years was approaching. As it turned out, reproduction did not keep pace in the 1930–1940 decade with the number of *Issei* who died or left the country, and the total number of Japanese dropped by 12,000. This is the statistical setting for a penetrating look into the Japanese American communities of the West Coast, where the vast majority lived, during the years the *Nisei* were growing up.

In 1930 fewer than 4,000 *Nisei* in the entire United States were of voting age. The *Issei*, in their productive prime, were firmly in control of their communities. Their wandering days were ended; their little businesses in Los Angeles, Fresno, San Jose, San Francisco, Stockton, Sacramento, Portland, Tacoma, Seattle, Spokane and way points provided them a measure of security and a sense of permanence that they had never known previously. Despite the land laws, they had sunk their roots in the soil of valleys with names like Imperial and San Joaquin, Yakima and Puyallup; they had learned to gauge the weather and they won as often as they lost in the gamble on market prices which is all a farmer can expect. The *Issei* held the purse strings. They established standards of behavior, planned the routine of their community life, ruled their families. Their world was a potpourri of the Japanese culture in which they had been reared and which they remembered and revered with a fierce tenacity until oftentimes the memory was more vivid than the reality; the American culture that had rubbed off on them and which they absorbed into their lives, sometimes unconsciously; and finally, the pressures that compressed them largely into their own ethnic communities.

The result for the *Nisei* was a world that was both secure and confining, comfortable and frustrating, challenging and stultifying, warm and hostile. In a word, although they rarely had either time or inclination to brood about it, theirs was a confusing life. Pervading all was the influence of the public schools. They learned English in their classes and spoke Japanese at home; in time, as English won the linguistic tug of war, the parents spoke to them in Japanese and they replied in English and somehow they understood each other very well. They took peanut butter and jelly sandwiches to school for lunch and for supper shoveled rice into their mouths with chopsticks together with fish or vegetables flavored with soy sauce.

The shock absorber that enabled them to survive the jolting and buffeting of divergent cultures was the home, reassuring despite its meager comforts, warm with often unarticulated love even though both parents worked themselves close to exhaustion, close-knit and secure because of—as well as in spite of—outside forces beyond their control.

For the *Issei*, home was security after the daily struggle of making a living in a white man's world where the language was difficult and strange, the competition harsh, the laws and those who enforced them hostile. At home the *Issei* could eat his rice with hot tea and make his delicious *tsukemono* pickles in a malodorous jar of fermenting *nuka* without prying blue eyes to embarrass him. He could listen to the wailing music that had soothed and moved his parents and grandparents before him and evoked memories of home. He could observe his own holidays, like New Year's Day which in Japan is New Year's, Thanksgiving, Labor Day and two or three other holidays all rolled into one. On New Year's Eve he observed the tradition of paying off as many of his debts as he could, so their burden would not follow him into the upcoming year; scrubbed and dusted his shop or office or home from top to bottom; luxuriated in a long hot bath to rid himself of the past year's grime —a symbolic rite since he bathed daily—and at midnight shared with his family a large pot of buckwheat noodles floating in chicken broth. His wife, meanwhile, was cooking all the wonderful and traditional dishes of the New Year's feast—bamboo shoots and taro, kelp neatly rolled and tied, spicily flavored burdock root, shrimp, a lobster if she could afford it, whole red snapper grilled after it had been trussed to make it look as if it were alive and flipping off the platter, filet of raw tuna and seabass, salted herring roe soaked in soy sauce, fried soybean cake, black beans and chestnuts, fishcakes, vinegar-flavored rice wrapped like a jelly roll in sheets of seaweed, and *mochi*—rice pounded into a glutinous mass and shaped into little buns. City people bought their *mochi* in the stores. Country folks gathered a few days before New Year's in gay, boisterous *mochi*-making parties not unlike husking bees in early America.

Early on New Year's Day—it would not do to linger in bed, for what one did on January 1 set the pattern for the rest of the year —the *Issei* man of the house would don his best suit and pay formal calls on his employer, his neighbors and friends. He followed an age-old ritual, bowing deeply, repeating the prescribed phrases: "*Akemashite omedeto gozaimasu:* Happy New Year. I am much indebted to you for your many favors the past year. I ask your benevolence once again this coming year." Then, with the host and hostess apologizing profusely for the "untasty, miserably prepared, unworthy food," he would be invited to sample the feast laid out in colorful array on huge platters. He could not tarry long. There were many calls to be made, and he had to hurry home to receive guests, too. In the afternoon the whole family might visit relatives or particularly close friends, gorge themselves, reminisce, play Japanese games.

As the years slipped by, the reminiscences about Japan grew less frequent; in their stead stories about adventures and amusing times in America in the earliest years were told with pride and relish as the *Nisei* listened in fascination. Memories grew mellow, the loneliness and pain and frustration, the humiliation of being denied service in public accommodations and of being relegated to "Nigger heaven" in the movie theaters, could be forgotten on happy occasions. They even laughed when they told about being stoned and beaten by hooligans on the street just because they were Japanese, and many men related stories like these because it was a common occurrence. But they laughed even harder when they recalled how a self-appointed squad of young *Issei* judo experts turned the tables on the roughnecks, prowling the alleys and backstreets and inviting attack, to which they retaliated with wondrous swiftness and dispatch so that in time the toughs came to associate judo with Japanese and left even the scrawniest specimen alone. And because their bellies were comfortably full, they could remember without pain how they had drooled in front of bakeries, torturing themselves with the aroma of cakes and cookies they couldn't afford to buy, and how they would slip into a restaurant booth to order a cup of coffee and then sprinkle sugar on the bread that was on every table and take these "sandwiches" outside to ease the pains of hunger.

Because of their *Nisei* children, the families found themselves celebrating Christmas, Thanksgiving and the Fourth of July with gusto comparable to that of the New Year festivities. But nothing quite replaced New Year's. If he owned a business, the *Issei* kept the doors closed at least three days, and New Year parties were celebrated throughout January and sometimes even into February.

Officers of the Sonoma County (Calif.) Japanese Association, taken in 1913.

The most important of these were staged by the *Kenjin-kai*, an association made up of people from the same prefecture. A *kenjin*, someone from one's own native prefecture, was almost like a blood brother even if he were a stranger—to be fostered, assisted when in trouble, to be trusted, tolerated, and to be treated gently and affectionately. Whenever possible, one took his business to a *kenjin*. An insurance agent born in Hiroshima or Okayama or Yamaguchi Prefecture, which had sent many *kenjin* to the States, was more likely to be successful than one from a prefecture that had exported few immigrants. People from other *ken* were Japanese, all right, but still they were considered a wee bit different from one's own kind, and various characteristics were attributed to the people of each prefecture. For example, Hiroshima people were said to be industrious and tight-fisted; Wakayama people aggressive and hot-tempered; Tokyoites generous, people from Kumamoto stubborn, Okayama shrewd and clever, the northern provinces patient as a result of their long, cold winters.

A *Kenjin-kai* New Year's party was like a clan reunion at which feasting, singing of ancient ballads, performances of traditional dances, and drinking (even during Prohibition years a generous supply of bootleg *sake* always seemed to be available, camouflaged discreetly by being served in teapots) helped the *Issei* to unwind and forget their pressing cares, however briefly. If the *Issei* father attended the party alone, he was given neatly packaged portions of food to take home to his family. More often, all the children went along, for these were primarily family parties and babysitters were unknown. These were customs that could be cherished and perpetuated in the cloistered security of the Little Tokyos.

The *Kenjin-kai* were also sponsors of elaborate outings each summer, with the various associations competing to see who could put on the biggest show. The young *Nisei* could appreciate these functions more than the New Year parties. The *Kenjin-kai* picnic was usually preceded by a shopping expedition on which each youngster was outfitted with a new pair of rubber-soled canvas shoes. Everyone called them tennis shoes, although few ever played tennis. The shoes, guaranteed to make even the dumpiest child a little lighter on his feet, were for the variety of footraces around a circular course marked by rope attached to posts hammered into the ground. The winners were given merchandise prizes and the also-rans were consoled with pencils and nickel tablets. It was astonishing how much loot even an unathletic family could gather in the course of a day. The picnics were also an opportunity for *Issei* mothers to assemble magnificent Japanese lunches—including fried chicken and potato salad—which were packed into treasured lacquer boxes. The food was washed down with an endless supply of free lemonade and topped off with free ice cream and watermelon. Before the Depression, several of the larger *Kenjin-kai* in Seattle customarily chartered excursion boats to take their members and their families to picnic sites on beaches across Puget Sound, no small undertaking even by today's standards.

The *Kenjin-kai* also served as welfare organizations. If a member became ill and could not work, the *Kenjin-kai* quietly offered help. When a member died, his compatriots made the funeral arrangements for the bereaved family. His friends came to the services with two or three dollars in an envelope which was dropped off at a desk set up to receive these offerings. After the funeral all those who had a part in making the arrangements would gather to enjoy a meal together, usually prepared by the ladies of the Christian church or Buddhist temple. Almost always there were enough cash offerings to pay all expenses and provide the widow with a small nest egg. In a way, these funeral offerings were like a mutual insurance policy. One paid a small premium each time a friend or *kenjin* died, knowing when his turn came, his family would be taken care of. That was the way the requirements of life and death had been met in the villages back home. Yet the bereaved family could not let such gifts go unacknowledged, even though the deceased may have been paying his "premiums" faithfully over many years. The *Issei's* sense of *on*, of obligation, required at least a token acknowledgement—a handkerchief for each person who had brought a contribution to the funeral, a tiny box of sweets, a little package of tea, and sometimes even a pound of coffee or a book of postage stamps.

These *Issei* customs, particularly the New Year parties and summer picnics, were matters the *Nisei* could understand, participate in and enjoy. But their first appreciable breach with their parents developed over language. The *Issei* who spoke English well was an exception; the linguistic problems that almost all immigrants face were complicated in this case by the total dissimilarity between Japanese and English. The fact that most *Issei* were confined to a racial ghetto where they lived, associated and did business with their own countrymen, made mastery of English largely unnecessary. The Reverend Daisuke Kitagawa, Japan-born Episcopalian minister who came to the United States in 1937, offers another explanation: "Because of his uncritical admiration for America and his neurotic desire to be able to speak English like an American, the *Issei* was overwhelmed by the tremendous difficulty of the English language—which no one can deny—and could not bring himself to speak it unless he could do so perfectly. Knowing that he could not possibly do so, he felt ashamed, and was afraid to open his mouth." Yet he could not avoid a certain absorption, and adaptation, of English to his needs.

"Oh lie," he would say when he meant "all right." "Thank you" became "sun kyu." If something went haywire, it was "waya." He said "osu mala you" when he asked his friend "what's the matter with you," and the reply might be "no guru" meaning "no good." He liked "cohee" with toast and "buttuh" for breakfast, and because he rarely had much money he ate hamburger steak which he called "hamboku stekki."

The *Nisei* had comparable trouble learning to speak Japanese adequately. As pre-schoolers many of them spoke Japanese better than English because this was the language of the family. But the Japanese they used was "baby talk," totally inappropriate and ridiculous coming from the mouths of adults or even teenagers. Professor Edward K. Strong Jr. of Stanford University, in his *The Second-Generation Japanese Problem* published in 1934, found "Japanese Americans are mastering neither language." Although he was writing about *Nisei,* he reported he "never met a Japanese who was free from accent, always used the article correctly, and did not occasionally employ the Japanese order of words in a sentence"—certainly an excessively broad evaluation based on limited observation. In ghetto type primary schools where the overwhelming percentage of pupils were of Japanese parentage—and there were many of these—Dr. Strong's observation could be applicable. However, it was the Japanese language that suffered as the *Nisei* progressed in school, wrote English, buried their noses in English language novels, read the daily English language newspapers, shouted and quarreled on the playgrounds in English, and resorted to Japanese only to communicate with their parents.

The *Issei* viewed this Americanization of their children with mixed emotions. They were proud that their offspring took so naturally to a language that they themselves were incapable of mastering. They knew their children must absorb the American culture, must be Americans, to make their way in the land of their birth. But they were also disturbed that the *Nisei* were ignoring, and in some cases rejecting, their Japanese heritage. The gradual change from Japanese-language-orientation to English-language-orientation was evidence of this change; how could one understand Japan when one could not even speak the language?

Basic to *Issei* concern was the feeling—the expectation, even the likelihood—that some day they would return to Japan with their families. Japan was still "home"; America was a temporary residence, and what would the children do if they could not read and write and speak Japanese? For most *Issei* this possible eventuality was a vague something in the distant future, and they had no way of knowing whether their decision, when the time came, would be voluntary or forced by even more oppressive legislation of the kind they had experienced. They were also acutely aware of the economic barriers ahead of their children despite their American citizenship and education. Few doors to jobs were open outside the communities. Everyone knew of older *Nisei* trained as engineers who were working in service stations, men with degrees in business administration helping run the family grocery. So *Issei* leaders pointed out that if one hoped to do business in the Japanese community, he had to know Japanese. And if he would capitalize on his knowledge of the English language and American customs to work for a Japanese trading firm, he still had to know Japanese.

Thus the *Issei* scraped up the tuition and the *Nisei* were sent to Japanese language school to learn the rudiments of this strange and difficult tongue. Until 3 P.M. the *Nisei* youngster was exposed to an education system calculated to make him as good an American as his classmates named O'Brien, Swanson, Santucci or Koblykovich. But when the bell rang and they ran off to play ball, many a *Nisei* trudged off for another hour or two of classes.

Understandably, many *Nisei* resented the time they had to devote to Japanese language school as well as the discipline they had to endure. Charles Kamayatsu, now a Los Angeles businessman, recalls that he took the negative side in a language school debate on the question as to whether knowledge of Japanese was essential in the United States. Kamayatsu made a strong case, but wandered off the subject somewhat by criticizing the teaching staff as incompetent. The next day the principal appeared at Charles' home and sternly warned his father that the boy was not only rebellious but seemed to be harboring radical ideas and would bear watching.

How ineffective these language schools were was not revealed until many years later. In the early days of World War II, the U.S. Army interviewed 3,700 *Nisei* in a search for men to be recruited for intelligence work. Only 10 percent were sufficiently fluent in Japanese to be useful to their country. These *Nisei*, and many others who were made proficient in Army Intelligence cram courses, helped write a brilliant chapter in American military history. Their accomplishments will be detailed later in this volume.

In most instances the schools did more than simply teach the language. Isao Horinouchi, in a paper published by the Sacramento Anthropological Society, tells us that *Shushin*, the study of morals, was "an important part of the curriculum of the Japanese language schools in America." He writes: "Apart from the formal course, moral principles were woven into the general curriculum and into school life in any way the ingenuity of the educators could devise. Although it was formally taught in school, one was constantly reminded both at home and in the community of his duty to respect his parents, teachers, and all elders. The highest authority in the home that demanded respect and honor was the father. Next in order was the mother, followed by the older children. The morality taught in the *Shushin* textbooks was basically Confucian. The teachings were exhortations to filial piety and respect for teachers and elders."

Monica Sone, in her autobiographical *Nisei Daughter*, writes vividly of a *Tenchosetsu* program sponsored by the Japanese language school in Seattle, honoring the Emperor's birthday. (It is perhaps significant that the school was named *Kokugo Gakko*, meaning National Language School.) Attendance at the program was compulsory, she reports. The youngsters sat bored and uncomprehending as community leaders conducted, as solemnly and formally as a religious rite, the reading of the Imperial Rescript on Education. "We did not understand a single word of the Imperial message since it was written in a style of speech used exclusively by the Emperor," she says. Then the assembly sang the Japanese national anthem and shouted three *banzais* for the Emperor's health. She recalls that some of the older *Nisei* girls once showed up wearing hats, as was proper at an important American afternoon affair, and were loudly ordered by the chairman to bare their heads and censured for "insulting" the Son of Heaven. The *Nisei* attitude toward the entire program can be summed up in the words of a boy who exclaimed on dismissal: "Thank God that's over. Come on, Bozo, let's get going."

Bozo was much easier to pronounce than whatever his true name may have been. Most *Nisei* were burdened with cumbersome Japanese names which were promptly shortened when they went to school. Makoto became Mac, Isamu naturally was changed to Sam, Shoji was easily altered to George. Nicknames also came easily: Masahisa became Mud, Kanetada became Kelly, Hisao became Horse and when the object was a short, stout young man Hitoshi easily became Hippo. Nor were the girls immune, although the transformation was usually more kind. Yuriko became Lily and Sumire became Violet, for they mean the same. Many adopted names—James and John, Mary and Esther, for much the same reasons that Americans of other ethnic groups chose them.

Perhaps it was a mistake that the Rescript Monica Sone mentions was not read in English translation for the benefit of the youngsters, for despite a strong nationalistic and racial tone, there were elements of value in it. The Rescript was promulgated in 1890 to give the Imperial stamp of approval to the concept of universal education, a necessity if Japan were to attain equality with the Western world. In part, the Rescript read:

". . . Ye, our subjects, be filial to your parents, affectionate to your brothers and sisters; as husbands and wives be harmonious; as friends, true . . . pursue learning and cultivate arts, and thereby develop intellectual faculties and perfect moral powers; furthermore, advance public good and promote common interests; always respect the Constitution and observe the laws; should emergency arise, offer yourselves courageously to the State; and thus guard and maintain the prosperity of our Imperial Throne coeval with heaven and earth . . ."

Horinouchi observes that in Japan "success in education and through it, the achievement of social status are regarded as bringing great honor to the race."

But many *Nisei* were much more pragmatic: "Why do I want to go to college? Because I don't want to get stuck on the farm. I don't want to spend my life in stoop labor like my folks."

Obviously, a large element of optimism prevailed. Realistically, the *Nisei* knew the odds were against them. But they and their parents felt that some day, somehow, prejudice would disappear, and they wanted to be ready to seize opportunity when it knocked at their door—as it did after World War II. Time and again *Nisei* heard their parents say: "If I could only speak English like you, I would have amounted to something." It was a spur that goaded the *Nisei* to scholastic excellence.

Whatever the chief incentive might have been, the *Nisei* as a group did remarkably well in grade and high schools. A disproportionate number of them became valedictorians and salutatorians with straight A grades. Stubborn persistence had as much to do with their success as brilliance. "I studied hard because I felt it was the thing to do," a *Nisei* explains. "It was important to succeed in school. I enjoyed seeing those A's on my report card, but a big part of the pleasure came in seeing how pleased my parents were. I guess you might say I worked for good grades because it made my parents happy."

Another *Nisei* recalls that he was competing in school against his *Nisei* friends. The grades that his Caucasian classmates made didn't seem to make much difference; his parents wanted to know whether he did as well as Mr. Suzuki's son and Mr. Yamada's daughter. In class the *Nisei* youngsters were inclined to be quiet, attentive, seldom volunteering recitations although they did well when called on, more inclined to absorb what they read or were told than questioning and challenging, obedient, rarely a discipline problem. At home he had been taught to respect his teachers, and he did.

In later years the "strong family system" would be credited with the exemplary conduct of the *Nisei*, their scholastic achievements and their ability to stay out of trouble with the police. Asked just what the "strong family system" involved, many *Nisei* were unable to explain. It was so much of them, such a natural part of their life, that it seemed to defy definition.

In essence, it was based on strong paternal dominance of the family's affairs in which, as Professor Miyamoto phrases it, "the father is the chief symbol of status and of the duties and privileges which are a part of his heritage." In practice, according to Miyamoto, it works this way:

"The male head assumes dominance over the children, and the mother as a representative of the father reflects a certain amount of this authority. By comparison with white-American children, the activities of Japanese children are generally more regulated by their parents. In extreme instances, though these are infrequent, this authority extends itself into a practical control over every important action of the children."

(One *Nisei* recalls that when as an eleven-year-old he told his parents he wanted to join a baseball team, his father insisted on attending a meeting to see for himself what kind of club it was.)

"The result is either docility on the part of the growing boy or girl to parental regulation, or an underlying irritation from it that threatens to break out in overt rebellion and necessitates a constant readjustment of relationships between them.

"The parents, on their part, rationalize this authoritarianism on an ethical basis, for the Japanese parents conceive their chief duty to be a concern over the welfare of their children. The apparent lack of regulation by American parents of their children's lives is interpreted by the Japanese as being an insufficient concern about the children's welfare.

"The strength of this authority lies not alone in the dominant role assumed by the parents, but even more in the reinforcement given by the community to this parental status. Upon every public occasion at which parents and children are gathered, the tendency is to remind the young of the virtues of obedience. Every visitor in the home is careful to make observations concerning the quietness of the children, or of their obedience, and the parents are prone to discuss the matter with hidden pride. In the Japanese schools, the Japanese churches, and in any organizations where the older generation has a part, the subject of obedience and filial piety is frequently brought to the forefront. It is thus through constant discussion and agreement over these basic ideals that their importance becomes impressed upon the children . . ."

The pressures for compliance were external as well as internal. Miyamoto goes on:

". . . since status in the community depends upon the observance of these basic ideals, another means of parental control exists in an appeal to the children's sense of respect for the family name. Every caution and every reprimand, therefore, is accompanied by a reminder of the necessity for preserving the status of the name, and of attempting to raise it if possible. What others will think of one's behavior looms large in the minds of the Japanese and controls their behavior extensively. This pressure, undoubtedly, is of basic importance in explaining the strong Japanese interest in keeping up a front and preserving 'face.' Family control, therefore, is not simply parental control, but community control as well. It is the family in relation to the community that becomes the decisive force in regulating the behavior of individuals within the group."

Statistics in community after community indicate that the delinquency rate among *Nisei* juveniles was virtually nil, and these have been held up as evidence of the good citizenship of this group. Professor Wilson suggests that the record may not have been as clean as the statistics indicate. The community and the family, he contends, had a way of taking care of troublemakers before they came to the attention of the authorities and thus caused the entire group to lose face. Perhaps a visit to the Buddhist priest or Christian minister helped straighten out the youngster. Or in some instances when the parents realized that the demands of making a living prevented them from devoting necessary time with a wayward offspring, he was shipped off to grandparents in Japan. Hopefully, he would be isolated from bad companions and become more manageable. In any case he did not become an American delinquency statistic. And in some instances the simple threat of being sent away from home was enough to improve a child's behavior.

Generally speaking, however, the period of growing up for most *Nisei* was reasonably pleasant. Home offered warmth and security if not luxury. If father was authoritarian, he also provided the restraints that most children seek, at least subconsciously. The community provided plenty of activity. Because only the exceptional *Nisei* was big enough physically or sufficiently skilled to make high school teams, community leagues were organized where boys of ordinary ability could compete against each other. Football, baseball, basketball and track were popular in California. In the Pacific Northwest track was ignored, but it was the Northwest that took the initiative in sponsoring an intersectional tour for a *Nisei* team. Although combination *Issei-Nisei* baseball teams had gone to Japan, it was not until the mid-thirties that George Ishihara, the volunteer czar of *Nisei* sports in Seattle, arranged for a visit by the Mikados, *Nisei* basketball champions of the San Francisco Bay area. The Mikados swept easily over all their Northwest opponents to everyone's amazement but their own.

Nisei life in this period was relatively uncomplicated. For most of them, the Japanese community was the center of activity, and by staying within its confines, one avoided the barbs of prejudice. For recreation, one went to a movie, fished, organized a beach party, took a drive, played ball or watched others play. There was nothing more pleasurable than stuffing oneself at a Chinese dinner—bean cake and pork, sweet and sour ribs, cold boiled chicken, shrimp chow mein, egg foo yung, rice, barbecued pork loin—in the company of family or friends. It was a not unhappy life.

The characteristics of the *Nisei* were alleged to vary from place to place, tending to be influenced by the environment. Los Angeles *Nisei* were said to be "fast," casual, interested in a good time. San Francisco *Nisei* were considered sophisticated, conservative, conscious of the need for good grooming and dressing well. Seattle *Nisei* had a reputation for being friendly but naïve, unsophisticated, even backwoodsy. At the author's request, Mary Oyama Mittwer has recalled what it was like to be a *Nisei* in Los Angeles in the 1930's. She writes in part:

"Li'l Tokyo in Los Angeles was a busy, buzzing little place as

the center of California's Southland for *Issei* and their *Nisei* offspring. The *Nisei* were already beginning to hold big-time dances
with full orchestra, renting ballrooms with glass floors and fancy
settings as contrasted with the more modest, small-scale dances in
the later 1920's. *Nisei* social life also centered around the churches
such as the Union Church (originally Congregational) in Li'l
Tokyo, in uptown West-side's Japanese Methodist Church (now
Centenary), and St. Mary's Episcopal Church.

"The Japanese Community's shopping and trading, especially for
the *Issei*, centered around the hub of the East First and San Pedro
intersection. The landmark Miyako Hotel, the Asia Company dry
goods store, the theater where Japanese movies were shown, restaurants and cafes, the professional offices, drew the Japanese populace from the rest of the city and the surrounding rural areas.

"City kids used to say they could tell country *Nisei* who came
to town 'because they wear white hats and white shoes.' Some of
the latter, as well as the locals, would stop at Tomio's department
store, dine at the Kawafuku, while bachelor fieldhands on weekends would drink in small cafes or shoot a round in the local pool
halls. Young Christians and their Buddhist counterparts held large
annual conventions, using their own churches, or renting Caucasian
churches or buildings in the smaller colleges.

"As a whole, *Nisei* in Los Angeles lived in fairly new, better and
more comfortable homes than did their counterparts in Northern
California. Their homes were *hakujin* (white people) style, with
trees, lawns and ample back yards rather than being in old, de-
crepit buildings in the shabby part of town as in other Japanese
centers. This was because in the 1930's Los Angeles was still a
wide-spaced, green-lawn town, horizontal, and with lots of room
for expansion. The Japanese also were beginning to acquire cars,
one to a family, to meet the transportation needs of the sprawling
city. Going to dances in a streetcar (wearing long dresses) as the
Nisei did in the late 1920's was becoming just a memory. To the
Issei, it seemed the *Nisei* were always running around. They
grumbled, 'One o'clock, two o'clock—never come home. Too
much-i dan-su, dan-su.'

"But somehow the *Nisei* survived their rounds of sports events,
dances, conventions and other activities without becoming delin-
quents.

"Toward the later 1930's the Los Angeles *Issei* and *Nisei* com-

In the 1930s merchants in the Los Angeles L'll Tokyo area sponsored "Nisei Week" celebrations complete with queen contests. The 1938 queen was Margaret Nishikawa, sitting in center of rear seat. (Los Angeles County Museum of Natural History)

munity inaugurated the annual Nisei Week Festival highlighted by a queen contest, baby show, and Japanese folk dances in the streets. The non-Japanese public came to see, buy and dine in Li'l Tokyo, and Japanese businessmen smiled happily. Life was fairly comfortable in our comparatively insulated world which we at that time did not recognize as being an ethnic ghetto in today's connotation of the expression."

Yet, outside the community, even in the democratic island of the schools, pain and disappointment often lurked. There are many stories about *Nisei* athletes who were highly thought of by their teammates, but couldn't join them in an end-of-season swimming party because the pool barred "Japs"; of *Nisei* members of high school clubs asked not to attend a party, of students left behind on field trips because their presence might embarrass the host. These, of course, are experiences familiar to Negroes in predominantly white schools in the immediate postwar era.

When Monica Sone applied to a Washington State Vocational School for secretarial training, she was told that there was a quota of six *Nisei* girls that year. "I don't want you to think that we are discriminating against people of your ancestry," the counselor said, with a straight face, "but from our past experiences, we have found it next to impossible to find jobs for you in the business offices downtown. We must ask the *Nisei* to find their own jobs among their own people." Because the school prided itself on placing a high percentage of its graduates, Monica was told she would have to come up with a promise of a job before she could be accepted for classes. Jobs for secretaries in *Issei* businesses were scarce. She went to the local branch of Mitsui, the giant Japanese trading firm where she was promised consideration "if there happened to be an opening" when she was graduated. She got the necessary letter and the man who signed it admitted he had written dozens of such letters.

A classic case of school discrimination is the story of John Aiso, now a distinguished Los Angeles jurist. In the fall of 1922 he was elected president of the student body at Le Conte Junior High School in Hollywood. Parents of other students protested so violently that the principal was forced to hedge. He said Aiso was not president because there was no such office at Le Conte, but that he was one (although the most prominent) of twelve commissioners. Apparently egged on by their parents, some students petitioned that Aiso be removed from whatever office he had been elected to. The petition, revealing some fine adult touches, read in part:

"We students want an American president of the student body and consider it a serious matter, and a bad example, for any American boy or girl to submit passively and take no part in the effort to remove the boy from the presidency of the student body of our school. We stand for America and want no other but an American as our student body president . . . The reasons for a recall are based upon those principles of freedom for which American patriots sacrificed their lives and fortunes."

Faced with a threat to remove Aiso or be removed himself, the principal declared that the *Nisei* had lost the confidence of his constituents, that chaos was developing, and that student government was being suspended for the semester. Aiso shrugged off this crushing experience and quickly ran into another. He was a debator at Hollywood High School and in 1926 won an oratorical contest. This entitled him to be sent to the national finals in Washington, D.C. At the last minute he was replaced by his debating partner, Herb Wenig, for no reason other than that he was not of the right race. Wenig went on to win the national contest. Of Wenig, Aiso says "We are still friends." The subject of the oratorical contest, ironically, was "The American Constitution." Despite the doubts of his junior high school classmates, Aiso went on to serve his country in a capacity that shortened World War II by months if not years and saved thousands of American lives. The detailed story of his wartime role will be reserved for another chapter.

Throughout the period of *Nisei* development, and despite the cruel rebuffs, the benevolent interest of the Caucasian community penetrated the *Issei-Nisei* world in numerous ways. Their dedication, concern and affection for the Japanese Americans is exemplified in the lives of two women who must be recognized.

One was Ada J. Mahon, principal for more than a quarter century of Main Street School and later Bailey Gatzert School in Seattle whose enrollment was usually about 95 percent Japanese. She was the symbol of the American educational system for the *Issei;* under her direction Caucasian teachers took *Nisei* youngsters, many of whom spoke no English, and prepared them for life in America. The community felt a sense of obligation to her, and in 1920 when it became necessary to replace Main Street School, the Japanese offered to raise $10,000 to help pay for a new building. When the offer was declined, the parents contributed an expensive motion picture projector. Later, the community raised funds to send Miss Mahon on a tour of Japan as a gesture of appreciation. At least one former pupil, Mrs. Ruth Yamada Hashimoto, now of Albuquerque, N.M., named one of her children Ada after Miss Mahon.

The other was Nellie G. Oliver of Los Angeles who first encountered *Nisei* as a kindergarten teacher in 1916. One of her former charges says: "She taught us manners, culture and the American way of life through physical fitness. She felt that the young *Nisei* were the neglected members of the community. With her meager earnings, she organized the youngsters into youth clubs at the old Daiichi Gakuen Building, and before she was through she had organized eight groups divided by age—seven boys' and one for girls, all known as the Olivers—which turned out some of the Southland's top *Nisei* athletes. Most of these youngsters grew up to be responsible citizens of the community." Miss Oliver died almost penniless in 1947 when her boys and girls were still scattered as a result of the Evacuation. Ex-Olivers in Los Angeles, including many substantial businessmen, now present an award each year honoring Miss Oliver's memory to the outstanding Japanese American high school athlete in Southern California.

But such friends could do only so much for the *Nisei*. As more and more of their numbers reached maturity they became aware of the problems they had inherited from their *Issei* parents. The *Nisei* were American by birth, education, outlook and inclination. But there was no denying their Japanese features, their culture and their communities. Thus they were made heirs to the decades of discrimination and prejudice that had been the lot of their parents. They had heard of these things, but most of them could not feel the full impact until they left school and began the search for jobs. Then they discovered the shocking truth that the business world is different from the campus. The attitudes of the white community had changed but little. The doors to social acceptance and economic opportunity were only slightly wider ajar than in the time of their parents; not many *Nisei* could slip through.

The Depression compounded the *Nisei's* plight, but you couldn't blame the Depression for the fact that a white classmate who just barely made it through could get a job while you, with a Phi Beta Kappa key, had a choice of going back to the farm or stacking oranges at a fruitstand.

Among many older, job-seeking *Nisei* the decade of the thirties was a time of questioning and soul-searching.

"What is my future in the sweet land of liberty?" they asked. "Am I condemned by racial discrimination to the ghetto? What good is an education when the only job a *Nisei* can get is as a menial? Was the Pledge of Allegiance with that bit about 'liberty and justice for all' a pile of baloney?"

12

THE SEARCH FOR IDENTITY

IN THE DECADE following 1930, particularly in the latter half of that ten-year span, the *Nisei* spent a great deal of time planning and going to conferences. These conferences, encompassing the *Nisei* of a city, an area, a state or even several states, were sponsored by both Christian and Buddhist churches, by student organizations, by the Japanese American Citizens League, and even by *Kenjin-kai*. And almost invariably the main topics had to do with some variation of the questions, "What's wrong with the *Nisei?*" and "What is in the *Nisei* future?"

Although the expression had yet to be popularized, the *Nisei* were searching for an identity. They were expressing the doubts and fears of youths who were American in citizenship and outlook, yet linked inextricably with Japan by blood. This was an uncomfortable position to be in, particularly because of rising international tension stemming from Japanese aggression on the Asian mainland. If the *Nisei* had been content to remain within the cultural and economic ghettos that existed in the main cities of the Pacific Coast states, they would have been spared the necessity of asking searching questions about themselves. In their schools, however, they had been taught to believe in the American doctrine of freedom of opportunity; they shared in the American dream of progressing as far as their God-given abilities and energies could take them. Yet, the reality was that outside the classroom America was a racist society where skin pigmentation and facial conformations often were more a factor than a person's ability. And when the *Nisei* began to suspect that, for them, what they had been taught in school was largely a myth, the questions were inevitable.

In seeking to learn what had gone wrong, it was natural that first they should look inward. They did not like much of what they found. For one thing, they discovered they were painfully shy, which may have been the result of their youth, the influence of their culture, the effect of the times in which they lived, or perhaps a combination of these and other factors. They were inclined not to speak up—in class, in social gatherings, even in their meetings when they were discussing their own shortcomings. The bulk of the *Nisei* were the despair of their own discussion leaders; they simply sat on their hands. As a group the *Nisei* were not outgoing. They were inclined to be clannish. Some said they were too earnest and serious; they didn't know how to relax and have fun; they were born old. Others said they were overly self-centered; that they lacked aggressiveness, that their interests were too narrow, that they suffered from an inferiority complex. A few demanded that the *Nisei* break out from the influence—and protection—of their communities, tear away from the domination of their parents, and make their way in the white community.

While many of these criticisms had a certain basis of fact, their individual shortcomings were really no greater than those to be found in any group of adolescents and young adults. Their doubts and their persistent self-analysis were largely a reflection of the pressures to which they were subjected.

That they lived under unusual cultural, social and economic pressures is undeniable. Their Japanese cultural heritage demanded respect of elders, filial piety even to the point of sacrificing one's personal desires and ambitions, unquestioning respect of authority, a deep sensitivity to the opinions of one's peers, a sense of group rather than individual responsibility.

But in school the *Nisei* were taught to question and challenge, encouraged to make their own decisions, to be aggressive, to assert their individuality. To make matters even more confusing, the parents whom one was taught at home to honor, respect and obey, in turn urged the *Nisei* to honor, respect and obey the teachers who, unconsciously and unintentionally, were indoctrinating the youngsters in a conflicting philosophy.

Home life was equally ambivalent, although there the clash of cultures was not without its charm. In an article published in the magazine *New Outlook* in 1934, Aiji Tashiro wrote of his youth in this manner:

"My home life was a queer mixture of the Occident and the Orient. I sat down to American breakfasts and Japanese lunches. My palate developed a fondness for rice along with corned beef and cabbage. I became equally adept with knife and fork and with chopsticks. I said grace at mealtimes in Japanese, and recited the Lord's prayer at night in English. I hung my stocking over the fireplace at Christmas, and toasted *mochi* at Japanese New Year . . . I was spoken to by both parents in Japanese or in English. I answered in whichever was convenient or in a curious mixture of both."

Tashiro is unusual for a *Nisei* in that he was born in New England where his father ran a restaurant. After his father's death Tashiro's mother moved her family west to Seattle where the children were exposed for the first time to larger numbers of other Japanese. The impression they made on young Tashiro, an outsider and yet one of them, is pertinent to this report. He wrote in the article:

"There was a class of Japanese that I called 'Typs.' This was an abbreviation for 'typical Jap.' A 'Typ' usually needed a haircut or had too obviously just had one . . . His father ran a grocery store; his sisters finished high school and worked in a market. The 'Typ' was enviably proficient in math and in art; totally lacking in the finer points of social grace. His clothes were incongruous and misfit. He either slunk timidly in the society of Americans or assumed a defiant, truculent air. He was impervious to self-consciousness, if the latter class, and persisted in jabbering loudly in Japanese in the presence of Americans. All 'Typs' cliqued together in school and out. The timid kind went on to college and became Phi Beta Kappas and 'Doctors.' The brazen variety became the denizens of pool halls and street corners. I decided that I was not a 'Typ.'" (The Japanese language school in Seattle where Tashiro grew up was widely referred to as Typ School.)

Tashiro went on to study architecture and landscape architecture in an Eastern school and has been practicing at North Wilkesboro, North Carolina where not only are *Nisei* scarce, but he is the only architect in the county. Tashiro's description of his compatriots was cruel but not inaccurate. There were Typs, of course, myopic, earnest and uncomfortable. But there were also the blithe spirits. Aiji Tashiro's brother Kenji, for example, known as Kazunk. Dr. Kelly Yamada recalls that on a summer work trip to an Alaska salmon cannery in 1925, Kazunk would enthrall the boys with skillful recitations of the *Cremation of Sam McGee* and *The Shooting of Dan McGrew*. Kelly Yamada himself delighted in playing hymns on a saxophone during Episcopal church services, and served in the Coast Guard for many years before he became an optometrist.

In Los Angeles a group of *Nisei* in the early thirties banded together and published a quarterly literary magazine. They called themselves the *Nisei* Writers Group and their magazine *Leaves*. Yasuo Sasaki and the late Carl Kondo were the editors. The magazine was mimeographed and hand-bound, and distributed to a small but appreciative list of paid-up subscribers, mostly in Southern California, but as far away as Seattle, Arizona and Colorado. Some of the contributors were Chiye Mori, Toyo Suyemoto and Lucille Morimoto who wrote poetry, and writers Eiji Tanabe, Ambrose Uchiyamada, Larry Tajiri, Mary Oyama, Bunichi Kagawa, Edo Mita, Kondo and Sasaki. They wrote short stories and sketches about everyday *Nisei* life, and also translated contemporary Japanese literature. The poems were mostly romantic, reflecting both general and *Nisei* emotional reactions to the problems facing young people. Remarkably, few were morbid. Tajiri also edited the English section of the *Kashu Mainichi*, a daily Japanese language paper, and on Sundays he published a remarkably readable "literary" page where aspiring *Nisei* writers could reach an audience. Sasaki went on to earn an M.D. as well as a Ph. D. in biochemistry, and is in general practice in Cincinnati.

Many of the writers were also members of the Little Tokyo Players, a group so fascinated by the drama that they'd get together after work and stage plays like *Charlie's Aunt* as well as more sophisticated fare. When Joe Hirakawa, a drama major from the University of Washington joined the group, they were astonished to hear him recite long passages from Shakespeare and promptly made him their director. There were romanticists like Joe Oyama who read books about the vagabond life written by unemployed newspapermen and dreamed of distant strands. In real life Joe worked in his father's modest cosmetics plant in Los Angeles. Once a month he would load a small truck and make deliveries to exactly 104 Japanese dealers in California—he still remembers that number —stretched out from Mexicali, on the border, to Auburn in the foothills of the Sierra Nevada. Finally sick of the routine, although there were other *Nisei* who gladly would have traded jobs with him, Oyama joined the restless flood tide of young Americans seeking their personal rainbows, hopping a freight until the wanderlust left him. Oyama today operates a Japanese provisions store in New York City.

It was when searching for a job that the *Nisei* felt the walls closing in on him. Unlike today's hard-core unemployed, the *Nisei* even of that time had many skills to sell. They wanted to work. They were able. But the doors of opportunity simply would not open to their knocking. Their *Issei* parents were acutely aware of their own lack of formal education. So they made great sacrifices to educate their children, denying themselves material comforts, even dipping into the nest egg that was to take them back to Japan in order to send their youngsters to college. One remarkable case in point is Kikumatsu Togasaki, the pioneer merchant. All nine of his children went through college. Of his six daughters, three became doctors of medicine, the others registered and public health nurses.

The *Nisei* themselves realized their job opportunities were limited. The crafts were closed by the unions that controlled them. If they were to move ahead, they would need all the education they could get, and many made their way through college on the money earned by summer labor on farms and in canneries, waiting on tables and washing windows, paying for room and board by working as houseboys and housegirls, skipping quarters to work in the family shop and making their laborious way back to the campus when they had a few dollars put away. But their college experiences were not normal in other regards, for most of them were in school, but not of it. In grade and high school they had been able to mix naturally with their white classmates. But many of these friends did not go on to college; they were of a socioeconomic group that sent few members on to an advanced education. The *Nisei* went to extraordinary lengths to find the money to continue their schooling, and even if there had been no barriers, few could have kept up socially with their classmates. After lectures or a lab when white students relaxed at a fraternity or sorority house, the *Nisei* went to the Japanese Students Club. *Nisei* Charles Kambe, an honor student in high school, received a mailed invitation to visit a fraternity during rush week. When they saw his face they said they were so sorry, it must have been a mistake. Kambe is now a prominent physician in Philadelphia.) The *Nisei* went to the rally before the Big Game between Cal and Stanford or USC and UCLA, he sang the Alma Mater song with as much fervor as his blond lab partner, but when the game was over each went back to his separate world.

Degrees were no assurance of success. *Nisei* English majors went to work in fruit markets when they found their Phi Beta Kappa keys would not open the door to decent jobs. Why would a *Nisei* major in English? Because he was interested in the subject, and many pursued their interests without regard to the practical considerations, feeling somehow that things would work out for them. The self-employed fared best. The Little Tokyo communities needed doctors, dentists, attorneys, accountants. Since they had to be far above average students to be accepted into their specialties, they were good. But the majority were doomed to disappointment when they sought employment in their chosen fields. Aiji Tashiro, with a degree in architecture, was offered a job as a valet, a wrestler, and giving ukulele lessons under a Hawaiian *nom de plume*. World-famous architect Minoru Yamasaki couldn't get a job in Seattle after graduation from the University of Washington. He went to New York in search of work and fended off starvation by unpacking china for an import firm. Such stories are legion, and it was inevitable that some *Nisei* should look to Japan as a market for their abilities.

Since childhood they had been told they would be a bridge across the Pacific, a link between East and West, the emissaries of understanding between two nations to which they were attached by birth and heritage. Many *Issei* felt that their children never would be accepted fully into American life, and that they must turn ultimately to Japan for fulfillment. In any case, *Issei* leaders felt the *Nisei* should learn at least something of Japan and encouraged visits to that country. Kyutaro Abiko's *Nichi Bei* was among early sponsors of *Nisei* tours to Japan. A young *Nisei* coed, Miya Sannomiya (now Mrs. Kikuchi of Los Angeles), was a member of the 1925 tour. In meetings with prominent Japanese leaders she voiced her confusion about her future. "I respect Japan, the land of my ancestors," she told them. "But I know nothing about her.

I cannot even speak Japanese. In spite of all our difficulties, I love America. I prefer to do my best in America."

Without exception her stand was applauded. Admiral Uriu told her: "Go back to the United States and become the best student, the best worker in your chosen field, the best wife when you get married, the best mother, and the best American citizen you know how to be. Then I am sure that the United States will be glad to have you there and all of us in Japan will be proud of you because you proved yourself to be such a good citizen of the United States. If the *Issei* and *Nisei* become the best citizens in America, they will have nothing to worry about."

Prince Iyesato Tokugawa, then president of the House of Peers, urged: "Work hard and make yourselves such fine citizens of the United States that you will be liked, respected and welcomed everywhere. I will be happy and the whole country of Japan will be proud to see them become good U.S. citizens."

Count Ayske Kabayama, a graduate of Amherst College and board chairman of Japan's Society for International Cultural Relations, advised her: "Tell the *Nisei* to stay right where they are and see to it that they become loyal citizens in the country in which they live. That's the only way they will ever become accepted as an integral part of American life. No one can live with divided loyalties and expect to succeed. Tell them that we in Japan expect them to do it that way."

In subsequent visits to Japan, and a period of employment in Tokyo with the Society for International Cultural Relations, Miss Sannomiya found that "most of the mediocre educators and leaders in Japan . . . looked down upon the *Nisei*" because of their American ways, their ignorance of Japanese customs and etiquette, their inability to speak the Japanese language properly, and because they were the offspring of socially inferior peasant emigrants. Thus the *Nisei* were stymied in their native America and scorned in ancestral Japan.

A few went to Japan and made good. Charles Yoshii was one. A graduate of the University of Oregon, the best job he could find was manual labor in a Los Angeles wholesale produce market. He was desperately looking for something better when Yosuke Matsuoka, a top Japanese diplomat who also had been educated at Oregon, visited the Yoshii home in Portland. When he heard about

Charles' difficulties he invited the *Nisei* to Tokyo. Yoshii became a top English language radio announcer. But far greater numbers of *Nisei* who went to the ancestral homeland in search of opportunity returned to the United States in total disillusionment. Ted Ohashi is a good example. A University of California basketball star from Stockton, Ohashi was a campus hero who was ignored by alumni when it came time to pass out jobs. Ohashi went to Japan in the late 1930's and worked briefly as a rewrite man for the Domei News Agency's English language service. But he had no liking for either Tokyo or working in Japan. The Japanese police state—the police checked him regularly—repelled him. Ohashi was well over six feet tall, which made his adjustment to Japanese ways and Japanese architecture even more difficult than average. He came home in disgust, and now is in YMCA work in the San Francisco Bay Region.

So far we've been writing about adult *Nisei* who went to Japan voluntarily as tourists, in search of work, or to study. By and large they had completed their American education and their thought patterns were set. Most of them found considerable trouble adjusting to Japan and the Japanese standard of living. Many of them hated Japan and counted the days until they could go home to America. There was another group of *Nisei* faced with altogether different problems. These were the children who went to Japan with their families, or were sent to Japan to live with grandparents, in their formative years. Their American education was incomplete; many, in fact, had been to grade school for only a few years if at all. They lived in native Japanese homes and went to Japanese schools. They were reared like Japanese children and were *Nisei* only in a technical sense. Yet, because they possessed American citizenship, they were permitted to return to the United States. After reaching adulthood many did, and they found themselves totally out of step with *Nisei* their age, as lost in America as the *Nisei* were in Japan. Their thinking was Japanese. Their English was inadequate. Unable to find a niche in *Nisei* society, unable in some cases even to develop warm relationships with American-educated siblings because of their completely different interests, they tended to congregate in their own groups. These were the *Kibei*, a term that has a place along with *Issei* and *Nisei*, and they found themselves in a peculiar predicament as World War II approached.

As for the *Nisei*, maturation was accompanied by growing friction between them and their parents over subjects as widely separated as dancing and Japanese militarism, the rising tide of labor unions and wedding customs. Despite strong family ties, the generation gap was a real and vexing matter magnified by *Issei-Nisei* differences in education, language, interests, customs, age—in fact almost the entire spectrum of human relationships. The wonder is that they got along as well as they did.

Western dancing was, of course, alien to the *Issei* culture and many considered the sight of their children dancing with arms around each other a disgusting public display of affection. When Caucasian children learned dance steps, they went home and happily demonstrated for their parents. Many a *Nisei* learned to dance in secret, as if it were a vice to be kept from parental knowledge. Normal boy-girl relations among the *Nisei* also made their parents nervous. Coming from a culture in which one's mate was chosen by a third party and courtship followed the marriage ceremony, the *Issei* found the free and easy American customs difficult to accept. The ancient traditions were hard to shed and some older *Nisei* found themselves being steered into matrimony by well-meaning family friends who acted as go-betweens (*baishakunin*). The go-betweens served a function beyond that of simple marriage brokers. Although their investigation in America may have been perfunctory, they tried to make sure that neither of the parties was cursed by "bad blood"—that there were no epileptics in the family, that there seemed to be no predisposition to insanity or tuberculosis, that the father was not an alcoholic, that the intended was not of the Eta (pariah) caste. Later, if the marriage should encounter rocky times, the go-betweens felt an obligation to step in and try to get the couple to patch up their troubles.

Charles Kamayatsu enjoys telling with great gusto how he happened to get married. "I was invited to this dinner," he says, "and among the guests was this girl, Yuki Kuwahara. We had a fine banquet, and after a while the host turns to me and points at the girl and says, 'Charlie, do you like her?' Well, I knew her and I didn't dislike her. I got the idea what he was driving at and I wasn't particularly interested in getting married at that time. But there she was sitting across the table, looking down at her lap. How could I answer no when she was right there? So I said yes, and he said,

'Okay, you two get married.' So I shook hands with her." It must have worked out pretty well because they're still married.

In later years it became customary for *Nisei* to court in the American style, then name go-betweens as window dressing in respect to tradition. Early *Nisei* weddings also were marked by elaborate reception banquets, with *Issei* parents vying with each other to see who could put on the grandest function, often going into debt for years to pay for it. This, it should be noted, is not a strictly Japanese practice. Later, *Nisei* were able to convince their parents of the folly of such spending and more reasonable reception came into vogue.

Somewhat more acrimonious were the *Issei-Nisei* arguments over Japanese foreign policy. The 1930's, it must be recalled, were the years of fascist aggression that led ultimately to World War II. Japan was slipping out of the hands of its civilian leaders. Late in 1930, after Japan ratified the London Naval Treaty, Premier Hamaguchi, a civilian, was assassinated. Within a year the Japanese Kwangtung Army had seized Manchuria. In January, 1932, the Japanese attacked Shanghai, and a few months later Premier Inukai was slain by military reactionaries, marking the effective end of party government. By 1933, Japan had attacked Jehol and withdrawn from the League of Nations, and Adolf Hitler became chancellor of Germany. Three years later, February 26, 1936—the infamous Two-two-six Incident—an uprising of young Army officers led to the assassination of many liberal leaders in the government and set Japan on a course of aggression that led to the Sino-Japanese war in 1937.

The *Issei* read about these developments in dispatches from Tokyo published in the Japanese language press. What these dispatches said was often in contradiction to what was published in American newspapers which the *Nisei* read. The reports of inspiring Japanese military victories over "Chinese bandits violating treaties," Japanese troops sweeping over the Chinese mainland defeating the "corrupt, pillaging mercenaries" of Chiang Kai-shek, made heady reading for the *Issei*. A powerful Japan was a source of pride. Their experience had shown that an aggressive Japan meant greater security for them. Japan's military victories were triumphs they could identify with in lives that were marked by many defeats and frustrations. They could not understand why there was so much American hostility toward Japan, why China was winning so much sympathy, why there was growing sentiment for boycotts against Japanese goods and an embargo against shipment of steel and oil to Japan. And when the *Nisei* took the popular American stand against Japanese aggression in dinner table discussions, many *Issei* complained bitterly that their sons and daughters were being misled by the biased and inaccurate accounts inspired by Chinese propagandists and published in the American press. Yet, while arguments raged at home, few *Nisei* spoke out in public against Japanese militarism. Perhaps they felt the need for a united community front against an unsympathetic world. Perhaps they did not want to seem to be defying their parents in public, or perhaps they failed to understand the significance of their failure to take a position.

Issei reading was confined largely to Japanese language dailies published in Los Angeles, San Francisco and Seattle, and to periodicals imported from Japan. Few read English well enough to be steady followers in American newspapers, magazines or books. Since the Japanese language papers were Japan-oriented in their coverage of world news and depended on Japanese sources for much of this, they did little to expand their subscribers' understanding of American viewpoints. The *Nisei*, on the other hand, read virtually no Japanese, so their sources of information were the daily newspapers and magazines. Realizing the desirability of attracting *Nisei* readership, Kyutaro Abiko started an English language section, the first of its kind, in the *Nichi Bei* in 1925. At first it occupied a space only three columns wide and ten inches deep. Dr. James A. B. Scherer, historian and author of a number of books on Japan, was the first editor. He was assisted by the late Kay Nishida, who later edited the section. A year after he launched the section, Abiko began publication of the *Japanese American Weekly*, usually running about six pages, providing *Nisei* news and offering aspiring *Nisei* writers an opportunity to be published. In its time the *Nichi Bei* English section achieved a high level of competence. Among those who worked on it before World War II were Kimpei Sheba, ex-editor of the Asahi Evening News in Tokyo; Iwao Kawakami; Miya Sannomiya; the late Dr. Kazuo Kawai; T. John Fujii, former wire service employee and now correspondent for Fairchild Publications in Tokyo; Larry Tajiri, drama editor of *The Denver Post* at the time of his death in 1965; Larry's brother Vince Tajiri,

picture editor of *Playboy* magazine; Robert Tsuda; Howard Ima-
zeki; the late Sam Horii; Haruo Imura, and Harry Honda, who
succeeded Larry Tajiri as editor of the weekly *Pacific Citizen*,
organ of the Japanese American Citizens League.

In time all the leading Japanese language newspapers published
English language sections, usually amounting to one page in an
eight-page paper, or a page and a half in a twelve- or sixteen-page
paper. The "news" they covered, however, was largely bulletin
board type information about club meetings and election results,
local sports events, personals and items about local individuals, who
had gained a measure of recognition. (It is only since World War
II that the English sections began to publish any substantial amount
of wire service copy.) The names of local scholars who made the
honor roll were always published, a practice not without its editorial hazards. Since lists published in the daily papers had to be
gleaned for Japanese-sounding names, it was almost inevitable that
Finnish-American children named Maki and Italo-Americans
named Cassai or Chiyoda should appear along with the Morimotos
and Watanabes.

On January 1, 1928, a different kind of *Nisei* publication made
its debut. It was called the *Japanese American Courier*, an all-English weekly, and it was published by a blind former prizefighter
named James Yoshinori Sakamoto. Sakamoto had gone to New
York City after graduation from high school in Seattle and worked
as English editor of the *Japanese American News*. He also boxed
professionally and was the first *Nisei* to fight at Madison Square
Garden. His eyesight failing from blows received in the ring, he
returned to Seattle in 1927. He saw the need for a *Nisei* organization and he realized the *Nisei* needed a voice. And so, with his
limited publishing experience and the meager savings he had
accumulated, he launched *The Courier* to give *Nisei* that voice.
The Courier was never a financial success in the 14½ years of its
existence—the Evacuation closed its door forever—and many times
it was on the verge of bankruptcy. Sakamoto preached a militant,
uncomplicated Americanism and played a major role in shaping
the Japanese American Citizens League as a national organization.
That story will be told in another chapter. As a newspaperman,
however, he was more idealistic than practical. He insisted on
devoting a large amount of space to matters that failed to interest

the majority of *Nisei*. Accounts of national and international
events, rewritten from the daily papers, took up a large part of
The Courier's front page. On page 2 were lengthy editorials about
such matters as tariffs, Europe's political issues, the activities of
Congress, the Supreme Court and the President, and occasionally
solemn and usually abstract treatises on problems of the "second
generation." Sakamoto was proud of the *Nisei's* Japanese heritage,
but he believed they should be 100 percent American. In line with
this reasoning the word *Nisei*, not being English, was taboo in *The
Courier*, making headline writing something of a problem. The
succession of *Nisei* newspapermen who worked for Jimmie Sakamoto argued often for a more popular level of editorial content,
but he insisted that the *Nisei* must be made aware of the greater
world of issues and problems about them, and that they should get
this information in his paper. It was a noble ideal, but the *Nisei*
were scarcely ready for such a reading diet in a four-page weekly
edited by one of them.

Page 3 was devoted to community sports and the back page to
community news not much different from that which was published in the daily English sections. Not many *Nisei* had two dollars
to pay for a year's subscription to such a newspaper. Those who
did took *The Courier* largely out of personal admiration for and
loyalty to Jimmie Sakamoto.

The unhappy experiences of *Issei* with labor unions undoubtedly
delayed *Nisei* contact with these organizations. Fearing Japanese
workmen would take jobs away from whites, labor unions were in
the forefront of the attack on the *Issei* almost from the very beginning. A mailing made in 1907 by the Fresno Federated Trades and
Labor Council, affiliated with the American Federation of Labor,
is typical of labor's attacks. The Council was notifying merchants
that it had passed the following resolution:

"Whereas, the Japanese in this country have by their arrogant
and insulting manners become a menace to the best interests of
good society, and

"Whereas, the merchants of this city, knowing full well that this
class of people are a detriment to the community, do employ or
cause to be employed, in their places of business these undesirable
people, therefore be it

"Resolved, that we, the delegates to the Federated Trades and Labor Council of Fresno, in regular session assembled, do pledge ourselves not to patronize any place of business where there is employed a Japanese; and further be it

"Resolved, that we request the affiliated unions of this Council to endorse our action in this matter, and that they be further requested to make it a part of their by-laws, 'That to patronize a place of business wherein there is employed a Japanese will be a violation of the trade rules of their respective unions.'

"Employ none but White Labor and the Japanese question will solve itself. These undesirable people, finding themselves without employment in America, will return to their own country. Stand by White Labor and White Labor will stand by the Employer."

In view of the long tradition of paternalism and labor contractors, it is understandable that the first *Issei* organization in this field was not a true union. Karl G. Yoneda, a farm labor organizer in the thirties and author of *History of Japanese Labor in the United States*, says some 300 *Issei* farm workers in the Vacaville area were organized into a "union" in 1892 by the contractors. Their purpose was to establish a uniform contractors' fee for supplying Japanese workmen, to maintain discipline among the Japanese, and to charge certain fees in handling personal matters for the workers such as mail services, sending money home to Japan, and buying clothing and food. Yoneda says: "The word union was used to counteract anti-Japanese feeling already sprouting at the time. There is not a single word about improving working conditions in the published bylaws.

"The first time Japanese farm workers were truly organized was in Oxnard in 1903. There were several hundred Japanese working in the sugar beet fields and ten or more Japanese contractors were making large fortunes from the rake-off system. The beet owners decided to hire the workers directly, thus cutting off the contractors. The contractors retaliated by calling off their men and asking recognition and more pay for their workers. The 'strike' ended successfully for the contractors as well as the workers and on February 11, 1903, they formed the Sugar Beet and Farm Laborer's Union of Oxnard. Kosaburo Baba was elected president."

But the union received no encouragement at all from the American Federation of Labor. When Secretary J. M. Larraras of the union wrote for a charter, President Samuel Gompers replied: "Your union must guarantee that it will under no circumstances accept membership of any Chinese or Japanese." Gompers contended "the American God is not the God of the Japanese."

Issei and *Nisei* alike were barred from unions controlling the various crafts, such as printing, plumbing, carpentry, bricklaying, electric wiring, painting and the like. If they wanted to learn these skills, they had to work in nonunion shops and projects. When Seattle *Issei* operators of cleaning and pressing plants were organized by Dave Beck's Teamsters, they were segregated into a Jim Crow union which had the privilege of paying initiation fees and dues, but not of voting.

In 1937, with the infant Committee (later Congress) of Industrial Organizations challenging the strongly entrenched American Federation of Labor, a major power struggle broke out in Seattle for control of the Alaska salmon cannery workers. By this time Filipino workmen outnumbered *Issei* and *Nisei* by about 3 to 1 and were organizing rapidly. Still, *Nisei* leaders could see that unless they joined the union movement to protect the rights of the Japanese, a substantial number of them would be frozen out of summer jobs as the union sought to bypass the Japanese contractors and deal directly with the cannery operators.

Three *Nisei* college students, George Taki, George Minato and Dyke Miyagawa decided something had to be done. In a letter to the author, Miyagawa recalled those days:

"At first, being full-time students, we couldn't do much organizing, even of ourselves. About all we had time for was to insinuate ourselves into the circle of 'progressive' Filipino leaders. This was a tactical necessity anyway, so we concentrated on internal politicking and learning a few things about the politics and power balances among the waterfront unions (Sailors Union of the Pacific, Longshoremen, Marine Firemen, Fishermen, Ship Scalers, etc.) that were solidly established and had the power to help make or break a union entity. Our worth and usefulness depended not only on being possibly able to deliver *Nisei-Issei* membership, but also on our capacity to contribute to the advancement of overall union aims and interests, not just protect the Japanese community interest in the salmon packing industry."

By the end of the year Taki was elected vice-president; Minato, Miyagawa and Yukio Kumamoto were named to the executive board. Thus entrenched, the *Nisei* set out to recruit Japanese members. The rival AFL also got busy, but they made the mistake of opening two recruiting offices, one for Japanese, the other for Filipinos, thereby underscoring the racial split and provoking fears that this would be a "contractors' union."

Miyagawa writes "the *Issei* and *Nisei* never actually resisted being organized into a union, although most of them did not embrace it with wild passion. They accepted the development as an inevitability, which it was, and quickly recognized the need to become card carriers if they were to retain summer jobs."

The big question was which card, AFL or CIO, and the campaign stirred a good deal of heat—probably the first time a Japanese community had been split by union rivalry. The AFL faction took advantage of the widespread belief that the CIO was Communist-infiltrated to play on the conservatism of the Japanese community. The AFL organizers also indicated that the CIO was committed to boycotting Japan-made goods and was generally anti-Japan. Miyagawa recalls that "people I had known since the first grade would cross the street or suddenly become hypnotized by a store window when they saw me on the street.

"The only counter possible was to make ourselves familiar, to humanize ourselves and to let people see for themselves that we wore no horns or tails, especially red ones. There were very few conferences of religious groups, sports tournament dances, or socials at which we did not make a calculated appearance. We arranged to be included formally in the program at as many functions as we could, and that failing, made sure we would be heard as non-panel participants at round-table discussions. Not all cannery workers were proper uptowners. So we also spent a lot of time getting better known around the gambling tables in Chinatown and in the beer joints and pool halls of Lower Jackson Street. In such places, in nearby restaurants and rundown hotel lobbies, we kept in touch with bachelor *Issei*, did small social service type favors for them, and simultaneously solicited the allegiance of the Filipinos who abounded in the area."

The CIO won the National Labor Relations Board election and approximately a thousand *Issei* and *Nisei* were unionized, the first major movement by a Japanese group into a national labor union. When the world did not come to an end, as some *Issei* businessmen had feared, other groups of Japanese workers approached Taki and his associates for help in organizing. "We were too busy to do more than advise," Miyagawa says, but shortly the idea of unions ceased to provoke tension and controversy in the community and Japanese-operated restaurants were organized almost without notice. At the request of CIO officials, the *Nisei* cannery union leaders visited sawmill and logging camps and with Tom Marutani, a bilingual *Nisei*, helped organize Japanese workers in that industry.

Miyagawa made a trip to Los Angeles in 1939 and met some *Nisei* who were seeking to organize the fruit and vegetable markets. They asked him to help them prepare a leaflet, but no one had a typewriter. Miyagawa walked into the offices of the *Rafu Shimpo*, the leading Japanese-English newspaper in the city, borrowed a typewriter, and wrote the copy. Miyagawa's friends, who were under the impression that the *Rafu Shimpo*, representing the Establishment, was hostile to unions, were amazed by his audacity.

At this point it should be apparent that there were many matters on which the two generations of Japanese, one immigrant, one native, did not agree. We turn now to the Reverend Daisuke Kitagawa, the Episcopalian minister, for an analysis and explanation. Father Dai, as he was better known, was neither *Issei* nor *Nisei*. Born and ordained in Japan, he came to the United States as a young man for further study at General Theological Seminary in New York City. In 1939 he was named resident minister of a small mission serving Japanese farmers and their families in the White River Valley between Seattle and Tacoma, Washington. He was evacuated with his congregation, and he has written perceptively of his experiences in a book titled *Issei and Nisei, the Internment Years*. As an outsider and a trained observer, he was able to see both *Issei* and *Nisei* with detachment.

Father Dai found Japanese communities in America "extremely static," made up of people unchanged from the time they left Japan. "The racial prejudice and discrimination in American society had pushed them back into segregated communities that invariably were nothing but reproductions of the Japan they had left," he writes. "Japan, of course, kept on moving, changing for better or for worse. Consequently, each year the sociocultural distance between the actual Japan and the Japan in the memory of the immigrant Japanese in America grew wider and wider. I knew instantly when I first came in contact with him that the immigrant could no longer fit into contemporary Japan. From the point of view of contemporary Japan, the Japanese in America was an extrahistorical, if not anachronistic, being.

"This situation inevitably resulted in, among other things, a poverty of ideas among the Japanese in America. The Japanese community was not participating in the ongoing life of either America or Japan. Such being the case, there was little possibility that any new ideas would emerge. The Japanese in America was exclusively preoccupied with the cold business of making a living and raising his family, trading and associating almost exclusively with his fellow countrymen. His community could not escape becoming ingrown."

Father Dai says the *Issei* said to himself, *Shikataganai* (It cannot be helped) and bore the affronts, the discrimination, and the injustices of America stoically. But he vowed that for the *Nisei*, it would be different. "The *Nisei* gave positive meaning to the *Issei's* life. The *Issei* parents lived simply to see their *Nisei* sons and daughters grow up into first-rate Americans, so that they could shout from the housetops to all the world, 'See, we knew it all the time!' To achieve that, they did not mind paying any conceivable price."

But the dream was not to be. The *Nisei*, on the basis of race, if not by law, was prevented from choosing his place of residence, selecting a mate, or working at the kind of job he was prepared to handle. "For all practical purposes," Father Dai observes, "he was not much better off than the *Issei*." This led many *Nisei* to spend a great deal of time "trying to convince both himself and the American public that despite his looks and his parents, he was really American." Father Dai goes on:

"Many a time I heard the *Nisei* emphatically answer, 'I am an American,' when asked by a somewhat bewildered Caucasian whether he was Chinese or Japanese. It sounded perfectly silly to me, for while in New York, I had been so used to hearing Americans say, 'I'm Irish,' 'I'm Italian,' 'I'm English.' Was it not perfectly natural in the West, where Japanese, Chinese and Filipinos were found in such a mixture that people should ask whether he was Chinese or Japanese? Of course, it is quite possible that some people had in mind the nationality, and others, the race or national origin. Whichever it was, what should it matter? Yet the *Nisei* found it next to impossible to answer quietly and unassumingly, 'I am Japanese.' He had to say in no uncertain terms, 'No! I am an American.' "

This defensive stance resulted from a desire to assert his status as a citizen, to differentiate for the questioner's benefit and education between citizens (with certain rights) and aliens (who had been subjected to legalized discrimination); it was an effort to win acceptance as an American despite his physical characteristics. Father Dai points out that every immigrant is urged to discard his national culture and heritage and "turn into a colorless American." This was true of Europeans, but not Asiatics. The Asians were set apart by color and considered unassimilable. The *Nisei* sought to show that they could indeed be assimilated culturally, and in their zeal many made it a point of rejecting their Japanese heritage, asserting with pride that they spoke no Japanese and knew nothing about Japan. Many years were to pass before *Nisei*, from a position of security, could take pride in their ancestral culture and try to interpret it for their fellow Americans.

This was the position of the *Nisei* as the 1930–40 decade neared its end. In America, they were still in search of their identity, seeking to make reality of the textbook ideals of Americanism. Yet even in such mundane matters as buying life insurance, their difference was evident; some firms refused to insure *Nisei* lives and others demanded extra premiums, presumably because they posed a higher risk. Meanwhile, in the Far East earthshaking events that would alter their lives were beginning to take shape.

13

THE BIRTH OF JACL

IN THE FALL of 1918 a small group of *Nisei* in San Francisco began to make a habit of meeting together for lunch. They were mostly recent college graduates, just starting out in business or having recently opened a practice. Among them were Dr. Thomas T. Yatabe, fresh out of dental school; Tom Okawara, attorney; Dr. Tokutaro Hayashi; Dr. Hideki Hayashi; and Kay Tsukamoto. When he returned from service with the U.S. Army in Europe after the Armistice, George Kiyoshi Togasaki joined the group. They talked of many things, but invariably their conversation would return to the future of the *Nisei* in the United States. Sometimes they became so engrossed in their discussions that after work they would meet again at the Japanese YMCA to talk some more.

This group included some of the very first *Nisei*, born before the turn of the century. They had grown up in a period of persecution; some had been among those banished to the segregated Oriental school. They had seen their fathers beaten for no reason other than that they were Japanese, their family businesses picketed and boycotted, the windows of their homes smashed while police officers looked the other way. These *Nisei* knew they were American citizens, but few others seemed to know or care. They were accustomed to having well-intentioned strangers ask: "When did you come to the United States? What is Japan like?" In their bull sessions the *Nisei* asked themselves: "What good is our citizenship? Are we going to live with the same discrimination that our parents experienced? What should we, as *Nisei*, do?" Many admitted there had been times when they resented their Japanese blood because they felt it was a handicap in their efforts to become good Americans. Although the members of the group were only in their early twenties themselves, they were deeply concerned about the future of *Nisei* boys and girls who were still in school, those who were just being born, those who were yet to be born.

Out of their discussions came a determination to claim their rights as Americans, to let others know that they were Americans. As few as they were, they realized they would be more effective if they organized. So they founded an association that they first called the American Loyalty Club. They debated that name for quite a while; after all, they weren't really a club. So they changed the name to American Loyalty League, laughing about such a high-sounding title for such a small and insignificant organization. The members were inexperienced but they were fortified by the idealism of youth. They had no bylaws, no real organization as such; they were united only by a desire to participate more fully in all the fine things that were American, and to try to make the way to that goal easier for other *Nisei*. One of their first activities was a speaker's bureau that would go around telling the story of the *Nisei*. But few people were interested in what they had to say. So they booked some speaking dates with church groups through the YMCA and told their story to whoever would listen.

Early in their program they realized that to assert their rights they must register as voters, become interested in political matters, and cast their ballots wisely. Dr. Yatabe remembers the day he went to register. The clerk took his name and address and asked his race.

"I'm Japanese," Dr. Yatabe replied.

"There is no listing for the Japanese race," the clerk replied. "You've got to be white, black or Mongolian."

"I'm not Mongolian. And I'm not white and I'm not black. I'm an American of Japanese parentage," Dr. Yatabe insisted.

The clerk was puzzled. She called a superior and they went into a huddle. After a while they accepted Dr. Yatabe's contention that he was Japanese rather than Mongolian and wrote it onto the form.

Despite its promising start, the American Loyalty League of San Francisco was short-lived. As their businesses and practices picked up, the members found less and less time for serious discussions. The League was virtually inactive when Dr. Yatabe moved to

Fresno in 1922 to open a practice, and his departure sounded the death knell. But the League had served its purpose; it was the first civic organization of Americans of Japanese ancestry. Its efforts marked the first time the *Nisei* had tried to do something about their own welfare in organized fashion.

About the time the American Loyalty League was going into its decline, *Nisei* in Seattle, with no knowledge about what was going on in San Francisco, organized what they grandly called the Seattle Progressive Citizens League. This was partly at the instigation of two long-time *Issei* community leaders, Henry H. Okuda and Chusaburo Ito who were concerned about legalized discrimination against "aliens ineligible to citizenship." Proponents of an anti-alien land law were threatening to make it a reality in Washington. Business licenses were being denied *Issei* on the ground that they were aliens. Okuda and Ito considered an organization of *Nisei* voters as an arm with which to fight discrimination, but Seattle *Nisei* of legal age also saw the advantages of banding together even though there were only about a dozen of them. The League was founded in 1921 with Shigeru Ozawa as president, George Ishihara secretary, and Miss Yuki Higashi treasurer. Okuda and Ito were two of three *Issei* advisers. However, they apparently did little advising, for the League held only three meetings between 1921 and 1928.

Meanwhile, another *Issei*, Tamezo Takimoto of San Francisco, also realized the advantages of an organization of American citizens of Japanese parentage. Takimoto was secretary of the Japanese Association of North America. Soon after Dr. Yatabe moved to Fresno, Takimoto asked him to return to San Francisco to address a meeting of *Nisei* from many parts of northern California which he would convene. Dr. Yatabe wrote back that he couldn't afford to make the trip. Takimoto offered to pay his expenses. That clinched the deal. Actually, it didn't take much persuasion. The girl Yatabe hoped to marry was in San Francisco.

At the meeting Yatabe found most of the *Nisei* delegates were teen-agers. Virtually all of them had come because their parents had ordered them to. They had no experience in organization, no ideas as to what they should do about fighting discrimination. Under the circumstances, Dr. Yatabe, a 25-year-old dentist just barely able to eke out a living, made what would appear to be a sensible suggestion. "You fellows go home and think about it," he told the delegates. "We'll have another meeting next year. Meanwhile, remember that you are Americans, that you must be recognized as Americans. Go out and tell everybody who will listen."

The delegates, plus some new recruits, met again in San Francisco early in 1923. This time *Nisei* from nine or ten localities—including San Francisco, Stockton, Sacramento, Livingston, San Jose and Fresno—agreed to set up chapters. But all except one were stillborn. That exception was Fresno where Yatabe was on hand to lead the way. He wanted to visit and encourage the other groups, but he couldn't afford the cost. Of those days he says:

"Most of the *Nisei* in the Fresno area were about ten years younger than I was. Even so, they were older than the San Francisco *Nisei*. Many of their folks were landowners and some were fairly well-to-do. Yet they had virtually no contact with the white community. I called an organization meeting to be held at the Buddhist church. The *Nisei* came because their parents told them to attend. I guess the other communities didn't have an older *Nisei* to call a meeting."

Yatabe still liked the name, American Loyalty League. The American Loyalty League of Fresno was organized in 1923, and it had grown into a thriving group when the Japanese American Citizens League became a national organization—meaning three states—in 1930. The JACL traces its origins to Fresno's American Loyalty League because the history of earlier groups had been disrupted by long periods of inactivity.

Yatabe in this period was faced with two problems—how to build up his own clientele, and how to get the *Issei* and *Nisei* more closely integrated into the white community. One day he asked a young Italian-American attorney, Joe Catania, who had just opened an office nearby, what he could do to attract some white patients.

"You were born in California, weren't you?" Catania asked.

Yatabe allowed as he was. In 1897.

"Well, you ought to join the Native Sons of the Golden West. That way you'll get to know a lot of the finest people around here. Let me put your name in for membership."

Yatabe smiled to himself and agreed, although he knew the Native Sons were violently anti-Japanese and he was sure to be blackballed.

A few days later Catania came into Dr. Yatabe's office with a stunned look on his face. "I had no idea they were that kind of a group," he explained. Yatabe found many other well-meaning Caucasians were equally unaware of the problems the *Nisei* faced. Now he was more sure than ever that he was on the right track when he urged *Nisei* to tell their story.

Meanwhile, the American Loyalty League found a purpose that extended beyond the Japanese community. It joined with Negro, Italian, Mexican, Chinese and German-Russian ethnic groups west of the tracks to ask the mayor for better street lighting. The mayor was amazed; no one had ever complained about conditions in that part of town. Better lights were quickly installed.

By 1926 Yatabe began to hear about another *Nisei* in San Francisco who seemed to share many of his ideas about the value of citizenship and what the *Nisei* had to do to protect their rights. His name was Saburo Kido, a native of the Hawaiian Islands, who had come to California to study law. He had opened a practice in San Francisco and was struggling to make a living, spending much more time than he could afford thinking and talking about *Nisei* problems. Tamotsu Murayama, a *Nisei* newspaperman, brought the two men together. Yatabe was tall, urbane, a polished speaker. Kido was slight, short, dapper, and he had never lost his Hawaiian accent. Yet the two liked each other immediately. They would work together closely in the years to come.

Then, even though Yatabe and Kido knew nothing about it, things began to happen again in the Northwest. The activity was touched off by the return to Seattle of a fun-loving, hard-drinking, hard-driving *Nisei* prizefighter who suddenly had been sobered by the shadow of approaching blindness, Jimmie Sakamoto.

Sakamoto had been born in Seattle in 1903, the son of Osamu and Tsuchi Sakamoto who had migrated to the United States from Yamaguchi Prefecture in 1894. The older Sakamoto had worked on a farm and in a sawmill, opened the first restaurant serving Japanese food in Seattle in 1896, operated a hotel and a secondhand furniture store. Jimmie was a football and baseball star in high school, although he weighed only 120 pounds. After graduation he went to New York, as he once said, "to study and loaf." While working for the *Japanese American News* in New York he spent one night a week teaching boxing at the Japanese Christian Institute, at the time meeting at the Dutch Reformed Church Hall on

West 123rd and Lenox Avenue. Sakamoto also boxed professionally, casually taking on bantamweights, featherweights and junior
lightweights—whoever the matchmakers picked for him. In correspondence with the author shortly before his death in 1955, Sakamoto said he could not recall how many professional fights he had,
"but they were not too many." He did meet some well-known
pugilists of the day, and once fought the special feature just before
a world's championship fight at Madison Square Garden. The ring
wars left him with two badly cauliflowered ears and ultimately
blinded him.

Apparently the eye injury started sometime in 1926. The retina
of his left eye was damaged. Unaware that a detachment had
started, Sakamoto continued to fight until he took a blow to the
head that detached the retina of his good right eye. Doctors told
him his left eye was deteriorating rapidly, and nothing could be
done to save its sight. Almost totally blind, he returned home to
Seattle in November, 1927, preparing for the inevitable darkness
by blindfolding himself and running up and down stairs and turning into rooms and hallways of the old house in which he lived.
It was about this time that he married a remarkable *Kibei* woman,
Misao Nishitani, who was to be his good right arm, his eyes, and
his support until he was hit by an automobile and killed on his way
to work one foggy December morning in 1955.

The way Sakamoto tells it, he returned to Seattle to find the
Japanese community split by a bitter rivalry between two sports
factions, the Nippon Athletic Club and the Taiyos. Sakamoto's
history was that of a protagonist rather than a mediator, but on
the strength of his not inconsiderable status and his neutral stance,
he sought to heal the breach. In the course of his efforts he heard
about the all but defunct Seattle Progressive Citizens League. The
idea of an organization of American-born Japanese stirred Sakamoto's imagination. Even at that time he could visualize a coast-
wide alliance. Sakamoto had been toying with the idea of sinking
his meager savings into an all-English weekly newspaper for the
Nisei; now he had a reason for launching such a project. A league
of *Nisei* citizens would require a voice, and he would provide that
voice through his newspaper. On January 1, 1928, he published the
first issue of *The Japanese American Courier*. The lead editorial
called for reorganization of the Seattle Progressive Citizens League.

A month later the group was revived and revamped with Clarence Arai, an attorney, as president; George Ishihara, vice president; Kimi Takayoshi, secretary; Yuki Higashi, treasurer. Soon afterwards, Arai went to Portland—a good seven-hour drive in those days—and helped the *Nisei* there organize the Portland Progressive Citizens League.

The Seattle group had been founded in 1921 to combat anti-Japanese movements. Largely at Sakamoto's insistence the orientation was changed from its original negative viewpoint to one of positive Americanism. Oddly enough this was the same tack that Dr. Yatabe had taken, unknown to the Seattleites, some years earlier. Sakamoto said: "Instead of worrying about anti-Japanese activity or legislation, we must exert our efforts to building the abilities and character of the second generation so they will become loyal and useful citizens who, some day, will make their contribution to the greatness of American life."

This was in 1928, less than fourteen years before the Japanese attack on Pearl Harbor catapulted the United States into World War II. Fourteen years was hardly enough time to build a positive image of the *Nisei* after decades of violent hostility. What would have been the course of their history if the *Nisei* had been given another decade—a mere quarter of a century—to build their image as loyal American citizens, to strengthen their economic position, to develop their political strength? There are no answers, but the questions make for interesting discussion. The fact is that the *Nisei* could not have started any sooner than they did; they just weren't old enough. Their rendezvous with destiny came a decade too early; they were born a decade too late.

In mid-1928 the Seattle group received an invitation from the American Loyalty League of Fresno to send delegates to a conference of *Nisei* leaders that August. Arai and Ishihara were en route when the meeting was cancelled. Nonetheless, on instructions from Seattle they continued on to San Francisco and Los Angeles, talking up the idea of a coast-wide *Nisei* citizens' movement at every stop. In San Francisco the two Northwesterners met with Kido, Dr. Henry Takahashi, Susumu Togasaki and others and agreed to another meeting the following April.

Dr. Yatabe, Kido and Arai were the Big Three of that April conference. Arai was armed with three major proposals: That a national *Nisei* organization be formed; that it be called the Japanese American Citizens League, and that a founding convention be held in Seattle in the summer of 1930.

No one opposed the first proposal, but Kido and Yatabe engaged in a lively debate over the name. Kido wanted to emphasize the word Japanese as an adjective that would describe the ethnic ties of the organization. Yatabe argued that any reference to Japan and the Japanese ought to be avoided. The final decision was to call the national organization the Japanese American Citizens League, but the various chapters could call themselves by any name they chose. Fresno proudly retained its original name, American Loyalty League.

At this point the *Nisei* leaders had agreed to set up a national organization with no membership and no local chapters. Kido saw nothing wrong in this. He contended that if the framework for a national organization could be put together, a slate of officers named, a policy established and leadership provided, various local groups would take shape. As it turned out, he was right. Arai, then twenty-seven years old, representing the host group, was named president pro tem of the League and he hurried home to prepare for the founding convention. Delegates arrived the next summer from Brawley, Fresno, Los Angeles, San Francisco, Newcastle, Stockton and San Jose, California; Portland, Oregon; Bellevue, Foster, Wapato, Auburn, Spokane, Vashon Island, Fife, Tacoma, Kent, Winslow and Seattle, Washington. Tasuke Yamagata represented Hawaii, Seichi (Bud) Konzo showed up from Urbana, Illinois, where he was going to the University of Illinois, and Tokutaro Nishimura Slocum registered from New York. Slocum was a Japan-born veteran of U.S. Army service in World War I—in the same regiment with Sgt. Alvin York. His outlook was *Nisei*. When he spoke, no one doubted that he had been a sergeant major. But technically he was an alien. His primary interest was in acquiring citizenship for himself and his buddies. Dr. Yatabe was not among those present. His financial position had improved considerably, but he was at home in Fresno waiting for his wife, Mary, to deliver their first child.

It is perhaps significant that the delegates, after approving the idea of a national JACL, adopted resolutions demonstrating the importance they placed on the privilege of American citizenship.

They petitioned Congress to amend the so-called Cable Act to permit *Nisei* girls who had married alien Japanese to regain their citizenship. And they urged that Oriental-born men who had served in the United States armed forces in World War I be granted citizenship.

Both measures subsequently were enacted into law, but not before some strenuous efforts on the part of the infant JACL. The Cable Act, passed in 1922, provided that "any woman citizen who marries an alien ineligible to citizenship shall cease to be a citizen of the United States." Nor could she become a citizen during the life of the marriage. This meant that either a *Nisei* or a Caucasian woman who married an *Issei* lost her citizenship. If she were widowed or divorced, a Caucasian woman could apply to regain her American citizenship. A *Nisei* woman in the same circumstances, being of a race ineligible to citizenship, could not! The JACL had somewhat less than $1,000 in its treasury, but the officers felt strongly enough about the issue to send Suma Sugi of Los Angeles to Washington, D.C., to point out the injustice of the law to members of Congress. She, thus, was the first *Nisei* lobbyist, and she made her point well for the Cable Act was amended early in 1931.

Because of his personal interest, and his gift for oratory, Slocum appeared to be the logical person to carry the ball for the JACL's efforts to gain naturalization privileges for *Issei* war veterans. He was commissioned to visit various gatherings of veterans' organizations to drum up support, but some felt that his effectiveness was impaired by his understandable urge to socialize a bit too intemperately with his old comrades in arms. This caused him to run out of expense money frequently with the result that Yatabe and Kido finally dug into their own pockets to provide Slocum's fare from a Texas encampment to Washington, D.C. In his way, Slocum was an extremely effective lobbyist, and he paved the path for ultimate passage of a bill that enabled some 700 *Issei* to become citizens.

The second national JACL convention was held in Los Angeles in 1932 with Dr. George Y. Takeyama as convention chairman. Under the precedent set with the election of Clarence Arai, Dr. Takeyama was also named national president for the subsequent biennium. Dr. T. T. Hayashi was chairman of the 1934 convention in San Francisco, and it was at this gathering that a constitutional provision for elective national officers was adopted. It seemed particularly appropriate that Dr. Yatabe should be elected president. Yet, the JACL was such a small organization that no vice president was chosen until the 1938–40 biennium when Ken Matsumoto of Los Angeles was named. Susumu Togasaki of San Francisco was the first treasurer (1932–38) at a time when finances were a pressing and persistent problem, and Saburo Kido was elected executive secretary.

The *Nisei* of this period were just beginning to feel their way into the involved world of politics and pressures outside their communities. Of those days, Mary Oyama Mittwer has written: "Between wienie bakes and the beaches and dances, *Nisei* would gather at church and JACL meetings to ponder ways of getting out the *Nisei* vote, planning ways of putting up Japanese American candidates for political offices, mixing more into the larger American community, talking about the future of Japanese churches and citizenship for the *Issei*."

The JACL tried valiantly to get the *Nisei* interested in political matters. It was easy enough to get *Nisei* registered to vote, but rounding them up for a meeting with candidates was a more difficult problem. On many an occasion candidates for local, county and state offices showed up to address JACL-sponsored political meetings only to find a mere handful of *Nisei* present. And more than once the chairman had to explain somewhat lamely that the *Nisei* in the audience were representatives of various community organizations who would carry the message back to the far larger number of voters in the respective groups.

Any analysis of the JACL and the *Nisei* communities in this period must be made with an understanding of the times. The nation was caught deep in an economic depression. Men sought work, could find none, and were reduced to selling apples on street corners or restlessly wandering from one town to the next aboard freight cars in search of jobs. Striving for security and opportunity, the labor unions became more militant than ever before. In Washington, President Franklin Delano Roosevelt consulted his "Brain Trust" and came up with drastic—for the times—New Deal regulations and reforms designed to crank up the economy and restore public confidence in the nation and its government. One of Roosevelt's first measures after he took office in 1932 was to declare a "bank holiday," a moratorium designed to halt the run on banks by panicky depositors and save them from going bankrupt. For many businesses the moratorium came too late. How bank failures affected the Japanese communities can be illustrated in the story of Sakamoto's *Courier*, a shaky business at best. Late in October, 1931, the Japanese Commercial Bank in Seattle closed its doors. There was no such thing as deposit insurance. All the *Courier's* and Sakamoto's personal funds were caught in the bank failure. Sakamoto had issued a number of checks on the bank; now he had to dig up funds and make those checks good. Many of his advertisers and subscribers were also hit by the bank failure, so he did not issue bills for several months. When a little money began to come in, it was deposited at another bank. But sixty days after the first bank failure, the second bank was forced to close. Sakamoto had to pay some bills three times before his creditors received their money.

Because the Japanese communities were so close-knit socially, so closely integrated economically—existing largely by taking in each other's washing, as it were—economic disaster such as failure of the local bank was a crushing blow that affected almost everyone. Under such circumstances it was virtually impossible for *Nisei* to be thinking big thoughts, to be dreaming big dreams, to be making big plans. Yet Sakamoto, who was elected the JACL's second national president in 1936, succeeding Dr. Yatabe, was audacious enough to launch an ambitious but unfortunately abstract "Second Generation Development Program" that called for the *Nisei* to become loyal American citizens by:

—Contributing to the social life of the nation, living with other citizens in a common community of interests and activities to promote the national welfare.

—Contributing to the economic welfare of the nation by taking key roles in agriculture, industry and commerce.

—Contributing to the civic welfare as intelligent voters and public-spirited citizens.

The goals, like motherhood, were beyond challenge and controversy but no one quite knew how to achieve them, particularly when the economic and social hostility against the *Nisei* was intensified by the pressures of the Depression. How could one contribute to the social life of the nation when one was not accepted into that life? How could one contribute to the economic welfare when one couldn't get a job? The JACL, which had established the goals, was no more effective than anyone else in showing how those goals could be reached. Professor Miyamoto describes the activities of a typical JACL chapter:

". . . The high points of the organization's activities were the national and sectional conferences, the annual New Year's dance under their sponsorship, and the 'Japan Day' at a local recreation park. Among other activities of prominence were the outings during the summers, their annual dinners, and the occasional gatherings to hear some speakers. Their monthly meetings were drab affairs at which a monotonous round of old and new business would be gone over, the major portion of which seemed concerned with the various conferences, or the preparation for some social event. For the majority of *Nisei* who participated in the functions of the group, it fulfilled a social purpose and meant little else. To be sure, the JACL constantly tried to stimulate political interest among the *Nisei*, and they often invited prominent candidates for elections to speak at their meetings . . . The significant fact is that despite the dissatisfaction among the membership, there was little understanding of how to change the organization for the better . . .

"Such, in brief, is the confused, insecure course that the Seattle JACL and its leaders followed in the years prior to the outbreak of war. If the JACL was an opportunistic, unstable organization, the fault lay not merely with its leadership, but the bulk of the *Nisei* population in Seattle were confused concerning their national and social identity and they extended these characteristics into their major organization. One might say that almost all the characteristics of the JACL, good or bad, derived more or less directly from the characteristic mental state of the *Nisei* . . ."

Miyamoto's reference is limited to Seattle but his findings would have been equally applicable to the *Nisei* of other communities along the Pacific Coast. Despite their individual differences, they faced a notably similar set of problems and reacted in an equally similar way.

Into this depressing milieu, late in the decade, there rode a brash, outspoken, sometimes delightfully devious *Nisei*. He had grown up in Utah and had had little contact with other *Nisei*. He knew virtually nothing about the history of the Japanese in the United States. He spoke no Japanese. He was largely unaware of the frustrations and the confusion of the *Nisei*. Yet, when he visited the Pacific Coast, he sensed immediately that something was drastically wrong. More important, he was young enough and inexperienced enough to think he had some answers, and he was anxious and willing to do something about the situation. His name was Mike Masaru Masaoka.

Mike was the fourth offspring of Eijiro and Haruye Masaoka. Eijiro had migrated to the United States from Hiroshima in 1903 and his bride, from Kumamoto, arrived two years later. In time they were to have eight children. Mike was born October 15, 1915, in Fresno, California. When he was three years old the family moved to Salt Lake City where Eijiro operated a small fish market until he was killed in an automobile accident in 1924. The burden of supporting the family fell to Joe Grant, the firstborn, and the widowed Haruye. Mike was then nine years old, and there were four younger children. Mike went through the Salt Lake City public schools and the University of Utah where he attracted enough attention as a debater to be invited to join the department of speech as an instructor.

While Mike was still in high school, Tamotsu Murayama, the newspaperman, visited Salt Lake, met with a group of *Nisei*, told them of the infant Japanese American Citizens League movement just taking shape on the West Coast, and asked Utah residents to join. Masaoka could see no need for such an organization and said so. Some time later, Thomas Yego of Placer County, California, and president of the California Federation of *Nisei* Farmers came to Salt Lake. He spoke of the JACL movement not in ethnic terms, as Murayama had, but as a channel that could be useful for protecting *Nisei* liberties and expanding their rights. Masaoka still had his doubts, and expressed them to Walter Tsukamoto, a Sacramento attorney, who had been invited to Salt Lake City to tell a gathering of Utah and Idaho *Nisei* about the JACL. Tsukamoto, executive secretary of JACL at the time, urged Masaoka to attend the organization's national convention scheduled in Los Angeles the summer of 1938 and state his feelings.

Since Masaoka was planning to visit California anyway, he

showed up at the convention and asked for the floor at a National Council meeting. By this time he was not entirely opposed to the idea of a Japanese American Citizens League but immodestly found several things wrong with it. He noted the JACL was strictly a West Coast organization and it ought to be made national if it hoped to accomplish its objectives. He also urged that if it really wanted to end discrimination, the membership ought to be opened to all persons, not just the *Nisei*.

At this point Susumu Togasaki, who felt the Council had much more momentous business on its agenda, demanded to know by what right Masaoka, who was not a member, was taking up the Council's time. Masaoka replied that he had been invited to speak by Tsukamoto. Togasaki pressed his protest and President Jimmie Sakamoto overruled Tsukamoto and asked Masaoka to leave. (Sakamoto and Tsukamoto, as well as Thomas Yego mentioned above, are now deceased. Both Masaoka and Togasaki long ago became firm admirers of the other's not inconsiderable talents.)

Masaoka naturally felt aggrieved about being kicked out and, characteristically, set out to see what he could do to make his views heard. Checking over the organizational structure of the JACL, he discovered that it took only three chapters to set up a District Council, and the chairman of such a council automatically became a member of the National Board. The young man who had been hostile to the idea of a JACL promptly hurried home to organize what became known as the Intermountain District Council, and was elected its first chairman late in 1939. (The Intermountain District, with chapters in Salt Lake City, Ogden, Boise Valley, Idaho Falls, Mount Olympus, Pocatello, Rexburg, and the Snake River Valley area of eastern Oregon, was the only district council in operation during the Evacuation years and, together with Arizona chapters, sustained the national organization.) At the next biennial convention, in Portland, Ore., in 1940, Masaoka appeared as a full-fledged member of the National Board. What he said must have impressed President-elect Saburo Kido because a year later, when it became apparent that the JACL needed a full-time staff employee—its first—the man who came to Kido's mind was Masaoka.

The two men met again in midsummer of 1941 at a District Council meeting in Monterey, Calif., convened under ominous conditions. German armies had invaded Russia along a 2,000-mile front in late June. The following day the Vichy government acceded to Japan's demand for military control of all French Indo-China. Alarmed by an escalation in Japanese aggression on the Asian mainland, the United States on July 26 abrogated its treaty of friendship and commerce with Japan, freezing all Japanese credits in the U.S., and halting all shipping between the two countries. Since a quorum of the National Board was present at Monterey, Kido called the members together, reviewed the mounting tension between the United States and Japan, touched on the problems that could be expected to arise if relations between the two countries deteriorated further, and proposed Masaoka be hired. Masaoka said he might be interested, but he wanted to go home and think about it.

Ironically, Kido chose Masaoka for the very reasons that had caused him to antagonize many *Nisei* on first meeting. Masaoka was cocky, aggressive, bursting with enthusiasm and ideas. He was articulate and had no hesitation about expressing his thoughts. "There was no one like Mike among the *Nisei* on the Coast at that time," Kido explained later. "He was an extrovert whereas most *Nisei* were shy, retiring. We needed that kind of assertive person who wasn't afraid to speak up."

Masaoka was reluctant to leave Salt Lake City but he thought enough of Kido's offer to discuss it with friends. Perhaps the man who most influenced him to accept was Utah's senior senator, Elbert D. Thomas, who had been a Mormon missionary in Japan in his youth. On his return Thomas had taught political science at the University of Utah and there he took a lively interest in Masaoka, one of his students. Thomas could see that difficult times were ahead for the Japanese in the United States. He could see the vast challenge that faced a spokesman for Japanese Americans, and the tremendous amount of good that such a person could accomplish. He expressed these thoughts to Masaoka, and the more he thought about Thomas' advice, the more enthusiastic Masaoka became. In August, 1941, he resigned from the University of Utah and headed for San Francisco to work for the JACL. His salary was $135 a month, somewhat less than the University had been paying him. He was not quite twenty-six years old.

14

THE LONG HOT SUMMER OF 1941

THE HOT, hectic summer of 1941 was no time for the faint of heart. War-weary Britain was under siege by Hitler's forces, a threat only slightly eased by the German invasion of Soviet Russia. Hitler's Panzer divisions had seized most of the Ukraine and other columns were converging on the city that would be known as Stalingrad. Shipping between Japan and the United States was at a standstill following the abrogation of the trade treaty on July 26, a move which President Roosevelt followed up on August 17 with a warning to the Japanese ambassador, Admiral Kichisaburo Nomura, that any further military expansion in Asia by the Japanese would force the U.S. "to take immediately any and all steps necessary" to safeguard American rights.

In Japan itself hundreds of *Nisei* were trying frantically to get back home. They besieged the offices of the Nippon Yusen Kaisha for news about a resumption of shipping. They called on the American embassy and consulates for advice and found scant encouragement. One ship was on the high seas when the treaty was suspended. It cruised off the Hawaiian islands for a time, awaiting word as to whether it would be safe to put in at Honolulu. One day when the sun shifted to the port side and remained there, indicating the ship was sailing westward back toward Japan, many *Nisei* passengers wept. Some of the *Nisei* and *Issei* were in Japan as tourists or on visits with relatives. Some had gone on business.

In the United States *Issei* and *Nisei* read the signs and while logic told them Japan and America were on a collision course toward war, such a conflict was unthinkable and therefore they believed that some miracle would come at the last moment and everything

A Nisei who volunteered for military service prior to Pearl Harbor comes home to visit his mother near Florin, California. (National Archives)

would be all right again. Strange as it may seem, few if any *Issei* were making frantic attempts to return to the shelter of Japan before the storm broke. Somehow, America seemed to be where they belonged. For an explanation, let us turn once more to Father Kitagawa who writes in *Issei and Nisei:*

"The pathetically ingrown and inwardly divided Japanese community in America, the atmosphere of which was getting rather stale, suddenly acquired new vigor when, under the Selective Service Act, a number of *Nisei* boys were called to military service in 1940. The *Issei* was psychologically prepared to face that eventuality. It was another case of *shikataganai* ("it cannot be helped") that his son should serve in the U.S. Army, for he was an American and not a Japanese. Not only that, but it might very well turn out to be a unique opportunity for the *Nisei* to be fully accepted into American society. If so, that would be a tremendous blessing for the Japanese community."

Kitagawa writes of attending a going-away party for two *Nisei* draftees in the fall of 1940, attended by all elements of the community. An elderly *Issei* spoke. Kitagawa recalls: "It was to the effect that the *Issei* was wedded to the United States and therefore, though Japan had remained his 'original' home for these many years, his 'true' home was none other than the United States. The traditional Japanese teaching emphasizes that, once married, the bride must accept her husband's parents as her own, his home as hers; and her primary and ultimate loyalty must be to his parents and his home. 'So,' said he, 'we the *Issei* gladly offer you, our sons, to the cause of the United States. Be brave and prove yourselves loyal citizens of this country, for by so doing you will prove worthy inheritors of the best of the Japanese heritage as well.' . . .

"The metaphor of marriage hit the nail on the head for the *Issei* much harder than the elder might have expected, for it was very pertinent to his situation. When he saw his son standing proudly in a U.S. Army uniform, he knew that he had been wedded to the United States for all these years, even though there had been many in-laws, as it were, who mistreated him. Characteristically Japanese, he would say, 'If I were alone, I might choose to return to Japan, but now I have these children, for whose sake I will stick it out to the bitter end.' . . .

"At that moment the *Issei* was in a frame of mind that would easily have led him to fight the Japanese forces, should they invade the Pacific Coast. Emotionally it would have been an extremely painful thing for him to do, but he would have done it just the same, for he saw quite clearly that it was the only thing for him to do as one who had been 'wedded' to the United States. The traditional Japanese ethic, when faithfully adhered to, would not only justify, but more positively demand, his taking the side of the United States. No *Issei*, however, articulated his feelings on this extraordinarily touchy subject. Yet, amazingly, this sentiment, in almost everybody's heart, quickly dominated the climate of opinion without anyone's expressing it. There could have been no split within the Japanese American family insofar as the issue of war between the United States and Japan was concerned, for in that eventuality the *Issei* would stand solidly behind the *Nisei*."

Something dramatic had come over the *Issei*, and the direct cause that triggered the action was their *Nisei* children. Once their families became established, a people who had come to America only as birds of passage, intending to go home as soon as they had made their fortunes, discovered themselves gradually changing their outlook and their plans. The dream of a homecoming grew progressively more dim, and they were not entirely dismayed. Their roots had been sunk into American soil deeper than they themselves realized.

This is not to say that the *Issei* felt completely at home in the United States. Dr. Miyamoto contends the *Issei* have never been at ease in the U.S. They lived with the memory of the Japan of their youth, a memory that grew stronger with the years. Yet, in the United States, language, culture and appearance set them apart, and the gap defied closure. They appreciated things Japanese in their communities; when they were able to afford it, they created a bit of Japan to enjoy—restaurants, the prefectural organizations, the public baths, the arts. Still they wanted to live in the United States, despite all the hostile pressures, and enjoy its material comforts. They had even come to feel a pride in American accomplishments, had taken an interest in political campaigns in which they could not participate, to relish the ball games and the holidays and the freedoms that permitted them to live in a fashion that was part Japanese, largely American.

It was into this atmosphere that Mike Masaoka arrived on the West Coast in August of 1941. Still only vaguely familiar with the JACL, he expected to find spacious, comfortably furnished headquarters in the glamorous city of San Francisco. Headquarters was a corner of Saburo Kido's second-floor law office in a rickety old house on Webster Street. The office was jammed with dusty files and piles of yellowing papers, and a couple of ancient typewriters and a bulky mimeograph machine were the total of office equipment. Kido gave Masaoka no time to be dismayed. He plunged his new aide into an intensive cram course about the Citizens League and the Japanese in America.

Masaoka had grown up in an inland community where there were few other Japanese families. He had mixed easily with Caucasian friends and their families (Senator Abe Murdock's son had been his friend and debating team partner), and most of the time he was unaware that he was "different." In San Francisco he found the *Nisei* being held together by ethnic ties rather than by intellectual interests or socioeconomic status, which was the case among his friends back home. Their common racial heritage made them a close-knit group regardless of their other interests. He found many *Nisei* were uncomfortable with non-Japanese. They couldn't or wouldn't articulate their thoughts in a mixed group and preferred to be among their own kind. He also discovered most *Nisei* were polite, conservative, reliable but quite unaggressive. They seemed to lack spontaneity. They, with a few exceptions like his blunt friend Susumu Togasaki, were careful not to embarrass anyone. In other words, not to cause anyone to lose face.

Masaoka was too busy to try to analyze his observations, but it is just as well, for Professor Miyamoto, a trained sociologist, has done it for us. He suspects that the relative inability of *Nisei* to articulate—despite the adeptness with which they handle most fields of endeavor—may be traced to lack of communication with parents during the formative years. A language barrier rose between the two generations as soon as creature needs ceased to be the main reason for communication. The parents were able to provide guidance in the personal affairs of their children, but the inability to talk to each other about abstract ideas blocked attempts at much intellectual stimulation at home, Miyamoto says. Thus the *Nisei* grew up on their own in many cases, turning to reading for intellectual stimulation, but without the visceral experience of having been reared in a family where politics, religion, economics or social issues were vigorously discussed, without having encountered firsthand the excitement and frustrations of being part of a family where being a Democrat or Republican was important. Those able to overcome the need for ethnic ties drifted out the communities in search of the imaginative, stimulating associations that they were unable to find in them. For those who felt a need to retain their ties, it was easy to fall into the *Issei* mold that counseled conservatism whereby one kept out of the line of fire, didn't rock the boat, and tried not to attract undue attention, because don't we have enough trouble as it is?

This attitude has been described in part by Prof. Harry H. L. Kitano, sociologist on the faculty of the University of California at Los Angeles, as the *Enryo* Syndrome, *enryo* being a Japanese word meaning reserve, restraint, deference or diffidence. Kitano contends that the Japanese were so meek and humble, so tradition-ally obedient to authority, that during the Evacuation "if the U.S. government wanted to run death ovens we would have marched quietly to our doom with only slight hesitation."

In his book, *Japanese-Americans: The Evolution of a Subculture*, Kitano says: "*Enryo* helps to explain much of Japanese American behavior. As with other norms, it had both a positive and negative effect on Japanese acculturation. For example, take observations of Japanese in situations as diverse as their hesitancy to speak out at meetings; their refusal of any invitation, especially the first time; their refusal of a second helping; their acceptance of a less desired object when given a free choice; their lack of verbal participation, especially in an integrated group; their refusal to ask questions; and their hesitancy in asking for a raise in salary—these may all be based on *enryo*. The inscrutable face, the noncommittal answer, the be-havioral reserve can often be traced to this norm so that the stereo-type of the shy, reserved Japanese in ambiguous social situations is often an accurate one . . . It has helped the Japanese 'look' good in Caucasian eyes because of its lack of aggression and high con-formity, but for the Japanese American the cost of the goodness may have been very high. A full development of an individual's potentialities would surely be hindered under such a norm."

Miyamoto says the "other side" of the *Enryo* Syndrome is that the *Nisei*, being unaggressive and therefore not offensive were more quickly welcomed into American society when the time was ripe.

Be that as it may be, Masaoka quickly proved his contacts were valuable. Within a few weeks after he reached San Francisco he was notified by Senator Thomas, a member of the Senate Educa-tion and Labor Committee, that the President's Commission on Equal Employment Opportunities was holding hearings in Los Angeles, and the JACL was invited to appear. Masaoka testified ably that qualified *Nisei* were not being hired for defense jobs and that this was not so subtle discrimination. It was the first time the JACL had been represented before a federal commission. Shortly, *Nisei* began to get jobs in the aircraft and electronic industries. (The attack on Pearl Harbor abruptly halted the program. But *Nisei* leaving the War Relocation Centers discovered that the Fair

Employment Practices Commission's orders opening job opportunities for *Nisei* had never been rescinded and they found defense work in the Midwest and East.)

Whatever satisfaction Masaoka gained from this experience was quickly dissipated a few days later when a mysterious stranger appeared at the JACL office. He flashed impressive-looking credentials that identified him as Curtis B. Munson, representing the Department of State.

"The United States and Japan have some serious difficulties," he said after brief amenities. "There is a real possibility of war. You know of the experience we had with Germans in this country during the first World War. We are aware of the possibility of similar action affecting the Japanese. What suggestions do you have for the protection of the lives and property of the Japanese in the United States if worst should come to the worst?"

It was the first time either Masaoka or Kido had realized the situation was so serious. They were also surprised that their government would send a representative to seek their ideas. This had never happened before. Why had Munson come to the JACL? Obviously, because it was the only national organization of Japanese American citizens. But the security agencies also must have known that the JACL had declined an invitation to cooperate with the Japanese Association of North America, an *Issei* group, in a joint national fund-raising campaign. There was an element of rivalry in the JACL's refusal, but basic to its position was a feeling that it ought to be independent of *Issei*—and therefore alien—influence. The agencies likewise were aware that Kido, shortly after he had been elected national president, had turned down a Japanese government invitation to visit that country, with all expenses paid, for its 2,600th anniversary celebration. Later, it occurred to Masaoka that perhaps Senator Thomas might have had something to do with the government's interest in JACL. Munson quietly but firmly warned that no notes must be taken of their discussions, and that his presence must be mentioned to no one for fear of alarming the public. Then the three men talked for the better part of three days, Kido and Masaoka continuing to discuss the problems at night after Munson had returned to his hotel.

Out of these conversations several proposals were developed. Kido felt that if war came, acts of vandalism and violence against the *Nisei* and *Issei* would be more probable in the rural areas than in the cities, and he urged that sheriffs and other rural law officers be alerted to keep order. Masaoka asked that in event of war, the President or some high Cabinet member issue a statement pointing out the distinction between the Japanese enemy and the resident Japanese aliens and their American-born children, urging that no misdirected anger be vented on the innocent.

(Attorney General Francis Biddle did indeed make such a broadcast shortly after Pearl Harbor. Many months later, Masaoka met Munson, who was then wearing a Navy captain's uniform, in Washington. Masaoka recalls that Munson said most of what he had been told in San Francisco had proven correct, that many of the JACL's recommendations for keeping order had been adopted, and indicated this was one reason government officials continued to rely on JACL for counsel and advice.)

Meanwhile, in Los Angeles, H. T. Komai, publisher of the *Rafu Shimpo*, decided it was only prudent to take steps to remain in business even if war should come. The *Rafu* was the most influential Japanese language newspaper in Southern California at the time. It also had one of the better English sections, edited by Louise Suski and Togo Tanaka, a Phi Beta Kappa from the University of California at Los Angeles. Komai had heard that under a World War I law, a newspaper owned by an enemy alien might be permitted to continue publication under certain conditions. He asked Tanaka to go to Washington and find out about it. In October of 1941, Tanaka, accompanied by Gongoro Nakamura, president of the Central Japanese Association of Southern California, flew to Washington and made the rounds of government offices.

Tanaka learned more than he had bargained for. Interrogated by an Army intelligence officer, Tanaka was shown slides of the *Rafu's* English and Japanese sections, the first vigorously waving the American flag, the second full of fire-eating, militaristic dispatches from Tokyo. Which represented the *Rafu's* true position? Tanaka couldn't say. At the Justice Department, Attorney General Biddle asked Tanaka in his gentle way how he knew war was coming. "Why," said Tanaka in all innocence, "everybody knows that!" Tanaka returned to Los Angeles with no assurance that the *Rafu* would remain in business and with a new respect for the men in Washington.

In November, 1941, the Northern California District Council meeting of the JACL was held in San Mateo. Tanaka reported on his visit to Washington—few *Nisei* were privileged to make such trips in those days—and said many officials were predicting war with Japan. Some said it would come as soon as the following March.

This was warning enough to Masaoka that the JACL must prepare for difficult times. But how? By opening pipelines to various persons in authority, to ask their aid in case of trouble, to impress on them the loyalty of the great mass of Japanese Americans. By this time he was aware that no such pipelines existed in California where, despite their numbers, few *Nisei* had contacts with government officials. In Utah, Masaoka had developed such personal connections that he could pick up the phone and get through to Senators Thomas and Murdock and many others in important places. He knew that other *Nisei* in the inter-mountain area had contacts with political figures. But not those on the Coast. He urged the need for strengthening JACL chapters in Utah, and setting up new chapters wherever *Nisei* could be found. The National Council authorized him to make a recruiting drive.

Tanaka's experience with the military intelligence officer indicated that the federal authorities knew a great deal about what was going on in the Japanese communities. In fact, security officials had been active for months, and while they worked quietly, they made no great secret of their presence. One of them was Lt. Comm. Kenneth D. Ringle of Naval Intelligence stationed in Los Angeles. He had a number of *Nisei* contacts. Writing anonymously in *Harper's* magazine in October, 1942, he replied to charges that the *Nisei* had failed to cooperate with government operatives by asserting that many had assisted him in his official duties.

In San Francisco, Kido was questioned frequently by FBI and military intelligence officers about specific *Issei*. Would Kido consider them loyal to the United States? Would they be likely to commit sabotage in case of war? He gave them a firm answer: "I have absolute confidence the *Issei* will not participate in sabotage."

But there were more difficult questions: "If a Japanese landing party should come to the shores of California under cover of darkness, would this *Issei* report their presence immediately to the nearest sheriff's office or would he harbor them overnight?"

How could anyone fathom the thoughts or predict the actions of a specific individual in such a hypothetical situation? In honesty, Kido could not give a categorical answer. Nor could anyone. Yet the security agencies had to have answers, and when it could not get them, it was often charged—usually by those not directly involved—that the *Nisei* were not cooperative, that they refused to inform on their fellows, that the Japanese communities were under a conspiracy of silence.

This was not true, of course, and by his own testimony before a Congressional committee some weeks after Pearl Harbor, Tokutaro Slocum for one proudly identified himself as a zealous source of intelligence. Numerous federal and local officials have testified that the *Nisei* were cooperative about providing information. Galen Fisher, writing in *Christian Century in 1943,* stated without equivocation: "I personally know at least 15 intelligence officers who have received continual aid from the group of loyal and patriotic *Nisei* attached to each."

Just how useful this type of information was to government agencies is a matter of conjecture. The record shows that arrests of Japanese aliens after Pearl Harbor were on the basis of suspicion and potential danger rather than for the commission of any specific subversive acts. And suspicion had to be based on such tenuous "evidence" as a man's membership in a fencing or judo club in which manly virtues, Japanese style, were emphasized. Or the "evidence" might be linked to the vigor with which a suspect solicited funds; there were several groups whose members contributed a dollar a month to be used for the comfort and rehabilitation of wounded Japanese veterans. This was concrete evidence of sympathy for Japan in her war against China—while the United States was still at peace. In similar fashion, Morton Grodzins points out, millions of Germans and Italians in the U.S. sympathized with their mother-countries, so long as the war did not involve the United States. By the same token, many Americans opposed U.S. aid to Britain. But when the United States became a belligerent, it was an altogether new ball game with new rules for virtually everyone but the Japanese Americans. They continued to be judged by the old rules. As for the Li'l Tokyos, there was no equivalent of the German-American Bund. The *Nisei* knew nothing about potential spies and saboteurs in the grim summer of 1941 because there was nothing to know. It is ironical that the *Nisei* were held under suspicion in some quarters because they were unable to provide information that did not exist. In Masaoka's case, he was unfamiliar with the situation on the Coast, had few friends among the *Nisei*, and yet was accused of being uncooperative and evasive when he could not answer the questions fired at him by security agents. Unfortunately, it occurred to few persons in authority that perhaps the *Nisei* were telling the truth.

Actually, the security agencies knew more than most residents about what was going on in the communities, and they had scant need for the assistance of amateurs. Jim Marshall, a long-time resident of the Pacific Coast who numbered many *Nisei* among his friends, and a highly knowledgeable reporter, wrote in *Collier's* magazine in October, 1941, that *Issei* and *Nisei* had been under close scrutiny "for five years or more" and "the consensus among intelligence people is that an overwhelming majority is loyal."

It is likely Marshall was referring to the work of the Special Defense Unit of the Department of Justice which was activated shortly after Germany overran Poland in the fall of 1939. When it appeared that in time the United States would be drawn into war, the unit was given the responsibility of checking on anyone who might be dangerous to the national security. Eighteen months before the attack on Pearl Harbor, the Japanese communities along the Pacific Coast were placed under intense scrutiny. Three categories of danger—A, B and C—were established. Leaders of organizations with strong Japanese ties were automatically given an "A" classification; in case of war all "A" *Issei* would be picked up immediately. A "C" category might be applied to anyone—alien or citizen—who contributed to a Japanese cultural society, and he would be watched but not necessarily arrested. It was easy enough to list most contributors. The Japanese language newspapers usually published their names. As early as October 21, 1941, FBI agents visited Li'l Tokyo in Los Angeles, questioned officers of various Japanese organizations and seized records and documents for further study.

In addition to their own investigations, the intelligence agencies were obliged to check out any number of tips, and many of them were as sinister as the charge that an unusually large number of *Nisei* students at UCLA were studying German. The implication was that the Berlin-Tokyo Axis somehow passed through the UCLA campus. Investigation showed that UCLA in the fall of 1941 had about 200 Japanese students out of an enrollment of more than 8,000, and that five Japanese were enrolled in German literature classes, twenty-one were in German language classes, and total school-wide enrollment in German classes was 508. The registrar pointed out that since a foreign language was a requirement for graduation, it was not unusual for Japanese as well as other students to study German.

Most of Li'l Tokyo was of two minds. Those who took a long, realistic view of the situation realized the need of good public relations, no matter what transpired. Masao Satow, the Japanese YMCA secretary, was named chairman of a JACL speakers' bureau to broadcast the story of *Nisei* concern and loyalty as widely as possible. A more optimistic element, the Li'l Tokyo merchants, could see nothing but business as usual regardless of what was happening in Asia. In preparation for a banner Christmas season sale, they invested liberally in merchandise.

But the die had been cast long before this, cast for war even as most *Nisei* hoped against hope that somehow the cloud over their lives would go away, cast even as Masaoka struggled to transform a largely ineffective JACL into an organization that would be able to cope with the darkening problems ahead. In August, 1941, a Japanese intelligence officer, Ensign Takeo Yoshikawa, arrived in Honolulu under the cover name of Vice-Consul Morimura. His mission was to report the movement of U.S. ships in Pearl Harbor. John Dean Potter writes in his book, *Yamamoto, the Man Who Menaced America:* "He (Yoshikawa) used to strike up conversations with American sailors in bars. He cautiously tried to obtain information from *Nisei* girls who entertained American sailors. His first great disappointment came when he made tentative attempts to sound out these girls and other Hawaiian-born Japanese. To his astonishment he discovered they were fanatically loyal to the United States."

By September 6, 1941, Japan's topmost councils had agreed to go to war with the United States if negotiations seeking a free hand in China failed. Even then a surprise attack on Pearl Harbor was being debated by military commanders, and largely opposed by naval strategists as excessively dangerous. On November 3, thirty-five days before the attack, Admiral Isoroku Yamamoto won the Naval General Staff's permission to attack Pearl Harbor in case of war. Four days later Japan's trim gray war ships, singly and in pairs, began to slip out of Japanese ports for a rendezvous in Tankan Bay in the Kuriles. Their commanders still did not know the reason. After dark on the evening of November 26, the main body of the fleet under Admiral Chuichi Nagumo left Tankan Bay and headed into the foggy North Pacific. On December 1, Prime Minister Hideki Tojo's cabinet finally ratified the decision for war. Thereupon the coded message, "Climb Mount Niitaka" (Formosa's highest peak) was flashed to Nagumo's ships. The final "go" message, "East wind, rain," was heard only hours before the attack was launched just before dawn on the fateful 7th.

Shortly before 8 A.M. on the unforgettable Sunday of December 7, 1941, Japanese bombs dropped on sleeping Pearl Harbor. The time was 11 A.M. on the Pacific Coast, 2 P.M. in Washington. Even then, the hapless Japanese envoys in Washington were preparing to call on Secretary of State Cordell Hull with formal notification that relations would be broken.

In Seattle, a *Nisei* was raking dead leaves in his yard when he was called to the telephone. A friend asked whether he had been listening to the news on the radio.

"What news?" the *Nisei* asked.

"The Japs have attacked Pearl Harbor."

"Jesus Christ, no," the *Nisei* muttered. "Oh, Jesus Christ." The way he said it, it was part oath, part prayer.

PART TWO

the years of travail

15

DECEMBER 7, 1941

THE HORROR, the anger, the shock that reverberated throughout the United States in the wake of the news flash that Pearl Harbor was under attack was, for the *Issei* and *Nisei*, magnified manyfold by reason of their ethnic and cultural ties with the nation that had shattered the peace. Added to these emotions was a searing sense of shame and grief, and yes, fear. The *Nisei* knew they were Americans, but would their white neighbors agree? The *Issei* suddenly had become enemy aliens, a role they accepted unwillingly for they had no recourse. How could Japan have done such a thing? they asked. What will happen to us, people who are the same race as the enemy, wearing the same face as the enemy, yet bleeding for America, wanting desperately to tell Americans how sorry, how ashamed, how angry we are?

In Honolulu on that morning of December 7, 1941, a seventeen-year-old lad named Daniel Ken Inouye woke up early to go to church. Automatically he turned on the radio that was on the shelf over his bed. Suddenly he heard a frenzied voice: "Pearl Harbor is being bombed by the Japanese! I repeat: This is not a test or a maneuver: Japanese war planes are attacking Oahu!" In his biography, *Journey to Washington*, United States Senator Dan Inouye describes how he called his father, and how they listened to the announcer in horror, wanting not to believe but knowing what he said was true. Together they stepped out in the yard and stared toward Pearl Harbor, watching the black puffs of antiaircraft bursts, listening in disbelief to the distant crrump of bombs and the answering chatter of guns. Then the planes that had made the attack climbed into the sky and headed northward, over the

Inouye home. The red ball on the wings that identified them as Japanese was clearly visible. Inouye's father, Hyotaro, born in Japan, peered up at them. In shock and torment, he shouted: "You fools." Dan jumped on his bicycle and raced to the Red Cross station where he taught first aid. It was five days before he returned.

Six thousand miles away in Manhattan, Larry Tajiri was enjoying a relaxed Sunday afternoon when he also heard the first radio news flashes. He reacted like the crackerjack newspaperman that he was. He sped to his office in the New York bureau of the *Asahi* newspapers of Japan, scanned the Associated Press teletype machines which were rattling off details of the grim story, and with practiced skill punched off a bulletin to Tokyo: "ASSOCIATED PRESS REPORTS PEARL HARBOR UNDER ATTACK BY JAPANESE PLANES." It may well be that the *Asahi's* cable editor on the foreign desk in Tokyo was the first Japanese, outside of top government and military leaders, to hear of the attack. Tajiri fired off bulletin after bulletin as the AP's coverage took shape until, sometime late that long dark afternoon, the connection to Tokyo went dead.

Almost everyone who is old enough to remember Pearl Harbor Day can recall what he was doing when he heard the numbing news. Some sensed immediately that an era had ended. Others were only angry, or stunned. Here are the stories of a handful of *Nisei* on that day, *Nisei* who were in positions of prominence then, or who were destined for leadership.

Saburo Kido was attending a meeting in San Francisco that morning. The possibility of war bore heavily on his mind. He knew the San Francisco Japanese community was divided, nervous under international tensions, unwilling to pull together. So an *Issei*, Kuniji Takahashi, had taken the initiative of calling various *Nisei* and *Kibei* leaders to a unity meeting, and Kido was there as national president of the JACL. The meeting had hardly started when Dr. George Baba entered the room, excitement written on his face. As he was driving to the meeting he had heard that Hawaii was under attack by Japanese planes. Kido recalls saying:

"That's too fantastic to believe. The report must be wrong, probably just another rumor. Let's hear what H. V. Kaltenborn has to say when he comes on at 12:15."

Kaltenborn at that time was among the nation's top newscasters. He had a fast, staccato delivery that lent an air of excitement to even the most prosaic news. The meeting was recessed while everyone moved to another room to hear what he had to say. In stunned silence they heard Kaltenborn's tense, high-pitched voice confirm that Pearl Harbor and Clark Field in the Philippines had been attacked and even at that moment American ships were burning and American men were dying.

Ashen-faced, Kido hurried to the office of the *New World Sun*, a Japanese language newspaper. Kido was its legal counsel and in its English section he also wrote a daily column called *Timely Topics*. The telephone was ringing. Reporters for the San Francisco newspapers and the local correspondent of the New York *Times* were asking for a statement. Kido still could not believe war had come, but he composed himself quickly and issued a statement condemning the attack, pledging the loyalty of the *Nisei* and offering full support of the war effort. Then on behalf of the JACL he sent a telegram to President Roosevelt that was a model of sincerity and quiet eloquence: ". . . IN THIS SOLEMN HOUR WE PLEDGE OUR FULLEST COOPERATION TO YOU, MR. PRESIDENT, AND TO OUR COUNTRY . . . NOW THAT JAPAN HAS INSTITUTED THIS ATTACK UPON OUR LAND, WE ARE READY AND PREPARED TO EXPEND EVERY EFFORT TO REPEL THIS INVASION TOGETHER WITH OUR FELLOW AMERICANS."

As the afternoon and night wore on, Kido was gratified to hear both his statement and the message to the President mentioned on newscasts along with the latest war bulletins.

In the days that followed the JACL received many messages of reassurance and understanding of the difficult position of the *Nisei*. Among them were telegrams from Lewis B. Hershey, director of the Selective Service System, and the governors of California, Wyoming, Colorado, Utah, Montana and Oregon. Many weeks later, when the demand for evacuation of all Japanese Americans from the West Coast was in full cry, only one of the governors remembered his telegram. That was Ralph Carr of Colorado, who throughout his political life had demonstrated the courage to defend what he felt was right. He said the displaced *Issei* and *Nisei* would be welcome in his state when all other Western governors were throwing up their hands in horror at the very idea of accepting evacuees. Many Colorado observers believe this action cost Carr a seat in the United States Senate in the next election. Hershey, too, changed his mind. The Selective Service System soon classified all *Nisei* 4C—aliens not subject to military service.

By December 7, Mike Masaoka had progressed as far as North Platte, Nebraska, on his swing through interior America to recruit support for the JACL. On that Sunday morning he met with some fifty *Nisei* in the basement of the North Platte Episcopal Church. Word of his coming had preceded him, and for the first time in years *Nisei* had converged on North Platte from southeastern Wyoming and northeastern Colorado and far western Nebraska, seeking assurance that war would not come.

Masaoka had prepared well for the meeting. On the wall he had tacked a map of the Rocky Mountain area, and as he spoke he drew rings around places like Cheyenne, Denver, Pueblo and other communities where Japanese had settled. It didn't occur to him that Cheyenne was the site of Fort Francis E. Warren; Denver had Lowry Army Air Base; Pueblo had an ordinance depot and a major steel mill. Masaoka was making an eloquent case for JACL membership when the door was thrust open and several bulky men—Caucasians—entered.

"Are you Mike Masaoka?" one of them asked, glancing at the map.

Mike said he was. He thought the strangers were newspapermen.

"Could we see you outside a minute?"

"I'm right in the middle of some important business here," Masaoka explained, impatience rising in his voice. "Would you mind waiting outside for a little while."

"This is quite urgent."

Masaoka left the room with the men. Once outside the door they pinned his arms to his sides and in silence escorted him directly to the city jail. His question unanswered, Masaoka wondered if he had been picked up for failing to get a license for a public meeting. At the jail he heard for the first time of the attack on Pearl Harbor. The *Nisei* in the church, who still hadn't heard of the outbreak of fighting, were mystified when Masaoka failed to come back. After a while someone thought to tell them of the war, and that Masaoka was in jail. No one said anything for what seemed a long time. Then somebody said: "I guess we'd better get home to our families." They needed no further urging.

Among those at the meeting were Ben and Fred Kuroki, sons of Sam Kuroki, *Issei* potato farmer. Ben was a trucker, twenty years old, hauling cabbage and potatoes and other produce to market. He knew he couldn't continue trucking during the war. He asked his father what he ought to do, and the old man without batting an eye said: "Enlist in the Army, Ben. America is your country. You fight for it."

Ben and Fred got in a car and drove 150 miles to the nearest recruiting station to volunteer. The call-up never came. The Army wasn't taking "Japs." Weeks later the brothers went to the newly opened recruiting station at North Platte and were accepted. Fred went into the engineers. Ben became an Air Corps gunner, flying 30 heavy bombing missions in Europe, then fighting to be assigned to the Pacific, and flying 28 more missions against Japan. Kuroki came out of the war a hero. The story of his heartbreaking efforts to be accepted in the armed forces, to win the right to fight for his country, to overcome the wartime stigma attached to his ancestry, is told vividly by Ralph G. Martin in his book, *Boy from Nebraska.*

As for Masaoka, he was held incommunicado long enough to figure out how local police had known his name and whereabouts. He came to the conclusion that FBI agents had been following his progress across the country and knew where to find him at any time. Two days later he was permitted to telephone Kido, in San Francisco, but was warned not to reveal he was in jail.

"Sab," Masaoka said when the connection was made, "I was afraid you were worrying about me. I'm stuck here in North Platte, Nebraska. I'm at the, ah, the Palace Hotel."

Kido commiserated with him, figuring Masaoka had been delayed by disrupted rail schedules, and urged him to get back to San Francisco as soon as possible because there was a load of work piling up.

Later that day Kido attended a board meeting of the International Institute which had been called to discuss problems facing Japanese Americans. When he told the members of Masaoka's misfortune, someone suggested a collection be taken and a telephone call placed to him in North Platte to console him. Annie Clo Watson, a YWCA executive and long a friend of the *Nisei*, was delegated to make the call. Presently she returned with a bewildered expression on her face. "Mike's not at the Palace Hotel," she said. "He's in jail!"

Kido promptly got on the phone to seek Masaoka's release. It is significant that the two men he tried to reach for assistance were Senators Thomas and Murdoch of Utah; neither he nor Masaoka had any sort of access to any member of the California congressional delegation. Senator Thomas quickly arranged for Masaoka's freedom, and he was placed on a train for San Francisco.

At the next stop, Cheyenne, local police walking through the train saw Masaoka. They decided that since he was an Oriental he needed further looking into, and over Masaoka's strenuous protests took him once more to jail. It took another call to Senator Thomas to win his release. The senator, who had other things to do, arranged an FBI escort for Masaoka all the way back to San Francisco.

About the time Masaoka was being picked up in North Platte, Pvt. Harry Honda, now editor of the JACL's official organ, the weekly *Pacific Citizen*, was hunched over a portable radio in a barracks at Fort Warren, just outside of Cheyenne. He had been stretched out on his bunk reading a newspaper when someone shouted that the war had started. The first thought that came to Honda's mind was that he wasn't going to get his furlough. Honda was in a truck company, learning to double-clutch 2½-ton trucks up and down the rolling Wyoming hills. The men were entitled to a two-week furlough on completion of sixteen weeks of basic training, and he saw that prospect vanishing. Honda was also worried about a party that had been scheduled for that night. Miss Hisako Sakata, now of Washington, D.C., was secretary to the post chaplain, and she had helped the Japanese community in Cheyenne to organize a dinner and dance for some fifty *Nisei* GIs taking basic training at Fort Warren.

Despite the tension and confusion at the post, Miss Sakata enlisted the chaplain's aid in getting passes for the *Nisei* GIs to attend the party at the old Japanese Hall above the Hashimoto Dry Cleaners shop. The residents had prepared a handsome spread of Japanese food, and there was even a record player for the dance. But it was about the saddest party ever held. No one was in the mood to enjoy the food. No one could get up the spirit to dance, and everyone went home early. Next day all personnel at Fort Warren assembled in their regimental areas to hear the broadcast of President Roosevelt's address to Congress requesting a formal declaration of war. Honda remembers that the regimental commanders then made a point of declaring that the *Nisei* recruits on the post were Americans, and were to be treated as such.

Another *Nisei* GI, Vincent T. Tajiri, was with his company on the firing range at Fort Vancouver, across the Columbia River from Portland. The men in the company were taking marksmanship qualifying tests, an event considered so important that the normal Sunday day-off had been cancelled. One of the truck drivers who had a portable radio heard about the attack on Pearl Harbor and quickly circulated the word. There was little excitement on the range; the need to qualify had taken on a grim new urgency. Tajiri remembers that on their return to their barracks that evening the outfit was placed on one-hour alert. Shortly, the company was convoyed across the Columbia River to guard the Portland municipal airport. *Playboy* magazine, where Tajiri served many years as picture editor, had not even been conceived in the mind of Hugh Hefner that grim night.

Hundreds of miles to the south at Ford Ord, California, the pace on December 7 was somewhat more leisurely for the men of Co. C., 7th Medical Battalion. Corporal Akiji Yoshimura, who had been drafted the previous April, slept late and missed breakfast. He was wondering whether he ought to wander down to the mess hall for lunch, or catch the bus for Monterey or Salinas when he heard the news. "My reactions ran the gamut of shock, bewilderment, anger, shame and sorrow," he says. "But mostly, I felt deep anguish and despair because the land that I had been taught to honor by my parents had committed an act of war against the country that I loved."

The 7th Medical Battalion had a relatively large number of Japanese and Chinese Americans. For the most part relationships among the troops remained normal until a white GI made some derogatory remarks about the "Japs" in the company. Tension rose quickly. The next evening the battalion commander ordered all noncommissioned officers, including Yoshimura, to a briefing where he made it clear that he had every confidence in the loyalty of the *Nisei* and would tolerate no discrimination against them. Yoshimura and some other *Nisei* applied for Officer Candidate School in the Medical Administrative Corps, but they were not accepted even though white GIs with lesser qualifications were. Some time later the outfit was moved to Crissy Field, San Francisco. One day Yoshimura was told an FBI agent wanted to see him. Several nights earlier Yoshimura and a *Nisei* GI friend had gone into San Francisco to visit the friend's brother who, it turned out, was a Tenrikyo (a Shinto sect) priest. Yoshimura says:

"The interrogation went along smoothly enough until I was asked: 'Will you fight against Japan if you are called upon to do so?'

"I told him that of course I would, making it clear that I expected to serve America at any place, anytime, to the very best of my ability.

"With this the FBI agent blew his calm. He shouted at me: 'You sonovabitch, I expect you to say that you will shoot down the Emperor and tear down the Jap flag and stomp it into the ground!' I guess I failed to pass his patriotism test, because shortly I was transferred to 'the enlisted reserve at the convenience of the government.' In other words, I was mustered out of the Army and sent home. It was a bitter experience. It troubled me for months afterward."

Yoshimura later volunteered for military intelligence training, served in India, Burma and China, and won a battlefield commission.

The war caught up with other *Nisei* in a variety of ways. Hito Okada, then national treasurer of the JACL and later its president, had chosen December 7 to take his family from their home in Portland to visit in-laws in Seattle. While his wife and daughter visited, Okada rented a rowboat on the Seattle waterfront and went trolling for blackmouth salmon in Elliott Bay. Even as the first American battle of World War II raged in Hawaii, Okada innocently rowed back and forth off the huge Todd Shipyards where oceangoing vessels were being refitted. It would have been an embarrassing position in which to be caught, but no one noticed him. Fishing was poor. Late Sunday afternoon Okada rowed ashore, returned the boat and drove to Tacoma to visit his mother. He had parked his car and was walking up to her door when a total stranger stopped him and snarled: "I'll be back to get you with my gun!" Okada wondered what the man was talking about. Then his mother told him what had been coming all day over the radio.

Okada decided he should be back in Portland where he was employed by a Japanese firm that bought lumber for export. He reached his home about 11:30 P.M., telephoned his boss, H. Y. Kato, and made arrangements to meet him next morning at the office. A few minutes later Kato's maid called back. She said FBI agents had just picked up Kato.

In Tacoma itself, Shig Wakamatsu was sleeping late that Sunday in the little cubbyhole he used as a bedroom at the Farmers Market. He was a student at the College of Puget Sound and he worked as a combination watchman and night receiving clerk at the market where farmers brought their produce. The first words he heard that morning were those of someone shouting: "Hey, Shig, the Japs are bombing Pearl Harbor." He came awake in a hurry. That night there was a *Nisei* bowling tournament. He went through the motions, as though in a dream. The next day he asked for permission to address the student body at a special assembly on the College of Puget Sound campus. Wakamatsu poured out his anger and shame. He pledged his personal loyalty to the United States, and that of other *Nisei*. He concluded his speech with the Japanese American Creed, written only a few months earlier by Mike Masaoka. The last paragraph of the creed reads:

"Because I believe in America, and I trust she believes in me, and because I have received innumerable benefits from her, I pledge myself to do honor to her at all times and in all places; to support her Constitution; to obey her laws; to respect her flag; to defend her against all enemies, foreign or domestic; to actively assume my duties and obligations cheerfully and without any reservations whatsoever, in the hope that I may become a better American in a greater America."

As he returned to his chair, drained of emotion, his fellow students gave him a standing ovation.

Wakamatsu, now a chemist in Chicago, went on to become

national president of the JACL. Another future JACL president, from Chicago, Kumeo Yoshinari, was in similarly humble circumstances on Pearl Harbor Day. He was pruning trees in a pear orchard near Hood River, Oregon, trying to make a few dollars. When he returned home for lunch, his wife Mary told him the news. The first thing that came to mind was the admonition of his *Issei* friend, Masuo Yasui, to treasure his citizenship and become a 100 percent American. He also remembered the cynicism of other *Issei* who predicted the *Nisei* never would be accepted as Americans, that they would live forever under the cloud of racial discrimination. Fleetingly, he wondered who would be proven right.

But in Fresno, Tom Yatabe's long record of civic activity paid off. He got the news when he arrived at home after a morning of golf. Shortly afterward there was a telephone call from Long Beach. It was the mayor of Fresno, anxious about his friend. "Doc," he urged, "tell your people to stay home. Keep them off the streets. We don't know what the hoodlum element might do, and we don't want any trouble. I've already ordered patrol cars into the Japanese areas."

Later, when sheriff's deputies began a roundup of *Issei*, Yatabe pleaded: "Go easy on them. They're old folks."

"I know, Doc," an officer replied. "I know most of these people anyway, and they're all right. We're working under FBI orders."

That night, various *Nisei* gathered at Yatabe's home to talk and seek reassurance. "What are we going to do?" the younger *Nisei* asked Yatabe. He had no answer for them.

In Los Angeles, the reaction of *Nisei* was as varied as their number and background. Masao Satow, who had been making speeches pleading for understanding of the *Nisei*, heard the radio broadcasts with shock and disbelief. It did not occur to him at the time that there might be dire consequences for those of Japanese ancestry in the United States. He recalls carrying the news to his mother, and her first words were, "*Nihon baka da ne!*" (How foolish Japan is!). He took his mother to church to attend somber *Issei* services and there gained the impression most *Issei* felt the same way she did. That afternoon Satow met some *Nisei* friends and they could talk of nothing but the war. Yet, its possible effect on their lives in the days to come did not enter their conversation.

Satow served the evacuees through the YMCA during the war years, and in 1946 agreed to join the JACL national staff to help out for no more than twelve months. That year has stretched out for more than a quarter of a century.

In another part of Los Angeles, the war news struck Frank Chuman with far greater impact than it had hit Satow. Chuman was a second-year student at the University of Southern California Law School and part-time employee of the Los Angeles County Probation Department. He and his sister Yemi had attended morning services at St. Mary's Episcopal Church. On their return home just before noon he switched on the radio, and the news was like a slap in the face. The Chumans had their customary Sunday lunch together, picking at their food in fearful silence, subdued and shocked. After lunch, Chuman's parents agreed it would be prudent to destroy as much evidence as possible of family or sentimental ties with Japan. They burned letters, photographs, books and magazines. Of the rest of that day, Chuman writes:

"My father went to a dresser in his bedroom where he kept two *samurai* swords, one long for two hands, the other short. These were family treasures which had been handed down to him. His ancestors had been *samurai*, warriors of the Satsuma clan. I had looked forward to owning these swords some day, and many times had secretly taken them out to admire the magnificent blades. My father removed the swords from the beautiful inlaid cases and he and I took them out into the back yard. There he thrust both blades, bare and glistening, deep into the ground and we buried them. I was sad and disconsolate. Disposal of these beautiful pieces of Japanese workmanship seemed to be a symbolic rite. It was as though a tangible cultural tie with Japan were being severed.

"Later, I drove to Japanese town, in the area around East First and San Pedro, to see what was going on. It was like a ghost town. I felt very conscious of the fact that I had a Japanese face. I wondered how we would be treated by our non-Japanese friends and neighbors. I felt very much alone, silently hoping for some words of comfort but fearing that my features would cause me to be the target of hatred and suspicion for what the Japanese Navy had done." Chuman today is a prominent Los Angeles attorney, and he too served the JACL as national president.

The blank-faced stores and shops that Chuman drove past on December 7 were not all abandoned. Sitting at the fountain of the Iwaki Drug Company, Store No. 1, at the corner of East First and San Pedro Streets was the owner, Thomas Tozaburo Sashihara, whose face bore the expression of one whose world had just crumbled around him. Sashihara had struggled a long time and climbed a long way to reach the position he occupied on December 7, and so the fall was all the more painful.

Sashihara left the obscure village of Tani, in Oita Prefecture, when he was fifteen years old to join his father in America. Until then he had never been more than ten miles from home. He landed in San Francisco on July 4, 1915, a particularly propitious date. In Los Angeles, where his father lived, the young immigrant enrolled in the second grade and there acquired the name Tom when the principal found his proper name unpronounceable. Eight years later he joined the Iwaki Drug Company as a junior partner, serving an apprenticeship and attending night school to qualify as an assistant pharmacist. But when it came time to apply for a full-fledged pharmacist's license, Sashihara found that the state legislature had amended the pharmacy law to bar "aliens ineligible to citizenship." It took seventeen years to get the law changed, and in the summer of 1941 Sashihara was overjoyed to receive his license. By then he had a family, two drugstores in Li'l Tokyo, a five-and-ten-cent store on Crenshaw Boulevard, a mortgage-free home in Alhambra and a Plymouth sedan that he had purchased with cash. On the morning of December 7, he had broken 85 for the first time at the Montebello golf course, an event of considerable importance. After lunch he drove down to Iwaki Drug No. 1 to see how the pre-holiday sale was going. There was almost no one in the store. In fact the streets were almost empty. Someone showed him a Los Angeles *Times* "extra," and as he describes it, "the floor seemed to sink."

"This must be a mistake," he kept muttering to himself. "This can't be true." He hurried over to store No. 2 in the next block. It, too, was almost empty. But strangers were to be seen almost everywhere—tall, well-built men in dark suits who bore the stamp of law officers. Rumors flew from one store to the next—almost every prominent Li'l Tokyo merchant had been arrested by the FBI, a band of vigilantes was planning to burn down every shop on First Street, Japanese bombers were on their way to attack the Douglas aircraft plant in Santa Monica . . .

About 6 P.M. a pair of the tall men in dark suits came into one of the drugstores and flashed a badge. Sashihara expected to be arrested, but the officer said he was from the Board of Equalization. "You are ordered to withhold the sale of all intoxicating liquors until further notice," he said. Then, in a kindly tone, he urged Sashihara to lock up the store and go home.

A day of golf turned out equally as badly for Kiyoshi Patrick Okura, a personnel technician with the Los Angeles City Civil Service Commission. He had played 18 holes at the Lakewood Country Club with a group of *Nisei*. They heard the news as they came off the 18th green. Everyone rushed home without having their usual lunch together. Okura lived in the Wilmington harbor area. His car radio told him that troops already were patrolling key harbor spots and that the drawbridge between Terminal Island, site of a colony of *Issei-Nisei* fishermen, and Wilmington was under surveillance. At home Okura learned his bride of less than three months, Lily, and her sister Tomiko had gone to Terminal Island that morning to have their hair dressed. Okura telephoned the beauty parlor and instructed his wife to come home immediately. But when the women reached the drawbridge, Army sentries refused to let them leave the Island without some sort of clearance. Lily called her husband to report her predicament. Okura by now was almost frantic. He telephoned almost every Los Angeles official he could think of, and then it occurred to him that there was a federal prison and immigration office on Terminal Island. He reached his wife again and told her to seek help from the federal officials.

It was evening before the women were permitted to go home. They had been interrogated, photographed and fingerprinted. While at the federal facilities they had seen a number of fishermen and Japanese community leaders being brought in for detention. Many were family friends of the Okuras.

Okura had fallen into a troubled sleep some time after midnight when he was awakened by heavy knocks on both the front and back doors. "We are special agents of the Federal Bureau of Investigation," a voice shouted. "Open your doors." Okura also heard his father's voice asking that they be allowed to come in.

FBI agents had already visited the elder Okura's home. They had kept Pat's two younger brothers, two younger sisters and his parents in one room while they searched the house. They picked up letters from Japan and papers having to do with the activities of the Los Angeles Japanese Chamber of Commerce and the San Pedro Japanese Association. Then, because the elder Okura had been known to visit Pat frequently, the agents forced him to accompany them to the son's home. Pat Okura describes what happened after a group of FBI men burst into the house:

"Just as I was trying to get out of bed, a Los Angeles city policeman in uniform stuck a flashlight in my face and told me to stay put. I questioned his authority in Wilmington. He said he had been deputized as an FBI agent. While I remained in bed, shaken and angry, they went through all the dresser drawers, turning everything upside down. They said they were looking for documents that my father might have hidden in our house. They went through all our closets, opening boxes of wedding gifts that were still packed away, going through all the bookcases. Finally, when they could find nothing important, they allowed me to get out of bed and told me to instruct my father to pack a few clothes as he was to be held in detention."

Even more harrowing was the experience of Togo Tanaka, the *Nisei* editor who had gone to Washington to see what could be done to keep the *Rafu Shimpo* publishing in case of war. He was in the bathroom of his home in Glendale that morning preparing to shave when a friend on the staff of the Los Angeles *Examiner* telephoned to tell him all hell had broken loose at Pearl Harbor. Tanaka was in the *Rafu Shimpo* office within the hour. Less than twenty-four hours later he was arrested by the FBI armed with something called a "Presidential warrant." He was never charged with violation of any law, and the reason for his arrest was never spelled out in eleven days behind bars, first at the Central Jail, then the Lincoln Heights Jail, and finally the Los Angeles County Jail atop the Hall of Justice. During this period he was mugged, fingerprinted and questioned frequently by FBI agents but was not permitted to contact an attorney or get in touch with anyone, not even his wife Jean who was nine months pregnant with their first child.

"I was worried about my wife and sore as hell about what I considered an infringement on my constitutional rights as an American citizen," Tanaka says. "I kept wondering why I was being held, and nobody would tell me. I had written and signed many flag-waving patriotic editorials on behalf of the Stars and Stripes in the *Rafu Shimpo* English section. For years afterward I figured that a couple of my fellow *Nisei*, prominent in the national JACL and overzealous in their American patriotism, who took great pride in their close association with Navy intelligence officers, had bird-dogged a number of us whose pre-Pearl Harbor itinerary looked suspicious or confusing. I remembered, too, that I gave a talk to an Orange County service club just a couple of days before Pearl Harbor, and one of the daily papers ran a story about it saying that 'a Japanese editor' had predicted the outbreak of war. Hell, that was nothing new. Among the 81 people whom I met in Washington, I found 79 who definitely said that war was inevitable. You didn't have to be part of some insidious plot to know war was coming."

Tanaka's release was as sudden and unexplained as his arrest. On 30 minutes' notice on the 11th day he was told to get dressed, pick up his belongings and go home. Tanaka was in no mood to ask questions. He took the elevator to the lobby of the Hall of Justice and stepped out a free man. He was looking for a telephone so he could call his wife when he saw her standing by a phone booth. How she happened to be there at that moment is one of those weird, inexplicable things. No one had told her Tanaka was about to be released. She had just felt some mysterious urge to go to the Hall of Justice and look around, and so she had.

The Los Angeles Japanese community to which Tanaka returned was in confusion and chaos. Its solidarity had been its source of strength, but now the *Issei* leadership was gone, picked up in a series of swift roundups by FBI agents. The same was true in other communities. By 6 A.M. of December 8, 733 "Category A" Japanese nationals had been seized by the FBI on the mainland and in Hawaii. Within four days the number of Japanese detainees had climbed to 1,370. Before the program was completed, 2,192 Japanese enemy aliens plus a lesser number of Germans and Italians were to be arrested. Coast newspapers, from Seattle to San Diego,

Editors of the English section of the *Rafu Shimpo* in Los Angeles, Louise Suski (center) and Togo Tanaka (right), inspect last issue before the paper was closed down for the evacuation. (National Archives)

published pictures of bewildered, downcast *Issei*, dwarfed by their robust captors, being hustled into paddy wagons and booked by burly sergeants.

There were three reasons for the speed with which the Department of Justice moved. First was concern for the national safety. Incomplete reports—later proved false—from Honolulu told of widespread sabotage by Japanese residents, interference with defense traffic, even gunfire from civilian areas. The federal authorities did not know what might happen, and so they took no chances.

Second, they were afraid of danger to the resident Japanese in the hands of hysterical citizens or ill-trained local officials. An FBI directive notified all state and local authorities that "arrests and detention of Japanese aliens are to be made only through the FBI." The FBI's authority was a blanket "Presidential warrant," signed by Attorney General Biddle, authorizing the arrest of enemy aliens considered as a result of previous investigation to be "dangerous to the public peace and safety of the United States." Edward Ennis, chief of the Alien Enemy Control Unit, told Morton Grodzins while he was preparing *Americans Betrayed*, his authoritative book on the Evacuation: "We were jittery. We did not know what to expect. At the same time, we were afraid of vigilante action or indiscriminate arrests by local law-enforcement officers. Our policy was to act first and explain afterward."

The third reason was to assure the American public that even though the military had been caught napping in Hawaii, the home front defense against espionage and sabotage was secure and in good hands. The usually tight-lipped FBI saw that the arrests of Japanese aliens were liberally publicized.

Attorney General Biddle sought to assure both Japanese Americans and the general public with a statement that the federal agencies had the situation under control and urging understanding for loyal *Issei* and *Nisei*. "So long as the aliens in this country conduct themselves in accordance with law, they need fear no interference by the Department of Justice or by any other agency of the Federal Government," he said. "They may be assured, indeed, that every effort will be made to protect them from any discrimination or abuse . . . Inevitably, there are some among our alien population who are disloyal. The Federal Government is fully aware of the dangers presented not only by such persons but also by disloyal citizens. The government has control of the activities of these elements . . ."

No one found much comfort in the statement. Whites who were aware that the FBI had swooped down on the mild, inoffensive Japanese who had been running the corner grocery store for twenty years, couldn't help but think the worst of all Japanese. If the truck gardener who grew that beautiful lettuce, the friendly fellow who operated the cleaning shop, and the meticulous little gardener all had been picked up by the FBI, could any of the Japs be trusted?

And in the Japanese communities, Biddle's words had a hollow ring, for both *Issei* and *Nisei* knew that many of the men who had

been arrested had never harmed anyone, and never would. Some
had been sympathetic toward Japan in a sentimental way, or had
sympathized with Japan in the war against China, but most of them
would never lift a finger against the United States which would
have been their country if only it had seen fit to grant them citizenship.

Father Kitagawa writes of the *Issei* reaction: "Had their hearts
been more with Japan than with the United States, they would
have taken the FBI activity as quite justifiable and would have
endured it without complaint. Because they had so completely
identified themselves, in their own minds at least, with America,
they interpreted the action as hostile and as a betrayal of their
loyalty."

Those plucked out of the communities represented the first and
second echelons of community leadership. Most of those who had
been spared had never been in a position to lead; if they had, they
hardly dared raise their heads now for fear of being noticed by the
FBI. In panic, many burned priceless diaries, cultural books, letters
—anything linking them with Japan. Some lived in anxiety from
day to day, waiting for the knock in the night, the hand on the
shoulder, the appearance of the tall men in dark suits. Some packed
suitcases and waited fatalistically, and some of these men were disappointed and felt they had lost face—"Don't they think I'm
important enough to be picked up?"—when no one came for them.

In these circumstances the mantle of leadership fell by default
on the *Nisei* who, as a group, averaged barely eighteen years of
age. They were hardly ready to bear the responsibility. Today we
speak of a "generation gap" that defies understanding between
teen-agers and their parents scarcely two decades older than they.
In 1941, *Issei* in their fifties and sixties suddenly found themselves
removed from authority, and their places taken by their teen-age
children. The JACL was their only national spokesman. Inexperienced and naïve as its leaders were, the JACL was the only
organization the *Nisei* could look to for leadership. And the Federal
Government, which chose to look upon Japanese Americans as a
group rather than individuals, also found it necessary to turn to the
JACL. In retrospect, the wonder is that the communities averted
total disintegration.

Every *Nisei* old enough to remember what President Roosevelt called the "Day of Infamy" has vivid personal memories of what transpired, and after more than a quarter century many of those memories are still tinged with bitterness. Yet, much time has passed, a measure of which is the fact that *Nisei* men and women now in their middle years were too young in 1941 to grasp the significance of the event that shattered the world as they knew it. Nor are they able to recall details of the humiliation that followed. Jerry Enomoto, penologist with the California state prison system and national president of the JACL from 1966 to 1970, provides a case in point. He was a fifteen-year-old San Franciscan on Pearl Harbor Day. He recalls now that the outbreak of war was just another incident in his busy young life, that the curfew regulations were simply an inconvenience and the experience of evacuation and camp life was a ball.

It is not possible, unfortunately, to interview and record the stories of every *Nisei* in whose memory is seared a recollection of Pearl Harbor Day. Undoubtedly many of their individual experiences are more poignant, more moving, more touching than those whose stories are related in this chapter. Hopefully, someone will capture them in text or tape before they, too, grow dim.

16

THE UNHAPPY DAYS

NEWS of the Pearl Harbor disaster hit official Washington that lazy afternoon with stunning impact. Top government leaders rushed unbidden to their offices, doing what they knew had to be done, awaiting instructions and leadership from President Roosevelt. Among the earliest to react outside of the War and Navy Departments was Secretary of the Treasury Henry Morgenthau, Jr. In his first official action after the attack he ordered the Secret Service to double the guard at the White House. In his second order Morgenthau closed the nation's borders to all Japanese nationals and through his Foreign Funds Control Office, removed all licenses under which Japanese firms and individuals were doing business.

Of the various civilian departments of the Federal Government, Justice through the FBI had been the first to involve itself with the Japanese American minority after Pearl Harbor. Under authority provided by a Presidential proclamation, FBI Chief J. Edgar Hoover's office issued orders to execute plans drawn up in anticipation of this unhappy day, and special agents fanned out swiftly to round up enemy aliens who had been under surveillance for many months. The Treasury Department was only a half step behind. Officials of both quickly became aware, if they hadn't been already, of the ancient, smouldering anti-Japanese emotionalism of the West Coast that had been fanned into instant life by the outbreak of hostilities. It did not take long for that emotionalism to be felt in Washington. In the book *Years of War*, the third volume of the Morgenthau diaries, we find this passage:

". . . deep-rooted hostility to the Japanese generated frequent rumors about espionage and subversion and frightened demands for repressive treatment not only of local Japanese residents but also of *Nisei*, American citizens of Japanese descent. On December 10 some of the staff of Foreign Funds Control urged Morgenthau to take over thousands of small businesses owned by Japanese and *Nisei* in the area between the Pacific Ocean and Utah."

Morgenthau apparently thought the proposal was important enough to summon the FBI's Hoover to his office that evening to discuss it with him and two Treasury officials. That same night, perhaps by coincidence, a Treasury Department agent told West Coast military authorities that some 20,000 Japanese in the San Francisco metropolitan area were "ready for organized action."

"Without checking the authenticity of the report," the Army admits in its official history, *Guarding the United States and Its Outposts*, "the Ninth Corps Area staff (in San Francisco) hurriedly completed a plan for their evacuation that was approved by the corps area commander."

The Ninth Corps Area staff, thoroughly spooked, was jumping at shadows. The 1940 census shows a total Japanese population— men, women and children; the senile and bedridden as well as infants—of 12,644 in San Francisco and nearby San Mateo, Alameda, Contra Costa and Marin counties. But apparently no one on the staff bothered to check with Army Intelligence. The so-called "evacuation plan," which has never been made public, to be effective had to call inevitably for clearing of entire blocks at bayonet point, with troops hammering at doors in the middle of the night and families being rousted out of bed and herded into concentration areas. Fortunately, the order to execute the plan was never given.

The Army's official history tells us: "The next morning the Army called the local FBI chief, who 'scoffed at the whole affair as the wild imaginings of a discharged former FBI man.' This stopped any further local action for the moment, but the corps area commander duly reported the incident to Washington and expressed the hope that 'it may have the effect of arousing the War Department to some action looking to the establishment of an area or areas for the detention of aliens.' "

In his meeting with Morgenthau that night of December 10, Hoover argued that no further action against Japanese Americans was required at the time since his agents had the situation well in hand with hundreds of aliens considered potentially dangerous already in custody. Later, Hoover wrote a memo about the meeting to his chief, Attorney General Francis Biddle, reporting that Morgenthau had been in telephone conversation with one of his representatives in San Francisco, and that: "It was the opinion of Mr. X that there should be a roundup of the Japanese in San Francisco, Los Angeles and the Bay Cities . . . as well as certain sections of the San Joaquin Valley."

Morgenthau did not make a decision that night, but by next morning he had decided the proposal "was not only hysterical but impractical." His basic position was that moves to counter subversion and espionage were the responsibility of the Justice Department, and it behooved Treasury to confine itself to an interest in the financial affairs of any aliens of any country who were doing business in the United States. Morgenthau continues in his memoirs:

"Someone with 'some horse sense,' moreover, had to be sure that the Treasury was not preventing Japanese farmers from providing food for Los Angeles markets. Californians, Morgenthau said, 'were so hysterical they wanted the Army to go out and work the truck farms while they put the Japanese into a concentration camp.' He would have no part of that: 'We have just got to keep our feet on the ground.' "

When Edward Foley, the Treasury's general counsel, objected that it was no time to be thinking about civil liberties when the country was in danger, Morgenthau by his own account replied:

"Listen, when it comes to suddenly mopping up 150,000 Japanese and putting them behind barbed wire, irrespective of their status, and consider doing the same with the Germans, I want at some time to have caught my breath . . . Anybody that wants to hurt this country or injure us, put him where he can't do it, but . . . indiscriminately, no."

The charred wreckage of Pearl Harbor was not even cool and all the facts had not been tallied, but already a member of President Roosevelt's Cabinet was being pressured to seize *Issei* and *Nisei* businesses and lock up their owners and their families in concentration camps. Early news dispatches from Honolulu had repeated hysterical rumors of widespread acts of sabotage by resident Japanese coordinated with the aerial attack. These rumors were categorically denied by military and civilian defense officials weeks and months later, but the truth did not always catch up with the lies. The point of view expressed by Edward Foley was espoused by

For most Americans, caricatures of the enemy were easily and carelessly applied to the American-born Japanese and their parents. (National Archives)

many high officials and as we shall see, ultimately it was accepted by President Roosevelt. It is difficult to deny that this reflected unabashed racism. At best it was thoughtless racism. In retrospect, it seems likely that Foley and the other well-meaning individuals who thought as he did would not have been quite so willing to shelve civil rights had it meant restricting the freedoms of persons other than a faceless, powerless, relatively insignificant American minority which was of the same race as the enemy.

The *Nisei* were, of course, totally unaware of what was going on behind closed doors in Washington, but they were painfully cognizant of the need to improve their public relations. After the shock and numbness of December 7 had eased a bit—it was weeks before it could be said they had regained their emotional equilibrium—residents of the Japanese communities on the Pacific Coast hastened to repair their image scarred by a happening thousands of miles away. At this point the *Issei* were more realistic about their plight than the *Nisei*. The *Issei* could understand the inevitability of being treated as enemy aliens. But the *Nisei*, who had taken deep pride in their rights as citizens, were depressed and frustrated to find themselves being considered one with the enemy Jap. It was *their* country that had been attacked. It was *not* their country that had assaulted Pearl Harbor. Their experience having been what it was, they were realistic enough to see dark days ahead for themselves. Yet, not one in a thousand thought seriously that the time would come when their government would lock them up in concentration camps on the basis of race and race alone.

In seeking to analyze the reason why reaction against Japanese Americans was so intense, some observers have noted that Germany had Hitler and Italy had Mussolini, both figures that were easy to hate and easy to caricature. These caricatures could not be linked with German Americans or Italo Americans. But there were no such handy targets in Japan for America's patriotic ire. Tojo and Hirohito were virtually unknown to the American public. They had not appeared larger-than-life on American newsreel screens, ranting and posturing in front of phalanxes of uniformed henchmen. So an old stereotype was dusted off and the Japanese enemy pictured as a buck-toothed, bespectacled, monkey-faced sneak, a hateful racial canard that was easily applicable to the *Issei* and *Nisei*. Their racial homogeneity ("They all look alike to me," two generations of whites had complained without really trying to see individuals) made them perfect subjects for stereotyping. The physical characteristics of the Japanese made it simple to segregate them, just as with the Negroes. And in the stereotype mold, a *Nisei* instantly became a "Jap," no matter how many generations his family had been separated from the old country, no matter how wide the cultural and ideological gap that had been opened between him and his ancestral land. The caricature of the Japanese enemy was identifiable as the schoolboy, the vegetable farmer, the gardener and corner grocer in military uniform. Not so with Germans and Italians. Like other elements of the racial potpourri that is America, they come in many shades of white, in many suit sizes, their noses hooked or straight with their hair ranging from blond to darkest brunette. In the melting pot they quickly became indistinguishable. Morton Grodzins points out additionally that the German enemy (Nazi) and Italian enemy (Fascist) would be distinguished verbally from Germans and Italians in the United States, "but no such convenient nomenclature existed for the Japanese. In most public discussions both citizens and enemies were 'Japs.'"

Caught napping and humiliated at Pearl Harbor, albeit by a

Above and right, Burmashave sign read "Slap the Jap with Scrapiron, Burmashave." (National Archives)

dishonorable act, it was only human for Americans to point the finger of righteous anger at the treachery of the Jap in an effort to lighten the weight of their own culpability. And in an environment where anti-Oriental racism had been a seldom-questioned tradition—comparable to the Deep South's attitude toward Negroes —and a way of successful political life, it was inevitable that the racial stereotype should be projected onto the *Issei* and *Nisei* and their loyalty loudly challenged. On the West Coast this was as predictable as a knee-jerk is to the stimulus of a rap with a rubber hammer. There were whites who honestly believed they were helping to win the war by throwing a brick through the window of a Japanese grocery store or firing a shot from a speeding car into the home of a Japanese farmer; their mentality was little different from the sheeted and hooded night riders in the Deep South. After Pearl Harbor the *Issei* who had experienced the West Coast's racism feared the worst. The *Nisei*, too young as a group to be aware of the past, were less disturbed by the darkening clouds.

Their youth and immaturity was another key factor in the inability of the *Nisei* to stand up and be recognized as loyal Americans. Their parents for many reasons had kept largely to themselves and were little known outside their segregated communities. The *Nisei* had gone to school with white children, played ball with them, visited in their homes, but they were still strangers to the men in positions of authority and influence. There were too few *Nisei* like Tom Yatabe. Literally and figuratively, the *Nisei* had no Joe DiMaggio whose baseball brilliance all but obliterated the fact of his Italian immigrant heritage. No one would dream of suspecting Joe DiMaggio's father, much less the great Yankee Clipper himself, of disloyalty toward the United States even though the elder DiMaggio was an alien. (One small but significant point

needs to be made: Unlike the *Issei*, the elder DiMaggio had the privilege of naturalization. Up to 1941 he had not chosen to exercise it.) Yet the vast preponderance of *Issei* and *Nisei* were no less loyal than the DiMaggios, father and son.

The *Nisei* needed no prompting to demonstrate their loyalty, and Kido's telegram to President Roosevelt was only the start of a spontaneous, uncoordinated series of actions that were more notable for their sincerity than their effectiveness. In Seattle the JACL chapter formed an Emergency Defense Committee. Jimmie Saka-moto headed it for the simple reason that he was the first to see a need for such an organization and all other potential leaders were too busy with their own affairs. The committee quickly sponsored a community-wide loyalty rally at the Buddhist church. Mayor Earl Millikin, still free of the hostile pressures that were to weigh heavily on him shortly, was happy to address a crowd that packed the gymnasium and overflowed into the basement rooms and out onto the sidewalk. His audience, apprehensive at first, was relieved to hear a flag-waving speech expressing his faith in the American democratic system, and promising fair play. But within two and a half months Mayor Millikin was to have second thoughts. Appearing before the Select Committee Investigating National Defense Migration, better known as the Tolan Committee for its chairman, Congressman John H. Tolan of California, Millikin demonstrated he had been swept along by the rising clamor for evacuation. The good mayor confessed it was "utterly impossible" to weed out the dangerous ones among the people he had addressed as "my fellow Americans." And because of this inability to distinguish the good from the bad, he offered as the city's contribution to the evacuation program the services of the 500 horsemen of Seattle's "Cavalry Brigade" to lead every last Japanese American into exile east of the Cascade mountains.

In San Francisco *Nisei* were urged by their leaders to support the Hearst newspapers—those antagonists of long ago—in their widely publicized but largely unfruitful campaign to collect money to buy "bombers for Tokyo," and were duly photographed making their contributions. In Los Angeles the JACL chapter called a special meeting at which everyone fervently pledged his loyalty to the United States. An "Anti-Axis Committee" was organized with Tokie Slocum as chairman to ferret out "subversive activity," and this development was duly reported by local papers and the wire services.

Someone suggested it would make good publicity to get the Los Angeles County Board of Supervisors to join their *Nisei* constituents in signing a loyalty pledge. Masao Satow, who had known Board Chairman John Anson Ford through YMCA activities, was named to head a committee of three to call on the officials. The supervisors were more embarrassed than honored. Ford, who had—and has—an excellent civil rights record, said he was happy to vouch for Satow's loyalty because they were old friends, but he declined to be associated with the other two *Nisei* members of the delegation whom he did not know. In community after community *Nisei* made belated efforts to advertise their loyalty with rallies to which civic dignitaries were invited, with purchases of war bonds and donations of blood, with newspaper publicity about the extent to which *Nisei* had become assimilated into American life (the intended implication being that they couldn't possibly be disloyal), with statements condemning Japanese militarists and pledging fealty for the United States even unto death. Scores of *Nisei* volunteered for military service but they discovered, as the Kuroki brothers did, that suddenly they had become unacceptable to their country.

In one particularly ingenious publicity ploy, Ham Fisher, creator of the then popular Joe Palooka comic strip, was asked to work a *Nisei* GI into his story. Palooka, a somewhat simpleminded but clean-living, patriotic American had given up his heavyweight championship of the world to join the Army and it would not have been illogical for him to meet a *Nisei* at his training camp. Fisher graciously found reasons why this could not be done, but he drew a single panel in which Palooka recognized the loyalty of *Nisei* in American Army uniform, and the Seattle *Times* published it. Such efforts, unfortunately, were too little by far and much too late to do a great deal toward swaying public opinion.

The Treasury Department's blanket crackdown on aliens immediately following the outbreak of war had been applied indiscriminately in the case of Japanese against citizens and aliens alike. *Nisei* who went to draw money from bank accounts found their funds blocked for the reason that they had Japanese names. Purchase of food and other necessities became a problem almost instantly. In San Francisco Annie Clo Watson summoned heads of welfare agencies, outlined the problem and demanded assistance. Mrs. Eleanor Roosevelt, the tireless First Lady who served unofficially as the President's eyes and ears, happened to be passing through San Francisco. Only three days before the Pearl Harbor attack, on December 4, the New York *Times* had published a statement from her about the possible effects of war which she pointedly said had been cleared with the Departments of State and Justice:

"I see absolutely no reason why anyone who has had a good record—that is, who has no criminal nor anti-American record—should have any anxiety about his position. This is equally applicable to the Japanese who cannot become citizens but have lived here for 30 or 40 years and to those newcomers who have not yet had time to become citizens."

Now a *Nisei* delegation called on her to ask her good offices in getting funds, at least those of citizens, released. She promised to see what could be done. But no action had been taken when Mike Masaoka finally made his way back to San Francisco on Thursday, December 11. At Kido's bidding he got on the telephone once more to Senator Thomas in Washington and explained the problem. Precisely what Thomas was able to accomplish is unknown. At any rate, in a short while the Treasury eased its orders so that both *Issei* and *Nisei* could draw up to $100 a month for living expenses and most of their businesses were permitted to resume normal operations. In many instances, however, the thaw came too late to avoid costly losses. *Issei-Nisei* flower growers in California, for example, found many of their long-time customers had switched to other suppliers. With the Christmas season approaching, they couldn't afford to take a chance on losing a source of supply, and who knew what the government would do next? Workmen who had been trained over the years left their Japanese employers in fear that they would not be paid. Similarly fearful, suppliers demanded cash from Japanese customers whose credit record had been impeccable.

Tom Sashihara's experience was not untypical. While bank accounts were frozen he took home receipts from his three stores in Los Angeles and hid the money. Soon he had much more cash around the house than he was comfortable with. But let him tell the story in his own words:

"One day during the first week two federal agents came unannounced to my drugstore No. 1 and ordered immediate closing. Upon my exhortations and after much telephoning with their superior, they allowed me to pay $50 cash to each of my employees. The rest of the cash and all valuables were put in the safe, on which was placed a government seal.

"The agents also closed my store No. 2 and went right down the street closing all larger stores in Little Tokyo, one by one. On the third day they were about to padlock Kimura Brothers. Then a special dispatch came from Washington ordering them not to close any more stores, so Kimura and a few other fortunate ones down the street escaped. We were informed that reopening applications might be filed at the Federal Reserve Bank. It took three days of waiting in the corridor of the bank to obtain an application blank. The filing required more time and figuring than it took to fill out an income tax return. I kept on calling every day until the permit was issued on December 21 and the government agents broke the seals on our doors. When the stores were reopened the stagnant air mixed with the nauseating odor of spoiled food in the fountain was unbearable. It took a full day to put the store in shape. But I was thankful that we were allowed to open before Christmas, even though only three days of shopping remained."

Meanwhile the well-publicized FBI roundups continued amid periodic reports of suspicious activity. The press was filled with sensational revelations about mysterious goings-on. A flaming arrow pointing toward Seattle was reportedly touched off by fifth columnists in the wooded hills above Port Angeles. Tomatoes had been planted, the press reported, so they formed an arrow showing the way to a Southern California aircraft plant. The truth was that the "flaming arrow" was brush being burned by forest workers, and the tomato plants, capped with paper to protect them against frost, were planted in a field that came to a point. If one looked far enough, there were numerous other such tomato field "markers" pointing in every direction, even straight out to sea. The logical explanations, alas, were never as exciting as the original alarms and never attracted quite the same attention.

Other published reports had more substance but were equally misleading. The FBI announced it had seized a total of 2,592 guns from enemy aliens, 199,000 rounds of ammunition, 1,652 sticks of dynamite, 1,458 radio receivers, 2,014 cameras and other contraband items. Enough material to launch and guide a major insurrection! What was not explained until considerably later was that most of the guns were sporting weapons owned by persons who had every right to possess them, that much of the ammunition was picked up in sporting goods stores, that it was normal for farmers to have dynamite to blow up stumps on land being cleared. Attorney General Biddle eventually admitted that his men had been making searches without warrants in pursuit of fifth columnists, but they had uncovered "no Japanese saboteurs . . . and no illegal radio transmitter was found at all." He went on to say:

"We have not uncovered through these searches any dangerous persons that we could not otherwise know about. We have not found among all the sticks of dynamite and gun powder any evidence that any of it was to be used in bombs. We have not found a single machine gun nor have we found any gun in any circumstances indicating that it was to be used in a manner helpful to our enemies. We have not found a camera which we have reason to believe was for use in espionage."

Biddle's report was intended as a tribute to the preparedness of the FBI, but in effect it also absolved the *Issei*. But his words were heard and heeded by few. It was easier to remember all those guns and ammunition and dynamite the FBI had seized from those treacherous Japs. The public's apprehensions were whipped up even further when Secretary of the Navy Frank Knox, after a hurried inspection of Pearl Harbor and Honolulu, issued a report on December 15 that most segments of the press promptly interpreted as confirming earlier accounts of fifth column treachery on the part of Hawaii's Japanese population. Knox's official report made no mention of fifth column activity. In fact he praised Hawaiian *Nisei* who had rushed to man guns against the enemy. But in a press conference in conjunction with the release of his report, he was quoted as saying: "I think the most effective fifth column work of the entire war was done in Hawaii, with the possible exception of Norway."

In trying to keep customers and avert vandalism, owner of the Wanto grocery store in Oakland posted a huge sign. (National Archives)

Did he mean to say espionage—the kind of diplomatic spying that is an accepted part of international relations? Was the mention of "fifth column work" an unconscious slip of the tongue? If so, why was not the error corrected? Or was it an intentional slip calculated to whip up war fever and stir the national anger? These are questions that cannot now be answered, but Knox's statement was to come back to haunt the *Nisei* time and again as the first isolated cries for evacuation became a frantic chorus.

In its zeal the FBI was guilty of picking up some rather unlikely suspects. Take the case of Mrs. Tora Miyake, arrested in Portland. She was a frail, shy, middle-aged widow who owned a debt-ridden weekly Japanese language newspaper she had inherited from her husband. It was edited for her by an employee and she had virtually no control over its content. What little money the paper made was through its printing shop which she operated. To supplement her income she gave piano lessons and taught young *Nisei* at a Japanese language school. Several years before the outbreak of war she had gone to Japan to visit sisters she hadn't seen for more than twenty-five years, but was so disillusioned by her experiences that she cut short her trip. She had two adult children, a married daughter and a son in college. This hardly seemed to be the kind of background that made it necessary to arrest her as an alien dangerous to the safety of the United States. Friends who could never understand why the FBI seized her wondered if the similarity of her name, Tora, to that of her late husband, Taro, hadn't resulted in a ghastly error. Soon after she was taken into custody her son, Kenneth, quit school and enlisted in the U.S. Army where he served with distinction.

(Another case of confused if not mistaken identity is related by Yas Abiko, the San Francisco newspaperman whose father Kyutaro Abiko, had published the *Nichi Bei*. Kyutaro died in 1936. By strange coincidence, a Japanese named Kyuta Abiko published a newspaper, also called the *Nichi Bei*, in New York City. Perhaps because the authorities could not figure out the relationship, Yas Abiko was denied permission to enter states under jurisdiction of the Eastern Defense Command during the war.)

Meanwhile, the patriotic determination to win the war and avenge the perfidy of Pearl Harbor was being expressed in strange ways. Some hotels and restaurants fired their *Issei* chefs. *Issei* janitors were told their services were no longer needed. Railroads discharged *Issei* section foremen with service records unblemished for twenty or thirty years. Many municipalities cancelled business licenses to operate grocery stores, beer halls and cleaning shops. Some hospitals refused to accept Japanese patients. Each of these acts of misguided patriotism created a hardship. Many of the families of men seized by the FBI found themselves without funds. Japanese communities that had taken pride in avoiding the welfare rolls even in the depths of the Depression suddenly found many of their people in want. With *Issei* organizations decimated, JACL chapters took over in community after community, accepting contributions to be distributed to the needy, serving as a buffer between government officials and the *Issei*, operating as a clearing house for information. The Federal Government's several departments had many things to say to the *Issei* and *Nisei* but it had no line of communication. Metropolitan newspaper coverage of federal pronouncements was spotty and confused. Here again JACL stepped in. In San Francisco Kido and Masaoka gathered what information they could from federal officials. With the help of volunteers they cut stencils and mimeographed bulletins which were airmailed to JACL chapter officials up and down the Pacific Coast. In Northern California the Japanese newspapers had been closed down. In Southern California they were permitted to operate under federal supervision. Where there were no newspapers, local JACL leaders copied the bulletins from headquarters, had some of the information translated into Japanese and ran off their own mimeographed newsletters which were distributed door to door by Boy Scouts. With rumors thick in the air, authoritative information was necessary to prevent panic.

After Japanese language newspapers were closed down by federal authorities, there was no way to communicate with persons who read no English except by mimeographed bulletins issued by volunteers. Sadae Nomura examines a bulletin. (National Archives)

One of the most persistent rumors had it that all Japanese nationals—the *Issei*—were to be interned in concentration camps for the duration. Although no one could confirm the report and no one could trace it to its origins, it did not seem especially outlandish. After all the *Issei* were enemy aliens, and a goodly number of them were already under detention.

Then one day late in December, Kido had a caller. He was Fred Nomura, who operated an insurance business in the East Bay area. Nomura seemed to be deeply agitated. "Sab," he said, "I hear they're going to put all the Japanese in concentration camps. Do you know anything about that?"

"Who says so?" Kido challenged. He thought it was another wild rumor and was anxious to quash it.

"The chief of police in Oakland told me," Nomura said. "He told me everybody—*Issei, Nisei,* even the little kids—are going to be interned."

"He's crazy," Kido replied. "They can't do that to us. We're American citizens. We've got our rights."

17

THE RISING CRY

When one is born in America and learning
to love it more and more every day without
thinking it, it is not an easy thing to discover suddenly that being American is a
terribly incomplete thing if one's face is
not white and one's parents are Japanese of
the country Japan which attacked America.
—*John Okada in his novel,* No-No Boy

WE HAVE SEEN in the previous chapter that as early as December 10, 1941, three days after the attack on Pearl Harbor,
responsible Army officers were nearly panicked by a wild rumor
and drew up a plan overnight—literally—for immediate evacuation
of all Japanese Americans from the San Francisco Bay region.
Moreover, this plan was approved by the senior officer in charge,
the corps area commander, who was poised to put it into operation
in the dark of night. Apparently the nation was spared this horror
only by lack of time. With daylight the fearful apparitions vanished and cooler heads were able to take charge. That same night
a key member of President Roosevelt's Cabinet met with FBI
Chief J. Edgar Hoover to discuss a demand that businesses owned
by Japanese Americans be seized. At this stage, however, there
was no audible public outcry for mass security measures against
the *Issei* and *Nisei.*

Nonetheless, the man responsible for defending the West Coast
was deeply concerned about the possibility of civilians taking hostile action, particularly after the scare of December 10. Nine days
later, on December 19, the commander of the Western Defense

Command, Lt. Gen. John L. DeWitt, recommended in a memo to his superiors in Washington "that action be initiated at the earliest practical date to collect all alien subjects fourteen years of age and over, of enemy nations and remove them to the Zone of the Interior."

DeWitt's request must be viewed against the dark backdrop of Allied military setbacks. On the far-flung Pacific front the momentum the Japanese had built up in the attack on Pearl Harbor showed no sign of running out of gas. That Hawaiian base was still largely inoperative although men and supplies were beginning to arrive from the mainland in an encouraging stream. Guam had fallen and Wake was as good as lost. The Japanese had landed a large force in the Philippines and were advancing rapidly on Manila. Hongkong was under seige. In Malaya, Japanese bombers had sunk two of Britain's largest battleships with ridiculous ease and her troops were racing down the peninsula toward Singapore.

So impressively had the Japanese executed their military operations against objectives thousands of miles apart that an invasion of the United States mainland in force was not ruled out, and a hit-and-run carrier strike against the Pacific Coast was considered a serious threat. As late as February 21, 1942, when history shows that Japan had abandoned plans for all but sporadic harassing raids, Congressman John H. Tolan declared in San Francisco: "It is possible that the entire Pacific Coast may be evacuated. They tell me back in Washington that it is not only possible but probable that the Pacific Coast will be bombed. That has come to me from men who are supposed to know. So the evacuation may run into hundreds of thousands of people."

Although Tolan was unduly alarmed, the West Coast was particularly vulnerable. Nearly half the U.S. military aircraft output was concentrated in the Los Angeles area. Naval yards and port facilities from San Diego on the south to Puget Sound in the north were essential to the launching of any counterattack. The fleet depended heavily on oil pumped from California's coastal fields. DeWitt had the responsibility of protecting this coast and he did not have nearly as many men and weapons as he felt he needed. In fact, much of his manpower was being drained away to meet other urgent needs. He was understandably nervous about the presence of enemy aliens, especially in view of reports—later proved false—that hostile warships were cruising offshore, and he wanted to clear out potentially dangerous civilians as soon as possible. It should be noted that his memorandum proposed action against aliens of "enemy nations"; he did not specify which countries. And he made no mention of American citizens of enemy extraction.

Even so, he was talking about substantial numbers. According to the 1940 federal census, there were 126,947 persons of Japanese ancestry in the 48 states, and this total had not changed substantially by late 1941. Nearly all of them—112,353—lived in the three Pacific Coast States. Of this number 71,484 were citizens by birth and 40,869 were aliens denied citizenship by law.

In California alone, however, there were 51,923 Italian aliens—more than the total of Japanese aliens in the entire United States—and 19,422 German aliens. Except for a few late-comers they were aliens by choice for there was no law preventing them from seeking citizenship. In the city of Los Angeles, largest concentration of Japanese in the U.S., there were 17,528 German-born residents compared to 8,726 Japanese nationals.

While DeWitt made no distinction among the several enemy nations, he quickly learned there was little enthusiasm for removal of Italian and German aliens. He also learned there was considerable demand for lumping all Japanese—alien and citizen alike—in a single category. The official record shows that these Japanese were the subject of a lengthy telephone conversation on December 26 between DeWitt and Maj. Gen. Allen W. Gullion, Provost Marshal General in Washington. Gullion said he had been visited by a representative of the Los Angeles Chamber of Commerce who, the official U.S. Army History reports, "asked for a roundup of all Japanese in the Los Angeles area."

DeWitt firmly opposed such a move, and Gullion agreed with his stand. DeWitt expressed fear mass arrests "are very liable to alienate the loyal Japanese." He said that rather than intern men, women and children under military guard, it would be better if they were watched by the police and people of the communities in which they had lived for years. And he uttered these words which history has largely overlooked:

"An American citizen, after all, is an American citizen. And while they all may not be loyal, I think we can weed the disloyal out of the loyal and lock them up if necessary."

If DeWitt had maintained this stand, the recent history of Americans with Japanese faces would have run an altogether different course.

But he wavered.

His doubts grew under the pressures, the constant dinning of West Coast racists who warned that the Japanese by nature were treacherous, and because they were Asiatics they posed a special and far greater hazard to the nation than Germans and Italians whose white skins somehow made them less perfidious. It is reasonable to assume that deep in his awareness DeWitt had a fear of being caught off guard; it would be logical for him to reason that if the Japanese were as great a danger as they had been pictured, their removal from areas of his responsibility was justifiable regardless of cost or injury to principle, and it was his duty to see that this was done. DeWitt was not a moralist. He was not a profound man. He was a soldier; his mission in life was to defend his country. He had moved up the ladder of his career with the aid of good staff work—his aides provided him with information and he made his decisions on the basis of that information. The information he received about the Japanese, particularly that provided by important California civilian authorities who presumably were familiar with the issue, was ominous.

And so he changed his mind. He changed it completely.

By 1943, long after his command had uprooted every last Japanese from their homes in California and the western half of Oregon and Washington and shipped them off to inland concentration camps, he had achieved a 180-degree turn in his beliefs. He was able to appear before a congressional committee and utter these infamous words to justify his action:

"A Jap's a Jap. They are a dangerous element . . . There is no way to determine their loyalty . . . It makes no difference whether he is an American citizen; theoretically he is still a Japanese, and you can't change him . . . You can't change him by giving him a piece of paper . . ."

(The first sentence—"A Jap's a Jap."—does not appear in the official edited record of his testimony. However, it was played up in stories written by newspaper and wire service reporters who

Lieutenant General John L. DeWitt
He became a symbol of bigotry

covered the hearing. Grodzins observes: "This extraordinary statement followed not only the essential racial doctrine of the Third Reich, but almost the same figure and almost the same words as Adolf Hitler himself. In *Mein Kampf* Hitler mocked at the idea of giving German citizenship to a Pole, a Jew, an African, or an Asiatic.")

The general had dismissed citizenship as a scrap of paper even as *Nisei* volunteers in the same U.S. Army that he served were preparing for combat. And so among *Nisei* DeWitt became a symbol of American racism and bigotry and not one had a good word to say for him. It is difficult at this time, more than a quarter century after the event, to make unequivocal statements about the influences that caused the general to execute such an about-face. DeWitt is dead and cannot speak for himself. But there is merit in reviewing the record as set down by Stetson Conn, chief historian

Col. Karl R. Bendetsen
He drew up the blueprint for evacuation

of the Department of the Army, in the official publication, *Guarding the United States and Its Outposts*.

Conn tells us that by the third week of December the pattern of Japanese operations became known and "apprehensions" about an imminent and serious attack on the West Coast subsided. Reflecting receipt of this intelligence, DeWitt on December 31 notified his subordinate commanders that there was no longer any immediate danger of an invasion in force. Whatever danger remained from Japan, he said, was from the air.

DeWitt, however, continued to be worried about sabotage and espionage. He wanted the Justice Department to crack down on suspected aliens with spot raids. A meeting to work out effective measures was held between Justice and War Department representatives in San Francisco on January 4 and 5, 1942. DeWitt expressed concern with the alien situation, Conn reports, voicing particular distrust of both *Issei* and *Nisei*, but continued to oppose mass evacuation. Eventually the conferees agreed on a new program to register aliens, a step-up in FBI raids, and designation by the Army of strategic areas from which the Justice Department would be asked to bar enemy aliens. Among those attending the meetings was Karl R. Bendetsen, a graduate of Stanford Law School and at the time a major serving as chief of the Aliens Division of the Provost Marshal General's office. Conn says the proposal for the alien registration program and designation of forbidden areas came from Bendetsen.

Despite its plea of urgency, it was January 21 before the Army got around to designating eighty-six "Category A" zones in California from which DeWitt wanted enemy aliens excluded, plus eight "Category B" zones in which enemy aliens could remain only by special permission. The first two Category A zones included the San Francisco waterfront and the area around the Los Angeles Municipal Airport. Most of the other prohibited areas surrounded airports, dams, powerplants, pumping stations, harbor installations and military posts, encompassed no more than a few acres and in many cases were uninhabited. Nonetheless, some 7,000 persons would have had to be evacuated, more than half of them Italian aliens and about 40 percent Japanese aliens. The Category B areas would have affected some 28,600 Italians, 13,300 Japanese and 8,400 Germans. (It was not until February 3—nearly two months after the Pearl Harbor attack—that DeWitt designated restricted areas in Arizona, Oregon and Washington.)

The War Department took from January 21 to January 25 to approve DeWitt's recommendations and pass them on to the Department of Justice. Four days later, on January 29, Attorney General Biddle announced that Japanese, German and Italian aliens must leave the first two Category A zones before February 24. If removal of enemy aliens from these areas was a matter of compelling military urgency, the Federal Government's pace did not reflect it.

Meanwhile, voices which had been silent for nearly a month after the Pearl Harbor attack began to be heard, tentatively at first and then with mounting harshness. They charged that the continued presence of "Japanese" on the West Coast posed an intolerable danger because of patent disloyalty to the nation and demanded that drastic measures be taken. To support their demand they made wildly alarmist accusations that served to whip up the doubts and fears of an already nervous populace. The anti-Oriental racism, largely dormant since the Exclusion Act slammed the doors to immigration less than two decades earlier, was quickly whipped into life.

Grodzins, who made an exhaustive study of the California press, found that in the days immediately following Pearl Harbor many newspapers urged tolerance and understanding of Japanese Americans. But this was to change before long. Two nationally known commentators spoke out almost simultaneously. The first was Damon Runyon, the widely read and admired Hearst columnist. In his January 4 *The Brighter Side* column he wrote: "It would be extremely foolish to doubt the continued existence of enemy agents among the large alien Japanese population. Only recently city health inspectors looking over a Japanese rooming house came upon a powerful transmitter, and it is reasonable to assume that menace of a similar character must be constantly guarded against throughout the war." (Runyon was in error. No secret radio transmitter was ever found in Japanese American hands.)

The next day, January 5, a Mutual Broadcasting Company radio commentator in Los Angeles who had a program called "News and Views by John B. Hughes" began a series of almost daily broadcasts, the gist of which was that 90 percent or more of American-born Japanese were "primarily loyal to Japan" and that the Justice Department was neglecting its duty by failing to move vigorously against them. Grodzins says Department of Justice officials felt Hughes' broadcasts were to no small degree "responsible for arousing public opinion and flooding the California Congressional delegation with protests which had the tendency to push the government into hasty and ill-considered action."

Other voices swiftly took up the cry as the days passed until newspaper and radio commentators were baying like a pack of wolves on a hot trail, and about as susceptible to reason. A few samples will suffice. Syndicated columnist Henry McLemore demanded an immediate roundup of Japanese Americans and wrote: "Herd 'em up, pack 'em off and give 'em the inside room in the badlands. Let 'em be pinched, hurt, hungry and dead up against it . . . Let us have no patience with the enemy or with anyone

Multi-racial group of San Francisco youngsters pledge allegiance to their flag. Only those of Japanese extraction were evacuated. (National Archives)

whose veins carry his blood . . . Personally, I hate the Japanese. And that goes for all of them." Westbrook Pegler, Scripps-Howard columnist, told his readers: "The Japanese in California should be under guard to the last man and woman right now and to hell with *habeas corpus* until the danger is over."

Grodzins observes that once the trend started, "Except for a single friendly column by Ernie Pyle, another Scripps-Howard commentator, and a series of liberal articles by Chester Rowell, political writer for the San Francisco *Chronicle*, there were no newspaper columnists who expressed faith in the resident Japanese. Mr. Rowell was among the small group of persons who took a firm stand in opposition to evacuation."

In the Japanese American communities the *Issei* and *Nisei* viewed the rising tide of hate with dread. They felt abandoned, betrayed, persecuted. "We are Americans," the *Nisei* wanted to say. "We love our country. We know no other. We are not guilty of sabotage or espionage. We would do nothing to hurt America. We want to fight for America, and in this we are supported by our parents. Why do you accuse us of disloyalty?" But because they looked like the enemy, they found few who would listen.

If they looked to their elected representatives in Congress for help, the *Nisei* were sorely disappointed, for before long the most forceful demands for evacuation were coming from members of that august body. It was not that way at first. Congressmen Bertrand Gearhart and H. Jerry Voorhis of California and John Coffee of Washington read words of praise for Japanese Americans and pleas for understanding and tolerance into the *Congressional Record* in the days immediately following Pearl Harbor. On December 8 Congressman Coffee declared:

"It is my fervent hope and prayer that residents of the United States of Japanese extraction will not be made the victims of pogroms directed by self-proclaimed patriots and by hysterical self-anointed heroes . . . Let us not make a mockery of our Bill of Rights by mistreating these folks. Let us rather regard them with understanding, remembering they are the victims of a Japanese war machine . . ."

The plea made little impression on Congressman Leland Ford, representing Los Angeles county. One of his constituents was Leo Carrillo, the movie actor, and on January 6, Carrillo sent his congressman this rambling and sometimes ungrammatical telegram:

"Why not urge legislation to compel all Japanese truck farmers who control nearly every vital foot of our California coast line with their vegetable acreage to retire inland at a safe distance from the California coast which has been declared a combat zone. Mexico has done this as a precaution and to we Californians that seems good sense. Why wait until they pull something before we act. I travel every week through a hundred miles of Japanese shacks on the way to my ranch and it seems that every farm house is located on some strategic elevated point. Let's get them off the coast into the interior. You know and I know the Japanese situation in California. The eastern people are not conscious of this menace. May I urge you in behalf of the safety of the people of California to start action at once. Personal regards."

Only four months earlier, over the Labor Day weekend, Carrillo had addressed a JACL district convention at Long Beach. Being of Mexican origins, Carrillo said, he knew what it was to be persecuted and promised to help the *Nisei* fight discrimination.

Congressman Ford reacted immediately to Carrillo's message. That same day, displaying his ignorance about the functions of the various departments of government, Ford dispatched a letter to Secretary of State Cordell Hull demanding evacuation of Japanese Americans.

By mid-January Ford was peppering federal officials with demands that "all Japanese, whether citizens or not, be placed in inland concentration camps." Ford argued that if a *Nisei* were loyal to the United States, he should be willing to accept internment as "his contribution to the safety and welfare of this country." He contended this was a small sacrifice compared to that being made by "millions of other native born citizens [who] are willing to lay down their lives" in the armed forces, neglecting to say that nearly 5,000 *Nisei* also were in uniform. Ford followed up his letters with a speech in the House on January 20 and a radio address. He urged that mass internment of aliens and citizens alike was the "humanitarian way" because it would not break up families, and he argued that only the disloyal would oppose evacuation.

Ford quickly picked up the support of other West Coast congressmen, particularly after Attorney General Francis Biddle made it clear that until the writ of habeas corpus was suspended, he had no intention of undertaking mass internment of American citizens regardless of their ancestry. Aroused were deeply-ingrained suspicions that the Administration in Washington—any Administration—did not understand California's problems and moreover, did not want to. Congressman Clarence Lea, unofficial chairman of the California congressional delegation, mustered his forces behind Ford's campaign. At a caucus of members of Congress from the Pacific Coast, Senator Hiram Johnson of California, the senior lawmaker, appointed two subcommittees. Senator Rufus C. Holman of Oregon headed the group to study proposals for strengthening coastal defenses. Senator Mon C. Wallgren of Washington was named to chair the subcommittee to deal with the question of enemy aliens and prevention of sabotage. On February 4 these committees met with General Mark Clark and Admiral Harold R. Stark for a briefing on the military situation. Conn reports:

"General Clark said that he thought the Pacific states were unduly alarmed. While both he and Admiral Stark agreed the West Coast defenses were not adequate to prevent the enemy from attacking, they also agreed that the chance of any sustained attack or of any invasion was—as General Clark put it—nil. They recognized that sporadic air raids on key installations were a distinct possibility, but they also held that the West Coast military defenses were considerable and in fairly good shape; and as Admiral Stark said, from the military point of view the Pacific Coast necessarily had a low priority as compared with Hawaii and the far Pacific."

The legislators did not want to believe this. This high-level estimation of the military situation destroyed their contention that it was necessary to remove Japanese Americans from the coastal states because of the danger of invasion. So they ignored the testimony they had solicited when it did not meet their purposes. Wallgren's committee issued a statement recommending "the immediate evacuation of all persons of Japanese lineage . . ." How the committee reached this decision will be detailed later in this chapter.

General DeWitt, meanwhile, had been involved in a series of conferences on the evacuation question. On January 27, six days after he had approved the list of Category A prohibited areas, he had a long meeting with Gov. Culbert L. Olson of California who apparently impressed on the general the important political implications involved. DeWitt reported after their conference: "There's a tremendous volume of public opinion now developing against the Japanese of all classes, that is aliens and non-aliens, to get them off the land, and in Southern California around Los Angeles—in that area too—they want and they are bringing pressure on the government to move all the Japanese out. As a matter of fact it's not being instigated or developed by people who are not thinking, but by the best people of California." Parenthetically, it is interesting that DeWitt saw the *Nisei* not as citizens, but simply as "non-aliens."

DeWitt was right about the "best" people. Mayor Fletcher Bowron of Los Angeles, swept into office in a liberal reform movement, was making radio broadcasts declaring the Japanese "must go." He was opposed to the proposal for a permit system because it would damage the tourist industry. Bowron also called a meeting of Southern California newspaper publishers to hear John B. Hughes and urged them to stir up public opinion in favor of evacuation of all Japanese. Among others joining in the clamor were the California Department of the American Legion, the

Military Order of the Purple Heart, the Farm Bureau Federation, various produce growers' associations who had been bothered by *Issei-Nisei* competition, and such familiar pressure groups as the Native Sons of the Golden West and the California Joint Immigration Committee.

DeWitt continued to insist he was not seeking a mass evacuation program. He said he was concerned only with getting enemy aliens out of the sensitive Category A areas. He added: "I have made no distinction between an alien as to whether he is a Jap, Italian or German." The agitation to move *all* Japanese away from the coast, he observed, sprang from California civilians.

DeWitt also revealed that Governor Olson had some rather definite ideas about an evacuation program. He wanted to move both *Issei* and *Nisei* out of cities like Los Angeles and San Francisco and the coastal areas, but he didn't want to get rid of them entirely. He wanted to transplant them into the agricultural valleys of the interior for a very practical reason. This would enable California to maintain its important and lucrative agricultural production without importing large numbers of workers undesirable for other reasons, namely Mexicans and Southern Negroes.

In fact, Governor Olson had discussed such a proposal, although not in such frank terms, with *Nisei* leaders before meeting with DeWitt. Late in January he had summoned handpicked *Nisei* from various sections of California to Sacramento. Saburo Kido and Mike Masaoka represented the JACL. They had no idea why the governor wanted to see them. They did not know that other *Nisei* were to be at the meeting until they were ushered into Olson's office. Some two dozen *Nisei* were present, representing a geographic as well as occupational cross section. Olson reviewed the mounting demand for evacuation for all Japanese, professed his desire to help them in every way possible, then proposed what he described as a way the *Nisei* could silence their assailants while helping the war effort by producing badly needed food. As some of those at the conference understood it, Olson was suggesting a system of state-supervised concentration camps into which the Japanese would move voluntarily with their families, but during the day the men would be permitted to leave to work on farms, either their own or as hired hands. A number of the *Nisei* thought the proposal, in view

California's Gov. Culbert L. Olson
The *Nisei* didn't go for his proposal

of the dark uncertainties ahead, was worth considering. Others were outraged.

Kido, normally a mild-mannered man, reminded the governor sharply that the *Nisei* were American citizens entitled to equal protection under the law. "If you are so interested in our welfare," he asked, "why don't you give us the necessary police protection so we can remain in our homes? I consider it the responsibility of the state to safeguard its citizens."

This was a turn of events that Olson had not anticipated. The meeting broke up in turmoil with Olson complaining that the *Nisei* were ungrateful and uncooperative.

Up to this point it had been almost impossible for Kido and

Earl Warren, then California's attorney general
He charged *Nisei* were more dangerous than the *Issei*

Masaoka to believe that evacuation would take place. Olson's proposal opened their eyes. Back in San Francisco they talked late
into the night seeking answers to difficult questions. What could
the *Nisei* do to dramatize their loyalty and turn the tide of sentiment for evacuation? Would the Army accept an evacuation of
only strategic zones? If the *Issei* were ordered evacuated, should
the *Nisei* stand on their constitutional rights and try to remain
behind? Or would it be more humane to keep families together
and go along with the *Issei* to look after them? Should evacuation
be resisted physically?

Searching desperately for something to block evacuation, Masaoka came up with an idea for a "suicide battalion," to be made

up of *Nisei* volunteers, for combat against the Japanese. To guarantee their loyalty, they would leave their parents as hostages with the American Government. But military officials turned down the proposal saying it was not American policy to field segregated units except among Negroes, that *Nisei* troops in the Pacific would pose an identity problem, that there was no place for suicide units in American strategy and besides the U.S. was opposed to the concept of hostages. This idea was shelved almost as soon as it was born, but it was to be dusted off before too many more months passed and developed into the all-*Nisei* 442nd Regimental Combat Team whose military feats dramatized the loyalty of the *Nisei* as nothing else could.

Meanwhile, some high Army officers were becoming impatient with the slow progress of evacuation plans. They felt DeWitt would weaken the program if he accepted Governor Olson's plan to resettle the Japanese within California. And Bendetsen, in a memo to General Gullion, pointed out that evacuation of only the *Issei*—which DeWitt wanted—"would accomplish little as a measure of safety" since they were mostly elderly. Stetson Conn tells us:

"Colonel Bendetsen recommended the designation of military areas from which all persons who did not have permission to enter and remain would be excluded as a measure of military necessity. In his opinion, this plan was clearly legal and he recommended that it be executed by three steps: first, the issuance of an executive order by the President authorizing the Secretary of War to designate military areas; second, the designation of military areas upon the recommendation of General DeWitt; and third, the immediate evacuation from areas so designated of all persons to whom it was not proposed to issue licenses to re-enter or remain."

This, in essence, was the plan that ultimately was adopted. While it was being discussed, however, DeWitt's Category A and Category B plan was still in effect, and he was in the process of enlarging the prohibited areas to include all of Los Angeles, San Diego, the San Francisco Bay area, Seattle, Tacoma and Portland. Some 89,000 enemy aliens would have been affected, but only 25,000 would have been Japanese. There were, in fact, more Italian and German aliens than Japanese living in areas DeWitt considered critical to the national defense.

But to carry out such an evacuation program would have been

Secretary of War Henry L. Stimson
He got Roosevelt's permission

a political catastrophe. The Japanese were the intended target; regardless of the facts, they were the ones the public had been told, and the public believed, were dangerous. Besides, the Italians and Germans had far more political leverage. In Washington the War Department decided the time had come to take evacuation planning out of DeWitt's hands. Secretary of War Henry Stimson's diary shows that on February 11 he conferred with Assistant Secretary John J. McCloy and General Clark, after which a memorandum was drawn up for presentation to President Roosevelt. The memo took cognizance of rising sentiment on the West Coast and asked how far the President wanted to go regarding the evacuation of Japanese: Would he authorize the movement of citizens as well as aliens?

President Franklin Delano Roosevelt
"Be reasonable," he told his aides

Roosevelt, with direction of a global war on his hands, was too busy that day to see Stimson. Stimson then reached him by telephone and explained what the problem was. Roosevelt apparently felt the question was one that could be resolved without additional discussion. Stimson later recorded in his diary that the President "told me to go ahead on the line that I had myself thought the best." Roosevelt's only admonition had been: "Be as reasonable as you can." With the responsibility in his hands, Stimson made his decision. He ruled without further hesitation that it was necessary to evacuate both *Issei* and *Nisei* from critical areas.

In his book, *On Active Service in Peace and War*, published in 1947 with the cooperation of McGeorge Bundy, Stimson on page 406 says of his decision:

". . . mindful of its duty to be prepared for any emergency, the War Department ordered the evacuation of more than 100,000 persons of Japanese origin from the strategic areas on the West

Coast. This decision was widely criticized as an unconstitutional invasion of the rights of individuals many of whom were American citizens, but it was eventually approved by the Supreme Court as a legitimate exercise of the war powers of the President. What critics ignored was the situation that led to the evacuation. Japanese raids on the West Coast seemed not only possible but probable in the first months of the war, and it was quite impossible to be sure that the raiders would not receive important help from individuals of Japanese origin. More than that, anti-Japanese feeling on the West Coast had reached a level which endangered the lives of all such individuals; incidents of extra-legal violence were increasingly frequent. So, with the President's approval, Stimson ordered and McCloy supervised a general evacuation of Japanese and Japanese-Americans from strategic coastal areas . . ."

What Stimson ignored was the professional opinion of top Army and Navy commanders that by February there was almost no possibility of invasion. And before too many more years passed the political and moral climate in the United States was to be such that the Army, which in 1942 was ordered to remove citizens from their homes because of their race, would be called out again to defend at bayonet point the civil rights of a minority, namely the right of Negro children to attend desegregated schools in Arkansas in the face of "incidents of extra-legal violence."

As soon as Stimson made his decision McCloy telephoned Bendetsen in San Francisco. The words McCloy used were: "We have carte blanche to do what we want to as far as the President's concerned." The news was relayed to DeWitt who, two days later (February 13) airmailed a new recommendation to GHQ in Washington proposing for the first time the evacuation of American-born Japanese from the Category A areas he had established previously. For some reason this document was not received by GHQ until late afternoon of February 18. The previous day, however, General Gullion's Provost Marshal General's office had sent a confidential telegram to corps area commanders warning them that within forty-eight hours "orders for very large evacuation of enemy aliens of all nationalities predominantly Japanese from Pacific Coast" probably would be issued and asking how many they could house and feed. The evacuation decision had not been made public, but plans for implementing it were beginning to take shape.

News of possible evacuation made bannerlines day after day in West Coast newspapers, but was largely ignored elsewhere. Note that the word "Japs" was applied to both California residents and enemy in Java. (National Archives)

Meanwhile, the Justice Department continued to feel a mass evacuation was not necessary. In a memorandum to Attorney General Biddle, FBI Chief Hoover had written: "The necessity for mass evacuation is based primarily upon public and political pressure than on factual data. Public hysteria and, in some instances, the comments of the press and radio announcers have resulted in a tremendous amount of pressure being brought to bear on Governor Olson and Earl Warren, attorney general of the state."

On February 17, six days after Stimson made his decision, Biddle sent a detailed memorandum to the President. Its content and tone indicate that Biddle was not aware that Stimson had decided on mass evacuation with the President's blessing, or if he had heard unofficially, he was feigning ignorance. Because the memo is an excellent summary of the situation then existing, it is worth reproducing in entirety here:

"MEMORANDUM TO THE PRESIDENT

"For several weeks there have been increasing demands for evacuation of all Japanese, aliens and citizens alike, from the West Coast states. A great many of the West Coast people distrust the Japanese, various special interests would welcome their removal from good farm land and the elimination of their competition, some of the local California radio and press have demanded evacuation, the West Coast Congressional Delegation are asking the same thing and finally, Walter Lippmann and Westbrook Pegler recently have taken up the evacuation cry on the ground that attack on the West Coast and widespread sabotage is imminent. My last advice from the War Department is that there is no evidence of imminent attack and from the FBI that there is no evidence of planned sabotage.

"In view of the fact that you may be asked about it at your press conference, or may wish to say something about the steps being taken, I am supplying you with the facts.

"I have designated as a prohibited area every area recommended to me by the Secretary of War, through whom the Navy recommendations are also made. The less populated areas are already in effect and the remainder have been designated to be evacuated by February 24. I have also designated a number of restricted areas in which alien enemies may live only under rigorous curfew and other restrictions.

"We are proceeding as fast as possible. To evacuate the 93,000 Japanese in California over night would materially disrupt agricultural production in which they play a large part and the farm labor now is so limited that they could not be quickly replaced. Their hurried evacuation would require thousands of troops, tie up transportation and raise very difficult questions of resettlement. Under the Constitution 60,000 of these Japanese are American citizens. If complete confusion and lowering of morale is to be avoided, so large a job must be done after careful planning. The Army has not yet advised me of its conclusions in the matter.

"There is no dispute between the War, Navy and Justice Departments. The practical and legal limits of this Department's authority which is restricted to alien enemies are clearly understood. The Army is considering what further steps it wishes to recommend.

"It is extremely dangerous for the columnists, acting as 'Armchair Strategists and Junior G-Men,' to suggest that an attack on the West Coast and planned sabotage is imminent when the military authorities and the FBI have indicated that this is not the fact. It comes close to shouting FIRE! in the theater; and if race riots occur, these writers will bear a heavy responsibility. Either Lippmann has information which the War Department and the FBI apparently do not have, or is acting with dangerous irresponsibility.

"It would serve to clarify the situation in the public mind if you see fit to mention it."

Roosevelt did not see fit to mention it. The decision had been made.

Biddle's reference to Lippmann, a distinguished newspaper commentator, was regarding his column of February 12 in which he strongly advocated mass evacuation. Lippmann wrote a second column on February 20 in which he accepted Earl Warren's argument completely—that the fact there had been no sabotage on the Pacific Coast was "a sign that the blow is well organized and that it is held back until it can be struck with maximum effect . . ." In other words, he contended the fact that *Issei* and *Nisei* had *not* committed acts of sabotage was a sign of their disloyalty. Early in 1968, in response to an inquiry from Palmer Hoyt, editor and publisher of the Denver *Post,* Lippmann explained his position of 1942:

"I did indeed write the columns you speak about and I felt at the time great anguish at doing it. My reason was a belief that in the state of war hysteria after Pearl Harbor, Japanese who are easily identifiable by mobs, would not be safe. As there were continual threats, and rumors of Japanese submarines landing on the Pacific Coast, I felt that very great popular trouble might result. There is no doubt that the rights of the citizens were abridged by the measure, but I felt then, and I still do, that the temper of the times made the measure justified."

The same day that Biddle sent his memorandum to the President (February 17), Stimson met with McCloy, General Gullion, General Clark and Colonel Bendetsen, who had flown back from California, to discuss evacuation procedures. That night McCloy, Gullion and Bendetsen went to Biddle's home to confer with him. Also present were Tom C. Clark, later to become a Supreme Court Justice, who had been sent to the West Coast by Biddle to coordinate the department's alien enemy control program; James Rowe, Jr., assistant to Biddle; and Edward Ennis, chief of the alien enemy control unit. Biddle by then apparently had been apprised of Stimson's decision. Rowe and Ennis knew nothing of it. The conversation at first was concentrated on the possibility of evacuating enemy aliens under the program that DeWitt had proposed. Presently General Gullion read the draft of a proposed Presidential Executive Order which would empower the Secretary of War to evacuate both citizens and aliens from areas he would designate.

Grodzins reports: "Rowe was amazed. He actually laughed. He thought the matter absurd. His first impression, he said, was 'ridiculous'—the lawyer's impression that it was a very badly drawn order. But he and Ennis voiced full opposition and 'perhaps too strongly.' General Gullion became angry . . . Rowe was 'angry and hurt.' Ennis, as he made a last appeal for the individual examination of citizens, looked as if he were going to cry."

When Ennis and Rowe turned to Biddle for support, they found none. Biddle was willing to accept the decision of the President, and of Stimson. Twenty years later he was to write in his book: "If Stimson had stood firm, had insisted, as apparently he suspected, that this wholesale evacuation was needless, the President would have followed his advice. And if, instead of dealing almost exclusively with McCloy and Bendetsen, I had urged the Secretary to resist the pressure of his subordinates, the result might have been different. But I was new to the cabinet, and disinclined to insist on my view to an elder statesman whose wisdom and integrity I greatly respected."

And of Franklin Delano Roosevelt's reaction, Biddle wrote: "I do not think he was much concerned with the gravity or implications of this step. He was never theoretical about things. What must be done to defend the country must be done. The decision was for his Secretary of War, not for the Attorney General, not even for J. Edgar Hoover, whose judgment as to the appropriateness of defense measures he greatly respected. The military might be wrong. But they were fighting the war. Public opinion was on their side, so that there was no question of any substantial opposition, which might tend toward the disunity that at all costs he must avoid. Nor do I think that the constitutional difficulty plagued him—the Constitution has never greatly bothered any wartime president . . . Once he emphasized to me, when I was expressing my belief that the evacuation was unnecessary, that this must be a military decision . . ."

At this point let us return to the hallowed halls of Congress where the legislators in their wisdom were working out a recommendation in the national interest. Senator Wallgren's committee on February 10 agreed on a moderate resolution that recommended "the immediate evacuation of all persons, alien and citizen, from all strategic areas and that only such persons be permitted to remain or return to such areas as shall have been granted special license for that purpose." The resolution intentionally avoided naming the Japanese to avoid legal complications.

The West Coast delegation met three days later and rewrote the resolution to specify "the immediate evacuation of all persons of Japanese lineage and all others, aliens and citizens alike, whose presence shall be deemed dangerous or inimical to the safety of the defense of the United States from all strategic areas." The recommendation as adopted asked for evacuation from "the entire strategic area" rather than the entire states of California, Oregon, Washington and the Territory of Alaska as the Wallgren group had proposed. Grodzins explains:

"By specifically naming 'all persons of Japanese lineage,' the final recommendation satisfied the extremist group of the delegations. By omitting reference to a pass-and-permit system and by restricting the area recommended for evacuation, the final recommendation satisfied those who wished to avoid imposing hardships on business and social life of the Pacific Coast population."

Of all the legislators representing the three coastal states, only Senator Sheridan Downey and Congressman Voorhis of California and Congressman Coffee of Washington spoke up to express doubt as to the necessity of evacuation, but in time they were worn down by Congressman Ford's violent, shouted attacks. In Congress itself, the California position won vigorous support from three Southerners, Senator Tom Stewart of Tennessee and Representatives John Rankin of Mississippi and Martin Dies of Texas. All three were outspoken white supremacists and found it easy to shift their contempt and hatred of the Negro to the Japanese, particularly Rankin and Stewart. A few choice quotations from their speeches, duly recorded in the *Congressional Record,* should be edifying:

Senator Stewart: "They [the Japanese] are cowardly and immoral. They are different from Americans in every conceivable way, and no Japanese . . . should have the right to claim American citizenship . . . A Jap is a Jap anywhere you find him, and his taking the oath of allegiance to this country would not help, even if he should be permitted to do so. They do not believe in God and have no respect for an oath . . ."

Congressman Rankin: "This is a race war . . . The white man's civilization has come into conflict with Japanese barbarism . . . I say it is of vital importance that we get rid of every Japanese whether in Hawaii or on the mainland . . . Damn them! Let us get rid of them now!"

Both Rankin and Stewart argued that American-born offspring of Japanese "are not citizens of the United States and never can be." Senator Stewart could see no sense in recognizing citizenship because of "the mere accident of birth on American soil," and of "those whose parents could not themselves become naturalized."

Grodzins observes: "The Southern trio—Dies, Rankin and Stewart—were the only members of Congress outside the Pacific Coast delegations to show an appreciable interest in fostering the Japanese evacuation. If the group from the three Western states thus received only limited support, the more pertinent comment is that they received no opposition. The truth of the matter was that the vast majority of the nonwestern Congressmen and Senators were unacquainted with the Japanese problem or simply uninterested in it . . .

"For the Western members, the animus held by large segments of the general population against resident Japanese made evacuation a popular political issue . . . Evacuation was pleasing not only to the powerful economic groups who had long wished to put an end to the competition of American Japanese and not only to that large group who confused racial similarity with political allegiance and who viewed the 'yellow menace' in biological, rather than military, terms. The war added a new and all-important group: evacuation was also pleasing, or at least not displeasing, to the large numbers who were genuinely concerned with fifth-column rumors, the magnitude of the attack on Pearl Harbor, and the continuing successes of the Japanese enemy in South Pacific areas . . .

"The necessity for protecting coastal areas, the widespread hostility toward resident Japanese, racial animus, economic cupidity, fears of attack and apprehension over the growing victories of the enemy—these factors became so intertwined that their separation was impossible. Yet they all had the common feature of pushing in the direction of evacuation. And the political representatives of the Western states reflected these one-way pressures."

Even so, the War Department was ahead of Congress. It was February 13 when the West Coast delegation sent their recommendations for evacuation to President Roosevelt. Stimson had made his decision two days earlier. It was on February 18 that Rankin stood on the floor of the House to join in bitter invective against the government's delay in taking drastic action against Japanese Americans. But the decision for such action had been finalized in that memorable meeting in Biddle's home the night before.

18

A FAULTY DIAGNOSIS

THE DOCUMENT known as Executive Order 9066 was placed on President Roosevelt's desk on February 19, 1942. The order gave the Secretary of War the authority to designate certain "military areas" and to exclude "any or all" persons from them. This was the authority that Secretary Stimson had sought to remove Japanese aliens as well as citizens of Japanese blood from the West Coast. President Roosevelt had endorsed this proposal in principle. The Army lawyers who composed the formal authorization realized there was a very good chance the Supreme Court would find it unconstitutional. So they couched the order in the broadest of terms to avoid the charge that it was a discriminatory measure directed at persons of a specific race.

The day that President Roosevelt received the document was the seventy-fourth since the attack on Pearl Harbor; two months and twelve days had sped by. What had been feared in the early days of December had not come to pass; the Japanese had ventured no farther to the east after the strike that had launched the war. Even to armchair strategists it was evident that the Pearl Harbor attack was a hit-and-run effort to cripple the American fleet and destroy its principal base, after which the thrust of Japanese aggression was turned in the opposite direction. As costly as the Pearl Harbor attack had been for the United States, it had not achieved the results Japan had sought, for the U.S. carrier fleet was still intact. Nonetheless, Japan had directed the full force of conquest at Southeast Asia and the far Southwest Pacific, not the American mainland. By February 19, Manila, Hongkong and much of the Dutch East Indies were in Japanese hands. Singapore had been lost

Representative Francis E. Walter
He helped correct immigration inequities

just four days earlier, and it was evident that Burma soon would be captured. It was a time for action rather than introspection. So Franklin Delano Roosevelt signed Executive Order 9066 the same day he received it, indicating that he was familiar with its content and approved its purpose, or if this was not so, that he paid scant heed to its implications.

For the 110,000 persons of Japanese ancestry who were uprooted from their homes as the primary consequence of Roosevelt's action, his decision could not have been more important. Yet, even though their future was clearly charted by the act of signing Executive Order 9066, to the *Issei* and particularly *Nisei* evacuation still seemed to be an impossibility. Such a thing could not happen in America; it was a hideous nightmare that would vanish with the dawn.

Their hopes were buoyed when it was announced that a congressional committee, headed by Representative John H. Tolan of California, would hold a series of hearings "to inquire further into the interstate migration of citizens," and to look into the "problems of evacuation of enemy aliens and others from prohibited military zones."

Congressman John H. Tolan
His committee provided a podium

Thoughtful *Nisei* knew that the power to evacuate "any or all" in the interests of military security had been provided by Executive Order 9066. But no action had been announced. And so, their vision clouded by a large measure of wishful thinking, they believed that the findings of the Tolan Committee would have a large part in determining the government's policy. Up to this point hardly anyone in authority had listened to *Nisei* protestations of loyalty and innocence. Now the Tolan Committee was inviting them to speak. At last here was someone who would listen, and a forum in which to be heard. All along the coast *Nisei* leaders prepared feverishly to make their case and asked their friends—ministers, sociology professors, social workers, business associates—to appear and put in a good word for them.

The hearings opened in San Francisco on February 21. (Almost unnoticed the previous day, Stimson had designated DeWitt to carry out Executive Order 9066.) The testimony of the initial witnesses quickly set the tone for the balance of the hearings. Mayor Angelo J. Rossi was the first to speak.

Rossi pointed out the "seriousness of having alien enemies in our midst." He said the measures already taken against enemy aliens "have caused great anxiety and distress among this group of people," causing dislocation of families and loss of livelihood. But, he went on, "the great majority of non-citizens in this area is made up of elderly men and women whom I believe for the most part to be industrious, peaceful and law-abiding residents of this community. Most of them have native-born children. Many of them have sons in the armed forces and both sons and daughters engaged in defense industries and civilian defense activities. It is the well-considered opinion of many that most of these people are entirely loyal to this nation; are in accord with its form of government, believe in its ideals and have an affection for its traditions and that under no circumstances would they engage in any subversive activities or conduct.

"It has been said that the measures which are proposed to be taken against these aliens, instead of making for national solidarity and unity of effort in this emergency may cause dissatisfaction and resentment among those of alien parentage . . ."

So far, so good.

Then Rossi uttered the disclaimer that was to be heard again and again throughout the hearings. "In my opinion the above-mentioned facts apply particularly to the German and Italian alien problems. Their problems should be considered separately from those of the Japanese. The Japanese situation should be given immediate attention. It admits of no delay. The activities of the Japanese saboteurs and fifth columnists in Honolulu and the battle fronts in the Pacific have forced me to the conclusion that every Japanese alien should be removed from this community. I am also strongly of the conviction that Japanese who are American citizens should be subjected to a more detailed and all-encompassing investigation. After investigation, if it is found that these citizens are not loyal to this country, they, too, should be removed from the community."

Mayor Rossi was arguing that Italian and German aliens should be less suspect than Japanese aliens and their American-born offspring.

Why?

Because Italians and Germans are white, and the Japanese are of another race. Mayor Rossi was too intelligent to put it in such bald language, but the implication was clear.

California Attorney General Earl Warren, later to become an outstanding champion of civil rights as Chief Justice of the United States Supreme Court, was the next principal witness. His testimony, including a detailed written statement, covers fifty printed pages in the committee's published report. Warren went to considerable lengths to point out that Japanese farmers were clustered around a vast array of strategic installations—aircraft plants, airports, highways, dams, pumping stations, military bases, bridges, power lines and the like. When Congressman Laurence F. Arnold of Illinois asked if "it just couldn't have happened that way," Warren replied: "We don't believe that it could in all of these instances, and knowing what happened at Pearl Harbor and other places, we believe that there is a pattern to these land ownerships in California . . ." No one embarrassed the attorney general by pointing out that many of the areas had been wilderness when Japanese immigrants cleared the brush and leveled the land for farms—long before highways, military camps, power lines and the Wright brothers had appeared on the scene.

Warren also made much of the inscrutable Oriental who had baffled Californians for half a century, and fired a slanderous broadside at the *Nisei:* "I want to say that the consensus of opinion among the law-enforcement officers of this state is that there is more potential danger among the group of Japanese who are born in this country than from the alien Japanese who were born in Japan." When Congressman Arnold asked if there were any way of distinguishing between the loyal and disloyal, Warren replied: "We believe that when we are dealing with the Caucasian race we have methods that will test the loyalty of them, and we believe that we can, in dealing with the Germans and the Italians, arrive at some fairly sound conclusions because of our knowledge of the way they live in the community and have lived for many years. But when we deal with the Japanese we are in an entirely different field and we cannot form any opinion that we believe to be sound."

A few moments after he admitted there had been no sabotage and no fifth column activity in California, Warren charged that there were no informers among the Japanese to report "subversive activities or any disloyalty to this country." Then he indulged in an astonishing bit of logic in which he had the active support of the Congressmen. The following is taken directly from the Tolan Committee report:

"Attorney General Warren: . . . To assume that the enemy has not planned fifth column activities for us in a wave of sabotage is simply to live in a fool's paradise . . . I am afraid many of our people in other parts of the country are of the opinion that because we have had no sabotage and no fifth column activities in this State since the beginning of the war, that means that none have been planned for us. But I take the view that this is the most ominous sign in our whole situation. It convinces me more than perhaps any other factor that the sabotage that we are to get, the fifth column activities that we are to get, are timed just like Pearl Harbor was timed and just like the invasion of France, and of Denmark, and of Norway, and all those other countries. I believe that we are just being lulled into a false sense of security and that the only reason we haven't had disaster in California is because it has been timed for a different date, and that when that time comes if we don't do something about it it is going to mean disaster both to California and to our nation. Our day of reckoning is bound to come in that regard. When, nobody knows, of course, but we are approaching an invisible deadline.

"The Chairman (Tolan): On that point, when that came up in our committee hearings there was not a single case of sabotage reported on the Pacific coast, we heard the heads of the Navy and the Army, and they all tell us that the Pacific coast can be attacked. The sabotage would come coincident with that attack, would it not?

"Attorney General Warren: Exactly.

"The Chairman: They would be fools to tip their hands now, wouldn't they?

"Attorney General Warren: Exactly . . ."

There is no reason to believe Warren and Congressman Tolan

were other than sincere in their fears. They were so completely convinced in their minds that the Japanese in California were disloyal, they could rationalize that the fact nothing had happened was proof that something terrible surely would come to pass. The temper and hysterical pressure of the time was such that few dared to challenge their astonishing logic, a curiously distorted logic hardly calculated to prove an endorsement for the post of Chief Justice of the United States.

The suspicion is inescapable that politicians like Warren, Congressman Tolan and Governor Olson, being familiar with the history of California's discrimination against the Japanese, simply could not understand why they shouldn't be disloyal. Hostility toward their persecutors would have seemed to be the natural and inevitable reaction.

Mike Masaoka, representing the JACL, was the first *Nisei* to appear before the committee. He did not receive the prompting from the Congressmen that Warren had enjoyed. Rather, he was questioned sharply. Apparently Masaoka was the first *Nisei* several of the Congressmen had ever encountered. They indicated surprise that he spoke English so well, and were surprised again when he said he could not read, write or speak Japanese. The Congressmen had heard that *Nisei* had attended Japanese language schools where they learned loyalty to the Emperor. Masaoka said he had never attended Japanese schools. The Congressmen had heard that many *Nisei* had been educated in Japan. Masaoka said he had never been there. The Congressmen had heard that many Japanese were Buddhists or embraced Shinto, which they believed to be proof per se of disloyalty. When Masaoka was questioned about his religion he said he and several members of his family were Mormons, while others in the family were Presbyterians.

Appearing together with Masaoka were Henry Tani, executive secretary of the San Francisco JACL chapter, and Dave Tatsuno, the chapter president. Both were subjected to the same line of questioning as Masaoka. Tani said he had been born in San Francisco, received his degree from Stanford University, had never been to Japan, had attended Japanese language school for one year when he was six years old, that he was a member of the Evangelical and Reformed Church, and felt no allegiance whatsoever to the Japanese government. Tatsuno testified he had been to Japan for six months when he was ten years old, was an American college graduate and an elder in the Presbyterian Church. The nature of the questioning showed the Congressmen were surprised, but not convinced that these witnesses with Japanese faces were really as free of Japanese influence as they seemed to be.

Over the years JACL and Masaoka have been accused of failing to oppose the evacuation strongly enough, of agreeing too readily to cooperate in the government's evacuation plans, in short, of selling the *Nisei* down the river. In view of these charges, the significant portion of Masaoka's prepared statement presented to the Tolan Committee as the position of the JACL, is reproduced here for the record. Speaking on behalf of "the 20,000 American citizen members of the 62 chapters of the Japanese American Citizens League," Masaoka said:

"When the President's recent Executive Order was issued, we welcomed it as definitely centralizing and coordinating defense efforts relative to the evacuation problem. Later interpretations of the order, however, seem to indicate that it is aimed primarily at the Japanese, American citizens as well as alien nationals. As your committee continues its investigations in this and subsequent hearings, we hope and trust that you will recommend to the proper authorities that no undue discrimination be shown to American citizens of Japanese descent.

"Our frank and reasoned opinion on the matter of evacuation revolves around certain considerations of which we feel both your committee and the general public should be apprised. With any policy of evacuation definitely arising from reasons of military necessity and national safety, we are in complete agreement. As American citizens, we cannot and should not take any other stand. But, also, as American citizens believing in the integrity of our citizenship, we feel that any evacuation enforced on grounds violating that integrity should be opposed.

"If, in the judgment of military and federal authorities, evacuation of Japanese residents from the West Coast is a primary step toward assuring the safety of this nation, we will have no hesitation in complying with the necessities implicit in that judgment. But if, on the other hand, such evacuation is primarily a measure whose surface urgency cloaks the desires of political or other pressure groups who want us to leave merely for motives of self-

interest, we feel that we have every right to protest and to demand
equitable judgment on our merits as American citizens."

The statement was clear enough. If the United States declared
evacuation was a military necessity, the *Nisei* would have no choice
but to accept it. This is a point that none of the *Nisei* witnesses
challenged. But Secretary Stimson already had declared evacuation
was necessary to the national defense. The Tolan Committee hearings could not affect the decision in any way. In this sense the
hearings were a sham, a forum for expression of opinions and
prejudices, for the voicing of pleas for justice as well as the cries
of bigotry, none of which could have any effect on the issue.

Yet it was important that the public be heard, pro and con. The
Tolan Committee, like a traveling medicine show, moved from San
Francisco to Portland to Seattle to Los Angeles and back to San
Francisco. The hearings were concluded on March 12, and the
testimony taken was printed in three booklets totaling 965 pages.
The hearings were only half completed when, on March 1, General
DeWitt issued Proclamation No. 1 designating the western half of
California, Oregon and Washington and the southern third of
Arizona as military areas from which all persons of Japanese an-
cestry eventually would be removed. One day before the hearings
ended—March 11—DeWitt established the Wartime Civil Control
Administration with Colonel Bendetsen as director, to carry out
the evacuation program.

The San Francisco hearings established a pattern that was followed in each of the other cities. Municipal and county officials,
local peace officers, members of the Joint Immigration Committee
in California stirring the ashes of old campaigns, veterans' groups,
chambers of commerce, representatives of floral and agricultural
organizations competing with the Japanese, even service clubs (the
Downtown Seattle Kiwanis Club, for one) added their voices to
the demand that all Japanese be evacuated. Federal agricultural and
labor officials testified briefly on the effect evacuation of Japanese
would have on the local situation. And spokesmen for the *Nisei*,
joined by ministers, college professors and sometimes by CIO labor
leaders, argued *Nisei* loyalty and pleaded for justice.

The demands for mass evacuation of all Japanese fell into four
general categories:

First, they stressed the danger of sabotage, espionage and fifth column activity by the Japanese and the need for removing this potential from a war zone.

Second, they argued for mass evacuation because of supposed inability to distinguish the loyal from the disloyal.

Third, a large part of the testimony was devoted to declaring that evacuation of Japanese would not be detrimental to the economy of the West Coast.

Fourth, mass evacuation was urged as a humanitarian measure to keep families together, to protect them from vigilante action, and as an opportunity for the *Nisei* to demonstrate their loyalty by accepting incarceration.

Let us examine each of these arguments briefly.

First, the danger of hostile activity. Time and again witnesses charged that the Japanese were guilty of sabotage in Hawaii during the attack on Pearl Harbor, and cited the danger of the same thing happening on the mainland if it were bombed or invaded. Even members of the committee threw this charge at *Nisei* witnesses who spoke of their loyalty. "What about your people at Pearl Harbor? Did they remain loyal Americans?" Congressman Tolan challenged Masaoka in San Francisco. "There are authentic pictures during the attack showing hundreds of Japanese old automobiles cluttered on the one street of Honolulu so the Army could not get to the ships. Are you conversant with those things?" And in Seattle, Congressman Arnold lectured Jimmie Sakamoto: "Of course, you probably recognize that if the Japanese in Honolulu and Hawaii had not conducted themselves as they did on December 7, that perhaps such drastic action would not be thought of in this area of the United States at this time." Sakamoto asked: "Do I understand from that, that the Americans of Japanese ancestry in Hawaii did not contribute loyally toward the defense effort on that day, at the time of the attack?" Congressman Arnold replied: "Well, there is a good deal of evidence to that effect, yes."

The *Nisei* on the mainland, as well as the general public, had no information to contradict the Congressmen. They had to assume members of Congress knew what they were talking about. But the facts are that the Congressmen and others who repeated as truth rumors of fifth column activity in Hawaii were wrong. Many weeks later, much too late to prevent the evacuation, officials in a position to know categorically denied the accusations. In response to an inquiry by Congressman Tolan, Secretary of War Stimson wrote: "The War Department has received no information of sabotage committed by Japanese during the attack on Pearl Harbor." Here are some other responses:

"Mr. John Edgar Hoover, director of the Federal Bureau of Investigation, has advised me there was no sabotage committed there (in Hawaii) prior to December 7, on December 7, or subsequent to that time."—James Rowe, Jr., assistant to the attorney general.

"There were no acts of sabotage in the city and county of Honolulu December 7, nor have there been any reported to the police department since that date."—W. A. Gabrielson, Honolulu chief of police.

"There have been no known acts of sabotage, espionage or fifth column activity committed by the Japanese in Hawaii either on or subsequent to December 7, 1941."—Col. Kendall J. Fielder, chief of military intelligence, Hawaii Department.

So thoroughly were the rumors implanted, however, that even today there are many Americans still convinced that some Japanese in Hawaii guided enemy planes to Pearl Harbor by cutting arrows in sugar cane fields, blocked traffic to delay rescue efforts, set fires and otherwise sabotaged the defense effort. Nothing like this ever took place. In fact, many Japanese Americans were cited for rushing to the defense of Hawaii.

On the mainland, as we have seen, even California's Attorney General Warren conceded that there had been no fifth column activity, an admission confirmed by General DeWitt. But they saw this as an ominous sign rather than a reassuring one.

DeWitt also charged that "for a period of several weeks following December 7, substantially every ship leaving a West Coast port was attacked by an enemy submarine. This seemed conclusively to point to the existence of hostile shore-to-ship communication."

Here again DeWitt was either misinformed, or speaking loosely in an effort to reinforce the argument for evacuation. Stetson Conn tells us in his official history that nine Japanese submarines arrived off the West Coast about December 17 and remained about a week. Only four of the subs made attacks and they sank two tankers and damaged one freighter off California. During the same period dozens of Allied ships were being sunk by German submarines in the western Atlantic. The Army's complaints about suspicious radio transmissions were investigated by the Federal Communications Commission's monitors, using highly sophisticated stationary and mobile equipment. A total of 760 reports were investigated, and in 641 cases it was found no radio signals were involved. In the remaining 119 investigations, 21 were found to be legal transmissions from U.S. Army stations, 8 from U.S. Navy stations, 12 from local police stations, 65 from U.S. and foreign commercial licensed stations, 3 were short-range transmissions emanating from home record players, and 10 from Japanese stations in Japanese territory!

Chairman James L. Fly of the FCC wrote the Attorney General: "There were no radio signals reported to the Commission which could not be identified, or which were unlawful. Like the Department of Justice, the Commission knows of no evidence of any illicit radio signaling in this area during the period in question." Fly complained bitterly about the "lack of training and experience" of military monitors. "Frankly, I never have seen an organization that was so hopeless to cope with radio intelligence requirements," he said. "They take bearings with loop equipment on Japanese stations in Tokyo . . . and report to their commanding officers that they have fixes on Jap agents operating transmitters on the Pacific Coast. These officers, knowing no different, pass it on to the General and he takes their word for it. It's pathetic to say the least."

It was more than pathetic; it was tragic. Fly's report was not made public until long after the evacuation was carried out. DeWitt's charges were widely circulated and an unfortunate coincidence provided what seemed to be the stamp of authenticity to what he was saying. On February 23, a submarine shelled oil installations at Goleta, near Santa Barbara, California, but fled after a few ineffective salvos. It was the only Japanese attack on the American mainland while the *Issei* and *Nisei* were at liberty. But it took place twelve days after Secretary Stimson received President Roosevelt's approval for evacuation; it could not have entered into deliberations as to the military necessity of evacuation. There were only two other Japanese attacks on the mainland. On June 20, 1942, fifteen days after the last person of Japanese ancestry who lived on the West Coast was in detention, a submarine shelled shore batteries near Astoria, Oregon. And on September 9, 1942, three months after the Japanese were locked up, a submarine-based plane dropped incendiary bombs on Mount Emily in Oregon in an attempt to start forest fires. Both attacks were ineffectual.

The second argument for evacuation had to do with inability to distinguish the loyal from the disloyal.

Many months before the attack on Pearl Harbor, the Federal Bureau of Investigation as well as the military intelligence services had begun a systematic probe of Japanese American communities. When hostilities broke out, the FBI quickly rounded up all persons it considered potentially dangerous. Commander Ringle of Naval Intelligence reported the great majority of *Issei* and *Nisei* were beyond suspicion. But this did not satisfy the politicians, the Army, and men like Attorney General Warren. While piously admitting that undoubtedly many were loyal, they contended it was impossible to separate them from the disloyal. In effect they were saying that because it was not possible to distinguish the sheep from the goats, all must be considered potentially dangerous. Grodzins tells us that when Senator Sheridan Downey turned to Congressman Leland Ford and said he was quite sure there were many Japanese Americans who were just as loyal citizens as himself or even Congressman Ford himself, "Ford roared a protest." The FBI had applied rigid criteria—some perhaps excessively harsh —to *Issei* its agents had observed on an individual basis over a long period. But others wanted blanket condemnation based on rumor and misconceptions.

Much was made of the fact that an organization called the *Butoku Kai* existed in some communities. Translated literally, which is what intelligence authorities did, it means Society for Military Virtue. In reality the *Butoku Kai* were athletic clubs where fencing, judo and wrestling—skills valued by the warrior class in feudal times—were taught and practiced. As one observer has noted, these clubs were "no more related to militarism in modern Japan than the buttons of the sleeve of an American male's business suit today are connected with dueling." Without this knowledge, however, the presence of *Butoku Kai* in various Japanese American communities resurrected visions of thousands of Japanese military reservists drilled and ready to rise against the United States, a phantasm that had been conjured originally by alarmists in the Yellow Peril era.

Earl Warren was among those who felt the *Nisei* were a greater hazard to the national security than the *Issei*. Those who espoused this point of view cited two factors, the Japanese education of many *Nisei* and dual citizenship.

A number of *Nisei* had received a portion of their education in Japan, but there was considerable confusion about the number involved, and the period of time they had spent in Japan, and the effect of this experience. A federal study made after the evacuation showed that nearly three out of four *Nisei*—72.7 percent—had never been to Japan. Another 14.4 percent had visited Japan briefly. And only 12.2 percent had three or more years of schooling in Japan. One-fourth of this last group were forty years of age or older, indicating they had studied in Japan before the rise of militarism. On the other hand, less than 2 percent of those under twenty had three or more years of education in Japan, proof that the practice of sending youngsters to school in Japan had largely ended by the 1940's.

Nor could it be said that the 12.2 percent of *Nisei* who had studied in Japan all had been exposed to, or accepted, Japanese nationalistic propaganda. Many were apolitical. Many others were repelled by the rising tide of Japanese militarism and could not get back to the United States quickly enough. Still others hurried home to the States to avoid military service in Japan.

Nisei who had gone to school for any substantial length of time and then returned to the United States were known as *Kibei*. The "Japanese-ness" of the *Kibei* depended on several factors, among them the age at which they had left the United States and the length of time they had spent in Japan, but this was no test of loyalty. Naturally those who had spent a large part of their lives in Japan were the most fluent in the Japanese language, and many of them proved to be extremely valuable to the United States as language instructors, radio monitors, propaganda and psychological warfare specialists, and military intelligence service interpreters and translators. They performed a service for which few Americans were qualified.

This is not to say that some *Kibei* did not become provocateurs under the abnormal conditions of the relocation camps. These almost invariably were *Kibei* who had been unable to make a cultural adjustment to life in the United States and the indignity of the evacuation stirred their hostilities rather than severed their loyalties. Prior to the evacuation the loyalty to the United States of the great majority of *Kibei* was unquestionable, and the doubtful ones were well-known. It was as wrong to condemn the *Kibei* as a group as it was to make blanket accusations against all *Nisei*.

The matter of dual citizenship was equally confused. It was charged that most if not all *Nisei*, while claiming American citizenship, were considered Japanese subjects under Japan's statutes, and that therefore their loyalty to the United States was suspect. Some legislators demanded that dual citizens be stripped of their U.S. citizenship while others wanted dual citizens to be treated as aliens. As a matter of fact, dual citizenship was not unique to the *Nisei*. Dual citizenship was possible under the laws of many European nations, including Germany and Italy. In fact, when Japan was codifying its laws in 1899, it copied common European practice when it adopted the so-called *jus sanguinis* rule that provided that "a child is a Japanese if his or her father is a Japanese at the time of his or her birth." In the United States and in many Western Hemisphere countries, citizenship is determined by birth on the soil of the nation (*jus soli*) regardless of ancestry. Thus the American-born children of Japanese immigrants, as well as the offspring of immigrants from many other countries, were claimed as citizens by both the United States and the ancestral land.

Sensing the complications that might arise, Japanese residents of the United States petitioned Tokyo to liberalize the nationality code and make expatriation or single citizenship possible. In 1924 Japan amended its laws. A child born of Japanese parents in the United States, Canada and many South American countries no longer would be claimed as a Japanese subject unless the parents indicated within fourteen days their intention of claiming Japanese citizenship for the child. In practice, it meant taking a positive action, registering the child's birth at the nearest Japanese consulate. The law also provided that those born prior to 1924, who consequently possessed dual citizenship, could cancel their Japanese citizenship by filing a notification. No figures are available, but a great many *Nisei* did take steps to rid themselves of Japanese citizenship. It is safe to say that of those who did not go through this process, the majority were unaware that they were dual citizens, and of those who were aware, many thought so little of their Japanese citizenship that they didn't bother to do anything about canceling it. After 1924, it was a rare parent indeed who went to the trouble of notifying a consulate of intent to accept Japanese citizenship for his child. Many *Nisei* were quite unaware there was such a thing as dual citizenship until politicians raised the issue as another reason for doubting their loyalty.

A surprisingly large number of witnesses based their argument for evacuation on the contention that removal of the Japanese would not hurt the West Coast's economy. Most outspoken were representatives of a variety of farm organizations—the Western Growers Protective Association, the Grower-Shipper Vegetable Association in the Salinas Valley, the California Farm Bureau Federation, and others—who obviously would profit by the elimination of competition by Japanese growers. What these witnesses overlooked—and members of the committee ignored—was that the expendability or the indispensability of the Japanese on the West Coast was not the issue. The question was whether it was necessary to remove the Japanese Americans for reasons of national security. If the answer was yes, they had to be removed regardless of cost, and the effect of evacuation on the economy should not have entered consideration. The fact that so much stress was placed on the possible economic effects of evacuation lent weight to the *Nisei* charge that powerful interests who would benefit by the expulsion of Japanese had a big part in forcing the decision.

If there was any doubt, it was dispelled by an article by Frank J. Taylor in the May 9, 1942, issue of the *Saturday Evening Post*. Taylor interviewed Austin Anson, managing secretary of the Grower-Shippers, and quoted Anson:

"We're charged with wanting to get rid of the Japs for selfish reasons. We might as well be honest. We do. It's a question of whether the white man lives on the Pacific Coast or the brown men. They came to this valley to work, and they stayed to take over. They offer higher prices and higher rents than the white man can pay for land. They undersell the white man in the markets. They can do this because they raise their own labor. They work their women and children while the white farmer has to pay wages for his help."

The argument most difficult to answer—because it was emotional rather than logical—was the contention that the *Nisei* could demonstrate their patriotism by accepting evacuation. Coupled with this viewpoint was a warning that the Japanese might be subjected to mob or vigilante action, particularly if the mainland were attacked, and it was to their interest to accept "protective custody." Governor Olson advanced these arguments in his meeting with *Nisei* leaders in Sacramento, and they were voiced many times by members of the Tolan Committee as well as witnesses.

The gist of *Nisei* replies was that they wanted to be treated like any other group of citizens, sharing the war burdens and seeking neither special consideration nor discrimination. They wished to remain in their home communities, they said, and help the victory effort in whatever capacity they could. As for the threat of mob action, Joseph Shinoda of Los Angeles expressed more faith in the good sense of Californians than the Congressmen. Shinoda, a large-scale flower grower appearing as a representative of the United Citizens Federation, told the Committee in reply to a direct question: "Personally I don't fear for my safety here among Californians who know us, who have seen many Japanese and who would not feel that an imperial army representative arrived every time they saw a strange face. I would feel much safer here, from a protection standpoint, but I also feel that even if the legal aspects of our civil liberties are more or less in a state of suspension, the average human being in Los Angeles County is to be depended upon. I haven't lost faith in the human beings here if sometimes I do doubt what they have done to us. I think that in time to come the complete and utter disregard for our right to make a living, to share in the defense effort in this area where we make our homes, where we pay our taxes, will some day appear as a very black page in American history."

Grodzins reports that seven Japanese Americans were slain, all in California, between December 8, 1941, and the end of the following March. In all, he says, there were thirty-six cases of violence that might be considered vigilante-type action with one-third occurring over the Christmas-New Year holidays. Grodzins concluded: "Seven killings in almost four months was no portent that 'the entire Jap population is going to be massacred,' as one constituent of Congressman Tolan wrote. Seven killings and twenty-nine additional cases of extralegal action in the first four excited months of war would not seem to justify the protective evacuation of 110,000 persons . . . the danger of vigilantism existed more in the minds of those demanding evacuation than in the facts as such."

The *Nisei* witnesses uniformly opposed evacuation of citizens, but no one suggested he would defy a federal evacuation order. Masaoka had made the JACL's position clear and his stand was backed by *Nisei* witnesses not associated with the organization. In San Francisco, Michio Kunitani, representing the *Nisei* Democratic Club, declared he wanted to "live as Americans in America," but declared his group would accept evacuation "if the military authorities of the United States deem it necessary." In the Seattle hearings Tom Marutani representing a CIO local of the Industrial Woodworkers of America declared: "For the preservation of democratic ideals, we are willing to abide by any decision handed down by the government." In Los Angeles, the Reverend Lester Suzuki, a Methodist minister, pointed out the Americanizing influence of Christianity and added: "We want to reassure you that whatever the federal government thinks ought to be done, we will do." Shinoda said he would accept the evacuation decision in principle but urged individual hearings: ". . . since our Constitution even now would protect us from dispossession and confiscation, it would be only fair to give us some consideration or some form of trial so that at least when we leave we don't leave under the cloud of disloyalty."

Congressman Carl T. Curtis of Nebraska summarized the government's position when he replied to Shinoda in these words: "I don't believe anything will be gained by assuming that everyone who has to be evacuated is disloyal. These military decisions must be made upon the basis of the best judgment of those military authorities who are in charge. All the rest of us will have to comply. It will be tough, it will be cruel, there will be hardships . . . I don't mean to sermonize, but the point is that I hope that the loyal Japanese will feel that in complying with a military situation, that in that very compliance you are rendering a service to your country."

But the *Nisei* felt then, and feel today, that they had been called on to render a service that was discriminatory and, more important, unnecessary.

Tom Clark had told the Committee in San Francisco: "If the military authorities, in whom I have the utmost confidence, tell me it is necessary to remove from any area the citizens as well as the aliens of a certain nationality or of all nationalities I would say the best thing to do would be to follow the advice of the doctor. Whenever you go to a doctor if he tells you to take aspirin you take aspirin. If he tells you to cut off your leg so you can save your body you cut off your leg."

The *Nisei* had no choice but to follow the doctor's orders. But they believed the doctor's diagnosis was wrong because, as so often happens to the best of them, the diagnosis was based on misinformation, incomplete information, and pressures and hysteria that should have had no part in the making of such a critical judgment. Tom Clark lived to admit he had been wrong. In 1966 he said the Evacuation decision had been a major error of World War II.

19

THE EXODUS

I don't like Japan, Mommy. I want to go
home to America.

—Sansei *child after her first day
in a U.S. evacuation center.*

IN THE YEAR 1863 Brig. Gen. James Carleton became convinced that the Navajo Indians posed a danger to the national security along the western frontier of the United States. He decided the best way to remove the danger was to evacuate the Navajos from the land of their forefathers. That winter, federal troops forced 9,000 Navajo men, women and children—all they could round up—to leave their desert homes in what is now Arizona, southern Utah and western New Mexico, and herded them on foot to Fort Sumner in southern New Mexico. The Navajos were made up of scores of unorganized nomadic clans. The miserable conditions at Fort Sumner, where many died of disease, heartbreak and starvation, persuaded the clan leaders to organize as a tribe. They chose Barboncito as their chief, and he and his lieutenants went to Washington for talks with President Andrew Johnson. As a result, a treaty was signed in 1868 under which the United States recognized the sovereignty of the Navajo tribe and their right to return to their homes. Some 7,000 Navajos, all that remained, started back to the desert in a straggling, jubilant 10-mile-long column on the now storied 300-mile Long Walk, fording the Rio Grande in flood near Albuquerque.

Seventy-nine years after General Carleton banished the Navajos the United States Army prepared for another evacuation of an entire people. This time, as in 1863, the Army had Presidential approval, the acquiescence of Congress and the enthusiastic support of white civilians in the affected areas. Yet the Army in 1942 was just as unequipped to bear the responsibility of removing civilians as it had been in 1863. General DeWitt had been advocating the evacuation of enemy aliens from the West Coast since December, 1941, as an urgent military necessity. But more than two months later, when Secretary of War Stimson empowered him to carry out an evacuation, DeWitt had no plan ready.

DeWitt's first public step was to announce, on March 2, the delineation of two military zones. Military Area No. 1 included the western halves of Washington, Oregon and California and southern Arizona. Military Area No. 2 covered the eastern portions of the coastal states and northern Arizona. The announcement said persons of Japanese ancestry soon would be removed from Military Area No. 1. Meanwhile, they were urged to move voluntarily into the interior.

"In all probability," the announcement said, they would "not again be disturbed." Obviously the Army was hoping that a substantial number would move out of Military Area No. 1 voluntarily, thus reducing the burden on the government.

Nine days later, on March 11, DeWitt announced formation of the Wartime Civil Control Administration to handle the evacuation program. Colonel Bendetsen, called by historian Conn the Army's "most industrious advocate of mass evacuation," was named to head the WCCA with headquarters in San Francisco's Whitcomb Hotel. By then, the Army apparently had changed its mind about not disturbing voluntary evacuees, many of whom had moved into the eastern half of California. DeWitt's directive to WCCA was succinct and clear: "To provide for the evacuation of all persons of Japanese ancestry from Military Area No. 1 *and the California portion of Military Area No. 2* (emphasis provided) of the Pacific Coast with a minimum of economic and social dislocation, a minimum use of military personnel and maximum speed; and initially to employ all appropriate means to encourage voluntary migration." If the intent to evacuate all of California was publicly announced at the time, it was largely overlooked for small numbers of Japanese Americans continued to migrate into eastern California until such movement was prohibited. As a matter of fact, Conn says DeWitt's ultimate intention was to remove or confine all Japanese in his entire eight-state Western Defense Command, and then evacuate all German and Italian aliens from ap-

Evacuation orders (right) share space on a brick wall with air raid warning instructions. (National Archives)

proximately 1,000 prohibited zones. Fortunately, he was overruled.

Early in 1968, Bendetsen was asked by the author to evaluate his role in the evacuation decision and to comment on Conn's statement. Bendetsen at the time was chairman of U.S. Plywood-Champion Papers Inc., and living in New York City. He replied that he had long followed a policy of declining to discuss the evacuation "either generally or in detail," but he departed from the policy to write:

"I am familiar with the quotation to which you have reference describing me as the 'most industrious advocate' of mass evacuation. This would have to be the *opinion* of the author. It cannot be anything else because the fact is that I was not an advocate at all. My assignment was to develop, in a staff capacity only, at the War Department staff level, at the specific request of my superiors, the various considerations of how to go about it if it was finally concluded by them to be essential. Finally, I was given the responsibility for carrying into effect the decision reached by them."

Bendetson also reminded the author in the same letter that "hundreds upon hundreds of Japanese and their families, under my direction and with the help of my organization, moved as individuals in family units in their own cars over the highways to places in Utah, Colorado and the Middle West and elsewhere to accept jobs which we had helped them find—none of them were ever under guard—we did not require it, nor did any of them ever go through any of the evacuation procedures." He referred to the official document, *Final Report: Japanese Evacuation from the West Coast,* issued over General DeWitt's signature, as "an entirely factual report." The following passage appears on page 107 of this document: "Thus, nearly a month after the original announcement of the intended evacuation of Military Area No. 1, and three weeks after Proclamation No. 1, only 2,005 Japanese had moved out of the area and reported this fact. With approximately 107,500 Japanese residing in Military Area No. 1, it was quite apparent that voluntary migration was completely ineffective as an evacuation device. Now apparent, it was creative of social and economic problems in the areas to which the Japanese were going." As for the "help of my organization," page 104 of the same document contains the following paragraph: "Only a small proportion of all individuals who left Military Area No. 1 prior to controlled evacuation applied for any assistance or advice. Many of the migrants were persons with some financial independence or with relatives and friends in the area of destination. To June 5, 1942, the Bureau of Public Assistance reported that a total of 125 relocation plans had been approved—92 during the voluntary evacuation period—and that approximately $10,200 had been expended in assistance on such plans." And on page 41 there appears this sentence: "The voluntary movement did not gain momentum because means had not been provided on the ground for aiding evacuees in the solution of personal problems incident to their voluntary exodus."

There would appear to be considerable difference in the way Bendetsen remembered the voluntary evacuation program in 1968 and the way it was evaluated in 1943 when the official report was written.

Bendetsen concluded his letter to the author with this paragraph: "One must view, if an event is to be fairly viewed, the events and conditions at the time, not those of today. On the other hand, of course, were it not for the pressures, the time and the circumstances, it would not have been done at all."

An interesting sidelight is provided by *Who's Who in America.*

The entry for Bendetsen in Vol. 25, 1948–49 includes this information: ". . . with 4 other officers, assisted in establishing and organizing Office of Provost Marshal General . . . initiated proposal for application of Geneva Convention relative to prisoners of war and civilian internees by U.S. and other warring nations; prepared exec. order authorizing creation of military areas; organized Civil Affairs Div. and Wartime Control Administrn. of Western Command; conceived method, formulated details and directed evacuation of 120,000 persons of Japanese ancestry from military areas. Received Distinguished Service Medal."

In the next edition, Vol. 26, 1950–51, the same section of Bendetsen's entry had been changed to this: ". . . one of four officers assigned to establish the Provost Marshal Gen.'s Dept., Army Mil. Police Corps and Sch. Mil. Govt., World War II. Directed evacuation of Japanese from West Coast, 1942 . . ." Persons selected for listing in *Who's Who* generally supply their data and verify their sketches.

There was never any question about Bendetsen's qualifications as a staff officer or his ability to handle all the complex logistical problems involved in the mass removal of an entire people. He lost no time in getting the WCCA machinery into high gear. By March 21 the first group of *Nisei* volunteers from Los Angeles were on their way to the Manzanar Assembly Center operated by the Army in the high, parched Owens Valley of eastern California to prepare the way for others who would be evacuated under the compulsory removal program. This program got under way in earnest three days later, March 24, when GIs in battle dress wheeled their jeeps over pleasant, pine-covered Bainbridge Island across Puget Sound from Seattle. Bainbridge Island is a place of summer homes and small farms hacked out of logged-over land. It also lies athwart the approaches to the Bremerton Naval Yard. On utility poles, at the post office and the ferry landing, the soldiers tacked up freshly printed posters headlined "Instruction to all Persons of Japanese Ancestry." The posters said they must leave the island by March 30—six days later.

As early as February 6, the Navy had recommended that Bainbridge Island be named a "military area" and that its Japanese residents, a handful of *Issei* and their *Nisei* offspring, mostly berry and truck farmers, be evacuated. The Justice Department, which was

Guard watches over abandoned homes in San Pedro after residents were evacuated on short notice. (National Archives)

still in charge, declared that if the Navy felt removal of Japanese aliens alone was sufficient, it was prepared to take the necessary action. But Justice stated flatly it had no authority to designate prohibited areas for American citizens. James Rowe suggested to the Navy that the only way *Nisei* could be removed was to declare the area a military zone from which all civilians would be excluded except those specifically issued passes by the military. But if this course were taken, the matter would have been entirely out of the Justice Department's hands. Apparently the Navy was not prepared to assume the responsibility, for no decision was made on Rowe's letter. However, Bainbridge Island remained on the military's top urgency list and Colonel Bendetsen selected it for the initial movement.

March 30 was a raw, overcast day, not uncommon for the Puget Sound country at that time of year. Although the Japanese had been given less than a week in which to settle their affairs and pack, they began to gather at the assembly point long before the designated hour, each of the fifty-four families carrying only the meager items authorized by the Army—bedding, linens, toilet articles, extra clothing, enamel plates and eating utensils. All else, the possessions collected over a lifetime, had to be stored with friends, delivered to a government warehouse, sold or abandoned. Farms developed over decades were leased or simply left to be overgrown by weeds.

Armed soldiers herded the bewildered and forlorn evacuees—children too young to comprehend, weeping schoolgirls (there were thirteen graduating seniors), sturdy young adults and the work-worn elders—aboard a ferryboat as their neighbors stared in compassion or curiosity. The ferryboat hooted and eased out of its slip and some of the *Nisei* looked back for the last time on the island that had been their only home. On the mainland the evacuees were transferred to dilapidated railroad coaches for the long, miserable ride to Manzanar.

The Bainbridge Islanders were the first to be evacuated by the Army but they were not the first evacuees. On February 14, the Navy had "condemned" Terminal Island, a spit of land across the channel from San Pedro, California. The notices said residents must leave by March 14; they were given a month to make arrangements for closing their homes, moving their belongings, finding new places in which to live and new jobs to keep families fed. This last item was of particular importance, for a large number of Terminal Island's *Issei* men had been picked up in the FBI raids. Like Bainbridge Island, Terminal Island was a sensitive spot. It formed the east shore of the channel to Wilmington, the Port of Los Angeles. Not far to the east was Long Beach Naval Station. Some 500 Japanese families lived on Terminal Island. Most of the men were fishermen, manning oceangoing tuna clippers. Many of the others worked in the fish canneries. Being a largely self-contained group, Terminal Islanders retained many of Japan's social customs. If there were any potentially disloyal Japanese in the community—as the Navy suspected—it was prudent to move them to a less strategic area. The condemnation notices did not say where the Japanese should go. (At this time Secretary of War Stimson had received President Roosevelt's verbal approval to evacuate aliens and citizens alike, but only top War Department officials had been informed and no firm evacuation plans had been made.) The residents knew only that they would have to leave their homes on Terminal Island. And so, shortly after the notices were posted, they began to trickle away, most of them heading for Los Angeles where they had friends and hoped to find jobs, where they knew they could get shelter in church basements and in the classrooms of Japanese language schools which had been disbanded.

At three o'clock the quiet afternoon of February 25, officials appeared without warning on Terminal Island with new posters.

As evacuation day approached, Japanese Americans sold their possessions for whatever they could get. Refrigerators and washing machines often went for $5 and $10. (National Archives)

The new orders said all Japanese must be off the island by midnight February 27. About 300 families were already gone. The 200 families remaining suddenly learned that the deadline for their departure was not seventeen days in the future, but a mere two days and nine hours away. The reaction was predictable. Near-panic swept the community, particularly those where the family head was in custody. Word spread quickly and human vultures in the guise of used-furniture dealers descended on the island. They drove up and down the streets in trucks offering $5 for a nearly new washing machine, $10 for refrigerators, $25 for pianos—pittances for household goods which soon could be resold for many times the price. And the Japanese, angry but helpless, sold their dearly purchased possessions because they didn't know what to do with their goods and because they sensed the need in the uncertain days ahead for all the cash they could squirrel away. Even so, an employee of the Federal Security Agency visited the island the day after the Japanese had left and found all manner of household equipment and enough expensive fishing nets and rubber boots to fill eight trucks—abandoned because there was not time to get it moved and no custodians to take possession.

In San Francisco, JACL leaders heard of the incredible confusion and tragic property loss. They realized the government was not yet prepared to supervise an orderly evacuation and that untold hardships and misery lay ahead unless order could be drawn out of chaos. In private conversations military officials had indicated to Masaoka in unmistakable terms that if the Japanese did not cooperate, the Army was prepared to remove them swiftly, efficiently and mercilessly—at bayonet point if it came to that. "This is a military necessity," he was told. "We have our orders. Any resistance will be interpreted as acts of disloyalty and will be met with appropriate action." Implicit in this warning was the threat of violence, the possibility even of heavy loss of life.

In an emergency meeting convened in San Francisco, JACL leaders from all sections of the Pacific Coast agreed unanimously that repugnant as the evacuation order was, they had no alternative but to cooperate with their government. There was reason to hope that by working with the military in this emergency, they could expect sympathetic consideration from civilian arms of the government when the pressures had subsided. Some persons had urged a court test of the evacuation order, even a token challenge for the record. But in the end those at the meeting decided there was more to be gained by cooperation, and JACL's leaders would be of greater service in their communities and in the evacuation centers rather than in jail. It was voted to move headquarters to Salt Lake City, safely out of the evacuation zone, while Masaoka would be dispatched to Washington.

Early in February the Justice Department had severely restricted the movement of enemy aliens, requiring them to be in their places of residence or employment at night, and prohibiting unauthorized travel. These restrictions were extended to cover the *Nisei* on March 24. General DeWitt issued a proclamation requiring Japanese, German and Italian aliens "and all other persons of

Japanese ancestry"—the proclamation did not recognize that they were American citizens—to be in their homes between 8 P.M. and 6 A.M.

By this time the Army's legal position had been strengthened considerably beyond Executive Order 9066 which even War Department attorneys recognized as an extremely far-reaching extension of Presidential powers. Many felt that congressional approval of Executive Order 9066 would buttress its legality. Thus a measure known as Public Law 503 was drawn up making it a misdemeanor for anyone to violate orders of military commanders prescribed under the executive order. Public Law 503 was approved by voice vote in both houses of Congress on March 19 and signed by Roosevelt on March 21. It provided for trial of violators in federal courts—thus freeing the military of that responsibility. Maximum penalty for each offense was set at $5,000 fine and one year imprisonment.

DeWitt's curfew order in specifying "all other persons of Japanese ancestry" segregated the *Nisei* on the basis of race. They were the only citizens covered by the order. Two of them, each without the knowledge of the other, decided to test the constitutionality of Public Law 503. They sought to challenge the authority of the military to order civilians around without invoking martial law. They also contended that since the curfew order was aimed only against citizens of a particular race, it violated the requirements of equality inherent in due process of law.

One was Gordon K. Hirabayashi, a student at the University of Washington and a member of the Quaker faith. He had never been to Japan, and he felt strongly enough to defy both the curfew and evacuation orders. He was apprehended, tried and sentenced to three months' imprisonment on each charge, the sentences to run concurrently.

The other was Minoru Yasui. Born in Hood River, Oregon, he had been graduated from the University of Oregon law school in 1939. On graduation he was also commissioned a lieutenant of infantry in the U.S. Army Reserve through the reserve officer training program. At that time graduates awaiting bar examinations were being paid $25 a month as law clerks. Yasui took a $150-a-month position with the Japanese consulate in Chicago to handle correspondence and other routine matters requiring the use of English.

On Pearl Harbor Day Yasui found himself out of a job. A month later Yasui received Army orders to report for active duty at Fort Vancouver, Washington. Immediately on arrival he was put in charge of a platoon of troops but within 24 hours, before he could be formally inducted, he was told he was unacceptable to the Army. By the time the curfew was invoked, Yasui was angry enough to challenge the military's authority.

Yasui notified the FBI and the U.S. attorney that he intended to violate the curfew. He walked the streets of downtown Portland until 11 P.M., having a friend telephone the FBI periodically as to his whereabouts, but no one paid him any attention. Finally he found a Portland city patrolman and asked to be arrested. As Yasui tells it, the officer said: "Go home, Sonny, or you'll get in trouble." However, on Yasui's insistence, he was duly arrested, charged with violation of the curfew order, and freed on bond. In November, 1942, Yasui was escorted from Minidoka Relocation Center in Idaho back to Portland for trial in United States District Court.

The court determined that under a precedent set during the Civil War, the military could not issue orders binding on civilians in the absence of martial law. But the court also ruled that this precedent did not apply to Yasui because, having been employed by the Japanese consular service, he was not a citizen of the United States.

Yasui had made his point regarding the military's jurisdiction over civilians. But the court stunned him by ruling that he had lost his American citizenship. He had no choice but to appeal to the Circuit Court of Appeals in San Francisco which promptly requested the Supreme Court to take direct jurisdiction. Meanwhile, Yasui was confined in Multnomah County Jail in Portland, kept alone in his cell and denied a haircut, a razor, fingernail clippers or even a typewriter. He was held in this condition for nine months, dirty and hirsute as a hippie, until August, 1943, when the Supreme Court heard both the Yasui and Hirabayashi appeals.

In Hirabayashi's case, the Supreme Court ruled only on the curfew order. It found that a special danger existed and "reasonable and prudent men charged with responsibility for our national defense had ample ground for concluding that they face the danger of invasion." The Court chose not "to sit in review of the wisdom of their action or substitute its judgment for theirs." In other words, the Army had a right to order a curfew specifically for the *Nisei*, and Hirabayashi was guilty of violating it.

Both findings in Yasui's trial were reversed. The high court ruled Yasui had not lost his citizenship, and that the Army did indeed have the authority to issue orders binding on civilians even in the absence of martial law. Yasui was fined $5,000, which was suspended, and he was freed on the ground that he had served nine months in prison while waiting for his appeal to be heard. Yasui estimates it cost him and his family $10,000 to carry his case through the courts. He returned to Minidoka before relocating in Chicago where, among other things, he worked as a laborer in an ice plant. By 1945 Yasui was living in Denver. He took the examination for admission to the Colorado bar and scored the highest marks of all the candidates, but was denied a license. The stated reason was that Yasui had a criminal record. Yasui suspects the real reason was that he happened to be of Japanese descent. Only after vigorous appeal to the State Supreme Court was the license issued.

Actually the *Nisei* did not have to go looking for harassment. It was unavoidable. The experience of Kiyoshi Patrick Okura is a startling example. A graduate of U.C.L.A., Okura was employed by the Los Angeles City Civil Service Commission as a personnel technician. His primary responsibility was testing job applicants. Early in February, 1942, Drew Pearson charged in one of his broadcasts that a Japanese American, passing himself off as an Irishman named K. Patrick O'Kura, had wormed his way into the Los Angeles city government, had familiarized himself with the city power and water system, and had installed a ring of fifty saboteurs within the Bureau of Water and Power who were poised to blow up the entire system when the word came.

Like so many loosely made charges, Pearson's "revelations" held a measure of truth. Okura jokingly had been called the Japanese Irishman by his friends. He had conducted examinations among applicants for jobs like cable splicer, lineman and reservoir keeper in the Bureau of Water and Power. And over a period of time some fifty *Nisei* had entered the Los Angeles civil service system and were working in various departments.

When Pearson's charges were published in the Los Angeles newspapers the next morning someone on Mayor Bowron's staff apparently became very nervous. Okura received a telephone call from the mayor's office suggesting that it might be a good idea for him to resign, thus setting an example for the other *Nisei* on the city payroll. Okura demanded to know on what grounds his resignation was being sought. The official replied delicately that the resignation of all *Nisei* might save the city a good deal of embarrassment. Okura then declared he had done nothing wrong and would not resign, reminding his caller that the proper procedure for discharging a civil service employee was to bring charges before the merit board.

A few days later Okura was summoned to the mayor's office and Bowron himself asked for Okura's resignation. Again Okura refused. When word spread, the entire staff of twenty-five in Okura's department announced they would resign en masse if he were fired. Soon, however, it became apparent that evacuation orders would be issued shortly, and Okura asked for and was given a leave of absence for the duration of the war. Although his skills were badly needed by federal agencies, word of the furore apparently destroyed his chances of government employment. He and his wife Lily were evacuated to the assembly center at the Santa Anita racetrack, then relocated to Boys' Town near Omaha, Nebraska, where he was employed as a psychologist.

Similar activity was under way in Sacramento where *Nisei* in state civil service were being threatened with discharge. Some of them appealed to Saburo Kido for help, and he in turn brought the problem to the attention of James Purcell, then a 36-year-old native San Franciscan whose grandparents had migrated from Ireland. Purcell had been associated casually with Kido in several court cases, but his only other contact with the Japanese had been in his youth when he became friendly with several *Issei* who worked on his cousin's ranch in northern California. Purcell had been linked with various civil rights causes and when it became apparent that the *Nisei* were being pushed around, he drove to Sacramento and talked with several score of them in a mass meeting. There he learned that the *Nisei* had been required to fill out a lengthy questionnaire purportedly to determine their loyalty. They were asked whether they had ever been to Japan, whether they had attended Japanese language schools. They were asked about their religion, the magazines and newspapers they read, the occupation of their parents and date of arrival from Japan and a great many other questions not being asked any other group of employees.

Purcell's sense of justice was outraged, but the evacuation orders were issued before he could do anything about saving *Nisei* jobs. One day he visited some of the *Nisei* being held at the Army's Assembly Center at Tanforan racetrack. What he saw horrified him. It also filled him with anger. Even now he bristles over the memory: "This was just a racetrack, with thousands of people confined inside it. They'd put a family in a stall big enough for one horse, with whitewash over the manure. Guards with machine guns stood at the gates. I couldn't understand why innocent citizens were being treated this way."

The knowledge that the Government of the United States was, in effect, presuming a person to be guilty—or at least suspect—of disloyalty simply because of his Japanese blood, ran counter to everything that Purcell believed in. So he set out to do something about it, and his path took him ultimately to the Supreme Court of the United States. How he got there, and what he accomplished— which was a great deal—will be related in another chapter.

Meanwhile, as the Army rushed to complete its plans, all reports indicated the voluntary evacuation program was a failure. It was as *Nisei* spokesmen had warned the Tolan Committee: Many Japanese families were willing to leave the West Coast, but where should they go? In the Seattle hearings the JACL statement had said in part: "The Japanese feared with reason that, forced to vacate their homes, unable to find a place to stay, they would be kicked from town to town in the interior like the 'Okies' of John Steinbeck's novel. Others envisioned the day when inhabitants of inland states, aroused by the steady influx of Japanese, would refuse to sell gasoline and food to them. They saw, too, the possibility of mob action against them as exhausted, impoverished and unable to travel further, they stopped in some town or village where they were not wanted."

And this had come to pass. Signs reading, "No Japs Wanted Here" greeted families heading for Idaho, Utah, Colorado and other states. Angry townspeople held mass meetings. Some travelers experienced difficulty buying gasoline. They slept in their cars when they were denied hotel and motel accommodations. Refused service in restaurants, they bought provisions in grocery stores and

Link between purchasing war bonds and evacuating Japanese is hard to see, but was typical of the feeling of the time. (National Archives)

Innocent victims of the war waiting to be evacuated. Photo was taken in Sacramento. Note sign advertising sale of metal beds and plants. (National Archives)

Humans were not the only creatures affected by the evacuation orders. Homes had to be found for pets. (National Archives)

munched cold sandwiches. Residents of interior states could hardly be blamed for refusing to welcome a people who the government had declared were too dangerous to be allowed to stay on the West Coast. And so on March 21 Bendetsen recommended that voluntary evacuation be halted. All free movement out of Military Area No. 1 was banned effective March 29. From that date it became illegal for Japanese to leave the area, and soon it would be illegal for them to remain; they had to sit tight and wait for the Army to move them. (Voluntary movement in or out of the California portion of Military Area No. 2 was banned on June 2, trapping those who had hoped to escape confinement by moving away voluntarily from coastal areas as the Army had urged.)

In the communities, commerce all but came to a halt. Businesses had to be disposed of. Stocks of merchandise had to be sold or stored away, homes had to be leased, furniture stored or sold, pets put in the hands of friends. This waiting period was particularly hard on farmers who, even then, were being urged to produce food for victory. Yet it cost them money to plant and cultivate crops, and they had no assurance whatever that they would realize any-

On Grant Avenue in San Francisco, the owner of a Japanese store had to liquidate his stock prior to the evacuation. Next door, it was business as usual for the Peking Bazaar Co. where the proprietor posted a sign identifying it as a Chinese store. (National Archives)

thing from the harvest. One *Nisei* complained with not a little frustration that the Navy was asking him to increase his planting of onions at the same time the Army was trying to push him off the land.

WCCA divided the coastal zones into 108 exclusion areas. Starting with Bainbridge Island, a series of "Civilian Exclusion Orders" were posted, sweeping across the country with clockwork precision to remove Japanese from each of the exclusion areas. Each area was established to include roughly 1,000 Japanese—250 families —although the numbers varied from less than 500 to more than 1,500. The evacuation procedure started with the posting of the exclusion order which instructed each single person and the head of each family to register at the WCCA control station in the area, usually a public hall or school gymnasium staffed by personnel borrowed from a variety of federal agencies plus *Nisei* interpreters to help with those who understood little English. Registration consisted primarily of filling out forms, being assigned a family number, and picking up tags for identification and baggage. D-day usually was set for a week after evacuation notices were posted—

Under the watchful eye of an armed soldier, Japanese residents of San Francisco wait to be registered for evacuation at a Wartime Civil Control Administration office. (National Archives)

Nisei Grill in San Francisco announces new management as the previous operators prepared to be evacuated. (National Archives)

Mr. and Mrs. K. Iseri say goodby to patrons of their drugstore in Los Angeles. (National Archives)

one week to pay bills, store treasured belongings, purchase work clothes and heavy boots, say goodbye to old friends and neighbors, close up the house, get rid of the car and present oneself at the assembly point to be checked, doublechecked and loaded into buses under the watchful eye of military policemen for the ride to the Assembly Center.

In many areas the Army and Public Health Service were unable to provide necessary health services. JACL chapters opened free

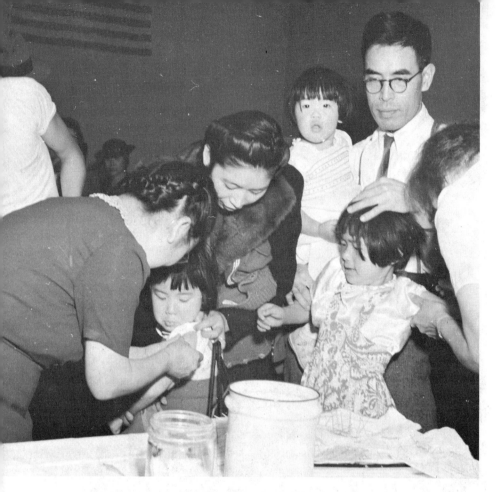

Federal government was unprepared to provide adequate medical service to evacuees. Volunteer *Issei* and *Nisei* physicians gave evacuees smallpox and typhoid fever inoculations. (National Archives)

clinics, staffed by doctors who donated their services, to give smallpox vaccinations and typhoid inoculations.

The Assembly Centers were just what their name implies—temporary camps where the evacuees could be assembled and held until semi-permanent camps were ready. Only four considerations went into selection of the sites. They had to have preexisting facilities so a minimum of building had to be done. Water, power and sewage facilities were needed. They had to be close to Japanese population centers, and there had to be enough room so the evacuees wouldn't be penned up like cattle in a corral. The Army quickly moved in on fairgrounds and racetracks, throwing up row

Armed military policemen supervise loading of evacuees into busses in
San Francisco. There was no violence. (National Archives)

Soldiers oversee loading of baggage as evacuees in San Francisco wait outside their homes for arrival of busses. (National Archives)

on row of crude barracks-like shelters partitioned into what the Army euphemistically called apartments. At the racetracks, horse stalls were converted for human occupancy. At other centers raw lumber was used in construction and as it dried, gaping cracks appeared in walls and grass grew up through the floor.

The Army built fifteen Assembly Centers plus camps at Manzanar, California, and Poston, Arizona which were to be operated by the Army in the initial stages of the evacuation. Manzanar was transferred to the War Relocation Authority (WRA), a civilian agency charged with operating the semi-permanent camps, on June 1, 1942, while Poston came under WRA jurisdiction from the beginning. Both inducted evacuees directly from their homes—9,830 to Manzanar and 11,711 to Poston. The Assembly Centers (from north to south), population and dates of occupation were:

Evacuation orders made no exceptions for age. If a person was of Japanese blood, he was evacuated. (National Archives)

The confusion and heartbreak of evacuation. Scene at Centerville, California. (National Archives)

Japanese-owned hotels and rooming houses were taken over by new operators who lost no time in identifying their race. (National Archives)

NEW MANAGEMENT
WHITE AMERICANS

FREE ROOM RENT
THE 3RD WEEK

ROOM · CLOSE · IN
CLEAN · MODERN

In eloquent protest, veteran of service with the U.S. Navy in World War I wore uniform and decorations on the day he was evacuated. (National Archives)

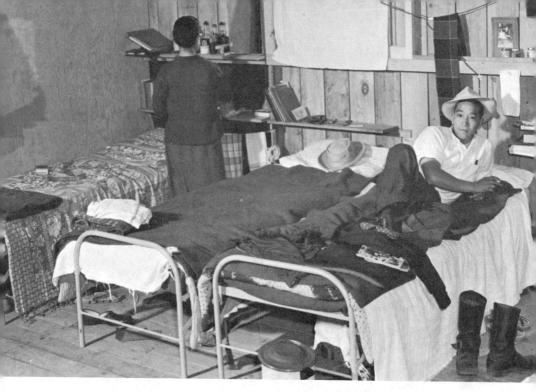

Interior and exterior of "apartments" at Salinas Assembly Center, where evacuees were sheltered until War Relocation Authority camps could be prepared in inland desert areas. (National Archives)

Assembly Center	Maximum Population	Occupied
Puyallup, Wash. (fairgrounds)	7,390	Apr. 28 to Sept. 12
Portland, Ore.		
(livestock exposition hall)	3,676	May 2 to Sept. 10
Marysville, Calif.	2,451	May 8 to June 29
Sacramento, Calif.	4,739	May 6 to June 26
Tanforan Racetrack, near		
San Francisco, Calif.	7,816	Apr. 28 to Oct. 13
Stockton, Calif.	4,271	May 10 to Oct. 17
Turlock, Calif.	3,661	Apr. 30 to Aug. 12
Salinas, Calif.	3,586	Apr. 27 to July 4
Merced, Calif.	4,508	May 6 to Sept. 15
Pinedale, Calif.	4,792	May 7 to July 23
Fresno, Calif.	5,120	May 6 to Oct. 30
Tulare, Calif.	4,978	Apr. 30 to Sept. 4
Santa Anita Racetrack,		
Los Angeles	18,719	May 7 to Oct. 27
Pomona, Calif.	5,434	May 7 to Aug. 24
Mayer, Arizona	245	May 7 to June 2

One day these Japanese Americans were free citizens and residents of communities, law-abiding, productive, proud. The next, they were inmates of cramped, crowded American-style concentration camps, under armed guard, fed like prisoners in mess hall lines, deprived of privacy and dignity, shorn of all their rights. Mine Okubo, a *Nisei* artist, in a sketch-and-text book published by the Columbia University Press in 1946, told vividly and effectively what it was like to be evacuated. She called her book *Citizen 13660*, which was the WCCA number assigned her. She was evacuated from Berkeley, California to Tanforan and assigned to Barrack 16, Room 50. But let her tell the story:

"The guide left us at the door of Stall 50. We walked in and dropped our things inside the entrance. The place was in semidarkness; light barely came through the dirty window on either side of the entrance. A swinging half-door divided the 20 by 9 ft. stall into two rooms. The roof sloped down from a height of twelve feet in the rear room to seven feet in the front room; below the rafters an open space extended the full length of the stable. The rear room had housed the horse and the front room the fodder. Both rooms showed signs of a hurried whitewashing. Spider webs,

Evacuees await inspection on arrival at assembly center set up in the Santa Anita racetrack. The Army had promised that if the Japanese Americans did not cooperate, they would be evacuated forcibly. (National Archives)

horse hair, and hay had been whitewashed with the walls. Huge spikes and nails stuck out all over the walls. A two-inch layer of dust covered the floor, but on removing it we discovered that linoleum the color of redwood had been placed over the rough manure-covered boards. We opened the folded spring cots lying on the floor of the rear room and sat on them in the semidarkness. We heard someone crying in the next stall."

Later, Mine Okubo joined a line of 5,000 evacuees being fed at the central mess hall. Dinner was a boiled potato, canned Vienna sausages and two slices of bread. When she went to draw a mattress, she was given a bag of ticking and told to stuff it with straw. The toilets were lined up in rows, back to back, but eventually parti-

These are evacuee quarters at Tanforan racetrack near San Francisco where artist Mine Okubo was sent. Below, Miss Okubo after her release shows one of the sketches from her book to Reed Lewis (left) of the Common Council for American Unity. (National Archives)

Military sentries at Santa Anita Assembly Center. Machine guns appeared after Japanese troops landed in Aleutians. (National Archives)

tions without doors were erected between them. She wrote: "At first the women were very self-conscious and timid about using the showers. The men's showers were in one large room but the women's showers were slightly partitioned. The older women preferred the good old-fashioned bathtubs to showers. It was a common sight to see them bathing in pails, dishpans, or in tubs made from barrels."

Outside the barbed wire, life went on as usual. Mine Okubo was moved to write: "We were close to freedom and yet far from it. The San Bruno streetcar line bordered the camp on the east and the main state highway on the south. Streams of cars passed by all day. Guard towers and barbed wire surrounded the entire center. Guards were on duty night and day."

The Puyallup camp, ironically named Camp Harmony, was divided into four fenced sectors—in the main fairgrounds and on three parking lots. Rows of neat residences lay between the camp areas in a checkerboard pattern. At dinnertime cooking odors drifted from these homes into the camps. The sounds of children at play and being called home to meals, the music of radios at night, the soft conversation of citizens rocking on their porches, drifted through the barbed wire fences to remind the evacuees of a life that had been. Sometimes the children would line up at the fences "to go look at the Japs" as though they were animals in a zoo.

Rain made the camp areas a quagmire through which the evacuees had to wade to get to the central toilets and mess halls. Summer's heat turned the shacks into bake ovens, for roofs of a single thickness of lumber and tarpaper provided little protection against the sun. The partitions between units in most cases did not go up to the ceiling; a child wailing at one end of a 100-foot long barracks disturbed everyone. Yet with remarkable fortitude the evacuees pitched in to make the best of their lot. Men who had owned restaurants or worked as chefs volunteered to man the kitchens. Others labored as dishwashers, garbage collectors, pot scrubbers, vegetable peelers—all the menial work that had to be done to keep the evacuees fed. Others organized recreation programs, taught classes for children, cleaned out the toilets and washrooms, repaired the plumbing, worked in makeshift dispensaries, took roll morning and evening, distributed the mail, delivered messages, translated instructions from the administration for the benefit of the older people, staffed the clinics, served as clerks in the offices. For this they were paid $8 per month in the unskilled classifications, $12 for the skilled, $16 per month for professionals including physicians, dentists and engineers working side by side with Caucasians drawing full civil service pay.

The Army's own report contends the equipment and supplies in the camps "were those to be found in any well ordered community in sufficient quantity to maintain health, sanitation and reasonable comfort." But then it adds somewhat self-consciously, "Physically, all Assembly Centers are more ideally suited for troop use than they were for the housing of families." The truth was that the Army had no experience in running concentration camps for entire families, with the population ranging from the senile aged to infants. (One day early in the program JACL headquarters in San Francisco received an anguished plea from an evacuee in one of the Assembly Centers: Couldn't something be done to get a supply of sanitary napkins? Mike Masaoka could get no satisfaction from Army officials. Finally, "out of sheer guts and frustration," he put in a call to the White House, was connected with a staff official, and was promised quick action.) Without the cooperation of the evacuees themselves, the evacuation program would have been pure chaos. The Army was concerned only with moving the people; it had not even considered ways of keeping the evacuees busy. The official report says: "It was brought about that, though no formal system of education or recreation had been contemplated in the original planning, and no initial budget provision made, an effective program was developed under the direction of the WCCA with the active cooperation of the evacuees, using their various training, skills and experience."

How much "direction" was provided is open to question. In many instances it was a matter of helping themselves or doing without, and many evacuees found themselves working in spite of their resentment. Patrick Okura was one.

"I was quite bitter when I went into the Santa Anita Assembly Center and had decided to simply sit out the war and not lift a finger," he says. "After the first week, seeing the chaos and confusion, I couldn't sit back any longer. I took it upon myself to talk to a number of friends and got their support to suggest a self-government program to help the Caucasian administrators. We divided the camp into eighteen districts and held open elections for district representatives. I was elected representative in my district, and then elected chairman of the council. In this capacity I worked closely with the administration, so closely that I was accused by some of the evacuees of being on the federal payroll. One day the military guards ordered a crackdown on 'weapons,' and went from family to family picking up anything they considered dangerous—kitchen knives, scissors, even crochet and knitting needles and hotplates mothers were using to warm milk for their babies. We not only were able to get the confiscation order tempered, but we persuaded the administration to set up milk stations instead of each family trying to handle its own."

Colonel Bendetsen completed the evacuation of Military Area No. 1 on June 7. By early August, Military Area No. 2 in California was cleared. A total of 110,723 persons had entered the centers. Another 6,393 had been evacuated without entering a center—117,116 in all. The Army had encountered many problems outside the expected—mothers about to give birth who could not be moved, inmates of tuberculosis hospitals and mental institutions, the Caucasian spouses of Japanese and their mixed-blood children,

This was the "apartment" of Pat Okura (in T-shirt) and his bride Lily (left) at Santa Anita. Mayor Fletcher Bowron of Los Angeles demanded Okura's resignation from a city job following distorted charges by Drew Pearson. Okura refused. (National Archives)

Japanese orphans being reared by Caucasian foster parents. Policies and exemptions had to be established for each of these categories. For example, families consisting of a Japanese wife and a non-Japanese husband were exempted; families consisting of a Japanese husband and a Caucasian wife were required to be evacuated. But a Caucasian widow of a Japanese husband and her mixed-blood children could remain on the coast. Another category, underlining the racist nature of the evacuation order, exempted "mixed-blood (one-half Japanese or less) individuals, citizens of the United States

"Self government" of sorts was practiced in the camps. Candidate Satoshi Iiyama's poster announces a platform of "equality of rights, opportunities, representation." (National Archives)

or of friendly nations, whose backgrounds have been Caucasian."

The summer dragged past. In the far Pacific the Battle of the Coral Sea on May 7 sent 100,000 tons of Japanese shipping to the bottom and blunted the threat against Australia. Early in June a Japanese naval force attacking Midway Island was defeated, and in the process U.S. defenders destroyed a large part of Tokyo's carrier fleet. On June 12, Japanese invaders occupied Attu in the Aleutian Islands, thousands of miles from the U.S. mainland, but at the Assembly Centers machine guns suddenly appeared in the watchtowers. In August, American Marines landed in the Solomon Islands, and at long last the United States was on the offensive. There was no longer any remote possibility that the Japanese would try to invade the American mainland.

But deep in the American interior, hundreds of carpenters—anyone who could swing a hammer—were busily pounding together vast cities of tarpaper-covered barracks. These were the War Relocation Centers to be operated by a new civilian agency, the War Relocation Authority. And soon long trainloads of evacuees would begin the long, weary ride into exile in these camps.

20

BEHIND BARBED WIRE

Snow upon the rooftop,
Snow upon the coal;
Winter in Wyoming—
Winter in my soul.

—*Miyuki Aoyama*

AT A CABINET MEETING on February 27, 1942, President
Roosevelt brought up the subject of the evacuation of Japanese
Americans from the West Coast. Eight days earlier he had signed
the Executive Order which had made this move possible. Now he
wanted to know what progress had been made, and what had been
done about transporting the evacuees out of military zones and
resettling them. Secretary of War Stimson had little to report
except that, despite the Army's plea of urgency, progress was
necessarily slow because of the size of the task and the limitations
of General DeWitt's forces. Stimson's notes after that meeting say:

"The President seized upon the idea that the work should be
taken off the shoulders of the Army so far as possible after the
evacuees had been selected and removed from places where they
were dangerous. There was general confusion around the table
arising from the fact that nobody had realized how big it was,
nobody wanted to take care of the evacuees, and the general weight
and complication of the project. Biddle (Attorney General Francis)
suggested that a single head should be chosen to handle the resettlement instead of the pulling and hauling of all the different agencies,
and the President seemed to accept this . . ."

The man who was picked a few days later for the assignment
without precedent was Milton S. Eisenhower, 42-year-old director

of information in the Department of Agriculture. He was destined to go on to become a noted educator and public servant although his brilliance was overshadowed by the career of his older brother, Dwight David Eisenhower. Milton Eisenhower worked informally on his new job out of his office until March 18 when another executive order, No. 9102, created the War Relocation Authority in the Office of Emergency Management, to assist persons evacuated by the military. Eisenhower was made responsible directly to the President although both he and his successor, Dillon S. Myer, worked through the director of the budget, Harold D. Smith, a man of many responsibilities in the White House inner circle.

One of Eisenhower's first actions was to concur with Colonel Bendetsen's recommendation that voluntary evacuation be halted in view of the ill feeling in interior states. Given a free hand to solve the resettlement problem—certainly one of the knottiest of World War II—Eisenhower's first idea was to set up from 50 to 75 small inland camps, not unlike the Civilian Conservation Corps camps, from which the evacuees would be moved out as rapidly as possible to resume normal life outside the Western Defense Command. But the hostility of public opinion as reflected in the press and in the comments of public officials in the mountain states, and the mounting threat of violence against the voluntary evacuees, caused Eisenhower to hesitate. On April 7, Eisenhower and other officials met in Salt Lake City with the governors or their representatives from ten Western states—Utah, Arizona, Nevada, Montana, Idaho, Colorado, New Mexico, Wyoming, Washington and Oregon. He explained that none of the evacuees had been charged with disloyalty, that they had been evacuated as a defense measure, and outlined his hopes of resettling them in inland states. The knee-jerk reaction was vehement. It was as though the officials had not heard Eisenhower speak, for they paid no attention to him. Some predicted violence. Others demanded guarantees that the evacuees would not buy land and would be required to leave after the end of the war. Still others declared they would accept evacuees only if they remained under military guard. The lone dissenting voice was that of Governor Ralph Carr of Colorado who not only said he had no objection to loyal Japanese Americans moving into his state, but that cooperation with the government's resettlement project was a citizen's responsibility.

As a result of the disappointing meeting, Eisenhower decided large-scale resettlement outside the centers would not be possible until time quieted the hysteria. He abandoned the idea of many small camps and settled on a lesser number of large, semi-permanent camps, with able-bodied evacuees enrolling in a "work corps." They would provide for the requirements of the camps, clear and develop land, and produce agricultural and manufactured products —such as tents, camouflage nets and cartridge belts for the war effort—for sale on the open market, and share in the profits. Less than a week after the Salt Lake meeting a search got under way for suitable camp sites. Certain basic requirements were enumerated. First, they had to be on government land so whatever improvements were made would become public. The site had to be large enough to accommodate 5,000 or more persons since this number could be guarded by a minimum unit of troops as easily as smaller groups. The site also had to be located at a safe distance from strategic installations, and it had to provide work opportunities. Some 300 sites were studied on paper and 100 examined by field crews. Predictably, some of the same officials who had opposed evacuees resettling in their states were extremely anxious to get a camp; a camp would be almost as stimulating to the local economy as a military base. By June 5, ten sites had been selected—Manzanar in the Owens Valley of eastern California and Poston in Arizona near the California line, both started as Assembly Centers by the Army but transferred to WRA; Tule Lake in northeastern California near the Oregon border; Minidoka in south-central Idaho; Heart Mountain just east of Cody, Wyoming; Granada in the Arkansas valley of southeastern Colorado; Topaz in central Utah; Gila River southeast of Phoenix, Arizona; and Rohwer and Jerome in the Mississippi bottomlands of Arkansas. All except the two Arkansas sites had one thing in common—they were in semi-desert country.

But even as site selection was under way, circumstances were bringing about a change in WRA policy. The work corps idea fell flat among the evacuees. Perhaps it smacked too much of permanent confinement. When it was given a trial introduction at the Portland Assembly Center, only fifteen men out of hundreds signed up. Almost simultaneously, however, farm officials from the very states which had opposed an influx of evacuees pleaded with WRA to make temporary agricultural labor available. After they had an opportunity to reconsider their problems, the prospect of evacuees moving into their states—temporarily—did not seem quite so repugnant. Thousands of acres of cropland were being overwhelmed by weeds or stunted by lack of care. The war effort required food, but it couldn't be grown without manpower. Many farm youths were in uniform. Others had gone to work in shipyards and aircraft plants. Suddenly the supply of manpower languishing in the Assembly Centers and starting to move to the WRA camps had become a very salable commodity. Perhaps there was hope of resettling the evacuees after all—not only in the fields of the West but in factories, stores and shops all over the country, wherever skilled hands were needed.

But first the needs of Western farmers had to be met. As a trial, a small group of men from the Portland Assembly Center was taken to Malheur County in eastern Oregon to investigate working and living conditions. Their favorable report led to scores of men, anxious for freedom, volunteering for farm labor. WRA quickly drew up "seasonal leave" procedures whereby evacuees could leave the Assembly Centers for temporary agricultural work, returning to the camp and their families when the job was finished. But now it was WRA laying down the conditions. WRA required that the governors, sheriffs, prosecuting attorneys and judges in the various localities certify that the safety of Japanese American workers would be guaranteed; that the going wage be paid; that transportation and adequate housing be provided. By the end of June 1,500 evacuees were working in Idaho, Utah and Montana. There were only a few minor incidents of local bullies threatening the Japanese, and when WRA threatened to withdraw the workmen, their employers quickly got matters straightened out. The evacuees were in such great demand that farmers even tried to lure them away from their neighbors!

By the middle of the fall harvest, 10,000 evacuees were on seasonal leave—one out of five of all males who had been evacuated were out of the camps helping to bring in the crops. Since there were some 20,000 male evacuees between the ages of twenty and fifty, approximately one-half the available manpower took part in the emergency farm labor program, forcing women to take over some of the heavy work in the camps. Even so, both WRA and the

When farmers in inland states issued a call for harvest hands in the fall of 1942, 10,000 *Nisei* and *Issei* volunteered from the camps. *Nisei* volunteers in Montana learn technique of topping sugar beets. (War Relocation Authority)

evacuees were criticized by local officials because more workers could not be provided!

Through the summer of 1942, barracks cities sprang up under Army direction on the sites selected by WRA. As crude and rudimentary as these settlements were, building communities to shelter from 8,000 (Granada) to 20,000 (Poston) residents was no simple matter. An adequate water supply, a major problem in some of the desert areas, had to be developed. A sewage disposal system had to be built. Electric power lines had to be strung. In a state like Wyoming, Heart Mountain with a projected population of 11,000 promised to be the third largest city, its residents outnumbered only by Cheyenne and Casper.

What was called a "modified theater of operations camp" was agreed upon to provide adequate shelter in communities that could be built speedily, cheaply and with a minimum use of critical materials. The typical center was made up of 36 or more "blocks." Each block had two sections, and each section was made up of 12 barracks served by one mess hall and a central H-shaped sanitation building housing men's and women's latrines, shower and laundry

Tarpaper-covered barracks housed 10,000 evacuees at Heart Mountain, Wyoming. Camp got its name from the peak in the background. (National Archives)

rooms, and a separate "recreation hall." The barracks were a standard 20 feet wide and 120 feet long, partitioned into six rooms, the smallest of which were 16 by 20 feet, the largest 24 by 20 feet. The exterior walls were wood sheathing applied on 2 by 4 studs and covered with black tarpaper. Uniformly drab black buildings, laid out in monotonously square formation, stretched over what had been sagebrush flats. None of the buildings was provided with interior walls, but in the northern camps wallboard was supplied and crews of evacuee carpenters hurried to build walls and ceilings before winter set in. Each room was furnished with a stove, one droplight and steel Army cots and mattresses—nothing more. The space allotment was one room per family; it was up to the family's ingenuity to build furniture and shelves from scrap lumber, arrange for the privacy of its members and make these bleak little boxes livable. In the 1960's such quarters would have been condemned as below the poverty level. There were no toilet or bath facilities in the rooms—these could be as much as 200 feet distant. The recreation hall was an unpartitioned barrack building and unequipped except for heating stoves. Each mess hall was designed to feed 300 persons.

Each camp site also had quarters for the Caucasian personnel who would supervise its operation, a camp somewhat separated from the evacuee area for a company of military police, an administra-

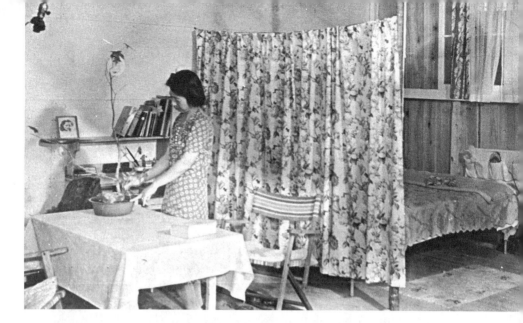

Despite the starkness of their barracks apartments, evacuees did their best to give them a homey touch and find a bit of privacy.

tion building, hospital and warehouses. The camp site and family "apartments," crowded as they were, were much roomier than those of the Assembly Centers but overall the WRA camps provided only for the most Spartan type of living.

The Army was anxious to get the evacuees out of the Assembly Centers and into the WRA camps as quickly as possible. Over WRA protests that the camps were not ready, the movements were under way in earnest by mid-June. Nearly every day contingents of roughly 500 were loaded into dilapidated railroad coaches together with military escorts, and steam engines, hissing and groaning, chugged off on the long, desolate road to exile. Mine Okubo wrote of her experience:

"The trip was a nightmare that lasted two nights and a day. The train creaked with age. It was covered with dust, and as the gaslights failed to function properly we traveled in complete darkness most of the night, reminding me of the blackout trains in Europe. All shades were drawn and we were not allowed to look out of the windows . . . The first night was a novelty after four and a half months of internment. However, I could not sleep and I spent the entire night taking the chair apart and readjusting it. Many became train sick and vomited. The children cried from restlessness. At one point on the way, a brick was thrown into one of the cars . . . In the late afternoon the train stopped in the desert somewhere in northern Nevada and for half an hour we were permitted to get off the train and walk around. Barbed-wire fences bounded the stretch on either side of the track and military police stood on guard every 15 feet . . ."

It might be well to recall at this point that two-thirds of these people were citizens of the United States and not one of them had been charged with a disloyal act.

Mine Okubo's trip from Tanforan to Topaz, Utah, was comparatively short. The rail journey from Santa Anita to Heart Mountain, Wyoming, sometimes by way of El Paso, Texas, took three days. Those being sent to the Arkansas camps were four days en route. Miss Okubo describes her first sight of Topaz which someone with a sense of humor had named "the Jewel of the Desert." After transferring from the train to buses, "suddenly, the Central Utah Relocation Project was stretched out before us in a cloud of dust. It was a desolate scene. Hundreds of low black barracks covered with tarred paper were lined up row after row. A few telephone poles stood like sentinels, and soldiers could be seen patrolling the grounds. The bus struggled through the soft alkaline dirt . . . when we finally battled our way into the safety of the building we looked as if we had fallen into a flour barrel."

Dust was with the evacuees at all the camps except those in Arkansas where the problem was mud. The desert, as the Soil Conservation Service well knew, was not meant to be disturbed. But bulldozers had stripped off the natural cover, trucks had trampled down the grass and churned up the earth. The slightest puff of wind lifted dust in suffocating clouds that drifted into the barracks under the loose-fitting window sash, under the doors, until the floors were gritty and even the bedding smelled of dust. In time the restless desert winds racing unimpeded swept the land bare, and on particularly turbulent days sand and even tiny pebbles were picked up and flung against the barracks.

Meanwhile, a significant change was about to take place in Washington. One Sunday evening in mid-June Mr. and Mrs. Dillon S. Myer hosted a party in their home. Most of the guests were associates of Myer in the Department of Agriculture and their wives. Ohio-born Myer was tall and white-haired. He wore rimless glasses and smiled easily and warmly. Early in adult life he had

Dillon S. Myer
As WRA Director, he defied the bigots

started work in Indiana with the Agricultural Extension service. During World War I he had been sent to Purdue University to train county agents to spur food production. He had served as a county agent in Ohio and as supervisor of county agents until he had been summoned to Washington by President Roosevelt's New Deal Administration to work in the program of revitalizing agriculture. One of the guests that evening was Milton Eisenhower, a neighbor who shared a car pool with Myer. When Eisenhower was named to head the WRA program, Myer had helped him select key aides from the Department of Agriculture, but outside of that Myer was only vaguely aware of the work that his friend was doing.

As Myer remembers it, Eisenhower sat down at the piano and played and he remained behind after all the other guests had gone home. Then he told Myer that Elmer Davis, head of the Office of War Information, had asked him to come to work as deputy. Eisenhower went on to say that in the few months he had headed WRA, he had become deeply involved in its problems and often had trouble sleeping at night. Eisenhower said he wanted to take the OWI job, but he felt a responsibility to leave WRA in the best possible hands. Then he asked Myer to take the WRA position.

Myer said he was interested, but wanted to think it over. Like most of the officials in Washington, Myer was largely unaware of any "Japanese" problem in the United States. He had known casually several students from Japan during his college days, but had had no dealings with Japanese Americans. The day after his party, Myer had another long talk with Eisenhower and finally agreed to take the directorship. Eisenhower on Tuesday recommended to the President that Myer be named to head the War Relocation Authority and on Wednesday the appointment was made. The two-sentence letter of appointment, dated June 17, 1942, read:

"Dear Mr. Myer:

"I hearby appoint you, effective this date, as Director of the War Relocation Authority established by Executive Order of March 18, 1942. In this position you will receive a salary of $10,000 per annum and will be entitled to actual and necessary transportation, subsistence, and other expenses incidental to the performance of your duties.

"Yours sincerely,
"Franklin D. Roosevelt"

This was the only guidance Myer ever received from the President. However, general guidelines were provided by the two-page executive order which gave the director broad powers to arrange "for the employment of such persons (the evacuees) at useful work in industry, commerce, agriculture or public projects, prescribe the terms and conditions of such public employment, and safeguard the public interest in the private employment of such persons." Myer also inherited a philosophy Eisenhower had developed even during his brief experience. On leaving WRA Eisenhower wrote to the President:

"The future of the program (WRA) will doubtless be governed largely by the temper of American public opinion. Already public attitudes have exerted a strong influence in shaping the program and charting its direction. In a democracy this is unquestionably sound and proper. Yet in leaving the War Relocation Authority after a few extremely crowded weeks, I cannot help expressing the hope that the American people will grow toward a broader appreciation of the essential Americanism of a great majority of the evacuees and of the difficult sacrifice they are making. Only when the prevailing attitudes of unreasoning bitterness have been replaced by tolerance and understanding will it be possible to carry forward a genuinely satisfactory relocation program and to plan intelligently for the reassimilation of the evacuees into American life when the war is over. I wish to give you my considered judgment that fully 80 to 85 per cent of the *Nisei* are loyal to the United States, perhaps 50 per cent of the *Issei* are passively loyal; but a large portion of the *Kibei* (American citizens educated in Japan) feel a strong cultural attachment to Japan."

Eisenhower went on to urge the President to take four steps:

1. Recommend to Congress a program of repatriation for those who prefer the Japanese way of life.

2. Issue a strong public statement in behalf of loyal American citizens "who are now bewildered and wonder what is in store for them."

3. Call for a more liberal wage policy for evacuees. The evacuees were to be paid $12, $16 and $19 a month depending on their skills, plus a small clothing allowance. They were, of course, also to be given shelter, food, medical care and education for their children without charge. WRA realized that with this kind of income the evacuees were dipping into their savings to keep up life insurance payments and to buy the little extras needed to brighten drab camp life. With no opportunity to save, their reassimilation into the American lifestream at the end of the war would be most difficult. Still, WRA felt that it could not pay the evacuees more than American servicemen whose basic pay was only $21 a month.

4. Ask Congress to enact a special program of rehabilitation after the war to help the evacuees find their place in American life.

Shortly after Myer took over, Tom Holland, one of WRA's top aides, returned to Washington from an inspection of several of the camps. His report, Myer recalls, was "a moving and articulate plea against keeping the evacuees in the camps for any length of time." Holland could see major problems developing in the unnatural atmosphere of the relocation centers. (The government persistently refused to call them concentration camps although others, including the evacuees themselves, did. There was a reason for official use of this euphemism. WRA felt it was easier to win public acceptance and find jobs and homes for "relocatees" from "relocation centers" than "prisoners" from "concentration camps.") Holland feared the development of new Indian reservations filled with Japanese Americans reluctant to leave, and urged that the WRA adopt a policy to permit the evacuees to move out on their own as rapidly as possible. Myer was convinced immediately that Holland's evaluation was right, and this conviction was strengthened after an inspection trip of his own. By July 20, hardly more than a month after he had taken over, Myer announced a program whereby citizens—but not *Kibei*—would leave the centers to take jobs outside the Western Defense Command. But resettlement obviously would be a long, slow process.

Simultaneously Myer plunged into the extraordinarily involved task of staffing the various centers, arranging for the logistics of feeding the evacuees as they continued to pour into the camps, and taking care of such matters as finding funds for building schools, organizing school systems and hiring teachers, and other human problems with which the Army hadn't concerned itself. Some 40,000 of the evacuees, nearly half of the total, were under twenty years of age—one-fourth were under fifteen—a fact accounted for by the *Issei* delay in starting families, and the problems of these youngsters differed greatly from those of their elders.

Then, in a four-day meeting in San Francisco with the men chosen to head each of the centers—their official title was Project Director—Myer and his aides hammered out an operations manual setting policy on everything from mess hall procedure to internal policing and fire control, freedom of worship to food production plans, requisitioning supplies to evacuee self-government. The rules had to be written from scratch, edited, printed and hurriedly distributed for the camps were filling up rapidly. There was no prece-

Even in the camps, education had to go on. Until more permanent school buildings could be built, classes were held in makeshift quarters like this. (National Archives)

dent to guide Myer, for never before had there been established within a period of a few weeks ten cities populated by people who were and were not prisoners, who did and did not have civil rights, who were unhappy and disillusioned and often bitter but who, remarkably, were determined to make the best of their misfortune.

The Project Director was in effect a city manager, but he held virtual dictatorial powers—within the limits of his operating manual —over the evacuees in his charge. He was surrounded by a staff of aides, all Caucasians, who headed the various departments. And running the departments under their direction were the evacuees. It was a three-caste system. First, there were the Caucasians who ate in their own dining room and had their separate quarters. They had free passage in and out of the camp, drew civil service pay and fraternized among themselves. Next were the evacuees who were the worker caste. They lived out in the "area," as distinguished from the administrative section. They were fed in mess halls where the cost averaged less than 45 cents per person per day. Many of the evacuees were better qualified by training and experience to run their departments than their supervisors. Yet the racially segre-

gated caste system decreed that they could never aspire to a supervisory job. The evacuees worked side by side with their supervisors
—running the accounting department, performing a surgical operation at the camp hospital, planning a long-range agricultural program, supervising the distribution of supplies from the warehouse,
overhauling a tractor, teaching in the schools—but they could not
be paid more than $19 a month. Nor, while in the camps, could
they ever leave their caste. Like their supervisors the *Nisei* were
American citizens, but the very fact of the evacuation and their
incarceration denied them equal treatment under the law.

Despite these inequities warm relationships developed between
the evacuees and their Caucasian bosses. Many of the Caucasians
had joined WRA from the Works Progress Administration and
other New Deal agencies where good work habits were conspicuous by their absence. These individuals were pleasantly surprised
by the competence, energy and sense of responsibility exhibited by
the evacuees. Whatever they were expecting, they quickly developed a respect for the people in their charge. And the evacuees
appreciated the friendship and trust their superiors extended, a
startling change from being kicked around back home on the Coast.

The third caste was the military, and they really have no place
in this account of WRA camp life. The military police were the
watchmen. They had been assigned by the Army to see that no
unauthorized persons entered or left the camps. Day after monotonous day they manned the gate and the watchtowers that surrounded the camps. At night they turned on floodlights that illumi-
nated the high barbed wire fences around the perimeter of the
"area." The soldiers were armed and it was their duty to mean
business. They demonstrated this at Topaz in Utah when they shot
and killed an elderly *Issei* who wandered too close to the fence.
There was nothing on the other side of the fence except more sand
and sagebrush. He could not have wandered far even if he had
climbed through the fence, but the sentry had to show that he
meant business. The fences and the towers were constant reminders
to the evacuees that they were prisoners and they had no desire
to fraternize, even if they were permitted to, with their jailers.
Even the WRA personnel did not fraternize with the soldiers.

By the first of November, 1942, the last trainload of evacuees
had been transferred from the WCCA Assembly Centers to the

relocation centers. Some 107,000 men, women and children had been moved, first from their homes to the Assembly Centers, thence inland. Even aside from the human cost, this had not been a cheap operation for the American taxpayer. Despite the primitive nature of the facilities, construction at the Assembly Centers had cost the Army $10,701,636. It had cost the Army another $2,281,976 for rail transportation to move the evacuees from assembly to relocation centers, and another half million to feed these people en route. The cost of building the ten relocation centers added another $56,482,638 to the total bill. The grand total spent by the Army in the evacuation program was $88,679,716. More significant, it had taken the Army until just seven days short of eleven months after the attack on Pearl Harbor to complete the job. By then the tide of war had turned completely in the Pacific. Even as the evacuation was completed, it could no longer be called a military necessity.

In the relocation centers, life settled down to a routine. After a series of chilly days, Minidoka finally got delivery of heating stoves for the barracks and the evacuees learned to bank fires so their rooms would stay warm all night. Some residents of Gila and Poston were able to buy electric fans which they rigged into crude evaporative coolers to take the edge off the Arizona desert's fierce heat. In the Arkansas camps plank walkways were laid to avoid the omnipresent mud. At Heart Mountain, where the temperature plunged as far as 30 below zero, everyone turned out one Saturday to "winterize" the barracks by shoveling dirt against the walls so the wind wouldn't blow under the floors, and some Californians had to be taught that coal would not burst into flames when a match was touched to it.

Americans everywhere were wrestling with the intricacies of "red points" for buying rationed meat, and the evacuees were under the same restrictions. An inordinate amount of what the Army Quartermaster Corps (which supplied the camps) called "edible offal" was served—pork liver, beef hearts, tripe. What red meat was available was so tough and stringy that the chefs had no choice but to throw it into stewpots. Toddlers learned to make do with suppers of frankfurters, sauerkraut and rice. When cold weather set in WRA issued Navy pea jackets and Army coats, all of which were too large. Since everyone wore trousers for protec-

The relocation camps were either too hot or too cold, too wet or too dry. These pictures were taken at Minidoka, Idaho. (National Archives)

tion against the cold, men were indistinguishable from women when they were muffled against icy, dusty winds and buried inside their government-issue coats.

Such hardships and inconveniences inevitably were a part of the frontier life of the WRA camps and were the result of a situation inherited—not created—by WRA. Myer and his staff labored diligently on two objectives: To make camp life less disagreeable, and to get the evacuees out of the camps as rapidly as possible. As we

War Relocation Centers provided little opportunity for a meaningful family life. This is a messhall scene. (War Relocation Authority)

have seen, before the evacuation program was completed evacuees were being released on temporary permits to work on the farms of the inter-mountain region. But even before this, a number of influential people had expressed concern for *Nisei* college students whose educations were being disrupted by the evacuation. Interest in their welfare came from unexpected sources, not the least important of which was California's Governor Olson.

Early in May, 1942, Olson wrote a letter to President Roosevelt relaying the concern of the Western College Association that due to the evacuation "the education of those who might become influential leaders of the loyal American-born Japanese will be abruptly closed. Such a result will be injurious not only to them, but to the nation since well-trained leadership for such persons will be needed after the present war." Olson went on to say that some 1,000 students were involved, and many of them would need financial aid to continue their studies even if they were accepted as students by Midwestern and Eastern schools.

Roosevelt replied promptly, saying: "I am deeply concerned

Harvey Itano, who established the highest scholastic record for the University of California Class of 1942, was unable to attend the graduation ceremonies to receive his degree in chemistry. President Robert Gordon Sproul said at the graduation: "Harvey cannot be with us today. His country has called him elsewhere." Photo was taken in the Sacramento Assembly Center. Itano went on to become a brilliant scientist. (National Archives)

that the American-born Japanese college students shall be impressed with the ability of the American people to distinguish between enemy aliens and staunch supporters of the American system who happen to have Japanese ancestry."

If he had taken this position five months earlier, the evacuation might not have taken place. By May, he had people around him who had gained an insight into the problems and pressures surrounding evacuation. There is reason to believe Eisenhower had a hand in drafting the President's reply to Olson, for Eisenhower already had asked Clarence Pickett, the prominent Quaker leader, to head a committee to devise plans for aiding *Nisei* students. By the end of May the National Student Relocation Council was organized at a meeting in Chicago and President John W. Nason of Swarthmore College was named chairman with headquarters in Philadelphia. By fall, hundreds of *Nisei* were enrolled in interior schools. Much of the field work, finding places for *Nisei* students and seeing that they were doing well, was undertaken by Robert W. O'Brien who as assistant to the dean of the college of arts and sciences at the University of Washington had learned a good deal about them. The *Nisei*, on their part, lost no time in fitting into the academic and social life of campuses all over the country, demonstrating an encouraging assimilability once they were freed of the strictures of the West Coast.

By October, WRA announced much more liberalized procedures for leaving the camps, enabling *Issei* as well as *Nisei* to apply. The main feature was security clearance by the Federal Bureau of Investigation. Evacuees seeking permission to take jobs outside the camps had their records checked by the FBI which also had access to the files of other U.S. intelligence agencies. If there was no derogatory information, and there was promise of a job, the evacuee was permitted to go out on "permanent leave." While such security checks were merely routine in virtually all cases, they were necessary to assure host communities the evacuees were "loyal." They were also necessary for the safety and welfare of the evacuees themselves because of the stigma attached to all Japanese Americans by the evacuation.

Myer explains why WRA was anxious to get the evacuees out into the American lifestream: "We recognized that loyalty could not flourish in an atmosphere of restriction and discriminatory segregation. Such wide and enforced deviation from normal cultural and living patterns might very well have lasting and unfavorable effects upon individuals, particularly children and young people. There was an obligation on the part of WRA, both to the evacuees and to the people of the United States generally, to restore all loyal citizens and law-abiding aliens to a normal useful American life. Confinement in relocation centers fostered suspicion of evacuee loyalties and added to their discouragement. We did

On the way outside: Mr. and Mrs. Tom Oki have their permit checked as they leave the barbed-wire confines of Heart Mountain WRA camp in search of a new life under the government's relocation program. (National Archives)

not want to be responsible for fostering a new set of reservations like those of the Indians."

Little by little, as WRA's effort to tell the true story of the evacuees began to take effect, offers of jobs began to filter in. In September, 1942, *Issei* railroad workers were restored to their jobs in eastern Oregon and two transcontinental lines asked for a thousand maintenance workers. But there were other employers who understood that all Japanese Americans were not laborers. Office workers were sought in Chicago, social case workers in New York City, a science teacher in North Dakota, an architect in Philadelphia, a linotype operator in Utah, a chemist in eastern Oregon. There were calls for diesel engineers, dental and laboratory technicians, draftsmen, mechanics—jobs which *Nisei* had prepared for and were anxious to fill.

By July of 1943 WRA had requests for 10,000 evacuees from the Chicago area alone, but now most of the jobs went begging. The demand reflected the efforts of the WRA, but more important, was the result of the superb records of the early relocatees who had gone out to demonstrate that they were good citizens and could do the work required of them. WRA hurriedly set out to learn why the evacuees were not leaving the camps in expected numbers. Myer says: "The principal deterrent proved to be uncertainty regarding public sentiment, which was quite understandable. Others were lack of funds, lack of information about conditions in the destination communities, fear about inability to support dependents, and worry about possible lack of living quarters. It was clear that the pattern of institutionalization, which many of us in WRA had feared almost from the beginning, was already well established."

This was true particularly of the *Issei*. For many of them evacuation was the first vacation they had ever enjoyed. They were provided shelter and food and they had plenty of time to visit with friends, play cards, take lessons in Japanese singing or brush painting and indulge in hobbies like wood-carving and building miniature gardens. On the "outside" they had worked from dawn to dusk to support their families and to try, usually unsuccessfully, to lay aside a small nest egg. Now the government had taken over their support and there was nothing anyone could do about saving money. And so they were reluctant to give up all this for the uncertainty of life in the hostile world outside the barbed wire where, regardless of where their sympathies lay, they were enemy aliens.

The *Nisei*, being younger, were more restless. They chafed at the aimless life inside the camps. They wanted to return to the "normal useful American life" that Dillon Myer talked about. One of those who did go was Robert Hosokawa who until the evacuation had never been farther east than Walla Walla, Washington. From Minidoka he relocated in Independence, Mo., attracted in part by the name, to work for a weekly newspaper. After he and his wife had been there several months he wrote in the *Christian Science Monitor:*

"We have made friends and have established ourselves fairly well. We are hopeful of the future and we will jealously fight for the perpetuation of true American ideals, opposing all the pseudo-democrats. During the months of confinement our minds lived in the future—not in the past—hoping, planning, dreaming and thinking. The freedom we had always taken for granted—as most Americans still do—began to take on deep meaning when we had been deprived of it. There were times when we began to lose faith in ourselves and our ability to take it. Life in the camps was not easy.

It was inadequate and morale-killing. But never in those months did we lose faith in America. Sometimes we were bitterly disappointed and enraged when we read the lies, distortions and testimony of un-American politicians and false patriots. If the government gives genuine backing to make a success of the plan for widespread resettlement, then the heartaches, losses and hardships will be partly compensated. If this fails, if Americans with Japanese faces are cast aside as unassimilables, as creatures to be shipped across to the land of their ancestors, despite their citizenship, then American democracy may as well throw in the towel. For what happens to one minority group will happen to another and the four freedoms will be enjoyed by only those powerful enough to keep it from the others."

There were many still in the WRA camps who felt similar doubts. They harbored deep fears about their acceptability and their future in their native land, fears that were stirred by a new wave of harassment and vituperation that made the pre-evacuation attacks seem mild by comparison. The voices of only a few West Coast members of Congress had helped bring about the evacuation. But now that evacuation was a fact, they were joined in attacking the evacuees by scores of others, by powerful newspaper chains, by the American Legion and other influential organizations.

Writing in the *Pacific Citizen*, weekly publication of the JACL, a *Nisei* columnist said: "These attacks that persist against us are more sinister than those that preceded evacuation, for now it is no longer possible to say that our persecutors are motivated by an honest if misguided patriotism. There has been plenty of time now to ascertain the facts. There is no reason after all these months for anyone to be morally honest and yet base his charges against us on misinformation."

In the camps the evacuees were convinced they had been driven out of California for economic and political reasons camouflaged by waving the red, white and blue flag of military necessity. Many believed the new campaign was launched to prevent their return to California, ever. But Carey McWilliams in his book *Prejudice, Japanese Americans, Symbol of Racial Intolerance*, says the real objective was "to prevent the release of any further evacuees from the centers and to drive back into relocation centers all those who had been released and relocated in the Middle West."

21

A TIME OF BITTERNESS, VALOR AND CONFUSION

Against the New Year sky,
Beyond the fence flutters
The Stars and Stripes.
                —*Haiku by Sankuro Nagano*

LATE IN NOVEMBER, 1942, shortly after the last of the evacuees had been transferred from Assembly Centers to WRA, the JACL was given permission to summon two of its leaders from each of the camps to a conference in Salt Lake City. JACL had little money to spend; all delegates were instructed to travel by bus or railroad coach. The men from Manzanar and Tule Lake were escorted to the California border before they were permitted to travel on their own. Some had expected to encounter hostility but the public took no particular notice of them. Only one man reported any kind of unpleasantness. During a rest stop at Evanston, Wyoming, Henry Mitarai from Heart Mountain went into a restaurant for a cup of coffee. The Chinese proprietor refused to serve him.

Nisei from Utah and Idaho hosted the visitors and had arranged a full social program but the events were poorly attended. The men from the camps held morning, afternoon and evening sessions, continued their discussions during meals, drifted out without pre-arrangement into the halls and cloakrooms during the socials for serious conversation that couldn't wait. There was much to talk about. How best could they help keep up evacuee morale in the camps? What role should JACL play in the limited self-government WRA permitted? What could be done to promote WRA's resettlement program? How should JACL combat the West Coast hate campaign aimed at preventing the return of the evacuees after the war? What should be done to defend the *Nisei's* most precious birthright, American citizenship, from further erosion?

The most intense discussion dealt with a proposal by Mike Masaoka: that JACL petition the President for reinstatement of *Nisei* under Selective Service.

This was a delicate issue, for the military had done little to endear itself to the *Nisei*. To begin with, the Navy and Marines had a policy of not accepting *Nisei* even before Pearl Harbor. And the Army had demanded evacuation and then carried it out. Shortly after Pearl Harbor the Selective Service System had changed the classification of all *Nisei* to 4C—aliens not subject to military service—thus imposing on them a blanket exemption from the draft. The *Nisei* had resented this discriminatory treatment deeply. On top of this, many *Nisei* already in uniform had been released from active service by transfer to the Enlisted Reserve Corps "for the convenience of the government"—a transparent euphemism for being kicked out. No explanation was ever given; the names of *Nisei* GIs (most of them *Kibei*) had been posted without warning at Army installations along the Pacific Coast and the next day they were on their way home. Other *Nisei* who remained with their outfits found themselves on permanent K.P. or yard detail, stuck with the most menial jobs. When their buddies were shipped overseas, the *Nisei* were transferred to other units.

Now Masaoka was urging that the delegates overlook this discrimination, overlook the fact that their people had been locked up, ignore all this and petition that these same people be conscripted to go out and fight for freedom. Some of the delegates said Masaoka's proposal was ridiculous and unrealistic, that the *Nisei* had every right to enjoy exemption from the draft since the government had made it plain they were not wanted. Others could see the long-range wisdom of Masaoka's argument that the *Nisei* needed a record of having fought for their country to bulwark their postwar struggle to win full citizenship rights, but they feared hostile reaction in the camps where long-suppressed resentments were bubbling to the surface.

For the most part, the Japanese Americans had submitted docilely to the evacuation order. Stunned and benumbed by the turn of events, they had been persuaded that their removal was a military necessity. Realistically, once the evacuation decision was made they had no choice but to comply; to do otherwise was to invite violence and charges of treason. In the early days of camp life the evacuees had been kept busy by the necessity of setting up a workable order, of making their quarters comfortable, of adjusting to the realities of their predicament. But when their lives had settled into a routine, there was time to think, time for anger and frustration to be given expression. Some of the delegates knew there would be trouble in the camps when it was learned they had endorsed Selective Service for the *Nisei*.

But Masaoka argued eloquently. Backed by Kido and others, Masaoka declared the *Nisei* must demand the right to fight for their country in its time of peril, must shed their blood if necessary, to nail down their claim to unabridged citizenship after the war. "There are politicians even now," he warned, "who are trying to pass laws in Congress to strip us of citizenship and ship us to Japan when the war is over. The most effective weapon against this kind of persecution is a record of having fought valiantly for our country side by side with Americans of other racial extraction."

In the end the delegates unanimously endorsed the proposal even though many of them knew they would face bitter criticism and perhaps violence when they returned to their camps. They also expressed their confidence in Dillon Myer and his policies, and urged that a plan be drawn up to separate the actively loyal from the others.

The apprehensions of some of the delegates turned out to be well-founded. Kido's quarters in Poston were invaded one night by a gang of *Kibei* and he was beaten so badly he was hospitalized for nearly a month. Eight men, ranging in age from eighteen to thirty-seven, were apprehended and confessed to having taken part in the attack. Like the young Japanese Army officers who staged coups in the 1930's, the *Kibei* declared they had taken the law in their own hands "for the welfare of the community." A somewhat similar attack was made against Dr. Tom Yatabe in the hospital at Rohwer WRA center where he was working, and in Manzanar, after Fred Tayama was severely injured, a number of aggressively pro-American *Nisei*, including Togo Tanaka and Joe Grant Masaoka, had to be moved out to a temporary camp in Death Valley for their own protection. Perhaps the chief agitator in Manzanar was Hawaiian-born Joe Kurihara, who had served in the U.S.

Army in World War I. Kurihara was deeply embittered by the evacuation and swore "to become a Jap a hundred per cent and never to do another day's work to help this country fight this war." "He was bitter, and the most eloquently persuasive fellow in Manzanar," Tanaka says. "We were no match for him, and so we JACL people were run out of camp." Later, Kurihara asked to be sent to the segregation camp at Tule Lake, renounced his citizenship and went to Japan. Tanaka recalls that while he was a volunteer worker with the American Friends Service Committee in Chicago, helping evacuees find jobs and housing, he received a request through the Red Cross in Switzerland asking him to submit testimony in behalf of Kurihara stating that at one time he had been a loyal American citizen. Tanaka says: "The Quakers are kind people. Under their influence I responded. What the hell."

The issue of segregation was a pertinent one. One of the most telling arguments for mass evacuation of *all* Japanese Americans from the Coast had been the contention that the "loyal" could not be distinguished from the "disloyal" in the limited time available, and therefore it was only prudent to put all of them away someplace where they could commit no mischief. Implicit, though unvoiced, in this line of thinking was the understanding that in time the sheep would be separated from the goats, and presently demands began to be heard that this be done. Oddly enough, this step was urged by both friends and foes of the evacuees, but for different reasons. Those friendly to the evacuees wanted the "disloyal" purged so the others could be certified as untainted and their return to normal life expedited. The hostile wanted the "disloyal" branded so they could be punished by deportation, and since they were expecting a substantial number to be found guilty, they weren't overly concerned about the loyal.

Not least concerned about segregation was the military, and the Army and Navy took somewhat different points of view. Commander Ringle, who had been detailed by Naval Intelligence to study the Japanese in California before the outbreak of war, was assigned briefly to WRA during its earliest days. He recognized that "at least 75 percent" of the *Nisei* were loyal to the United States, that the "large majority" of *Issei* were "at least passively loyal" and would not knowingly do anything to injure the U.S., that less than 3 percent of the total "would act as saboteurs or agents" and most of them were in custody. Ringle also declared the *Kibei* were the most potentially dangerous element. He said they should be looked upon as enemy aliens despite their legal citizenship and "many of them" should be detained. Ringle proposed that aliens and citizens alike be given an opportunity to announce loyalty to Japan with the assurance that they would be treated as internees and repatriated to Japan as soon as possible. In summary, Ringle declared that aside from race there was very little difference between *Nisei* and their Caucasian contemporaries, and that their ultimate outlook "will depend on the way in which they are treated now, and on how they are helped to meet the test of this war."

On the other hand, WRA received a proposal over General DeWitt's signature on December 30, 1942, that called for troops to take over the camps without warning on a designated day, institute "suitable security measures in order to insure against probable rioting and consequent bloodshed," and proceed swiftly with segregation. Those to be segregated would include all who requested repatriation or expatriation to Japan, all aliens paroled to WRA centers from internment camps, all evacuees with police records at the assembly or relocation centers, all listed as "potentially dangerous" by the intelligence services, and all immediate family members of those marked for deportation.

Myer quickly rejected what he called "this brazen and cold-blooded proposal." But it impressed on him again the need for a less drastic segregation program. About the same time, he received word the War Department was receptive to the formation of a volunteer all-*Nisei* combat unit to fight in Europe, possibly as a first step toward the restoration of Selective Service. Myer had been advocating a revision in the Army's policy since July of 1942 for the same reasons that Masaoka had expounded at the Salt Lake City meeting. But neither was quite sure how the *Nisei* would take to a segregated unit, the kind of outfit Masaoka had first proposed and was turned down on. However, both WRA and Masaoka, representing the JACL, endorsed the idea of a volunteer all-*Nisei* outfit, and on January 28, 1943, Secretary Stimson announced plans for what eventually was designated the 442nd Regimental Combat Team. Masaoka and his colleague, George Inagaki, were summoned to the Pentagon to hear the news before the public announcement.

Both volunteered on the spot. Masaoka in time joined the 442nd, and Inagaki went into the military intelligence program about which more will be heard later.

The Army's plans called on all male *Nisei* of draft age to fill out questionnaires which then would be evaluated to determine eligibility for work in defense plants as well as military service. Myer seized this as an opportunity to expedite WRA's leave clearance procedure and proposed that the questionnaires be presented to everyone—men and women, citizens and aliens—over seventeen years of age.

The proposal was adopted, but in its haste, WRA was guilty of two major errors. First, the questionnaires were labeled "Application for Leave Clearance." Many *Issei* did not want to leave the camps. In fact, they feared they would be forced to leave the security of the camps for an uncertain life among hostile people, and the questionnaire confused, frightened and antagonized them.

Second, questions which had been planned for *Nisei* men were submitted unchanged to women and *Issei*.

Question No. 27 asked: "Are you willing to serve in the armed forces of the United States on combat duty, wherever ordered?"

Question 28 asked: "Will you swear unqualified allegiance to the United States of America and faithfully defend the United States from any or all attack by foreign or domestic forces, and foreswear any form of allegiance or obedience to the Japanese emperor, to any other foreign government, power or organization?"

Having been forced to fill out dozens of forms and answer uncounted questionnaires, the evacuees had learned to be cautious. They were also quite literal. Women and the *Issei*, who averaged more than fifty years of age, read Question 27 and decided they were not about to volunteer for combat duty. Who could say what the government was plotting for them? The *Issei* had not been permitted to become American citizens, but Question 28 asked them to foreswear allegiance to the only country where they had citizenship status. Obviously an affirmative answer would make them stateless persons, and so they shied away from that question, too.

Even the *Nisei* were confused. Some contended that to reply affirmatively to Question 28, forswearing allegiance to Japan, would be an admission that such allegiance had existed. Others made conditional responses to Question 27: "Yes, if my rights as a citizen are restored," or "No, not unless the government recognizes my right to live anywhere in the United States." A number of *Nisei* answered the two questions in the negative, not because of disloyalty, but out of resentment against the way their country had treated them. But within the limited confines of a questionnaire, there was no room for explanatory ifs and buts, no place for conditional responses. And in the unfeeling process of statistical analysis, the No-No boys had to go down as disloyal. In this context, "disloyal" was an excessively harsh word, failing to allow for shades of meaning.

When the various troubles became evident, the *Issei* version of Question 28 was changed to read: "Will you swear to abide by the laws of the United States and to take no action which would in any way interfere with the war effort of the United States?" Most *Issei* found this acceptable, but by then the camps were in turmoil. There were numerous meetings with fiery speeches pro and con volunteering for military service. Often families were split, one brother ready to volunteer, another so bitter about the evacuation that he had registered a No-No protest, and parents caught in the middle.

In all, some 11 percent of those eligible to register—about 7,600 evacuees—gave "No" or qualified answers to the loyalty questions. At Tule Lake, some 3,000 refused to register, many of them intimidated by gangs of ruffians against whom WRA could not guarantee protection.

The "No" replies meant many things, Myer explained. He felt most of them were the expressions of people who had failed to become integrated into their prewar communities, who were weary of fighting against discrimination, who were unhappy with the way they had been treated in the Evacuation and angry with the government, who were discouraged about their future in the United States, even some who felt that they might have a more promising future if they went to Japan. But few were actively or even potentially disloyal to the United States; they were just fed up, and Myer could understand why they would be.

It was under these circumstances that President Roosevelt wrote to Secretary of War Stimson applauding the decision to form a *Nisei* combat team. Dated February 1, 1943, and addressed to "My Dear Mr. Secretary," it said:

"The proposal of the War Department to organize a combat team consisting of loyal American citizens of Japanese descent has my full approval. The new combat team will add to the nearly five thousand loyal Americans of Japanese ancestry who are already serving in the armed forces of our country.

"This is a natural and logical step toward the reinstitution of Selective Service procedures which were temporarily disrupted by the evacuation from the West Coast.

"No loyal citizen of the United States should be denied the democratic right to exercise the responsibilities of citizenship, regardless of his ancestry. *The principle on which this country was founded and by which it has always been governed is that Americanism is a matter of the mind and heart; Americanism is not, and never was, a matter of race or ancestry.* A good American is one who is loyal to this country and to our creed of liberty and democracy. Every loyal American citizen should be given the opportunity to serve this country wherever his skills will make the greatest contribution—whether it be in the ranks of the armed forces, war production, agriculture, government service, or other work essential to the war effort.

"I am glad to observe that the War Department, the Navy Department, the War Manpower Commission, the Department of Justice, and the War Relocation Authority are collaborating in a program which will insure the opportunity for all loyal Americans, including Americans of Japanese ancestry, to serve their country at a time when the fullest and wisest use of our manpower is all-important to the war effort.

> "Very sincerely yours,
> "Franklin D. Roosevelt"

The letter had been drafted in the offices of the War Relocation Authority for the President's signature. To make sure the letter was worded for the greatest public relations impact, Myer showed the draft to Elmer Davis, head of the Office of War Information. Myer recalls that Davis read it carefully, then whipped out a heavy black editorial pencil and wrote in the sentence that appears above in italics. Then he tossed the letter back on the table with the comment that perhaps it was his American Civil Liberties Union background that caused him to be sensitive to the essence of citizenship.

Although they were confined behind barbed wire and deeply resented deprivation of their rights, most evacuees continued to be loyal to the United States. Girls in a sewing class at Topaz WRA center in Utah sew a service flag. Below, Boy Scouts lead a Fourth of July parade at Tule Lake WRA center. (National Archives)

It was a happy contribution; the sentence, attributed to President Roosevelt, has been quoted scores of times.

Davis had come to bat for the *Nisei* on an earlier occasion. In a letter to the President on October 2, 1942, Davis noted that there were two bills in Congress, one seeking to strip the *Nisei* of citizenship, the other proposing to "intern" them for the duration. He felt these bills heightened the feeling that this was a racial war and

"No loyal citizen of the United States should be denied the democratic right to exercise the responsibilities of his citizenship, regardless of his ancestry.

"The principle on which this country was founded and by which it has always been governed is that Americanism is a matter of the mind and heart.

"Americanism is not, and never was, a matter of race or ancestry.

"Every loyal American citizen should be given the opportunity to serve this country wherever his skills will make the greatest contribution — whether it be in the ranks of our armed forces, war production, agriculture, government service, or other work essential to the war effort."

THE PRESIDENT OF THE UNITED STATES, FEBRUARY 3, 1943

In an effort to undo the damage done to the *Nisei* image by the Evacuation, the federal government issued posters like this one, quoting President Franklin Delano Roosevelt's letter endorsing *Nisei* war service. (National Archives)

asked F.D.R. for a brief public statement on behalf of loyal *Nisei*. He also urged that *Nisei* after individual loyalty tests be permitted to enlist in the Army and Navy.

"This matter is of great interest to OWI," Davis said. "Japanese propaganda to the Philippines, Burma and elsewhere insists that this is a racial war. We can combat this effectively with counter propaganda only if our deeds permit us to tell the truth. Moreover, as citizens ourselves who believe deeply in the things for which we fight, we cannot help but be disturbed by the insistent public misunderstanding of the *Nisei* . . ."

In the WRA camps the announcement of a *Nisei* combat team

was greeted by the predictable rumors—the *Nisei* would be used as cannon fodder, they would be employed as service troops because they would never be trusted enough to be thrown into combat, DeWitt would see to it that none of the *Nisei* would ever come back, etc., etc., etc. Most of the *Nisei* opposed the idea of a segregated outfit. They wanted to be treated in the same way as other Americans. Still, they admitted that the argument put forward by Army recruiting teams (including *Nisei* officers and noncoms) which visited the camps made sense: Dispersed among millions of Americans in uniform, the *Nisei* would be lost from view; concentrated in a combat team of regimental size, they could dramatize their loyalty. In the end more than a thousand *Nisei* stepped forth from behind the barbed wire fences that confined them—often resisting strong pressures from their peers—swore allegiance to the government that had evacuated them, and volunteered to fight for the freedom that had been denied them. These men were moved by more than an ordinary purpose. Many were married and had families. They understood, as some younger *Nisei* did not, the importance of securing the future of their children in the land of their birth. And they could see that military service was the surest way of securing that future. How these men wrote a stirring chapter in American military history with their blood will be related later.

As the first anniversary of WRA approached, Myer felt more deeply than ever that the relocation centers were unhealthy, undesirable communities and that they should be closed as soon as possible, particularly since there appeared to be little danger of the war effort being damaged by releasing the evacuees. He was distressed by the breakdown in the structure of Japanese American family life. With families eating in community mess halls and youngsters no longer dependent on parents for food and shelter,

Military recruiting teams visited the camps in an effort to sign up Nisei volunteers. Expressions reflect the doubts many Nisei felt.

Henry Sugimoto's painting portrays plight of Nisei wives who re-mained in the camps while their husbands volunteered for military service.

discipline problems increased. The concentration of thousands of persons of heterogeneous interests and backgrounds—citizens and aliens, farmers and urbanites, the well-to-do and the poor, those strongly oriented toward Japanese culture and those who knew nothing about Japan—into primitive camps led to what Myer called "widespread feeling of individual and collective insecurity and to frustrations, fears and bitterness." He decided it was time to take the first step to return the evacuees to their prewar homes, and on March 11, 1943, exactly one year after WCCA was formed, he wrote a long letter to Secretary of War Stimson proposing three possible courses of action.

Plan A called for a continuance of WRA's current program—relocating as many evacuees as possible, with volunteers going into specialized military units. The outlook was for relocating between

10 and 25 percent of the evacuees in the next four to six months.

Plan B would abolish restrictions applying only to the Japanese, permitting all evacuees to return to their homes except those ordered held by a joint board representing the Army, Navy and Department of Justice. Selective Service would be reinstituted for the men.

Plan C was a middle course. Evacuation restrictions would continue, but citizens cleared by the joint board, parents of servicemen and their immediate families would be permitted to return to the Coast. The WRA camps would be continued for those wishing to remain, and regular leave procedures would be applied to those seeking to settle elsewhere.

Myer hoped Stimson would agree to Plan C, moving toward Plan B "as soon as all real danger of West Coast invasion seemed to be eliminated." Stimson kept Myer waiting for two months. When the reply finally arrived, Myer with disappointment described it as "condescending." In essence, Stimson demanded a vigorous segregation program before anything else was done. He wrote in part:

"A serious deterioration in evacuee morale has been noted in recent months. This unsatisfactory development appears to be the result in large measure of the activities of a vicious, well-organized, pro-Japanese minority group to be found at each relocation project. Through agitation and by violence, these groups gained control of many aspects of internal project administration, so much so that it became disadvantageous, and sometimes dangerous, to express loyalty to the United States. The fact that these groups were permitted to remain in power not only shook the confidence of the loyal ones in their Government, but also effectively stifled the expression of pro-American sentiment . . . much trouble could have been avoided if these trouble makers had been removed from the relocation centers and placed in rigorous confinement . . . It seems clear to me that the problem of resettlement of persons of Japanese ancestry loyal to this country would be measurably simplified through segregation, as it would constitute an assurance to the American public that the bad actors had been effectively dealt with.

"The importance which the War Department attaches to segregation renders premature any consideration of relaxing the restrictions in force in the Western Defense Command . . ."

Myer was seething, but in a carefully restrained letter to Stimson he sought to set the record straight:

". . . I feel it is only fair to point out that if segregation could have been accomplished by the War Relocation Authority during 1942 and the early part of this year (1943) as easily as your letter implies, it could also have been accomplished by the War Department during the evacuation period. Substantially all the information about individual evacuees actually available to the War Relocation Authority prior to registration was available to the Army at the time of evacuation and later. If mass segregation on a fair and individual basis is so simple that the War Relocation Authority is to be criticized for not accomplishing it, it is difficult to see why a wholesale evacuation of all persons of Japanese descent was ever necessary. If the dangerous and potentially dangerous individuals may be so readily determined as your letter implies, it should have been possible to evacuate only the dangerous from the Pacific Coast area . . ."

Myer reminded Stimson that the military had made several segregation proposals affecting entire categories of the population rather than individuals. General DeWitt, Myer said, had proposed the segregation and repatriation of both *Issei* and *Kibei*, ignoring the obvious injustices of such indiscriminate action. Myer also termed as "over-simplification" Stimson's charge that a "pro-Japanese minority group" was disrupting the centers. He said some 100 aliens and 55 citizens had been determined to be trouble makers and placed in isolation centers. But most of those who had asked for repatriation and ostensibly were pro-Japanese, "generally have not been a source of trouble in the centers."

Myer also made a point that had largely been overlooked: The relocation program of moving evacuees out of the camps as rapidly as possible was, in fact, a segregation process and "the only process of whole segregation which has very much to recommend it."

Stimson, however, was far from being the greatest of Myer's concerns. By the first half of 1943 the anti-Japanese voices that had been stilled by the evacuation were being heard again, more raucously now, and joined in their shrill chorus by a motley assortment of demagogues, racists, sensation-seekers and hysterical little people. Most of the attacks were based on the thesis that the government's decision to evacuate Japanese Americans was proof of their disloyalty, proof of their undesirability, and ample reason for banishing them permanently from the West Coast. Looking back on this unbelievable period, one can only conclude that a not inconsiderable segment of the American people, including some of their political leaders and some of the press, had lost all reason on matters pertaining to the Japanese Americans. This was an excruciating time for the evacuees and for Myer who had come to identify with them far more completely than he had ever suspected he would. A book could be written about this period alone; here we shall try to cover it in a few paragraphs. Generally, the attacks can be categorized as follows:

—The politicians. If the loyalty of the *Nisei* could be gauged by the kind of politicians who were assailing them with reckless abandon, they would have come up with the highest possible marks. Senator A. B. (Happy) Chandler of Kentucky dashed in and out of several of the WRA camps and declared he had found 60 percent of the residents disloyal. He never explained how he had reached this conclusion. Representative J. Parnell Thomas of New Jersey, a member of the Dies Committee, hurried out to Los Angeles and without ever visiting a WRA camp, issued a series of press releases charging the Japanese were being permitted to return to the Coast in wholesale lots, that "fat-waisted Japs are being released while our American boys on Guadalcanal are barely receiving enough food to keep alive," and that wine was being served with meals in the camps. Senator E. V. Robertson of Wyoming, a naturalized citizen, ignored invitations to visit the Heart Mountain camp in his state but set himself up as a fountain of information about mismanagement, wasted food and coddling of the evacuees who, he said, are better housed "than are 75 percent of the people" of Wyoming.

California politicians, led by Earl Warren who by then was governor, were particularly active. Warren traveled to the National Conference of Governors in Columbus, Ohio, in June of 1943 to declare in a major address that release of Japanese Americans from WRA camps would lead to a situation where "no one will be able to tell a saboteur from any other Jap." He warned that "no more dangerous step could be taken" than the relocation of evacuees and announced that California would utilize every legal means to prevent their return. Congressman John Costello, another Californian, was chairman of a Dies Committee hearing on the West Coast that provided a podium for dozens of what Carey McWilliams calls "smear witnesses." Not to be outdone, State Senator Jack B. Tenney of Los Angeles County conducted hearings of similar low character and value by his "Little Dies Committee." And close behind him was Representative Chester Gannon of Sacramento County whose Gannon Committee badgered all those who dared speak up to ask fair play for the evacuees.

McWilliams comments: "The Dies Committee never intended to make an investigation of the evacuation program. It was summoned to California to make newspaper headlines and to keep the 'Japanese issue' alive, for political and other purposes . . . It is interesting to note how the whole tenor of the Japanese problem had changed since 1942 when, at the Tolan Committee hearings, all witnesses were treated with respect and when, so we are told, the evacuation of the Japanese was being ordered for their protection and as a matter of 'military necessity.' By December, 1943, witnesses were being browbeaten for defending the Bill of Rights and all Japanese were loathsome and immoral creatures whose homes 'smelled' bad."

—The pressure groups. Early in 1943, McWilliams reports, "literally hundreds of organizations" in California had passed resolutions criticizing WRA's handling of the evacuees, urging deportation of the Japanese, and generally pursuing the white supremacist line. The American Legion was in the forefront of this activity, and soon, McWilliams tells us, "resolutions and memorials began to flow from California; grand juries throughout the state began to adopt resolutions asking for the permanent exclusion of the evacuees; city councils, boards of supervisors, public officials, and lay groups began to take similar action . . . With scarcely a single exception, these protests, resolutions, and memorials are identical in character, and in most cases the same printed forms appear." McWilliams traces much of this activity to Dr. John R. Lechner, a former clergyman and founder of the Americanism Educational League with headquarters in Los Angeles. Lechner was an exceptionally nimble operator. He had offered his services to Japanese Americans to fight the evacuation movement before he moved to the other side of the street. Once he got up steam, he made scores of speeches in California, Arizona, Utah and as far east as Colorado about the "Japanese problem." He once boasted that his organization had mailed copies of a stock anti-evacuee resolution to some 900 service clubs and civic organizations. There were few persons in those days who had the courage to oppose such resolutions.

(Many years later a movement was started in the California legislature to cite Lechner for his long record of militant "Americanism." By then the JACL was strong enough to block the recognition.)

Lechner and the American Legion were among the more moderate of the antis, if that term can be used. Many of the others
bordered on the lunatic fringe. The California Citizens Council of
Los Angeles, for example, had as its slogan, "Remember a Jap is a
Jap." Windshield stickers were printed with this slogan and a picture of a rat with a Japanese face. San Diego had its No Japs, Inc.;
the Home Front Commandos urged Americans to "Slap a Jap Rat"
and charged that all Japanese are "treacherous, faithless, untrust-
worthy, irresponsible, inhuman, depraved, ungodly, soulless, disloyal and not fit to associate with human beings." The Pacific Coast
Japanese Problem League, founded by, among others, several prominent members of the Native Sons of the Golden West, had as
its spokesman the Reverend John Carruthers who told a State Senate hearing in urging the deportation of the evacuees: "It is our
Christian duty to keep the Japanese out of this western world of
Christian civilization." There were, unfortunately, many others of
equally intemperate views.

—The press. An important segment of the West Coast press during this period abandoned its tradition of supporting the underdog,
seeking the truth, unmasking the demagogues, and demanding fair
play. In fact, some newspapers seemed to be vying with each other
to publish the most sensational, if unsubstantiated, stories. The wild
charges of Senator Chandler, Costello, Tenney, Gannon and others
were taken at face value and printed without question or qualifica-
tion. An examination of Los Angeles newspapers reveals that re-
buttal stories failed to receive anywhere near the prominence given
to the original charges. Ray Richards, Washington correspondent
for the Hearst papers, followed few rules of objectivity in reporting Chandler's allegations for the San Francisco *Examiner* and the
Los Angeles *Examiner*. Warren Francis was equally guilty in his
dispatches to the Los Angeles *Times* which since has lived down
its past to become one of the nation's great newspapers. The same
could be said of the Denver *Post* which sent sportswriter Jack Car-
berry to make a cursory inspection of Heart Mountain, then published a grossly inaccurate "exposé" about hoarded food based on
the allegations of a WRA commissary department employee who

had been fired for incompetence. These newspapers at the time were not interested in producing a fair or accurate picture of the Japanese Americans. They were swept along by the hysteria and often contributed to it, and their performance is a shameful chapter in the history of the press.

Aside from slanted reporting, many newspapers pulled no punches in their editorial comments. The Denver *Post*, for example, demanded a "24-hour curfew" on "all Japs" in Denver. (Barron Beshoar, then working for the War Manpower Commission, was sent to the *Post* by his boss to suggest more temperate treatment—an unsuccessful mission, incidentally—and he recalls seeing on Editor and Publisher William C. Shepherd's desk a wooden cut-out of a Japanese soldier, about two feet high, with a monkey face and huge buck teeth. The *Post* changed completely after Palmer Hoyt became editor and publisher in 1946.)

The smaller newspapers had even fewer inhibitions. A classic example is a front-page editorial published in the Santa Maria (Calif.) *Courier* over the name of its editor and publisher, Edward R. Trebon. Trebon took after a reader who in a letter criticized something derogatory the newspaper had published about the Japanese and, with understandable discretion, failed to sign his name. Wrote Trebon:

"In the first place you're a dirty, rotten, low-down, pusillanimous SNEAK. You haven't any more decency about you than the dirty, yellow-bellied Japs you are upholding and fighting for—the enemies of America—the race that would make you a disgusting foreigner in your own homeland . . . but you wouldn't understand that, because you're just a Snake . . . And so, you Weasel, you mangy baboon, you warty lover of Hirohito . . ."

In fairness, it must be said that Trebon late in the editorial wrote that he had become acquainted with many Japanese Americans "whom we believe to be truly loyal to America. With them we have no quarrel and we respect them."

It was in this atmosphere that President Roosevelt, just before setting off for Mexico in the spring of 1943, asked Mrs. Roosevelt to visit one of the WRA camps. She chose Gila in southern Arizona, and Dillon Myer escorted her on a day-long tour. On the drive back to Phoenix Myer told Mrs. Roosevelt about some of his problems and said he would appreciate an opportunity to talk with the President about WRA. Some days later Myer received an invitation to lunch with the President at the White House on Mother's Day. It was a pleasantly warm Sunday, and Roosevelt, his daughter Anna, Myer and Mrs. Myer sat at one table on the White House lawn. At another table some distance away were Harry Hopkins and several other guests.

The President wanted to talk about his dog, Fala, and a variety of other things, but Myer finally steered the conversation around to WRA and its greatest problem of the moment—the wild charges that Senator Chandler was making as he galloped through his "investigation." Myer said he feared for WRA's resettlement program if Chandler's report was as irresponsible as his press releases. The President said he thought he could do something about that problem. Later, Myer heard that Senator Joseph O'Mahoney of Wyoming had been instructed by F.D.R. to talk to Chandler. The Chandler report bore little resemblance to the statements he had been making to the press. In essence, about all it said was that *Nisei* ought to be drafted for Army service, that the disloyal be segregated and interned for the duration, and that other evacuees be allowed to take private employment. Myer had reached almost the same conclusion months earlier. Chandler's huffing and puffing had served no purpose; his mischief had, in fact, seriously damaged an important national program.

The one point where Myer differed with Chandler was over a general segregation program. Myer continued to feel it was unnecessary and unfair. "These people may be resentful or angry about the evacuation and the situation in the camps," he said, "but they are not disloyal. We must be careful to distinguish the difference. If there were any enemy agents among the Japanese Americans, they would have left before the war, or have sought diplomatic repatriation. I cannot believe 100,000 people would jeopardize their future by failing to report enemy agents in their midst."

He expounded this point of view at a conference of WRA project directors in Washington over the Memorial Day weekend but these men, who were closest to the people involved, were solidly in favor of segregation. In the end, Myer could not ignore the unanimous judgment of his directors and agreed reluctantly to get a segregation program under way. When the Army refused to build a special camp, WRA picked Tule Lake to house the segregants, partly because it was a large center and partly because many of its residents were potential segregants.

The evacuees were on the move again in September, 1943. Thirty-three trainloads—15,000 individuals—were shuttled between Tule Lake and the other camps. But this exchange of human beings was far from a clear-cut segregation of the "loyal" from the "disloyal." Some 6,000 "loyals" departed Tule Lake but 4,000 others remained behind for a variety of reasons. Some did not want to leave California. Others were simply weary of being moved around. Still others, fearing they would be pushed out of the camps into an environment they feared, decided their best chance of remaining under government care was at Tule Lake. Nor were all the segregants "disloyal." Some, as we have seen, replied "No" to the loyalty question out of anger or bitterness or confusion. Some, like Joe Kurihara, were convinced there was no future for them in the United States. And many were the minor children of *Issei* parents who had decided that they were unwanted in America and it was the better part of valor to go to Japan.

Poignant scenes marked the exchange as friends of a lifetime parted. When would they see each other again? Nor were all the partings friendly. At camps like Gila and Granada and Minidoka, young *Nisei* waiting for an opportunity to enter military service taunted departing "No-No's" with, "Go on, you dirty Japs. We'll kill you the next time we see you."

Tule Lake wound up as an impossible can of worms. Hundreds of dissidents, many of them *Kibei*, were joined by about a thousand of their kind who had been shipped to the mainland from Hawaii. They quickly intimidated the non-activists and those who were seeking only peace and quiet. The dissidents were looking for trouble and they found fertile ground for it. Tule Lake was wracked by strikes, violent demonstrations and even bloodshed. WRA was never set up to cope with such a situation. For a two-month period the Army took over administration of the camp and rigidly restricted news of what was going on. Not even WRA knew the details. Denied access to accurate information, the West Coast press had a field day reporting rumors, speculation and conjecture, none of which did the evacuees a bit of good.

22

THE DEDICATED JACL-ERS

AS THE SORRY EXODUS of Japanese Americans picked up speed in the early summer of 1942, the Japanese American Citizens League sent its national secretary, Mike Masaoka, on a seemingly impossible mission: Find and cultivate influential friends, consult and cooperate with the Federal Government to get the most equitable terms possible for the evacuees. JACL's headquarters were moved to Salt Lake City where Masaoka had grown up and had friends. President Saburo Kido's family had moved from San Francisco to Visalia in central California where, the Army had said, evacuation was not likely. But when the Army changed its mind and decided to remove the Japanese from all of California, Kido's family was sent to Poston, largest of the WRA camps, and he decided to join them there.

Masaoka had never been in the East. He did not know what kind of a reception he would find. Judging from his experiences in North Platte, Nebraska, he could expect rough times from over-zealous local officials. He decided it would be wiser to travel with a companion and he chose George Inagaki, a nursery operator and JACL leader from southern California. Inagaki was married but he had no children at the time. He had enough money put away so that he did not have to depend on JACL's meager treasury for living expenses. Moreover, he owned a nearly new station wagon and thanks to the requirements of his business, he had a supply of gasoline ration cards. Inagaki could not turn down JACL's plea for help. He saw his wife off to Poston, and then he and Masaoka headed for Salt Lake and on to Cleveland, Ohio, where the JACL had been invited to speak at a meeting of the American Committee for the Protection of the Foreign Born. Masaoka was so naïvely eager for an audience that would listen that it never occurred to him to check his hosts' credentials. Only after he spoke and was turned down flat on what he considered reasonable proposals did it dawn on Masaoka that the Committee was a front organization bent on exploiting the plight of the *Nisei* to embarrass the United States. Being exploited was the last thing Masaoka wanted, but it was too late. Without telling him, the Committee placed Masaoka on its board. The presence of his name on the group's letterheads was to embarrass him for a long time afterward.

From Cleveland, Masaoka and Inagaki drove to New Orleans where the National Conference of Social Work was being held. Annie Clo Watson had managed an invitation, and this time Masaoka figured he could count on an attentive and legitimate if not a sympathetic audience. By the time they reached New Orleans the two were thoroughly discouraged. Their traveling allowance of five dollars a day did not permit them the luxury of a comfortable hotel. They ate as cheaply as possible and consequently were under the constant threat of both ptomaine and the patriotic zeal of local red-necks who did not take kindly to strange Orientals in their midst. With a little time to kill before his appearance, Masaoka and Inagaki went for a sight-seeing drive which took them to St. Bernard Parish just outside the city. What they did not know was that a German U-boat reportedly had ventured into the coastal waters of the area a day or two earlier and the natives were in a high state of excitement over rumors that Axis spies and saboteurs had been put ashore. Two Orientals in a car with California license plates, driving slowly and stopping at prominent landmarks, set off an instant alert. Masaoka and Inagaki quickly found themselves being marched to the St. Bernard jail at pistol-point by a very jittery deputy sheriff. Without being charged, they were locked in separate cells out of sight of each other. Bloodhounds patrolled the corridor outside the cells and as word spread that "a couple of Jap spies" had been captured, a noisy crowd gathered outside the jail. Remembering stories about lynchings in the Deep South, the two *Nisei* were not reassured. At first they shouted to let each other know they were all right, but when a jailer demanded that they be quiet, they signaled at intervals by flushing the toilet in their cells. In New Orleans, meanwhile, when

Masaoka did not appear for his speech, the program chairman notified the FBI who quickly traced down and rescued the missing men.

The next stop was Washington, D.C. Apparently local FBI agents had not been adequately briefed. Within minutes after Masaoka and Inagaki had checked into a modest hotel, FBI agents showed up to question them. This so alarmed the desk clerk that he insisted the *Nisei* leave that very afternoon. Masaoka remembers that a handful of *Nisei* was in Washington working at a variety of federal jobs, and most of them were afraid to have anything to do with him. Finally, Jack and Betty Murata made space for Masaoka and Inagaki in their modest quarters, and this was their base of operations until they could get an apartment of their own. Masaoka set out on the slow, delicate task of winning the confidence of first Milton Eisenhower, and then his successor, Dillon S. Myer, and establishing a pipeline to the decision-makers under the JACL's mandate of "constructive cooperation" with the government.

Masaoka's original plans were to spend only a few days in Washington, then go to New York to establish contacts with various religious, civil liberties and social work organizations before returning to Salt Lake City. But when he realized the need for keeping in daily touch with government leaders, he decided to stay on the East Coast. In one of his reports to the organization, Masaoka described his work in this manner:

"Because of its administration over the lives and futures of Japanese Americans, the national office of the War Relocation Authority was the major interest and concern of JACL representatives. Daily contacts were maintained with it. When reports of unsatisfactory conditions which could be corrected came in, calls were made on the proper officials in charge and the allegations submitted for their investigation, together with suggested action. When ideas as to policy or program occurred to us, or were sent in by National Headquarters or interested individuals, we would present them to the officers directing the section or division involved in their consideration. Sometimes we would be asked to supply some information on specific items or to make recommendations or suggestions on various topics of mutual interest. Although we may have differed on some subjects, in the main we cooperated wholeheartedly with them because it became apparent early in the program that this government agency, at least, was sincere and honest in its efforts to deal with one of the most difficult problems in the history of this country.

"The War Department, too, and particularly the offices of Assistant Secretary John McCloy was a 'must' for periodic visits and discussions, even though there was nothing of particular interest to canvass. These offices often made decisions of great importance to Japanese Americans and JACL could ill afford to miss such special announcements.

"Many other problems arose which were either outside the province of WRA or the War Department or were also a part of another agency's interests and jurisdiction, as, for example the manpower situation under the War Manpower Commission. When such problems became evident, JACL would try to contact the officials involved and make the proper representations. Moreover, we tried to meet and discuss our general status with every high government official who was willing or could be interested in listening to our presentation whether his department was directly concerned with Japanese Americans or not.

"Friendly and/or interested congressmen in both houses were contacted, with the exception of the rabid bloc from the West Coast, and our case presented as best we could . . ."

Masaoka also spent considerable time in New York City (Mr. and Mrs. Mervyn Suzuki often hosted him) where he consulted, and was particularly encouraged by, among others, Roger W. Baldwin of the American Civil Liberties Union, Author Pearl Buck, Reed Lewis of the Common Council for American Unity, that doughty liberal, Norman Thomas of the Post War World Council, Dr. John W. Thomas of the American Baptist Home Missions Council, and Annie Clo Watson who was on leave from the San Francisco International Institute to serve on the national board of the Young Women's Christian Association. JACL won the support of many other prominent Americans, including seventy widely known and respected men and women who became "sponsors." But the six persons named above, together with Clarence Pickett of the American Friends Service Committee headquartered in Philadelphia and Masaoka's old friends in Congress such as Senators Thomas and Murdock of Utah, formed an informal, unofficial advisory committee.

"George and I consulted with them individually before making major decisions or statements," Masaoka explains. "Since both of us were new and naïve in the kind of work we were attempting, whatever headway or success we may have achieved can be credited largely to these and other friends in the East. Similarly, most of the mistakes or errors of judgment made by us can be charged up to inexperience."

A particularly harrowing experience was Masaoka's encounter with a subcommittee of the Committee on Un-American Activities headed by Congressman Martin Dies of Texas. Congressman John M. Costello of California was chairman of the subcommittee whose professed purpose was to investigate un-American propaganda activities in the United States. The real purpose, judging from the list of witnesses and the type of questions asked them, was to harass and discredit the War Relocation Authority. Once again the Japanese were caught in the crossfire of an intramural fracas. The conclusion that these hearings were held with political intent is inescapable, particularly since more than half the testimony—which totals 922 printed pages—was taken in Los Angeles where the *Times* and the *Examiner* gave it extensive coverage, even though many of the witnesses had been summoned from Arizona.

The hearings opened in Los Angeles on June 8, 1943, extending through June 17 after which the committee moved to Parker, Arizona, for one day before returning to Washington. On June 11, representatives of the subcommittee appeared at 1324 14th Street N.W. in Washington, D.C., and knocked on the door of Apartment 5. This was the residence of Joe Tooru Kanazawa and his bride of a year and a half, Kentucky-born Emilie Aldridge Kanazawa. Joe Kanazawa, a struggling New York free-lance writer, had moved to Washington shortly after Masaoka's arrival to join the JACL as his assistant and the organization's eastern representative. Kanazawa's 14th Street apartment was both home and JACL office, and the organization's files remained there even though Kanazawa had entered military service late in May. The Dies people showed Mrs. Kanazawa a subpoena and seized the JACL files. (Masaoka says that despite strong protests many of the papers were never returned, leaving a documentary gap in the office history.)

Subcommittee investigators used the seized documents, largely copies of Masaoka's correspondence and memos to JACL headquarters, to try to prove that JACL through Masaoka "dictated"—the word is Congressman Costello's—the policies of WRA. The subcommittee also suspected an unholy alliance between WRA and JACL because WRA directives—which Myer later testified anyone could have on request—were discovered in the files. Masaoka had typed "Confidential" or "Strictly Confidential" on many of his reports, meaning in most instances that the information should not be released prematurely. However, the investigators saw this as further proof of unauthorized relationships between JACL and government agencies.

One memo in particular came in for detailed attention. Masaoka had written in part:

"Myer put this up to me directly and pointedly. He said that he and his staff deal with me on the same basis of confidence and mutual trust as they do among themselves.

"Up to now I have been permitted to sit down and discuss every major policy before it was finally passed on. Up to now no confidence has been betrayed. The War Relocation Authority desires to continue that fine relationship and will continue to do so as long as confidential matters are kept in confidence and as long as we sincerely try to cooperate with them on the improvement of conditions.

"He is afraid that certain guys in Congress would jump down their collective throats if they could only imagine a part of the part which we play in forming WRA policy . . ."

Myer was questioned about these statements by Robert E. Stripling, the subcommittee's chief investigator. The following is taken from the record:

"Mr. Stripling: Mr. Chairman, I would like to go into detail on this particular paragraph which I just read: 'He said that he and his staff deal with me on the same basis of confidence and mutual trust as they do among themselves.' Is that statement correct?

"Mr. Myer: I don't think that statement is correct.

"Mr. Stripling (reading): 'Up to now I have been permitted to sit down and discuss every major policy before it was finally passed on.' Is that correct?

"Mr. Myer: That is not correct."

Myer told the subcommittee he had discussed WRA policy with Masaoka many times, and commented as follows on Masaoka's reports to JACL headquarters:

"Well, I might say from the reading of the reports, I felt there were a good many places where Mike was rather expansive in his reports. He allowed his imagination to run wild, occasionally, on how much influence he had on WRA policy. There were times when he was reasonably factual. I might say, generally speaking, that that would be true of most any man if he were promoting certain policies, and a policy was finally adopted, he is absolutely sure that he is responsible for the adoption of the policy. I assume also, after having heard of some of the policies, he thought it was a good idea, or maybe thought that he was the one that proposed it. Now, I would say that, generally speaking, there were many statements in the reports that were exaggerations; statements that I don't think were malicious statements, but were simply imaginative statements that anybody could make."

The investigators pulled no punches in picturing Masaoka as a glory-seeker trying to impress JACL headquarters with exaggerated accounts of the fine work he was doing and the influence he wielded in Washington. Although it was a humiliating experience, Masaoka did not fight the accusation. "Well, everyone likes to pat himself on the back," he admitted at one point. "It is human nature."

No doubt there is a strong element of truth to the investigators' charges. But it is also apparent that, directly and indirectly, Masaoka was extremely effective in molding opinions and inspiring actions among important persons both in and out of government. These persons would have been embarrassed, and perhaps their effectiveness would have been impaired, if the full extent of Masaoka's influence had been bared. And so rather than endangering his allies, he accepted the role of the braggart and self-seeker. In response to the subcommittee's questions he was vague, he failed to recall names, he found difficulty in remembering details, all of which is totally uncharacteristic of Masaoka of the razor-sharp mind. None of that vagueness was apparent when Congressman Karl E. Mundt of South Dakota asked him to state his criticism of WRA.

Masaoka complained first that WRA was not releasing the evacuees from the camps rapidly enough. He said WRA should provide those wishing to relocate with more financial aid because camp life had depleted the resources of many. He urged that WRA be more aggressive about presenting the nation with a true picture of the loyalty and aspirations of Japanese Americans. In the camps, he said, the educational systems needed upgrading, and high school students should be permitted to attend classes outside the camps for "complete assimilation with the American people."

"On the Pacific Coast," he said, "persons of Japanese ancestry were accused of being clannish; yet the very program of WRA has tended to make them even more clannish. I am particularly worried about the breakdown in social controls. The evacuees are not living a normal American life, and every effort ought to be made to restore these people to that state."

Despite their differences in the hearings, it is significant that Myer and Masaoka, both in Washington, are today warm friends with sincere and solid respect for each other's talents. In 1946 Masaoka, on behalf of JACL presented to Myer at a testimonial banquet in his honor a citation which read: "To Dillon S. Myer, American and champion of human rights and common decency whose courageous and inspired leadership as national director of the War Relocation Authority against war hysteria, race prejudice, and misguided hate, as well as economic greed draped in patriotic colors, contributed mightily in convincing the American government and public at large that Americans of Japanese ancestry and their resident alien parents were, and are, loyal and sincere Americans worthy of every right and privilege of the American heritage, and aided materially in restoring faith and conviction in the American way to these same Americans of Japanese ancestry . . ."

As for Myer, he insisted on telling the Dies Committee precisely what he thought of its inquisition, an act that demanded no little courage in that period. Brushing off Congressman Costello's attempt to persuade him to postpone the statement, he said:

"The program of the War Relocation Authority has been under investigation for the past eight weeks in such a manner as to achieve maximum publicity of sensational statements based on half-truths, exaggerations and falsehood; statements of witnesses have been released to the public without verification of their accuracy, thus giving nation-wide currency to many distortions and downright untruths.

"This practice has fostered a public feeling of mistrust, suspicion and hatred that has had the effect of:

"Providing the enemy with material which can be used to convince the peoples of the Orient that the United States is undemocratic and is fighting a racial war.

"Undermining the unity of the American people.

"Betraying the democratic objectives which this nation and its allies are fighting to preserve."

Predictably, the subcommittee's report was sharply critical of Myer and WRA, charging them with ineptness and laxness, and taking at face value testimony by discharged employees about pampering, waste of food, and indifferent security measures. Much of the sting of the report was removed, however, by a minority report submitted by Representative Herman P. Eberharter of Pennsylvania. "I cannot avoid the conclusion that the report of the majority is prejudiced and most of its statements are not proven," he said. "It is my conclusion that considering the magnitude of its job, the difficulty of the legal issues involved, and the complexity and delicacy of the problem of resettling a large group of people in the midst of a war, the War Relocation Authority has acted, by and large, efficiently and capably, and has carried out the spirit and intent of the President's executive order under which it was established. I think it is better to let the War Relocation Authority carry on unhampered by unfair criticism."

JACL, meanwhile, proceeded with its work quietly and usually effectively despite the inclination of substantial numbers of evacuees to blame it for everything from the evacuation decision to inadequate food in the camps, snafus in the relocation program, hostility and job discrimination in the Midwest and East. Regional offices were opened with Joe Grant Masaoka in Denver, Dr. Tom Yatabe in Chicago, and T. Scott Miyakawa and later Peter Aoki in New York. They supplemented the work of WRA field offices, and of volunteer organizations like the Friends Service Committee, in helping relocatees find jobs and housing and adjust to life outside the camps. They appeared before service clubs, church groups, at schools and labor union meetings to tell the story of the evacuation and urge tolerance and understanding.

Under WRA's urging and the friendly encouragement of various volunteer organizations, a steady if not particularly large flow of *Nisei* left the camps, followed later by numbers of *Issei*, to seek a new life in the Mountain States, the Midwest and East. In essence, relocation differed little from the process by which convicts on parole were returned to normal life. The government provided transportation to the first destination and a little pocket money. At

Ruth Nishi was among evacuees who left a camp to take a war production job in Chicago. (National Archives)

first the promise of a job was a prerequisite to release; in the later phases of relocation employment was so easy to find that if a person's security record was clear, he could go out prospecting for work. In their search for a place to make a living, the relocatees congregated in the urban centers—Salt Lake City, Denver, Chicago, Cleveland, St. Louis. Once the original barriers to employment were broken down by the earlier relocatees, employers were delighted with the skill and capabilities of the *Nisei* in a time of critical manpower shortages and numerous other jobs opened up for them. For the first time in their experience many *Nisei* found employment in fields for which they had been trained—as teachers, stenographers, printers, machinists, chemists, architects—work which had been denied them on the West Coast. The WRA cautioned relocatees not to work for less than the going wage, nor to ask for more, but many were pleased to find they could draw premium pay for their superior qualifications. It was a heady experience.

Yet it was not all rosy. Robert M. Cullum, who manned WRA's Cleveland relocation office, recalls two *Nisei* employees of a shipyard in Camden, N.J., who were hauled up for a security check by military investigators. "When we win the war, would you agree it would be all right to kill all the people in Japan in retaliation for all the wrongs they've committed against Americans?" they were asked. One replied no, that would be unreasonable, and he was fired as a security risk. The other said: "I will go along with whatever my country wants to do." He retained his job. Later, he explained: "I knew the United States wouldn't do anything as barbaric as that agent suggested." Cullum also remembers a *Nisei* who slugged and broke the jaw of his steel-plant foreman who made the error of calling him a "damned Jap." The *Nisei* had the good fortune to be the star pitcher of his union's softball team. The union managed to get him a job at another steel plant and thus retained his services.

"The confounded *Nisei* were so darned good, it was unbelievable," Cullum says. "They were eternally on their best behavior, afraid that if they got into trouble they would hurt the relocation program, jeopardize the opportunity of others to leave the camps. Actually it was a relief to find them getting into trouble once in a while, like the softball pitcher."

Housing was a much more critical problem than employment, and race prejudice had little to do with it. There just weren't enough houses and apartments to rent. WRA put housing specialists in their offices. The more energetic among them hustled housing in every possible way. If they saw a "For Rent" notice while riding in a streetcar, they jumped off and signed up the property, then went looking for *Nisei* to move in. If they overheard someone on the street talking about moving, they buttonholed him quickly to ask about the apartment he was leaving. When the Cleveland Board of Realtors complained to Dillon Myer that too many Japanese were moving into the city and occupying too much of the available housing, he replied that the evacuees were Americans with every right to move where they desired, that WRA's job was to help them relocate, and if they didn't like it, blast away. The board pulled in its horns.

Many relocatees will never forget the hospitality they found in hostels operated by Quakers and various church groups. Usually they made beds available at nominal cost in a large old rented house. The relocatees slept and ate there, sharing in the housekeeping, cooking and dishwashing, while they looked for jobs and more permanent housing, encouraging each other, passing along tips about where to look and how to get there. Once they were established, the evacuees moved out to make room for others, and the married men could send for their families or their parents. Many *Nisei* girls took jobs as housemaids—repeating the experience of their parents decades earlier—while seeking more appropriate jobs. In time, as the evacuees sank their roots into the soil of new communities, as they progressed in their occupations, they were able to move into better homes. Summer's humid heat and the bitter cold of Midwestern winters became less unbearable, and large numbers decided they had found a permanent home in the American heartland.

All the while the organization that held the *Nisei* together, that kept them in touch with each other, was the JACL although many did not agree with its policies and some regarded it with bitter resentment. At its headquarters in Salt Lake City, Miss Teiko Ishida (now Mrs. Mickey Kuroiwa) a long-time JACL stalwart from San Francisco, took over as acting national secretary when Masaoka went into the Army. Hito Okada, then national treasurer, was office manager and bore the responsibility of keeping rent and telephone bills paid and meeting the payroll, meager as it was. JACL staff members were paid the munificent sum of $75 a month which was increased ultimately to $125 as living costs rose. Only an annual contribution of $10,000 from the ten chapters in the Intermountain district kept the organization solvent, and only an intense dedication kept the staff from accepting more lucrative positions.

Of particular importance at this time was JACL's national organ, *The Pacific Citizen*, better known as the PC. It had struggled along as an undistinguished monthly newspaper, first published in San Francisco, then for a while by Jimmie Sakamoto's *Courier* staff in Seattle. It attained editorial maturity under the editorship of Larry Tajiri.

Tajiri lost his job after Pearl Harbor when the Tokyo *Asahi's* New York bureau was closed. He drifted back to San Francisco, saw the need for a *Nisei* news organ, and volunteered to take over the PC. Out of an incredibly cluttered office in Salt Lake City, Tajiri and his wife Marion Guyo published a lively, newsy authoritative newspaper that dared to be aggressive in the finest traditions of independent American journalism. Some of the news was provided by correspondents. Much of it was gleaned by perusing the columns of several score newspapers from all parts of the country for items of interest to the *Nisei*. These newspapers, which accumulated at an astonishing rate, were stacked on desks and the floor and were hauled out and dumped periodically to make space for later issues. Masaoka and Kanazawa often provided the PC with news about WRA decisions even before they were known to the project directors. But perhaps the most important function of the PC was that it gave the *Nisei* a strong, clear editorial voice when it seemed that most of the nation's newspapers were against them, or at best, ignoring them. (This, of course, was only an impression. Many Midwestern and Eastern newspapers gave the evacuees considerable support. The stable of editorial writers at the Des Moines *Register & Tribune,* for example, turned in so many editorials sympathetic to the *Nisei* during one period that the editor in charge had to assign some of them to write on other subjects.) Tajiri was erudite. His writing was facile. He could be sharp or humorous. In his editorial columns he was a David shouting defiance at the bullying Goliaths of the newspaper world—the Hearst Press, the Los Angeles *Times,* the Denver *Post* and others—challenging them to dare to tell the truth, to look for the facts, to cease their distortions and live up to the canons of good journalism. He corrected their misinterpretations and lectured them on the responsibilities of a free press. With equal vigor he assailed the politicians, the racists, the professional hate-mongers who had found the evacuees a convenient target. Tajiri was great for evacuee morale; he was their spokesman who articulated their anger and resentment. In each of the camps the PC's arrival was awaited each week with keen anticipation. Evacuees who had relocated to places like Dayton, Ohio, and Buffalo, New York; in Marshalltown, Iowa and Providence, Rhode Island, kept in touch through the PC. The value of the Tajiris' contribution to *Nisei* welfare during the evacuation and relocation period is beyond calculation. In later years, after the Denver *Post* had been converted by Palmer Hoyt into a highly respectable newspaper, Tajiri joined its staff and distinguished himself as its drama editor. After his death following a stroke in 1965, his associates in the field of drama and entertainment established an annual Larry Tajiri Memorial Award to honor persons who have made exceptional contributions to the theater.

Mrs. Tajiri, who worked side by side with her husband on the PC, wrote the lyrics for the JACL Hymn, set to music by Marcel J. Tyrrel. The lyrics provide not only an eloquent summary of the *Nisei's* wartime travail, but are a part of contemporary Americana:

"There was a dream my father dreamed for me
A land in which all men are free—
Then the desert camp with watchtowers high
Where life stood still, mid sand and brooding sky
Out of the war in which my brothers died—
Their muted voices with mine cried—
This is our dream that all men shall be free!
This is our creed we'll live in loyalty
God help us rid the land of bigotry
That we may walk in peace and dignity."

It was the sacrifice of individuals like these, who stuck with JACL through the war years at great personal sacrifice, that enabled the organization to function and serve.

Precisely what was JACL's purpose outside of the immediate tasks of helping the *Issei* and *Nisei?* Masaoka once was asked that question and he replied:

"JACL is more than just another organization. It symbolizes an ideal to be attained, a crusade to be fought, a goal to be reached: the emancipation of all Japanese Americans from the stigma of limited citizenship and the cloak of questioned loyalty through their total assimilation into the general cultural pattern and their complete acceptance as co-Americans by their fellows. In a broader sense, JACL is but a part of the larger movement through which all minorities—racial, economic, political, religious—seek their just and rightful place in that heaven of human endeavor which must come."

It is a florid statement, but appropriate. For JACL is an organization unique among American minorities, perhaps for the reason that the problems of the *Nisei* which JACL was organized to solve, also were unique. At any rate, the Japanese American Citizens League has played a monumental role in the history of the Japanese in America, and certainly no recounting of that story would be complete without mentioning it prominently.

23

PROOF IN BLOOD

"I do not know of any group in the history of our country who has suffered so much without justification and has come out of it to make such a great contribution with never a scar of resentment or faltering their love of and loyalty to country. God bless the Japanese Americans."
—*Congressman Barratt O'Hara*
of Illinois, June 11, 1963

LATE IN THE SUMMER of 1940 Congress adopted a military conscription law for the first time in history while the nation was at peace. The peace was only technical. It seemed only a matter of time until the United States would be involved in the war being waged by the German-Italian Axis against Britain and France. In July the Democratic National Convention at Chicago had nominated President Roosevelt for an unprecedented third term, urging his reelection with a warning that to change horses in midstream at a time of great international peril would be disastrous. Two days after his nomination Roosevelt signed a bill providing for a vastly enlarged two-ocean navy as part of an extensive defense buildup. On October 16, some 16,400,000 American men between twenty-one and thirty-six years of age registered under the Selective Training and Service Act. A few days later the draft lottery got under way to determine who among these men would be first to begin their compulsory one-year military training program.

At this time *Nisei* were being drafted like other young Americans. Few thought it unusual or remarkable that GIs with Oriental faces should be among white boys learning to salute, march, bivouac and handle weapons for possible use against an enemy nation. (In fact the history of Japanese in U.S. military service goes back to the Spanish-American War. Seven *Issei* members of the crew of the battleship *Maine* died when she was blown up in Havana harbor in 1898. Other *Issei* served aboard U.S. warships in the Battle of Manila Bay on May 1, 1898.)

Among those whose numbers came up fairly early in the nation's preparedness program was a 31-year-old Los Angeles attorney named John Fujio Aiso whose name has appeared earlier in this volume. Aside from his age, Aiso was an unusual draftee in other respects. He was a *cum laude* graduate of Brown University in Providence, R.I., and he had a law degree from Harvard Law School. He had also studied at Seijo University and Chuo University in Japan, and had spent three and a half years at Mukden in Japanese-occupied Manchuria as head of the legal department of a subsidiary of the British-American Tobacco Co. In April, 1941, the United States Army made him a buck private and assigned him to a truck repair outfit in the Quartermaster Corps.

But the Army works in strange and wonderful ways. Even as John Aiso was learning the intricacies of truck repair, a tiny handful of Army Intelligence specialists was trying to alert superiors to the importance of training Japanese language interpreters and translators for the seemingly inevitable war ahead. Among them were Lt. Col. John Weckerling (later a brigadier general) and Capt. (later Col.) Kai E. Rasmussen. Both were on duty with the Fourth Army intelligence staff at The Presidio in San Francisco. They knew that only a very few Americans of European ancestry were familiar with the incredibly complex Japanese language. Japanese language programs in American colleges were elementary and had had far too few students to serve a national need. Even finding qualified teachers for a crash instruction program was a problem. But there might be one way to meet the need—use *Nisei* who naturally had a Japanese language background. Still, they were an unknown quantity to most highly placed officials. Could these youths of an alien race, only one generation removed from the ancestral land, be trusted in battle and in highly sensitive intelligence work against people of their own blood, against even cousins and brothers in some cases?

Weckerling and Rasmussen argued that the *Nisei* were loyal Americans. Rasmussen himself is of foreign birth, and he reminded his superiors that the United States is made up of immigrant groups. The War Department was hard to convince. Only after costly delays did the two officers win reluctant approval for a small-scale language school. Indicative of the Department's dim view, the school was placed under the Fourth Army, which had jurisdiction over only the West Coast, and not under the Army's regular Specialized Training Program. The initial appropriation was for only $2,000. Undiscouraged, the two officers fanned out to interview *Nisei* already in uniform to determine their proficiency in Japanese. One of the men Rasmussen talked to was Private Aiso.

Aiso's primary interest at the time was getting out of the Army which was releasing men over twenty-eight years of age. He was planning to be married and hoped to return to his law practice in Los Angeles. Thus, when he found orders to report at Camp Haan in Riverside, California, after completing maneuvers in the state of Washington in September, 1941, he figured he was being discharged. Instead he found new orders sending him to The Presidio. There he was told he was the brand-new head instructor of the brand-new Fourth Army Intelligence School. But because it would be unseemly for a buck private to be running a school in which full colonels might be among the students, Aiso was furloughed to the enlisted reserve "for the convenience of the government" and hired as a War Department civilian employee.

Aiso and two other *Nisei*, Aki Oshida and Shig Kihara, seated on empty apple boxes, held their first faculty meeting in a basement room. They worked up a curriculum and hurriedly mimeographed textbooks for a Japanese military language school. On November 1, 1941, scarcely five weeks before the outbreak of war, the school was opened in a converted hangar at Crissy Field, The Presidio. Half the hangar was used for classrooms, the other for barracks. More apple boxes and orange crates were pressed into service as chairs until furniture could be wangled. There were sixty handpicked students in that first class, fifty-eight *Nisei* and two Caucasians. All day and late into the night they studied Japanese reading, writing, interrogation, translation and interpretation; analysis of captured documents; Japanese geography and mapreading; Japanese military organization and technical terms, and the social, political, economic and cultural background of Japan.

Fifteen of the students couldn't keep up with the intensive pace and were reassigned. After six months, thirty-five of the graduates were attached to outfits going overseas to meet the Japanese in battle—half to a Marine division headed for Guadalcanal and the others to the 7th Division assigned to drive Japanese raiders out of the Aleutian Islands. The remaining ten men were added to the faculty to teach an enlarged second class.

The change in Aiso's military status did not alter his wedding plans. He and his fiancee, Sumi Akiyama of Westminster, Orange County, California, had set the date for December 14, Aiso's thirty-second birthday. Her friends scheduled a bridal shower for her on December 7. "On that Sunday," Aiso says, "I had a late breakfast at the base, then caught a streetcar for downtown San Francisco so I could send Sumi an appropriate telegram. I was walking down Market Street to a Western Union office when I heard radios blasting the news of the attack on Pearl Harbor. My first thoughts were: Could this be true? Was it another false alarm? But reason told me that what was coming sooner or later—and what my heart had hoped would never happen—had now come to pass. I had no doubt the *Nisei* in the Army would prove completely loyal to their native land. But I wondered whether the military authorities would give us a chance to prove our loyalty. I hurried back to the Presidio." Neither he nor his wife recalls whether he ever sent the telegram.

Aiso was uncertain as to whether he should go through with the wedding. He consulted his commandant who said. "John, this is going to be a long war. A man has to get married sometime. Incidentally, I want you to go to Los Angeles on official duty to interview three or four applicants for instructorships at the school." Then he added with a wink: "If you happen to get married on your leisure time, that's your business." A small family wedding was held. Then Aiso found that the government had banned travel for Japanese Americans and his air passage back to San Francisco was cancelled. Only after Fourth Army officials had telephoned the FBI in Los Angeles was he able to get train tickets to take his bride home.

Meanwhile, even as one branch of the Army was laying plans for the removal of all Japanese Americans from the West Coast as a matter of military necessity, another branch was searching for qualified *Nisei* to enroll in its now-urgent language and intelligence program. But the results were disheartening. The vast majority of *Nisei* were too thoroughly Americanized. Of the first 3,700 men interviewed, only 3 percent proved to speak Japanese fluently. The next 4 percent could be considered fairly proficient in the language. Another 3 percent knew just enough so that they could be thrown into intensive training; only one *Nisei* in ten understood a useful amount of his ancestral tongue. And even the best of them had to be taught military vocabulary and usage. Almost invariably the best qualified were *Kibei*, thanks to their education in Japan. Ironically, they as a group had been the first to be condemned as potentially the most likely to be disloyal.

Soon after Pearl Harbor the Selective Service System automatically reclassified all *Nisei* 4-F (those physically, mentally or morally unfit), and later as 4-C (not acceptable for military service because of nationality or ancestry). So great was the need for linguists, however, Selective Service rules were bypassed to induct qualified *Nisei* directly into the school.

As the evacuation got under way, the school was transferred to larger quarters at Camp Savage in Minnesota. By then the top brass could see the value of the program. It was reorganized as a Military Intelligence Service Language School under direct War Department supervision and on June 1, 1942—when the evacuation program was at its height—a second class of 200 men, virtually all *Nisei*—began their rigorous routine. Class sessions were held from 8 A.M. to 4:30 P.M. with additional classes in the evening. So rapid was the pace that even the more able students had to study every spare minute to keep up, often cramming by flashlight under bedcovers after the 11 P.M. lights-out. Weekends were usually spent in field maneuvers, for these men were expected to be soldiers as well as linguists.

Soon reports began to come back from the far-flung Pacific front. The *Nisei* were performing magnificently. "Send us more *Nisei* linguists," corps commanders ordered.

Most of the *Nisei* linguists worked in teams in the anonymity of command posts and rear echelon headquarters at the tedious and demanding job of translating captured documents. These included battle plans, defense maps, tactical orders, intercepted messages and diaries. Their efforts turned up a mass of information that enabled

American commanders to anticipate enemy action, evaluate their strengths and weaknesses, avoid surprise and strike where they were least expected. Headquarters duty alternated between utter boredom and a series of frenzied twenty-hour days when captured documents were rushed back following battle. Often, captured maps of enemy defense positions were translated and hurried to the front in time to turn the tide of battle. On the rare occasions when prisoners were captured, they were hurriedly interrogated by *Nisei*, then the information relayed to intelligence analysts.

The album of the Military Intelligence Service Language School says the *Nisei* "translated the entire Japanese battle plans for the naval battle of the Philippines. These plans were captured from the commander in chief of the Combined Japanese Fleets when the plane in which he was hurrying to join his fleet made a forced landing in the Philippines . . . Likewise, the complete Japanese plans for the defense of the Philippine Islands also were made known through the work of the language specialists from the School long before our forces had landed on Leyte."

The Japanese, lulled into a false sense of security in their belief that Americans could not fathom the complexities of their language, were extremely lax about their security. The abilities of the *Nisei*, plus the fact that Japanese codes had been cracked before Pearl Harbor, moved Maj. Gen. Charles A. Willoughby, General MacArthur's chief of intelligence, to remark: "Never before in history did an army know so much concerning its enemy, prior to actual engagement, as did the American Army during most of the Pacific campaigns."

In all, more than 6,000 *Nisei* were trained to serve with Allied forces in the Pacific during World War II in the school which, in later stages, was transferred to even roomier quarters at Fort Snelling just outside Minneapolis. Of that number, 3,700 served in combat areas before the surrender. In addition to rear echelon duties, they took part in every landing in the bitter island-hopping campaign up through New Guinea, the Marianas, Philippines and Okinawa, and finally participated in the surrender ceremonies in Tokyo Bay. The *Nisei* were assigned to the U.S. Joint Intelligence Center in Hawaii, to every Army division, to paratroop units and Office of Strategic Services (OSS) and Office of War Information (OWI) teams. Although the Navy did not accept *Nisei* enlistments, *Nisei* linguists were placed on loan from the Army in Marine divisions and task force flagships. Some were loaned to British, Australian and Chinese forces. Attuned to the Japanese tongue, the *Nisei* were the eyes and ears of Allied fighting forces throughout the Pacific and they saved countless American and Allied lives and helped shorten the war by many months.

Col. Sidney F. Mashbir, commander of the Allied Translator and Interpreter Service which was responsible for some 200 *million* pages of translations, says in his autobiography, *I Was an American Spy:* "Had it not been for the loyalty, fidelity, patriotism, and ability of these American *Nisei*, that part of the war in the Pacific which was dependent upon intelligence gleaned from captured documents and prisoners of war would have been a far more hazardous, long-drawn-out affair. The United States of America owes a debt to these men and to their families which it can never fully repay."

There was more than mere rhetoric in Mashbir's words. Aiso says to his personal knowledge at least two of his students serving in the Philippines ran into a blood brother in Japanese uniform. Kenny Yasui, about whom more will be heard later in this chapter, learned the Japanese division the Yanks were systematically chewing up in Burma was made up of men from the district where he had spent his youth. He expected momentarily to find his brother's body. He met a boyhood friend from his parental village while interrogating prisoners, and from him learned that the brother had been transferred to another division.

With victory the Military Intelligence Service Language School shifted its emphasis from military Japanese to general Japanese and civil affairs. The newest linguists were assigned to take part in the occupation and reconstruction of the defeated Japan. The *Nisei* were put to work interpreting for military government teams, locating and repatriating imprisoned Americans, in counterintelligence to nip the plots of dissidents, rounding up war criminal suspects and interpreting at their trials. They were as valuable in the clean-up after victory as they had been in combat. They helped to smash black market operations, evaluate Air Force bombing damage, train Japanese military police and supervise the repatriation of Japanese prisoners. Aiso, who was promoted to director of academic training, was commissioned a major and sent to Japan to

During the war in the Pacific and after the Japanese surrender, Nisei interpreters and translators were the "eyes and ears" of the U.S. armed forces. (U.S. Army Photo)

enforce the political purge as executive assistant to General Willoughby. He was relieved from active duty fourteen months later with rank of lieutenant colonel. The very presence of *Nisei* in the occupation army contributed much to the rapid democratization of Japan.

Yet, because of the secret nature of their work, the wartime contributions of the *Nisei* in the Pacific theater were not revealed to the nation at a time when the *Nisei* were most in need of publicity about their loyalty. During the fighting the linguists were under tight security wraps; after the surrender of Japan their story was largely forgotten in the flush of victory. And so their accomplishments remained unknown while the publicity spotlight was played on their brothers of the 442nd (Go for Broke) Regimental Combat Team which fought with such valor and paid such a price in blood in Italy and France.

The story of the 442nd actually begins in Hawaii in the tense summer of 1941 when the Hawaiian National Guard, made up largely of *Nisei*, was federalized. The unit distinguished itself on Pearl Harbor Day, and some of its members captured the first two prisoners of the war—two Japanese naval men who came ashore from a disabled midget submarine on Waimanalo Beach on the island of Oahu.

"When invasion of the Hawaiian Islands was believed imminent," says Congressman Spark M. Matsunaga who was a member of the National Guard, "all Americans regardless of race stood side by side in beach dugouts and trenches, fully prepared to repel the enemy. After the battle of Midway in June, 1942, when invasion by the enemy became a remote matter, our fellow Americans suddenly turned to us of Japanese ancestry and looked at us with a suspicious eye, almost as if to say, 'Why, he's a Jap.' It was shortly thereafter that all of us of Japanese ancestry who were in American uniform were given orders to turn in our arms and ammunition and were corralled at Schofield Barracks, an Army post about 22 miles northwest of Honolulu.

"Before we had any chance to bid goodbye to our loved ones, we found ourselves on board a troopship sailing for God-knew-where. Speculation was rife that we were headed for a concentration camp."

At a time when most American troops were headed westward across the Pacific, the *Nisei* were taken east and landed at Oakland, California. Several days later their trooptrain was unloaded at Camp McCoy, Wisconsin, where the *Nisei* were designated as a provisional battalion.

"We pictured ourselves as a battalion of forced laborers," Matsunaga says. "As time went on, we were put through close-order drill and trained with wooden guns. We wrote home of our great desire for combat duty to prove our loyalty to the United States. It was not known to us then that our letters were being censored by higher authority. We learned subsequently that because of the tenor of our letters, the War Department decided to give us our chance. Our guns were returned to us, and were told that we were going to be prepared for combat duty as the 100th Infantry Battalion. Grown men leaped with joy on learning that they were finally going to be given the chance on the field of battle to prove their loyalty to the land of their birth."

Meanwhile, after exhaustive study, the War Department on January 28, 1943, announced plans to accept *Nisei* volunteers for a special combat unit. Said Secretary Stimson: "It is the inherent right of every faithful citizen, regardless of ancestry, to bear arms in the national defense . . . Loyalty to country is a voice that must be heard, and I am glad that I am now able to give active proof that this basic American belief is not a casualty of war."

Each WRA camp proudly listed names of its men in service. This is the honor roll of Minidoka camp in Idaho. (National Archives)

Up until the time war broke out, nearly 3,500 *Nisei* had been drafted. After December 7 a number had been mustered out "for the convenience of the government," but the majority remained in uniform. Now these men, mainly noncoms in service command installations in all parts of the country, began in the early days of January, 1943, to get orders to Camp Shelby, Mississippi. They were to be the cadremen for the volunteers who would arrive shortly.

In Hawaii, which had been attacked by the enemy and where no mass evacuation had been ordered, the decision to accept *Nisei* volunteers was greeted enthusiastically. More than 10,000 men volunteered although only some 1,500 were being sought. Because of the response, their quota was nearly doubled, and in April, 1943, 2,686 Hawaiian *Nisei* arrived at Camp Shelby. There were joyful reunions with brothers and friends of the 100th Battalion who had been sent to Camp Shelby for the final phases of their training.

Soon the Hawaiian contingent was joined by some 1,500 main-land volunteers, selected from 2,500 young men who had stepped

forward to serve in the Army that had sent them and their families
into the evacuation camps. Nearly half were still residents of the
camps when they volunteered, leaving their parents and families
behind barbed wire to go out and fight for their country. This
response, one observer noted, while not as impressive as that of
Hawaii, was even more heartwarming for the mainland *Nisei* had
the courage and vision to see beyond the watchtowers of the
American-style concentration camps.

The *Nisei* outfit was designated as the 442nd Regimental Combat
Team. It was made up of the 442nd Infantry Regiment, the 522nd
Field Artillery Battalion, the 232nd Combat Engineer Company,
and the 206th Army Ground Forces Band. Its first commander was
Col. Charles W. Pence. Most of the officers, but not all, were Caucasians. Capt. Pershing Nakada commanded the Engineers Company and a number of *Nisei*, mostly trained in college Reserve
Officer programs, wore the bars of lieutenants and captains. The
great majority of the *Nisei* were small physically, but they made
up for lack of size in determination, stamina and intelligence. The
average IQ of the entire 442nd was 119, nine points higher than
that required for officer candidate school, and it was said that there
were more college graduates in the outfit—learning to become riflemen in infantry companies—than in any unit of similar size. Gradually, *Nisei* farm boys, students, sales clerks, fishermen, college
graduates, bookkeepers, florists, truck drivers, grocers, cooks and
pants pressers learned the fine art of combat. They seldom had to
be told anything twice. They had a special reason for being in
uniform.

Dan Inouye, who was to go on to become a war hero and
United States Senator from Hawaii, was one of the volunteers. In
his autobiography, *Journey to Washington*, Inouye writes:

"Day in, day out, our all-important mission was getting ready
to fight. In the field we put out as though every training exercise
was the real thing. Assigned a 25-mile hike with full packs, we
were out and back in little over seven hours, a new camp record.
What was really remarkable, though, is that every man in the outfit
made that march—cooks, supply sergeants, headquarters personnel—
and every man finished it, although a few had to be carried down
the home stretch, literally. In maneuvers against the 69th Division,
the 442nd was assigned the role of Aggressor Force, which meant

Nisei troops in Italy round up captured German soldiers. (U.S. Army Photo)

that we were only supposed to provide the opposition while the 69th, three times our strength, polished up its tactical skills. I guess we didn't follow the script or something, because by the time the exercise ended, the umpires were forced to rule that we had 'wiped out' two of the Friendly Force's three regiments."

But when other soldiers called them Japs, maliciously or out of ignorance, the *Nisei* forgot their discipline and waded in with fists swinging against men that outweighed them seventy-five or a hundred pounds. The 442nd's shoulder patch showed a white hand holding high a torch of liberty against a blue sky. It was framed in white and red. The regiment's motto was "Go for Broke," a Hawaiian dice-roller's pidgin phrase meaning "shoot the works" or "go all out." It was uniquely appropriate.

The 100th, more advanced in its training, left Camp Shelby in August, 1943, and landed at Oran, North Africa, on September 2 where it was attached to the 34th (Red Bull) Infantry Division. Three weeks later the 100th was blooded at Salerno, Italy, after which it saw action in rapid succession at Volturno, at the Rapido River, Cassino and the Anzio beachhead. These were some of the most difficult battles of the Italian campaign, and the 100th took heavy casualties who were replaced by men from the 1st Battalion of the 442nd. When the 442nd sailed for Europe in May, 1944, it was minus its 1st Battalion; virtually all its men already were overseas.

The 442nd landed in Italy on June 2, 1944. A few days later the 100th joined the 442nd as its 1st Battalion although retaining its special identification as the 100th in tribute to its combat record. Thus reinforced, the 442nd was made a component of the 34th Infantry Division and first went into action on June 26 north of Rome near the town of Suvereto. It pursued the enemy to the Arno River, participating with distinction in the battles for Belvedere, Luviana and Leghorn, and the crossing of the Arno. Its reputation as crack assault troops well established by this time, the 442nd was pulled out of Italy in September and sent to southern France where it became a unit of the 36th (Texas) Division for the thrust into the heavily defended Vosges Mountains. Entering combat on October 15, the 442nd captured the town of Bruyeres after three days of the bitterest fighting. The 7th Army report says: "Bruyeres will long be remembered, for it was the most viciously fought-for town we had encountered in our long march against the Germans. The enemy defended it house by house, giving up a yard only when it became so untenable they could no longer hope to hold it."

The 442nd's bloodiest single battle followed immediately. The 1st Battalion of the 36th Division's 141st Infantry Regiment was cut off in a heavily wooded section of the Vosges Mountains and was under withering enemy fire. The 442nd was assigned to relieve it. With the 2nd Battalion on the left flank, the 3rd Battalion in the center and the 100th on the right, the *Nisei* began a slow, painful assault through incredibly rugged forestland that had been mined and was dotted with strongpoints. German artillery shells exploded on contact with the trees and showered the troops with lethal shrapnel. Now word was received that the "Lost Battalion" was short of water and medical supplies with many wounded who needed attention. The 442nd was ordered to push on at any cost. After three days of intense fighting, often with grenades and bayonets, the *Nisei* broke through and rescued 211 men—all that remained of the battalion. Then the 442nd's 3rd Battalion pushed on to take the ridge that had been the Lost Battalion's original objective. The 442nd was not pulled out of the line until November

A quiet moment at an advanced aid station, operated by medics of the 2nd and 3rd Battalion of the 442nd Regimental Combat Team, just before the costly push to rescue the Lost Battalion in the Vosges Mountains of southern France in October, 1944. (U.S. Army Photo)

9, when it was sent to the Riviera to rest. In the 25 days of nearly continuous action it had suffered 814 casualties, including 140 dead. A thousand other men already were in hospitals from earlier actions. With nearly 2,000 men hospitalized, the 442nd was at half strength. By then, however, the enemy defenses were shattered, and other elements of the 36th Division had begun the push that took them eventually to the valley of the Rhine. How terribly the 442nd had been hurt is told in the combat team's history: "As a fighting unit, the 442nd was temporarily impotent. In the 3rd Battalion, where casualties had been heaviest, company strengths were fantastically low: Co. I had four riflemen and a light machine-gun section left on the line. Co. K had 17 riflemen and part of a weapons platoon. It was commanded by a buck sergeant, Sergeant Tsutomu Yoshida, who later was commissioned. The strength of the other battalions was correspondingly low."

Dan Inouye tells it more dramatically in his book: "When General Dahlquist (Maj. Gen. John E., commander of the 36th

Nisei infantrymen move up through mud of a heavily forested area in southern France during rescue of the Lost Battalion in October, 1944. (U.S. Army Photo)

The 442nd suffered brutal losses in the Vosges Mountains campaign. Survivors paraded after the battle to honor their dead and wounded comrades. (U.S. Army Photo)

Survivors of the Lost Battalion presented this silver plaque to their Nisei rescuers.

Nisei troops of the 442nd Regimental Combat Team attend a Christian service outside billets in France. Many *Nisei* were Buddhists. (U.S. Army Photo)

Division) called the regiment out for a retreat parade to commend us personally, he is reported to have said to the C.O., 'Colonel, I asked that the entire regiment be present for this occasion. Where are the rest of your men?' And Colonel Pence, as bone-weary as any dogface in the outfit, replied, 'Sir, you are looking at the entire regiment. Except for two men on guard duty at each company, this is all that is left of the 442nd Combat Team.' And there we were, cooks, medics, band and a handful of riflemen, a ragged lot at rigid attention, without a single company at even half its normal strength . . . My outfit, E Company, with a normal complement of 197 men, had exactly 40 soldiers able to march to the parade ground."

Such heroism did not go unnoticed. The men of the 36th Division declared all members of the 442nd "Honorary Texans" and survivors of the Lost Battalion presented a silver plaque to the *Nisei* to express their appreciation.

Rested and reinforced, the 442nd after a relatively quiet holding action in the Maritime Alps during the winter of 1944–45 returned to Italy in the spring in time to play a major part in the last big drive of that campaign. The Allies were now preparing to push the Germans out of all Italy. The western anchor of the Nazi Gothic Line in northern Italy had withstood Allied assaults for five months. The plan was to breach the line elsewhere and the 442nd, by then a part of the 92nd (Buffalo) Division, was assigned to launch a diversionary attack on the seemingly impregnable German positions hewn into the solid rock of sheer peaks. But the diversion turned into something else. After an eight-hour climb at night up a saddle between two strongly fortified peaks, a *Nisei* assault party seized positions behind the German emplacements. Then the 100th Battalion captured the keystone of the German defenses in a 32-minute final assault. Closing in to hand-grenade range, the *Nisei* captured one bunker after another, strongpoints that had resisted long-range artillery fire for months. In less than five days the men who were to be the decoys had turned their diversionary attack into a full-scale breakthrough, and the drive to Genoa was on at full speed. The war was almost over, but for the 442nd, the cost had been devastating.

In seven major campaigns, the 442nd had suffered 9,486 casualties—more than 300 percent of its original infantry strength—

Members of the 442nd Regimental Combat Team, led by the 100th Battalion, parade through ruins of Vada, Italy. (National Archives)

including 600 dead. Some of the men had three Oak Leaf Clusters to attach to the ribbons of their Purple Heart medals.

More than 18,000 individual decorations for valor were won by the men who served with the 442nd. Among them were one Congressional Medal of Honor, 52 Distinguished Service Crosses, one Distinguished Service Medal, 560 Silver Stars and 28 Oak Leaf Clusters in lieu of second medals, 22 Legions of Merit, 15 Soldiers' Medals, some 4,000 Bronze Star Medals and 1,200 Oak Leaf Clusters, 12 French Croix de Guerre and 2 Palms to the Croix de Guerre, and 2 Italian Medals for Military Valor, plus nearly 9,500 Purple Hearts including Oak Leaf Clusters.

As a unit, the 442nd won 43 Division Commendations, 13 Army Commendations, 2 Meritorious Service Unit Plaques, and 7 Presidential Distinguished Unit Citations, the last of which was affixed by President Truman in a rain-drenched ceremony on the White House grounds following a special parade. "You fought for the free nations of the world along with the rest of us," Truman told the *Nisei.* "I congratulate you on that, and I can't tell you how much I appreciate the privilege of being able to show you just how much the United States of America thinks of what you have done. You are now on your way home. You fought not only the enemy, but you fought prejudice—and you won. Keep up that

On their return home in 1946, veterans of the 442nd Regimental Combat Team were reviewed in Washington by President Harry Truman and other top officials. President Truman salutes the colors before pinning on the unit's seventh Presidential Citation. (Wide World Photo)

fight, and we will continue to win—to make this great republic stand for what the Constitution says it stands for: 'The welfare of all the people all the time.' "

A pertinent question at this point is why the men of the 442nd were awarded only one Medal of Honor while 52 received the next highest award, the Distinguished Service Cross. The fact is that a number of *Nisei* were recommended for the Medal of Honor, but in each case somewhere along the line the request was denied and the Distinguished Service Cross was presented instead. At the end of the war no *Nisei* had been awarded a Medal of Honor, and this fact was made known by Mike Masaoka, the 442nd's enthusiastic one-man public relations staff, to Senator Thomas when he visited Italy. Senator Thomas, as chairman of the Military Affairs Com-

An United States Army Transport was named the U.S.S. Sadao S. Munemori in memory of the first *Nisei* to be awarded the Medal of Honor. At right, holding framed portrait of his late brother, is Robert Munemori. Portrait and citation hang in the wardroom of the transport.

mittee, asked that an investigation be made. As a consequence, recommendations for decorations still under consideration were reviewed, and the Medal of Honor was awarded posthumously to Pfc. Sadao S. Munemori. An assistant squad leader of Co. A, 100th Battalion, he died in action on April 5, 1945, near Seravezza, Italy. His citation reads:

"When his unit was pinned down by grazing fire from the enemy's strong mountain defense and command of the squad devolved on him with the wounding of its regular leader, he made frontal, one-man attacks through direct fire and knocked out two machine guns with grenades. Withdrawing under murderous fire and shower of grenades from other enemy emplacements, he had nearly reached a shell crater occupied by two of his men when an unexploded grenade bounced off his helmet and rolled toward his helpless comrades. He arose into the withering fire, dived for the missile, and smothered its blast with his body. By his swift, supremely heroic action, Private Munemori saved two of his men at the cost of his own life and did much to clear the path for his company's victorious advance."

Munemori had been a technical sergeant assigned to intelligence training at Camp Savage. There he asked for transfer to a combat unit even if it meant he had to "take a bust to buck private," and he was permitted to join the 442nd at Camp Shelby. A troop transport was named the U.S.S. *Pvt. Sadao S. Munemori* in his memory.

Until the Vietnam war, where they served with distinction, only one other *Nisei* had won the Medal of Honor. He is Sgt. Hiroshi "Hershey" Miyamura, who served briefly with the 442nd. Recalled into service for the Korean War, he was a member of the 7th Infantry Division when his company was attacked near Taejon-ni the night of April 24, 1951. His citation reads: "Corporal Miyamura, a machine gun squad leader, aware of the imminent danger to his men, unhesitatingly jumped from his shelter wielding his bayonet in close, hand-to-hand combat, killing approximately 10 of the enemy. Returning to his position, he administered first aid to the wounded and directed their evacuation as another savage assault hit the line. He manned his machine gun and delivered withering fire until his ammunition was expended. He ordered the squad to withdraw, while he remained behind to render the gun inoperative. He then bayoneted his way through infiltrated enemy soldiers to a second gun emplacement and assisted in its operation. When the intensity of the attack necessitated the withdrawal of the company, Corporal Miyamura ordered his men to fall back while he remained to cover their movement. He killed more than 50 of the enemy before his ammunition was depleted and he was severely wounded. He maintained his magnificent stand despite his painful wounds, continuing to repel the attack until his position was overrun. When last seen, he was fighting ferociously against an overwhelming number of enemy soldiers."

Miyamura was captured and spent 29 months in a North Korean camp. Only after he was repatriated was it announced he had won the Medal of Honor. President Eisenhower decorated him in ceremonies at the White House in 1954. Miyamura operates a service station in Gallup, N.M.

The annals of *Nisei* military history are replete with tales of similar heroism and it would be an injustice to relate some here and not others. Yet many of them cry for retelling and four have been selected for their general interest. Two of these men died in action and two came home. Two served in Europe and two in Asia. Here, then, are their stories:

On the night of July 5, 1944, the 2nd Battalion of the 442nd infiltrated high ground not far from Livorno, Italy, flanking German positions. When they were discovered the *Nisei* came under heavy attack. Staff Sgt. Kazuo Masuda, a former truck gardener from Santa Ana, California, was manning a forward observation post. He crawled back 200 yards through heavy fire, picked up a mortar tube and ammunition and returned to his post. Using his helmet as a baseplate for the mortar tube, Masuda fired the piece single-handed for 12 hours, throwing back two counterattacks and leaving his position only to go back for more ammunition. Several days later he was killed on patrol along the Arno River when, as the album of the 442nd explains, "he deliberately sacrificed himself so that the men with him could return with valuable information." Masuda's Distinguished Service Cross was presented to his sister, Mary, by Gen. Joseph Stilwell, one of the outstanding generals of World War II, at a special ceremony on the front porch of the Masuda home. Some weeks earlier, when Mary had returned to California from the Gila WRA camp, a delegation of local men had threatened her with bodily harm if she insisted on remaining. General Stilwell, who had become acquainted with *Nisei* intelligence specialists in the China-Burma-India theater, was a charter member of the "pickax club" pledged to come to the aid of Japanese Americans being discriminated against by what he called "barfly commandos." "The *Nisei* bought an awful big hunk of America with their blood," he said. "You're damn right those *Nisei* boys have a place in the American heart, now and forever . . . We cannot allow a single injury to be done them without defeating the purpose for which we fought." Mary Masuda had no more trouble.

Sgt. Frank Hachiya of Hood River, Oregon, a graduate of the Military Intelligence Service Language School, volunteered to be dropped behind Japanese lines on the island of Leyte in the Philippines on an intelligence mission. Invading GIs mistook him for an enemy infiltrator—an ever-present danger facing the *Nisei*—and shot him as he was making his way back to American lines. Although mortally wounded, he delivered maps of the Japanese

Sgt. Hershey Miyamura, second *Nisei* to win the Medal of Honor, is congratulated by President Eisenhower after presentation ceremonies at the White House. Miyamura won the nation's highest honor for heroism in Korea.

defenses to an American officer, and no doubt saved the lives of hundreds of his fellow Yanks. Earlier, Hachiya's name, along with those of other *Nisei*, had been removed from the community honor roll of servicemen in Hood River by the American Legion. But the Army honored Sergeant Hachiya's service to his country with a Distinguished Service Cross, the highest decoration for valor awarded a *Nisei* in the Pacific Theater in World War II.

Staff Sgt. Kenny K. Yasui was born in Fresno, California but was taken to Japan when he was three years old after his mother died. By the time he returned to the United States in 1938, he was an adult with an excellent Japanese education but he could hardly speak English. The Army drafted him in April, 1941, then kicked him out after Pearl Harbor because he was a *Kibei*. Yasui, who stands barely five feet tall, was angry that his loyalty was being questioned. He was even more angry that *Kibei* as a group were being regarded with suspicion, and he vowed to prove his loyalty. When the Army issued a call for linguists, Yasui volunteered and easily passed every test. Yasui was among a small handful of volunteers sent to Burma. Most of them were assigned to Merrill's Marauders where the *Nisei* proved so valuable in the fight for Burma that half were rewarded with battlefield commissions. Yasui was attached to an OWI unit engaged in psychological warfare. Mopping up after the Irawaddy River campaign, Yasui was with a loudspeaker team trying to persuade diehard Japanese troops to surrender. Just when it seemed he would be successful, an American combat unit through some mixup opened fire on the Japanese. Yasui could see the OWI's entire program going down the drain. He knew this would be disastrous so he volunteered to swim out to an island with an officer and two GIs and bring in a group of Japanese holdouts. All four stripped and swam to the island with only their hand weapons. Yasui announced loudly that he was a Japanese colonel working with the Americans and ordered all soldiers to surrender. A Japanese noncom appeared out of the brush with a number of his men, all armed. Yasui was rounding them up and about to disarm them when a Japanese officer sprang from a thicket and ordered the men not to surrender. Yasui shot him. Two of the Japanese committed suicide with a grenade, but Yasui captured sixteen others. He took possession of the dead officer's sword, put the survivors through close-order drill to establish his authority, then boarded a raft and had the prisoners push him back across the river. Yasui, who went on to further distinguished service with OSS operatives in China, was awarded the Silver Star.

Dan Inouye was a chubby-faced eighteen-year-old when he volunteered for military service in early 1943 along with 10,000 other Hawaiian *Nisei*. He matured quickly under fire, and he was barely twenty when he won a battlefield commission. Nine days before the end of the war in Italy he led an assault against a German position on Mount Nebbione. Forty yards from the German bunkers, he stood up and threw a grenade into a machine gun nest, cutting down the crew with his tommy gun, but taking a bullet in the abdomen in return. Ignoring the wound, he charged up the hill

T/3 Kenny Yasui of Los Angeles was discharged from the Army after Pearl Harbor because he was educated in Japan. When the Army called for linguists, Yasui volunteered, was sent to Burma with an Office of War Information unit to wage psychological warfare. He was decorated for swimming out to an island to capture Japanese soldiers. (U.S. Army Photo)

and lobbed two grenades into a second machine gun emplacement. A German fired a rifle grenade from 10 yards' range and it all but tore off Inouye's right arm. He picked up his own grenade with his left hand and killed the German. Inouye directed the final assault which took the ridge, suffering another bullet wound in the right leg before being evacuated. Twenty-five Germans were killed and eight captured in this action. Inouye, who lost his arm, received the Distinguished Service Cross. Earlier he had been awarded the Bronze Star. His hopes of becoming a physician shattered by the loss of his arm, Inouye turned to law, became the first Congressman from Hawaii and was elected to the Senate in 1962. But on his way home in 1945, Capt. Dan Inouye, his empty sleeve pinned to a beribboned tunic, was denied a haircut in a San Francisco barbershop. "We don't serve Japs here," the barber said.

Within a year after the Army opened its ranks to *Nisei* volunteers, full Selective Service rights were restored to them. According to a Selective Service System monograph on special groups, some 33,300 *Nisei*—an astonishingly large figure in view of their total numbers—served in World War II. More than half were from the

Nisei women also served the U.S. Emiko and Rose Tanada were members of the Women's Army Corps. (National Archives)

mainland. They served in sundry ways—in the Women's Army Corps as well as in combat, as nurses and doctors, as therapists and pharmacists, in the merchant marine, as paratroopers and tank corpsmen. General Willoughby in his book, *MacArthur 1941–1951*, reveals that several FBI-trained *Nisei* operatives from Hawaii were sent to the Philippines before the outbreak of war to keep the Japanese population under discreet surveillance. Although he is still not permitted to discuss his activities in detail, Lt. Col. Richard M. Sakakida, commander of the Office of Special Investigations at the Presidio in San Francisco, no doubt was one of these men. In correspondence with the author in late 1968, Colonel Sakakida said he was one of fifteen members of the U.S. Army's undercover Counterintelligence Police in the Philippines in 1941. After the outbreak of war he was used to interrogate Japanese prisoners, translate captured Japanese documents and decipher Japanese military codes. He took part in the surrender of U.S. forces on Bataan, and after the surrender of Corregidor, he was placed in Bilibid Prison and remained in Japanese hands until rescued on September 25, 1945. Another *Nisei*, Sgt. Arthur S. Komori, also of Hawaii, was Gen. Jonathan Wainwright's combat linguist in the futile defense of Bataan until evacuated to Australia on General MacArthur's order.

There were *Nisei* who, inexplicably, escaped segregation and served in combat units like any other Americans. Colonel Paul Sakai, for example, fought as an enlisted man with the first U.S. troops to land in North Africa. He was commissioned and went on to make the Army his career.

And then there was Sgt. Ben Kuroki, the Nebraska farm boy who pleaded to get into the Air Force. He flew 30 missions—five more than required—as a gunner on a Liberator bomber against targets in North Africa and Europe, including the costly raid on the Ploesti oilfields in Romania. Although eligible for rotation to a safe job in the States, he insisted on and received an assignment in the Pacific. He flew 28 more combat missions in B29 bombers, many of them over Tokyo. For his 58 combat missions in two theaters, he was awarded the Distinguished Flying Cross with two Oak Leaf Clusters and the Air Medal with five clusters. Kuroki was one of four brothers who served in World War II. Early in 1944, after returning from Europe, Kuroki addressed the prestigious Commonwealth Club in San Francisco, telling about his war experiences and his two battles—"against the Axis and against intolerance." "They were really the same battle," Kuroki said, "for we will have lost the war if our military victory is not followed by a better understanding among peoples." San Francisco's "establishment" gave the *Nisei* aerial gunner a standing ovation, and many persons feel the tide of public sentiment turned for the Japanese Americans the day Kuroki spoke.

Five of Mrs. Haruye Masaoka's six sons were in combat with the 442nd. Ben Frank died in action in France. The others were Mike, Akira Ike, who suffered 100 percent disability, Henry and Tad. The Masaokas probably were the only American family with five brothers in a single combat unit. However, the record for most sons in service—nine—went to Mr. and Mrs. Ginzo Nakada who were evacuated from Long Beach, California. Yoshinao Nakada served with the Office of Strategic Services; Henry and George with the 442nd; John with military intelligence in Alaska; Saburo, Minoru, James and Yoshio with military intelligence in the Pacific, and Stephen with the language school.

The war took *Nisei* to strange and distant places. Sgt. Hatch

Air Force Gunner Ben Kuroki who flew missions both in Europe and the Pacific, addresses a meeting of the Community Council at Heart Mountain WRA center. (WRA Photo)

Kita of Seattle found himself in Borneo as an interpreter attached to British troops. Akiji Yoshimura of Colusa, California, another of those kicked out of the Army in the early days of the war even though he had never been outside the United States, volunteered when enlistment was reopened. He won a battlefield commission after taking part in five major campaigns with Merrill's Marauders in Burma and was sent to China as head of a detachment of *Nisei* interpreters. There he took part in the ceremonies for the surrender of all Japanese troops in China. Sgt. Fumio Kido was a member of a mercy team that parachuted down on Hoten Prison Camp at Mukden, Manchuria, at the end of the war to rescue American prisoners of war. Lt. Ralph Yempuku, a veteran of OSS projects in Thailand and Indochina, took part in a similar parachute mission to Japanese-held Hainan Island.

Nisei—and *Issei*, too—without uniforms also contributed mightily to the nation's defense. They were the civilian instructors in the

Herbert Miyasaki of Hawaii (left) and Akiji Yoshimura of California with Brig. Gen. Frank Merrill, commander of Merrill's Maurauders in Burma. Nisei were infantrymen as well as interpreters. (U.S. Army Photo)

Military Intelligence Service Language School and the language programs at the University of Michigan and the University of Colorado, employees of the Army Map Service, and civilians behind the scenes in OWI and OSS. Even during the war, *Nisei* announcers and writers beamed psychological warfare propaganda broadcasts to Japan and Japanese-occupied territories from OWI stations on the West Coast.

On June 11, 1963, twenty years after the armed forces were reopened to the *Nisei*, the House of Representatives set aside two hours from its normal routine to pay unprecedented tribute to Japanese American military service in World War II. Twenty-four Congressmen spoke to extoll the record of the *Nisei*, and particularly of the *Nisei* in the states they represented. In the absence of important debate or legislative action, sessions of Congress often

While most Nisei served in the infantry or military intelligence, a few were accepted into other services. Sgt. Masaharu Okinaka (l) and Sgt. Kazuo Komoto (r), admire medals won as radio operators attached to the 20th Bomber Command in India.

are sparsely attended. On that day, 351 members of the House answered roll call. One of them, Charles H. Wilson of California, declared:

"Our treatment of the *Nisei* is a shameful chapter in our national history . . . I think we can say with truth that it was the Japanese American fighting men that proved to our government of that day the loyalty and patriotism of the *Nisei*."

Which was precisely what the *Nisei* had set out to do—to prove that a person of Japanese ancestry seeking freedom and the blessings of liberty was basically no different from Americans of European ancestry. And in this mission, they had succeeded. Never again would their loyalty as a group be challenged.

24

TWO ANGRY IRISHMEN

JAMES PURCELL and Wayne M. Collins are both San Francisco attorneys of Irish descent. Both have a deep and long-time concern for civil rights. Each, almost unknown to most *Nisei*, played a major role in winning their ultimate release from the WRA camps and making possible their return to the West Coast. Both number *Nisei* among their friends. Where they differ is in their attitude toward the Japanese American Citizens League.

Purcell has a high regard for the JACL and a great personal affection and respect for Saburo Kido, its wartime president. In fact, it was Kido who was responsible for Purcell having become involved in a landmark legal case involving the *Nisei*. Collins, on the other hand, told the author he has nothing but "utter detestation for the JACL; they're nothing but a bunch of jackals." Pressed for specifics, Collins said: "The JACL pretended to be the spokesman for all Japanese Americans but they wouldn't stand up for their people. They didn't speak up for the *Issei*. They led their people like a bunch of goddam doves to the concentration camps."

At this juncture, what these two attorneys think of the *Nisei* is not particularly important. The important thing is what they did for the *Nisei* as a consequence of their profound love of democracy and their zealous regard for civil rights, the sanctity of the Constitution, and the inviolability of due process. It would be an error, however, to say they did what they did only because they were, and are, friends of the *Nisei*. Important democratic principles were involved, and particularly for Collins, this created a situation that could not be ignored. Collins' law practice encompasses many kinds of cases. Admiralty law is one of his specialties. But as early as 1929 he entered a case in defense of the right of free speech. He does not agree with the philosophy of Communists or Nazis, but he has gone to court in defense of their rights under the Constitution.

Purcell, as has been reported earlier, was asked by Kido early in 1942 to see what could be done to prevent *Nisei* employees of the state of California from being fired simply because they were of Japanese parentage. Before he could accomplish anything, the evacuation was ordered, and Purcell was appalled and angered when he went to visit some of his clients who were locked up at Tanforan racetrack. Purcell determined then that he would file a writ of *habeas corpus* demanding that the government free the *Nisei* or show cause why they should continue to be kept in custody.

He set out forthwith to build a case. The first step was to send out a questionnaire to the scores of *Nisei* who had been working for the state of California. Their loyalty had been challenged on the basis of their affinity toward Japanese culture. Had they attended Japanese language school? Did they read and write Japanese? Had they ever been to Japan? Did they have dual citizenship? Did their parents subscribe to Japanese language newspapers or belong to Japanese clubs and associations? Under the standards set up by the state civil service commission, a *Nisei* who could answer questions like these negatively was the least likely to be disloyal. Utilizing these standards, Purcell selected a young woman named Mitsuye Endo as his best bet for a test case. Not only could she answer correctly, but she had a brother serving in the United States Army. With her permission Purcell filed a *habeas corpus* petition on her behalf with the federal court in San Francisco in July, 1942.

The petition fell to the lot of Judge Michael J. (Iron Mike) Roche, a crusty, gruff veteran of the bench capable of overawing young lawyers. Purcell at the time was thirty-six years old. Judge Roche made it clear he did not look favorably on accepting such a petition. Civilians should not impede the war effort, he asserted, and the Army must not be attacked in its duty of defending the nation. But Purcell insisted on a hearing, and Judge Roche instructed Purcell to appear the following morning so a time could be set for argument on the petition.

When Purcell appeared the next day, Judge Roche told him to proceed with his argument.

"Your Honor, I understood the hearing this morning was for the purpose of setting a time for argument," Purcell said.

Judge Roche replied that Purcell had understood correctly, and that this was the time.

"He tried to catch me unprepared," Purcell explains with a smile. "Fortunately I had done my homework."

Purcell began to speak at 11 A.M., citing the Constitutional provisions for protecting the rights of citizens and the various precedents that had established those rights. Mitsuye Endo, he argued, by being confined in a War Relocation Center without a hearing, had been deprived unlawfully of the rights guaranteed to her as a citizen of the United States. As he progressed deeper into his argument, Purcell noticed the judge showing increasing interest. At noon Judge Roche interrupted Purcell to ask how much more time he would require. Purcell replied that he thought he could wind up his case in about another half hour. As Purcell remembers it, Judge Roche then said: "When this matter was first brought up, I was of the opinion that it was a frivolous action. I am no longer of that opinion." Turning to the United States attorney, Judge Roche said: "Be prepared to answer when court is resumed at 2 o'clock."

At 2 o'clock the courtroom was half filled with uniformed officers from the Army's judge advocate department. Judge Roche acknowledged their presence with a question: "To what do we owe the honor of the presence of this array of military brass?" The officers had been dispatched posthaste to the hearings to impress on the court just how seriously the Army considered this attack on the evacuation program. Purcell knew many of the men. They had been among his colleagues in San Francisco's legal fraternity before the Army had inducted them. Some of them approached Purcell when a short recess was called in mid-afternoon. One said: "Jim, you know we have one sure way of beating this case." He continued without smiling: "We can have you inducted."

Purcell replied quickly: "I hope you're joking, because I'd hate to have to tell the judge you're trying to intimidate me."

At the close of argument Judge Roche took the matter under advisement. About once a month after that Purcell would make discreet inquiry about the status of his petition on behalf of Mit-suye Endo, and each time he would be told the matter was still under study. Purcell was in no hurry. He realized it would take time for public opinion to change, and a delay would not damage his case. He had reason to be very much aware of public sentiment regarding the evacuation. One of his San Francisco neighbors threatened to shoot him for defending "Japs." At a cocktail party a family friend upbraided him for coming to the aid "of that Jap girl." Purcell corrected her: "We are talking about two different things. I am defending the legal rights of an American citizen who happens to be of Japanese parentage." The woman, Purcell told the author, has not spoken to him since.

In July, 1943, a year after the hearing, Judge Roche finally was ready to announce his decision. He denied the petition; he ruled that the United States Government was acting lawfully when it deprived Mitsuye Endo of her freedom. Purcell was disappointed but not dismayed. The American legal system provides several levels of appeal against a lower court's decision, a system designed to eliminate every possible chance of error, and Purcell promptly asked for a review by the Circuit Court of Appeals. The Circuit Court, stating it "desired instructions" on questions of law, then sent the case without acting on it directly to the attention of the Supreme Court of the United States. Legal machinery moves with majestic deliberateness. The wheels turned ever so slowly as Mitsuye Endo was evacuated from Sacramento to Tule Lake, and when the segregation program got under way, to Topaz in central Utah.

Meanwhile, a somewhat parallel case was making its way through the courts. Its principal was Fred Toyosaburo Korematsu, a native of Oakland and a high school graduate who was working as a ship-yard welder until he lost his job after Pearl Harbor. Korematsu did not want to be evacuated, but for him the issue was not primarily a principle of law. He was in love with a Caucasian girl. He hoped to change his name, remain in his home in San Leandro and marry the girl. When he failed to show up for evacuation, officials arrested him and Korematsu was convicted of remaining in a portion of a military area from which persons of Japanese ancestry had been ordered excluded and hustled off to an Assembly Center. Wayne Collins took his appeal to the Supreme Court.

Oral argument in the Korematsu case was heard October 11 and 12, 1944. The Endo case was heard October 12. Of parenthetical interest is an exchange that took place between Purcell and Mr. Justice Felix Frankfurter. As the justices often do, Frankfurter at the outset asked Purcell, "How did you get here?" meaning what legal steps had been taken before the case came to the attention of the Supreme Court. Purcell was allotted thirty minutes for verbal presentation; he devoted the first ten to a careful step-by-step explanation of the complex legal course that had been followed. Then he stopped, looked directly at Frankfurter and asked the eminent jurist: "Do you follow me? If not, I would be happy to go over this matter again."

Frankfurter smiled faintly at the attorney only slightly more than half his age and murmured, "I do. Proceed."

The decisions in both cases were returned on Monday, December 18, 1944, three years and eleven days after the attack on Pearl Harbor that had started all the trouble.

Korematsu was guilty of remaining in a prohibited area; the nation's highest tribunal recognized the right of the Army to order the exclusion of persons of Japanese ancestry from specific military areas.

Mitsuye Endo was ordered released from WRA custody; under the Constitution she as an admittedly loyal citizen should be free to come and go as she pleased. No one was more delighted than WRA's Dillon Myer, who now had a Supreme Court decision to help him empty the camps.

Because of the long-term significance of these decisions, it is pertinent to review the arguments of several of the justices. In the Korematsu case, Mr. Justice Hugo Black delivered the Court's opinion. He said in part:

"To cast this case into outlines of racial prejudice, without reference to the real military dangers which were presented, merely confused the issue. Korematsu was not excluded from the military area because of hostility to him or his race. He was excluded because we are at war with the Japanese Empire, because the properly constituted military authorities feared an invasion of our West Coast and felt constrained to take proper security measures, because they decided that the military urgency of the situation demanded that all citizens of Japanese ancestry be segregated from the West Coast temporarily, and finally, because Congress, reposing its confidence in this time of war in our military leaders—as inevitably it must—determined that they should have the power to do just this. There was evidence of disloyalty on the part of some, the military authorities considered that the need for action was great, and time was short. We cannot—by availing ourselves of the calm perspective of hindsight—now say that at the time these actions were unjustified."

But the unanimity of the Court on issues relating to wartime treatment of the *Nisei,* as demonstrated in the Hirabayashi and Yasui cases, was shattered by dissenting opinions from three justices, Owen J. Roberts, Frank Murphy and Robert H. Jackson. While all three had agreed that it was constitutional to keep people off the streets at night, they saw a clear violation of Constitutional rights in Korematsu's case.

Mr. Justice Roberts wrote: "It is the case of convicting a citizen as a punishment for not submitting to imprisonment in a concentration camp, based on his ancestry, and solely because of his ancestry, without evidence or inquiry concerning his loyalty and good disposition towards the United States. If this be a correct statement of the facts disclosed by this record, and facts of which we take judicial notice, I need hardly labor the conclusion that Constitutional rights have been violated."

Mr. Justice Murphy wrote: "No adequate reason is given for the failure to treat these Japanese Americans on an individual basis by holding investigations and hearings to separate the loyal from the disloyal, as was done in the case of persons of German and Italian ancestry. It is asserted merely that the loyalties of this group were unknown and time was of the essence. Yet nearly four months elapsed after Pearl Harbor before the first exclusion order was issued; nearly eight months went by until the last order was issued; and the last of these 'subversive' persons was not actually removed until almost eleven months had elapsed. Leisure and deliberation seem to have been more of the essence than speed. And the fact that conditions were not such as to warrant a declaration of martial law adds strength to the belief that the factors of time and military necessity were not as urgent as they have been represented to be.

"Moreover, there was no adequate proof that the Federal Bureau of Investigation and the military and naval intelligence services did not have the espionage and sabotage situation well in hand during this long period. Nor is there any denial of the fact that not one person of Japanese ancestry was accused or convicted of espionage or sabotage after Pearl Harbor while they were still free, a fact which is some evidence of the loyalty of the vast majority of these individuals and of the effectiveness of the established methods of combatting these evils . . .

"I dissent, therefore, from this legalization of racism. Racial discrimination in any form and in any degree has no justifiable part whatever in our democratic way of life. It is unattractive in any setting but it is utterly revolting among a free people who have embraced the principles set forth in the Constitution of the United States. All residents of this nation are kin in some way by blood or culture to a foreign land. Yet they are primarily and necessarily a part of the new and distinct civilization of the United States. They must accordingly be treated at all times as the heirs of the American experiment and as entitled to all the rights and freedoms guaranteed by the Constitution."

Mr. Justice Jackson's dissent points out a fact that has worried many observers—that the Court validated the principle of racial discrimination in an emergency, and that this principle is a "loaded weapon" available even today to anyone who can convince others by whipping up hysteria or by any other device that there is a need to use it again. His opinion asserted:

"I cannot say, from any evidence before me, that the orders of General DeWitt were not reasonably expedient military precautions, nor could I say that they were. But even if they were permissible military procedures, I deny that it follows that they are Constitutional. If, as the Court holds, it does follow, then we may as well say that any military order will be Constitutional and have done with it . . . A military order, however unconstitutional, is not apt to last longer than the military emergency. Even during that period a succeeding commander may revoke it all. But once a judicial opinion rationalizes such an order to show that it conforms to the Constitution, or rather rationalizes the Constitution to show that the Constitution sanctions such an order, the Court for all time has validated the principle of racial discrimination in criminal procedure and of transplanting American citizens. The principle then lies about like a loaded weapon ready for the hand of any authority that can bring forward a plausible claim of an urgent need. Every repetition imbeds that principle more deeply in our law and thinking and expands it to new purposes . . . A military commander may overstep the bounds of constitutionality, and it is an incident. But if we review and approve, that passing incident becomes the doctrine of the Constitution . . ."

In the Endo case, Mr. Justice Douglas read the Court's unanimous opinion, saying in part: "A citizen who is concededly loyal presents no problem of espionage or sabotage. Loyalty is a matter of the heart and mind, not of race, creed or color. He who is loyal is by definition not a spy or a saboteur. When the power to detain is derived from the power to protect the war effort against espionage and sabotage, detention which has no relationship to that objective is unauthorized . . . If we assume (as we do) that the original evacuation was justified, its lawful character was derived from the fact that it was an espionage and sabotage measure, not that there was community hostility to this group of American citizens. The evacuation program rested explicitly on the former ground, not on the latter, as the underlying legislation shows. The authority to detain a citizen or to grant him a conditional release as protection against espionage or sabotage is exhausted at least when his loyalty is conceded . . ."

Mr. Justice Murphy in a concurring opinion declared "racial discrimination of this nature bears no reasonable relation to military necessity and is utterly foreign to the ideals and traditions of the American people. Moreover, the court holds that Mitsuye Endo is entitled to an unconditional release by the War Relocation Authority. It appears that Miss Endo desires to return to Sacramento, California . . . and it would seem to me that the 'unconditional' release to be given Miss Endo necessarily implies 'the right to pass freely from state to state,' including the right to move freely into California."

Thus had the highest court in the land ruled that evacuation had been Constitutional, but conceded that loyal *Nisei* could not be prevented from returning to their homes.

Decisions of the Supreme Court traditionally are announced on Mondays. Because of the many ramifications attending Supreme Court decisions, no one outside the Court is supposed to know what will be said until the announcement is made. But someone leaked word of the Court's decision in the Endo case, or else the Army was possessed of extraordinary prescience, or there was an incredible coincidence, for on Sunday, December 17, one day before the Supreme Court spoke, the War Department announced the mass exclusion orders against Japanese on the West Coast would be revoked. The evacuees were free to go home, the effective date being set at January 2, 1945. Rumor at the time was that one of the justices close to President Roosevelt had notified him the Court would overturn the exclusion order, but it is altogether likely that because the decision affected a national defense measure, the Court felt that the President should be forewarned.

On the same day that the Supreme Court announced its decisions, WRA made it known that regardless of the progress of the war, all its relocation centers would be closed before the end of 1945, and June 30, 1946, was set as the target date for liquidating the entire WRA program.

Actually, the Army and WRA were not entirely unprepared for the Supreme Court's decision. Largely under the prodding of Dillon Myer, three government agencies closest to the evacuation —the War Department, the Department of Justice and the Interior Department (into which WRA had been absorbed)—had agreed in principle by June of 1944 that the time had come to rescind the West Coast exclusion order. But once again politics had reared its ugly head. Myer says: "Someone in the office of the President decided it should not be done before the November election in 1944. Nevertheless we did get the approval of the Army allowing certain selected individual evacuees who applied for permits to return to the West Coast during the fall of 1944. By the time of the announcement on December 17, there were already about 2,000 evacuees in the exclusion area."

The Endo decision was a great personal triumph for Purcell. Although a number of individuals and organizations had filed *amicus curiae* briefs on Mitsuye Endo's behalf (as was done in the Hirabayashi, Yasui and Korematsu cases), Purcell largely had carried the ball alone. "Nobody paid me a cent," he told the author. "I figure the whole thing cost me about $5,000, not counting my time. There were printing bills, travel expenses to Washington and for interviews, stenographic expenses, and the like, but the outcome was worth every bit of the time and effort."

Why did he do it? "I was mad—about how my client was treated and about the way I was treated. I didn't like them trying to surprise me. And an important principle was at stake."

Wayne Collins' fight for Fred Korematsu, supported by the American Civil Liberties Union for Northern California, was also a matter of principle, and he also was never paid for his efforts. "I still feel bitter about the evacuation," he says. "It was the foulest goddam crime the United States has ever committed against a wonderful people." Collins says to this day he has not met Korematsu. And although Purcell had correspondence with Mitsuye Endo and may have seen her when he first went to Sacramento to counsel *Nisei* threatened with discharge, he has no recollection of having met her.

Not long after the Supreme Court decision Purcell happened to be in Judge Roche's courtroom. Iron Mike recognized Purcell, motioned to him just before a recess and said: "Mr. Purcell, I would like to see you a moment." When they were alone, Judge Roche declared: "I see you have overruled me. Congratulations." He thrust out his hand, and the two men exchanged handclasps.

PART THREE

the years of fulfillment

25

JUSTICE IN THE COURTS

NEARLY THREE YEARS of exile from the West Coast ended for Japanese Americans on January 2, 1945. The Supreme Court of the United States had determined that it was a violation of their constitutional rights to keep them in confinement. And the Army, anticipating this ruling, had lifted the bars one day before the black-robed justices sat down to announce their verdict. The Court's logic was difficult to fathom. It had ruled that the military under the circumstances it faced had not infringed on the rights of *Nisei* when it evacuated them from the West Coast. But having suffered this indignity on a racial basis, the *Nisei* were entitled to freedom of movement; the Army must not prevent them from going home.

The Army's original action had been executed with the general approval of a West Coast public that had come to believe Japanese Americans were a danger to the national security. That opinion could no more be changed by the Supreme Court's decision than another of its rulings at a later time could bring about instant de-segregation of Jim Crow schools and lunch counters.

Acceptance would come slowly. It would come as the enormity of the *Nisei's* wartime sacrifices became understood. When in history had an American minority accepted banishment and incarceration as a demonstration of their loyalty? It would come as the significance of their quiet cooperation with the government became understood, as tales of their battlefield heroism became part of the American legend. It would come as the competence, the diligence, the skills of these Americans with Japanese faces in a thousand callings became apparent with the opening of doors to opportunity. It would come as this people, so insignificant in numbers, escaped their Oriental ghettos and found their rightful places in the vigorous stream of American life.

Some 110,000 persons had been evacuated in 1942. By the time the exclusion orders were rescinded only half that number remained in the camps. The others had struck out for freedom. Some had gone into the armed forces. The balance had scattered under WRA's relocation program from Alabama, Arizona and Arkansas to West Virginia, Wisconsin and Wyoming, and even to such unlikely areas as Maine, Mississippi and the Carolinas. Some 43,000 had resettled in just these nine states:

Illinois	15,000
Colorado	6,000
Utah	5,000
Ohio	3,900
Idaho	3,500
Michigan	2,800
New York	2,500
New Jersey	2,200
Minnesota	1,700
Total	42,600

In the main these resettlers liked their new homes. They found job challenges and opportunities that had been unknown on the Coast. Many had no desire to return and reopen the psychological scars of the evacuations. Others in time would be drawn back by ties of business and property, by the attraction of family and friends, or even by the lure of climate and booming economy that pulls an increasing number of Americans westward. But for the moment, return to the Coast was not a pressing matter.

For those still in the camps the Supreme Court decision held greater personal significance. Soon the WRA centers would be closed. Their landlord was urging them to find new accommodations, to locate jobs and rustle up their own meals.

And so the homeward trek started, slowly and hesitantly as compared to the military precision of the Evacuation, for much had changed and much else remained unchanged. In the tension-filled months after the attack on Pearl Harbor there had been some thirty-six authenticated instances of violence against Japanese Americans or their property. The danger of even more widespread violence had been cited as one reason they should be evacuated, and now violence against the returnees resumed without delay. On January 8, 1945, an attempt was made to dynamite a fruit packing shed owned by Japanese Americans in Placer County, California. More than thirty other terrorist incidents followed—shots fired at farmhouses from speeding cars in the dark of night, unexplained fires, a few beatings and any number of telephoned threats from anonymous callers. The war to safeguard the Four Freedoms had made little impression on some elements of America.

There were other problems. The ghettos the evacuees had abandoned in Los Angeles, San Francisco and other cities were filled now with black and brown people who could not be displaced overnight. The Japanese had lived in these ghettos because they were unwelcome elsewhere. Where now could they go?

Heartbreaking sights greeted many of the returnees. Robert Asazawa came home to his eighteen-acre fruit orchard in Placer County which he had left in the care of a tenant. The tenant was gone and most of the trees were dead. Asazawa had no alternative but to pull them out and start over. Yoshimi Shibata went back to his nursery in Mount Eden, California, and found his home in ruins, his 125,000 square feet of greenhouses requiring virtually complete reconstruction due to neglect and abuse by his lessee. The Sugiyama Sporting Goods Store in San Francisco had been broken into and vandalized. The Nichiren Temple in Los Angeles, where 600 families had stored household goods, had been ransacked. George Yanagimachi, whose father had been a pioneer oyster grower in the quiet bays of southwestern Washington, found that his oyster beds had been systematically pirated with a loss of nearly $100,000.

There were many other instances of festering hostility—merchants who refused to sell to the returnees, produce dealers who refused to buy from Japanese farmers, municipal officials who found reasons for delaying or denying business licenses.

But for each of these there were many heartwarming stories of neighbors, teachers, business associates and friends who welcomed the evacuees back into their communities, helped them reestablish their homes, trim the lawns, prune the trees, reopen the shops and pick up the strings of life. WRA employees from the camps and inland cities changed their scene of operations to the West Coast,

Students, Caucasian neighbors and friends ride out to fields with K. Funai, to help restore his Washington farm on his return from WRA camp at end of World War II. (National Archives)

rounding up local support for the returnees, speaking to service clubs and keeping newspapers informed, anticipating trouble and moving swiftly to avert it. In Seattle, when Teamsters Union officials organized a boycott of produce grown by returnees, Harold Fistere arranged for Caucasian friends to drive the trucks while the Japanese sat in the back and pretended to be helpers. In Visalia one night a mass meeting was called in the baseball park to stir up sentiment for keeping the "Japs" from returning. Bob Cullum, who had just been transferred from WRA's Cleveland office, went to the rally to see what was going on. Cullum was recognized by the local congressman and was invited to speak. Cullum climbed on the back of a truck being used for a platform, seized the microphone, and declared he had been sent to Visalia by the United States Government to open an office. His assignment, he said, was to help evacuees to reestablish themselves in their home communities, and anyone with questions was welcome to drop by and ask them. No one bothered to come in. The next few days Cullum called on local welfare and law-enforcement officials to acquaint them with the situation. When evacuees returned to Visalia a short time later in two railroad coaches, a few young hoodlums raced around the depot in their cars but the vigilantes were conspicuously absent.

From Chula Vista, hard by the Mexican border, up along the California coast where the cool winds blow, up through Los Angeles, Santa Barbara, Santa Maria, San Luis Obispo, up through the torrid interior valley—Bakersfield, Delano, Tulare, Hanford, Fresno, Merced—through the flat floodplain of the San Joaquin and the Sacramento, up into the wooded reaches of Oregon and Washington, similar scenes were repeated as the exiles came home. For the *Issei* and *Nisei*, this was a time of rebirth, and for many launching a new life was not easy. This was particularly true of the *Issei* who felt the weight of oncoming years. A new start meant rebuilding a clientele, reinvesting savings that had been eroded by the evacuation and devalued by postwar inflation. The refrigerator that had been sold in panic for $10 had to be replaced by one that cost $200. Like the servicemen who had been away, the evacuees found the American economy had left them far behind. But there was no mustering out pay, no GI Bill to help the evacuees catch up. There was only one thing to do and they did it. They attacked their problems with characteristic determination and vigor, the same kind of single-minded purposefulness that enabled distant cousins in Japan to rebuild a viable nation out of the ashes of defeat.

VJ-Day was an anticlimax for most Japanese Americans. They heard the news of American victory with relief and gratitude rather than elation. Japan's ultimate defeat had been apparent for months; the only questions had been when she would surrender, and how many more lives would be sacrificed before the firing would be halted. Now they could push on with the task of rebuilding their own lives and restoring the world.

Whatever problems the returnees faced, much more serious ones were being encountered by the small minority of evacuees who for a broad variety of reasons had asked for repatriation or expatriation to Japan. Segregated at the Tule Lake center, after Japan's surrender many of them began to have serious doubts about decisions made in disillusionment, bitterness or confusion. A staff of Department of Justice officials was dispatched to Tule Lake to grant hearings to those who wanted to change their minds. Of 3,186 persons who requested interviews, 2,780 were given releases to relocate anywhere in the United States. The officials agreed that there were many mitigating factors, that most of the renunciations had been signed for reasons other than any real loyalty to Imperial Japan.

Overall, a total of 4,724 Japanese Americans left the United States as repatriates or expatriates, categorized as follows:

1,659 aliens repatriated to Japan.

1,949 American citizens, virtually all minors, accompanying repatriate parents.

1,116 renunciants, 930 being between the ages of twenty and thirty-five. These were mostly *Kibei* who had most of their education in Japan.

Dillon Myer observed: "In view of all the bitterness, frustrations and pressures that the 120,000 Japanese Americans were subjected to, it is quite remarkable that less than 4 per cent of the total decided to cast their lot with Japan. Of this limited number, 1,800 were youngsters 18 years of age or under who felt they had no choice except to accompany their parents. The fact that so few renounced in spite of the pressures is a testament to their training and life in America. We believe it is also due in part at least to WRA policies."

One other set of figures is particularly pertinent. In 1959 the Justice Department announced that during the entire war period, including of course the turbulent registration episode in the camps, 5,766 *Nisei* renounced their citizenship, and 5,409 of them subsequently asked that it be returned. This means only 357 failed to apply. As of that date, 4,978 were able to regain their status as citizens—a net loss of 788, meaning that many renunciants who went to Japan succeeded in recovering American citizenship.

By the time WRA finally closed its books, it had spent $160,-037,030. It had cost the Army $56,482,638 just to build the ten relocation centers. Since the Army had spent a grand total of $88,679,716 in the evacuation, the overall cost to the American taxpayer was $248,716,746—nearly a quarter billion dollars in cash outlay on a program that history indicates was far from justified or necessary. There is no way to estimate the long-term economic loss to the evacuees themselves, although the Federal Reserve Bank made an arbitrary estimate of $400,000,000. Nor can a price ever be set on the hearts that were broken, the tears that were shed, the lives disrupted.

Meanwhile, *Nisei* leaders began to realize that the sacrifices of the evacuation would have been in vain if nothing were done to make a repetition of such an outrage impossible. They agreed the time was ripe to attack and eliminate the legal bases for discrimination against the *Issei*. The foremost issue was their right to become naturalized citizens. As citizens the *Issei* would be entitled to equal protection under the law. After that goal was achieved, perhaps it might be wise to launch a drive to eliminate the discriminatory features of American immigration laws. In the quiet of many long nights, Saburo Kido had lain awake planning ways of achieving these objectives. Mike Masaoka, with his persuasive talents and the familiarity he had gained of Washington before going into the Army, played a large part in Kido's planning.

Masaoka, however, was entertaining other ideas. Staff officers who had been impressed by the way he had handled the 442nd's public relations urged him to go into newspaper work after the war. Masaoka had been assured of a job with both the New York *Times* and the New York *World-Telegram*, and he expected to take one of the offers. But he failed to allow for the contagiousness of Kido's dedication.

"Our work is just starting," Kido argued when the two men met after the war. "First, we have to call a national convention and get a mandate for what has to be done. Now get going on the program." Masaoka quickly put aside plans for a newspaper career.

The first postwar convention of the Japanese American Citizens League was held in the spring of 1946 in Denver, where once the *Post* had demanded a "24-hour curfew on all Japs." Kido outlined a program that could be characterized only as audacious. A people only months out of the relocation camps was demanding that Congress give the *Issei* the right to become naturalized citizens.

"We have seen the ultimate in human tragedy," Kido declared. "*Nisei* in the uniform of the United States Army visited their parents in the internment and relocation camps before going overseas. Their parents urged them to be good American soldiers, to fight fearlessly for their country even though their own status in the United States was uncertain, when it was altogether likely that they might be left as people without a country. The *Issei* have earned the right of citizenship. The *Nisei* demonstrated their loyalty with their blood, but in reality they are Americans and this was their duty. The *Issei* made a choice."

JACL leader Saburo Kido (left) and S. Kubo from Gila WRA center attended a conference on inter-racial coordination during the war. (National Archives)

Kido also set as a goal revision of the 1924 immigration law which was discriminatory toward all Asians. World War II had wrought several changes. The door was opened a crack to permit entry of the Chinese who until then had been excluded just like the Japanese. Kido contended the United States must remove all racial discrimination from its immigration and naturalization code. He also set as JACL's objective indemnity from the government for monetary losses suffered in the evacuation.

Many *Nisei* shook their heads in disbelief. The objectives seemed grossly overambitious; the *Nisei* had barely escaped being stripped of citizenship, their enemies had been close to success in their efforts to deport them. And when had anyone ever collected an indemnity from the government? Wasn't it wiser to let well enough alone?

Kido's reply was to propose that Masaoka be dispatched to Washington to lobby for the entire program. He also asked that JACL raise $100,000—an insignificant sum for a national lobby, but the largest any Japanese American organization had ever sought— to finance the campaign. At least one *Issei* thought the budget was inadequate. Keisaburo Koda, pioneer San Joaquin Valley rice grower who had suffered a million-dollar loss as a consequence of the evacuation, urged that the budget be doubled. To supplement fund-raising efforts on the mainland a delegation was sent to Hawaii, and ultimately more than a quarter million dollars was collected.

Masaoka and his wife, Etsu Mineta of San Jose, went back to Washington. He had no idea how to achieve the goals Kido had set and the JACL had adopted. He had no idea how long the job would take, or whether it could be accomplished, but he was anxious to go to work. The Masaokas rented a small apartment, set up a typewriter on a dresser, and were in business.

A professional lobbyist might have launched his campaign with a 10,000-dollar cocktail party in a downtown hotel. Masaoka began by calling on key members of Congress, members of important committees who might be able to help him. Everyone who was acquainted with the Masaokas during this period emphasizes that Mike and Etsu worked as a team, she providing the quiet logistical support in the background while he trudged from office to office, testified at committee hearings, and put over his arguments in behind-scenes meetings. Many doors were closed to him at first, but he found help in unexpected places. A member of the Capitol guard, who had turned Masaoka away when he first came to Washington during the war, remembered him and proved extremely cooperative. Secretaries who saw Masaoka cooling his heels in outer offices day after day began to feel sorry for him, engaged him in conversation, and eventually they would put in a good word for him with their bosses. In time Masaoka became a familiar sight in the halls of the Senate and House office buildings. Lawmakers who never had occasion to talk to him knew him by name. Congressman Walter Judd of Minnesota, a onetime medical missionary in China, took an interest in Masaoka. Congressman Ed Gossett of Texas agreed to talk with Masaoka because he had heard of the 442nd's

A youthful Mike Masaoka happily makes a point during a Congressional hearing on a measure to extend naturalization rights to Japanese citizens. (Vincent A. Finnigan)

rescue of the Lost Battalion, and he became a strong advocate of liberalizing the immigration laws. Sheer persistence paid off in some cases. Masaoka had tried unsuccessfully for weeks to get an appointment with Congressman John Robison of Kentucky, a ranking member of the House Judiciary Committee which was involved with proposed bills for naturalization of *Issei* and evacuation claims. One day Masaoka saw Robison heading for the men's room. Masaoka quickly followed him, moved alongside and engaged him in conversation when he couldn't conveniently get away. Apparently he made an impression, for Robison invited Masaoka to go back to the office with him. In time he became a staunch supporter for the causes Masaoka was pushing.

There were many factors working for the *Nisei*. One was a growing realization that the evacuation had been a ghastly error, and some officials and prominent citizens were anxious to make amends. The pendulum, which had overreacted in one direction, was now swinging in the opposite direction. Another was the *Nisei* war record, a demonstration of loyalty that could not be ignored. One of Masaoka's close associates during this period was Cullum, the former WRA aide, who had joined the staff for the Committee for Equality in Naturalization. "Mike had a remarkable way of giving members of Congress the impression that he was on hand just to help them do the right thing," Cullum says. "He was able never to appear to be forcing anybody or anything. Mike was a prodigious worker, and he had a real talent for accepting advice without losing command of a situation. He soon gained a reputation for complete integrity. When you are playing on the side of the angels, you don't use a marked deck. All Mike had to do was tell the truth. But he told it well."

It is characteristic of Congress, perhaps, that it was able to agree on compensation for the evacuees before it did anything about their human rights. On July 2, 1948, President Truman signed into law the Japanese American Evacuation Claims Act. The evacuees were given until January 3, 1950, to file claims against the government. By that deadline they filed 23,689 claims asking a total of $131,949,176—one-third of the sum the Federal Reserve Bank had estimated they had lost. The amounts asked for broke down this way:

2,413 claims asked for sums of less than $500.

3,385 claims asked for sums between $501 and $1,000.

8,409 claims asked for sums between $1,001 and $2,500.

4,066 claims asked for sums between $2,501 and $5,000.

4,630 claims asked for sums between $5,001 and $100,000.

77 claims were for amounts in excess of $100,000.

The number of claims does not quite total 23,689, but federal records do not explain the discrepancy. At any rate, 60 percent of the claims were for less than $2,500—"pots and pans" claims for loss of household items—and 73 percent were under $5,000.

Predictably, the government was unable to find an easy way to settle these claims. In all of 1950 the Department of Justice heard only 211 claims and agreed to pay 137 of them.

These successful claimants had asked a total of $141,373—an average of $1,030 each. The government agreed to pay them $62,500—an average of $450.

Most appalling of all, it was costing the government about $1,400 per case to decide that a payment of $450 was equitable compensation!

Congress then approved a procedure whereby a "compromise" settlement could be made without lengthy investigation. The Attorney General was permitted to pay three-fourths of the amount of a compensable claim, or $2,500, whichever was the less.

In 1952, 15,354 claims were compromised and settled for a total amount of $18,255,768. The original amount claimed was $46,664,-332. By this time it took only $43.37 in administrative costs to settle an average claim for $773.65.

The final claim was paid late in 1965—more than thirteen years after the evacuation. It was a compromise payment to Ed Koda, son of Keisaburo Koda, and to Mrs. Jean Koda, widow of Ed's brother, William. Their original claim was for $1,210,000. They were paid $362,500, and the Kodas had spent almost that much in litigation.

The Koda case is a classic of fraud and double-dealing by persons who took advantage of the evacuation. Keisaburo Koda and his sons owned and operated the State Farming Co., which owned nearly 4,000 acres of rice land near South Dos Palos in the San Joaquin Valley. Their business was growing, milling and marketing rice. An indication as to the size of the operation can be seen in the fact that State Farm's net profit in 1941 was in excess of $52,000.

This was the business they left in the care of their attorney and others. But when they returned after the evacuation order was lifted, they found most of State Farm's assets had been sold, that the Kodas' stock had been transferred to others, that they had been swindled out of virtually everything. The documentation of their original claim to the government covered some 170 typewritten pages. Only the death of the key principals averted criminal prosecution.

In all, some $38,000,000 was paid out in evacuation claims—less than 10 cents for every dollar lost. Furthermore, claims were made on the basis of 1942 prices and payment was made in inflated post-war dollars. In terms of reduced purchasing power, the evacuees were paid only a nickel in compensation for every dollar they had lost as a direct consequence of the evacuation.

The government could have afforded to be more generous. Many families did not file claims because they could not document their loss; they had no record of furniture purchased, of inventory lost, of seed planted and left unharvested. Only one claimant was ever tried by the Department of Justice for a fraudulent claim, and a jury quickly acquitted the defendant. Justice would have been on the side of trying a large number of those who took advantage of the evacuees.

Masaoka observes: "This was not a generous program. But it represents a major triumph for the evacuees, and the JACL which pushed for compensation, in that Congress recognized the error of the evacuation and the justice of the claims."

Little by little, Congress moved to rectify the human wrongs that could be corrected by legislation. Through an amendment to the Soldier Brides Bill, the Japanese spouses and children of American servicemen were permitted to enter the United States without regard to the Oriental Exclusion Act. Alien Japanese who had lost the right to live in the United States as "treaty merchants" on the outbreak of war were given a stay of deportation, many of them having married American citizens in the interim. Individual members of Congress sponsored more than 200 private bills benefiting specific *Issei* and *Nisei*. Tenure, which had been cancelled as a result of the evacuation, was restored to *Nisei* in federal civil service.

Meanwhile, California itself was forcing a test of the constitutionality of its alien land laws although such a test was not the primary objective. The state legislature appropriated $200,000 to be used in investigating and filing escheat actions in prosecuting alleged violations of the alien land law. In practice this meant that property held by *Nisei* would be seized without payment by the state if it could be proved the land was purchased illegally by an *Issei*. To encourage prosecution, counties were offered one-half of the proceeds when the escheated property was sold. Between 1944 and 1948, some eighty escheat cases were filed. Seven pieces of property were escheated and sold for a total of $57,864 and twelve cases were "compromised" with the defendants settling the action by paying half of the appraised valuation of the land to the state. A total of $231,915 was paid to the state in these actions which amounted to no more than blackmail.

Because of the obvious unfairness of the escheat actions, many defendants chose to defend their land in court. The first of these to go to the United States Supreme Court was the case of *The People v. Oyama*. It involved eight acres of farmland near San Diego. In 1934, Kajiro Oyama, an *Issei*, bought six acres of land in the name of his six-year-old son, Fred Oyama. The purchase price was $4,000 and the deed was recorded in Fred's name. Shortly afterward the father petitioned a Superior Court to be appointed Fred's guardian, stating that Fred owned the six acres. The petition was granted. When Fred was nine years old, his father bought two adjoining acres for $1,500, also in Fred's name. The Oyama family was evacuated in 1942. In 1944, when Fred was sixteen years old, the attorney general of California filed escheat action contending the two parcels of land had been purchased in Fred's name "with intent to violate and evade the alien land law." The San Diego Superior Court ruled in favor of the state. On appeal, the California Supreme Court ruled that the state could constitutionally exclude ineligible aliens from any interest in agricultural land.

The case was appealed to the United States Supreme Court and argument pressed on three grounds: That the alien land law deprived Fred Oyama of the equal protection of the laws and of his privileges as an American citizen; that it denied Kajiro Oyama equal protection of the laws; that the property was seized after expiration of the applicable limitations period.

The U.S. Supreme Court, by a 6 to 3 vote, ruled that the escheat action was unconstitutional in that it denied the defendants equal protection. The decision declared in part: "The cumulative effect, we believe, was clearly to discriminate against Fred Oyama . . . In short, Fred Oyama lost his gift, irretrievably and without compensation, solely because of the extraordinary obstacle which the State set before him. The only basis for this discrimination against an American citizen, moreover, was the fact that his father was Japanese and not American, Russian, Chinese or English . . ."

Not long afterward, two other cases firmly established the unconstitutionality of California's alien land law. The first case involved Sei Fujii, *Issei* publisher of a Los Angeles newspaper, who bought an unimproved city lot and asked title to it. The state sought to escheat the property. The District Court ruled the alien land law "untenable and unenforceable" because it was a violation of the United Nations Charter. The court observed that the Charter, "which, as a treaty, is paramount to every law of every state in conflict with it," specifies that "everyone is entitled to all the rights and freedoms set forth in this Declaration, without distinction of any kind such as race, color, sex, language, religious, political or other opinion, national or social origin, property, birth or other status. Everyone has the right to own property alone as well as in association with others."

The Fujii case was a frontal attack on the alien land law, squarely asserting *Issei* rights. In a second case, *Masaoka v. California*, an effort was made to show that the alien land law abridged the rights of American citizens of Japanese ancestry. Akira Ike Masaoka and his wife, Sumiko, transferred title on an unimproved city lot in Pasadena to Mrs. Haruye Masaoka, an *Issei*. Her five citizen sons, Ike, Henry, Tad, Mike and Joe Grant, proposed to build a home on the property for her use during her lifetime, after which it would revert to the sons. Under the alien land law this gift was illegal. The mother would lose her home and the sons' investment would be escheated to the state. Under the law, this act of charity on the part of the sons—which would be considered meritorious if undertaken by Americans of other racial extraction—would make felons of the five sons. The Masaoka brothers asked: "Can the state of California by statute relegate citizens of the United States to a position inferior to that of other citizens and, in some cases, inferior to aliens, merely because of their racial origin, in the matter of the right to make and enforce contracts; in the matter of providing for the security of persons and property; in the matter of the right to purchase land, sell, hold and convey real or personal property, and in the personal relationship of those citizens to their own parents . . ." Their plea was dramatized by the fact that four of the sons were combat veterans and a fifth son had been killed in the rescue of the Lost Battalion.

The Oyama case established the escheat action as unconstitutional. The Fujii case found the alien land law unenforceable. The Masaoka case finally established the alien land law as unconstitutional. In another key case, *Takahashi v. Fish and Game Commission*, the right of *Issei* to engage in commercial fishing was upheld by the U.S. Supreme Court. California had denied commercial fishing licenses to "aliens ineligible to citizenship" on the pretext that this was a conservation measure. The Supreme Court held that this violated the equal protection clause and conflicted with the federal power to regulate immigration. There is a kinship between the Takahashi and the several land ownership cases in that they have a bearing on the right to make a living. In the Takahashi case the issue was discrimination regarding work in commercial fishing; in the Oyama case ownership of property was also related to livelihood by farming.

Following victory in the Oyama case, JACL was instrumental in persuading the California legislature to appropriate funds to reimburse those whose land had been escheated or who had paid money to effect a "compromise," and subsequently all other escheat cases were dropped. The California alien land law was effectively laid to rest when a State Constitutional Amendment (Proposition 15), an effort to strengthen the law, was defeated by the voters 1,143,-780 to 797,067. The JACL's Anti-Discrimination Committee spearheaded the attack against Proposition 15, and that effort marked the successful beginning of effective political involvement by the *Nisei*. In time the alien land laws of other states, almost all of them patterned after California's, would be struck from the statute books. The JACL might then have rested on its laurels, but now it was firmly committed to press for civil rights legislation regardless of which minority was involved. The organization filed briefs and became otherwise involved in all the hallmark civil rights cases, including the suits that outlawed racially restrictive housing covenants and the order desegregating schools and other public facilities.

After the alien land laws had been eliminated, there was one legislative goal left affecting Japanese Americans directly. It was the one that mattered most—elimination of race as a consideration in naturalization. Mike Masaoka's first objective was a simple congressional resolution to provide naturalization for all persons hitherto denied this privilege because of race. But that was too simple. Some of his friends, in Congress and out, declared naturalization should be tied together with a general overhaul of immigration and naturalization laws. Others were more concerned with doing something for refugees from Europe, and because they feared Congress would be reluctant to act on any measure favoring the Japanese so soon after the war, they wanted to keep the two matters separated. Masaoka explains his position:

"We were willing to accept almost any cooperation with the liberal elements, but we were most concerned that naturalization be granted our parents as early as possible since so many were in the twilight of their lives. Furthermore, if we could secure the repeal of the Japanese exclusion act of 1924, so much the better, for that would be Congressional recognition that the Japanese were 'good enough' to be admitted into our country and, subsequently, to become citizens. It was obvious that if postwar Japan was to emerge as a democratic state, its nationals could not be treated less worthily than the nationals of other countries. So our task was to try to gain our minimum goals while not alienating either the liberals or conservatives to the extent that no legislation would result."

Some Congressmen told Masaoka it was too soon after the war to do anything about naturalization other than to pass a few private bills for worthy individuals. Others suggested citizenship be extended only to parents of *Nisei* soldiers killed in action. Such proposals, of course, were far too restrictive.

In 1950 Congressman Walter H. Judd at JACL's request introduced a simple measure (H.J. Res. 238) that would authorize the naturalization of any qualified alien without respect to race or national origin. The House approved this resolution unanimously, but the Senate voted to limit its application to Japanese nationals then in the U.S. A joint conference committee restored the House language, but added certain "security" amendments that caused President Truman to veto the measure. The House overrode the veto, but the Senate again refused to act. This was the Senator Joe McCarthy era when Congress was seeing Communists under every bed. Citizenship for the *Issei* was denied once again, lost in a controversy over an issue that had no direct bearing on them. The "security" amendments, however, were expanded and subsequently passed as sections of the Internal Security Act of 1950, which became law over another Presidential veto.

Masaoka and his advisers decided to take a new tack—a direct assault on the immigration and naturalization laws. He had found a strong friend in Congressman Francis E. Walter of Pennsylvania.

Gen. Jacob L. Devers presents flag to mother of Pfc. Fumitake Nagato, first *Nisei* to be buried at Arlington National Cemetery. (U.S. Army Photo)

His counterpart in the Senate was Pat McCarran of Nevada. A JACL task force including Tats Kushida, Sam Ishikawa and Joe Grant Masaoka was dispatched to Nevada to talk to McCarran's friends and supporters and ask them to let the Senator know of their interest in a revision of archaic immigration and naturalization laws. The result was the Walter-McCarran Immigration and Naturalization Act of 1952. It provided for repeal of the Oriental Exclusion Act of 1924, extending to Japan and other Asian nations a token immigration quota. It also eliminated race as a bar to natural-

Mike Masaoka, Dean Acheson (later Secretary of State) and Charles A. Horsky, later a presidential assistant, discussing legislation for equality in naturalization and immigration. (Vincent A. Finnigan)

ization. Once again President Truman vetoed the act for reasons not linked to the Japanese. This time Masaoka and others cranked up a determined campaign to override the veto. *Nisei* all over the country were urged to seek editorial support in local newspapers for the measure. Masaoka reminded Texans of the rescue of the "Lost Battalion." Other veterans got in touch with men they had known in uniform and rekindled old memories. A flood of sentiment for the measure poured in on Washington, and Congress passed it over the veto, 278 to 113 in the House, 57 to 26 in the Senate. It was a supreme triumph for Masaoka's generalship.

In recent times there has been confusion over the Walter-McCarran Immigration and Naturalization Act of 1952, and the Internal Security Act of 1950, also known as the McCarran Act. The Internal Security Act of 1950 in its Title II provides for the detention of such persons as there is reasonable ground to believe "will engage in, or probably will conspire with others to engage in, acts of espionage or sabotage" in the event of invasion, declaration of war, or insurrection in the United States in aid of a foreign enemy. Some of these provisions, which make it known as the "concentration camp measure," were also included in the Walter-McCarran Act in 1952 though they were already in the 1950 Internal Security Act.

Masaoka explains: "We favored overriding the Presidential veto on the grounds that since the objectional provisions were already law, and would remain law regardless of whether the veto was upheld or not, we might as well get some good provisions out of the legislation. When the bill that subsequently became the Internal Security Act was first being debated, it did not include so-called Title II, which provides for the detention camps. This was added to the bill over the objections of Senator McCarran. Congressman Sam Hobbs of Alabama was the original author of what became Title II. JACL opposed not only Title II but also Title I, which was directed at controlling alleged subversive activities. In other words, JACL opposed this entire bill and in this respect, we also urged that Truman's veto of this bill be upheld. We were not successful in this particular effort." In 1968 a National JACL Committee to Repeal the Emergency Detention Act was formed to spearhead an attack on Title II. Through a vigorous educational campaign members of the committee drew national attention to the "concentration camp" law and Senator Inouye and Congressman Matsunaga introduced bills for its repeal. Title II was finally repealed in September, 1971, and President Nixon signed the bill in Portland, Oregon, while en route to welcome Emperor Hirohito in Alaska. It is particularly poignant that *Nisei* should have spearheaded the drive to outlaw political internment.

The Walter-McCarran Act was a giant step forward, but it still had shortcomings. U.S. immigration quotas continued to be heavily weighted in favor of north European nations under the so-called National Origins System. Critics charged that the system implemented "the racist theory that immigrants from Western and Northern Europe were superior to those from Southern and Central Europe, and that those from Europe were better than those from Asia and Africa." It also continued to discriminate with token quotas against the peoples of the so-called Asia-Pacific Triangle. These shortcomings were finally eliminated in the new immigration bill signed by President Lyndon B. Johnson in 1965. With the typi-

Proud of their newly acquired citizenship after more than half a life-time in the U.S., a group of *Issei* called on Vice President Nixon in 1953. (Harris & Ewing)

cal Johnsonian flair, he chose Ellis Island in New York harbor for the signing. One of the honored witnesses was Mike Masaoka. The immigration laws now specify that the 350,000 immigrants permitted to enter the United States annually will be admitted on a basis of their skills and relationship to those already here and not on the basis of race, creed or nationality.

Among the *Issei*, passage of the Walter-McCarran Act was the realization of something they had thought impossible. By the hundreds they enrolled in citizenship courses sponsored by churches, JACL chapters and other organizations. They learned that the government of the United States was divided into the executive, legislative and judicial branches; that each state is entitled to two senators but representatives are apportioned on the basis of population; that the Constitution is the basic law of the land and the first ten amendments are known as the Bill of Rights. If they wondered why the rights of their citizen offspring had been abridged in the hysteria of war, they were too polite to ask and too busy studying for their citizenship examinations to challenge the instructor. And in time, tiny old ladies bent by toil, gray-haired old men gnarled by a lifetime of labor, men and women in their sixties and seventies and eighties—usually accompanied by their proud *Nisei* children and even their *Sansei* grandchildren—stood before federal judges and took the oath of allegiance as America's newest citizens. It was a privilege and an honor that had been a long time coming.

26

HAWAII, THE CHANCE THAT WAS OURS

ONE OF THE GREAT inconsistencies—if not mysteries—of World War II is the fact that the Pacific Coast states were cleared of Japanese Americans while the Hawaiian Islands, closer by 2,500 miles to the war zone, were not. Hawaii was the first American territory to be attacked by the Japanese. When the tide of war turned, Hawaii became the staging point for the vast campaigns that ultimately brought the war to an end. These operations were planned in minute detail at CINCPAC (Commander in Chief, Pacific) headquarters at Pearl Harbor. Warships damaged in distant battles were brought back to Pearl Harbor for repairs. Men of the fleets came back to Hawaii for rest and recreation. The wounded were returned for hospitalization and the dead for burial. Hawaii was a bastion of defense and victory, and more than one-third of its 425,000 residents were of Japanese ancestry.

Why were they left on the islands undisturbed? Why were these Japanese Americans permitted to take part in the war effort while those on the mainland were shoved into American-style concentration camps?

There is no simple answer to these questions, for many factors were involved. We shall try to explore some of them in this chapter.

At the outset, it should be explained that there was limited evacuation from the Hawaiian Islands, but it was extremely limited. The FBI special agent in charge in Hawaii, Robert L. Shivers, told a congressional committee that out of a total population of 160,000 persons of Japanese extraction, only 981 were interned or sent to relocation camps on the mainland in the first weeks of the war.

Most of them were *Issei* or *Kibei*. But for many months the freedom of the remaining 159,000 was in jeopardy. On instructions from Washington, detailed plans were drawn up for evacuating some 100,000 of them to the mainland. Even closer to reality was a scheme to concentrate most of Hawaii's Japanese on an outlying island. President Roosevelt said in a memo to Secretary of the Navy Knox that it is an "immediate and present war emergency" to move "most of the Japanese" from Oahu (the island on which Honolulu and Pearl Harbor are located) to one of the other islands, preferably Molokai. Neither step was taken. Ultimately, the Army announced: "The shipping situation and the labor shortage make it a matter of military necessity to keep the people of Japanese blood on the island."

Irony of ironies! The Army also used the words "military necessity" to justify evacuation of the West Coast States. Obviously, it is an all-purpose phrase useful in a variety of situations.

To understand the situation that existed in the Territory of Hawaii in late 1941, it is necessary to review briefly the history of the Japanese in the islands. As we have seen in Chapter 4, shipwrecked Japanese fishermen rescued by American whalers visited Hawaii at various times early in the nineteenth century. The first organized group of contract laborers—141 men (one died en route), six women and one child, arrived on June 19, 1868. They were temporary workers rather than immigrants, recruited by one Kimura Hanbei to labor on Hawaii's sugar plantations. Oddly, not one in the group was a farmer. There were potters, merchants, cooks, tailors, even a barber and blacksmith as well as assorted vagrants picked up off the streets of Yokohama. These Japanese had been told Hawaii was *Tenjiku*, a heavenly place. They discovered a beautiful land, but on the plantations they found themselves little better than slave laborers. Hawaiian law held that a plantation was like a ship at sea, and all hands were subject to the same kind of discipline that seamen faced on sailing vessels.

Koji Ariyoshi, writing in the *Star-Bulletin and Advertiser* of Honolulu, says: "A contract laborer who claimed to be sick but who was considered by the plantation to be able to work was fined —and, if unable to pay, was jailed. The owner of the plantation who won that case posted house rules which said that for taking one stalk of sugar cane, a worker would be fined 25 cents—two days' pay. The same fine applied for curfew violations—smoking, making noise or entertaining visitors after 9 P.M. For each ten minutes that he was late to work, a laborer was fined one-fourth of a day's pay. If he lost, stole or carelessly broke a tool, his wages were deducted to cover the loss."

Within eighteen months seven men had died and many were ill. Whipped by a foreman, twenty of the Japanese retaliated and almost beat him to death. On the whole, however, the Japanese worked diligently and were much desired by plantation owners. When their work contract expired, many of the men and all but one of the women returned to Japan, happy to escape what amounted to bondage. The woman, Tome Ozawa, and her husband Kintaro, became the parents of Arthur Kinzaburo Ozawa, the first *Nisei* attorney in Hawaii. Most of the other men who remained married Hawaiian girls and in Ariyoshi's words, were "assimilated into the Hawaiian community."

These first Japanese to live in Hawaii were known as *Gannen Mono*, or "first year people" because they left Japan in the first year of the Meiji era. Because of the bad reports brought back by the workers, Japan refused to permit any more of its citizens to leave until 1885 when under a treaty with Hawaii, laborers were again permitted to go out on three-year contracts. Even then, however, these laborers were regarded in Japan not as immigrants, but *dekaseginin* (meaning "go-out-earn people"), a concept known even in feudal Japan when men left their native villages for temporary work in another part of the country.

On February 8, 1885, the ship *City of Tokio* arrived in Honolulu with 859 contract laborers, women and children. By 1890 there were some 7,600 Japanese contract laborers on the plantations, and each year saw many new arrivals. The turning point in Hawaii's history of Japanese immigration was 1900 when Hawaii was annexed by the United States as a territory, and the rigorous contract labor system was abolished. Many of the erstwhile contract laborers then made their way to the U.S. mainland. New arrivals thereafter came as free men.

The history of Hawaii is replete with stories of Japanese who rose from humble beginnings as plantation hands to become successful businessmen, merchants, contractors and the like. One of the most financially successful was Kikutaro Matsumoto, who came to Hawaii in 1891 when he was twenty-four years old, and worked in a guano fertilizer plant. In time he became a major building contractor and was considered the first Japanese millionaire by the time he died.

Nisei involvement in Hawaiian politics can be traced back to 1917, several years before the *Nisei* of San Francisco organized their American Loyalty League. In 1917 there were 179 registered voters among the *Nisei* in Hawaii, and Republicans and later the Democrats recruited some of them for membership in their parties. The first *Nisei* candidate for territorial office was James T. Hamada, Republican, who ran unsuccessfully for the House of Representatives in 1922. Four years later Thomas T. Sakakihara, also Republican, ran for the House and lost. Four *Nisei* Republicans sought House seats in 1928—James Moriyama, Sakakihara, Dr. Harry I. Kurisaki and Leslie Nakashima. All were defeated.

But the barrier was finally broken in 1930, about the time substantial numbers of mainland *Nisei* were first beginning to become aware of their political heritage as Americans. Noboru Miyake was elected county supervisor and Tasaku Oka was named to the House. Both were Republicans. And Andy M. Yamashiro, a Democrat, also was elected to the House.

In 1922, the first time a *Nisei* ran for territorial office, *Nisei* voters made up 3.5 percent of the total. In 1930, when three of five *Nisei* candidates were elected, 15.3 percent of all registered voters were *Nisei*. And by 1936, when nine *Nisei* were among Hawaii's ninety-three elected officials—thus claiming 9.7 percent of elective posts—24.9 percent of registered voters were *Nisei*. If they had voted as a racial bloc, they could have pushed many more of their number into office. But the fact is they did not vote as a bloc, and they never have. Their Democratic or Republican sympathies, not race, was the overriding factor.

Surprisingly enough, a number of Hawaii's first *Nisei* went into law although, as one observer notes, they had no models to emulate among their fathers. "It was a time," says George K. Yamamoto, "when the immigrant parents, mostly of village origins and used to conciliation as a mode of coping with interpersonal problems, felt a little uneasy about a profession where one 'took one side in opposition to the other regardless of who was right.'" Arthur Ozawa, son of *Gannen Mono* parents, won his law degree in 1910, but he died seven years later before any other *Nisei* passed the bar. In the 1920's men like Wilfred Tsukiyama, Masaji Marumoto and Robert Murakami became attorneys. Tsukiyama went on to become city and county attorney of Honolulu and chief justice of the State Supreme Court. Marumoto was elected president of the Hawaiian Bar Association in 1954 and two years later became the first *Nisei* justice of the State Supreme Court. Murakami in 1952 was named to the Circuit Court bench.

A few older *Nisei* moved ahead in medicine, business and a variety of other professions, but these were the exceptions. The bulk of the Hawaii *Nisei*, like their counterparts on the mainland, were just ordinary men and women with ordinary ambitions and problems. The main difference between mainlanders and islanders was that the Hawaii *Nisei* were exposed to a culture unique to Hawaii. They were, in fact, part of it. They helped shape a way of life that in the Polynesian tradition was in part langorously informal and easygoing, in part tirelessly hard-working in the Japanese tradition, in part efficient and businesslike in the American tradition.

The sons and daughters of the average plantation worker went to the public schools as well as Japanese language schools. The Hawaii *Nisei* was likely to have a better working knowledge of Japanese than his mainland cousin because it was inevitable that he should be exposed to it more in a population that was one-third of Japanese origin. Because he lived in a polyglot society, chances are that the English he spoke was largely pidgin. Senator Inouye's book tells how he was unable to make a "th" sound and spent much time during his recuperation from battle wounds practicing so he wouldn't say "Hey dere, what's dat?" He learned to say: "A man who aspires to life's heights begins to climb by expressing himself in clear, correct English," rather than, "Guy who want to get ahead bettah talk good."

In the thirties the growing power of *Nisei* in Hawaiian politics—a power that increased rapidly as more and more of them reached voting age—plus the hold they had on the island economy through sheer numbers, was bound to be of concern to persons who thought of Americans only in terms of white men. In 1932 Rear Admiral Yates Stirling, Jr., then Pacific area commander, articulated the doubts of many with these words:

"If these islands were populated, as are the states of our Union, by American citizens, comprised in large measure of the Caucasian race, their allegiance and loyalty to the welfare of the whole nation might not be questioned. But the fact of several claimed unassimilable races predominating in the civil population gives to the situation here a decided element of doubt, if not of actual alarm. We cannot disregard this fact through sentimental or altruistic ideas. The safety of the United States is far too important for us to close our eyes and refuse to appreciate the importance of this fact in the military problem in these islands. The large number of aliens in the Hawaiian Islands is a matter of grave concern to our national government, and years of study by civilian, military, and naval authorities, of the probable attitude of certain of the island-born Orientals has led to the conclusion that but doubtful reliance can be placed upon their loyalty to the United States in the event of war with an Oriental power. The presence of Oriental-language newspapers, of Buddhist temples, of Oriental schools, or Oriental organizations for various purposes, are indicative of the methods by which many of the island-born Orientals are being educated to consider themselves primarily subordinate to the country of their racial origin and tends to lessen to a considerable degree the so-called ties that might bind them to America . . ."

Once again Americans in authority were underestimating the appeal of a democracy, the influence of the American public school system, the attractiveness of the American dream in forging loyalties. It was beyond their comprehension that non-Caucasians who spoke an alien tongue could be good Americans.

Some whites, particularly long-time residents of Hawaii who daily witnessed diverse racial elements living in harmony, had no difficulty accepting Asians as Americans. When Tomekichi Okino of Hilo was named district magistrate in 1934, the first *Nisei* to be appointed to a judicial position in the Territory, the Honolulu *Advertiser* declared editorially:

"There is hardly a better way to bind the young Japanese, the young Americans of Japanese ancestry, to America than to assure them that we are sincere in regarding them as Americans; and the best proof of sincerity is deeds, not words. At the moment persons of Japanese birth or descent compose 40 per cent of our population; rather soon, as the years run, 40 per cent of our citizens will be of

Japanese blood. They are entitled to their share of public appointments, and they will elect their share of elective officials. Diehards —and we have them—should realize those facts and accept them gracefully . . ."

Many did not, and each time statehood for Hawaii was proposed, the spectre of a state whose politics and economy were dominated by Asiatics was dressed up as a reason for blocking the move. This was the situation in the darkening summer of 1941 when the *Nisei*, well aware of their precarious position, were doing everything possible to demonstrate their loyalty. In a five-week campaign late in 1940, more than 30,000 *Nisei* signed a petition asking Secretary of State Cordell Hull to negotiate a simple way for dual citizens to renounce the Japanese citizenship that most of them had acquired unknowingly in infancy. As the months slipped by, the Hawaiian Japanese Civic Association, the United States Japanese Society, the Young Buddhists' Association and other organizations urged their members to buy government bonds, grow more food to make the islands self-sufficient, participate in civil defense activities, and otherwise take part in preparing the islands for the possibility of war.

Six months before the attack on Pearl Harbor, Dr. Shunzo Sakamaki, a member of the University of Hawaii faculty and chairman of the Oahu Citizens Committee for Home Defense, told thousands of *Nisei* at a rally: "We want to carry our full share of the burden of national defense, and tonight we wish to think together how best we may serve our country, to determine what definite steps we can take to uphold and preserve those democratic traditions which represent our nation at its best. We are met tonight also to re-pledge, one with another, our unreserved loyalty to the United States. We do this freely, gladly, proudly . . ."

The United Japanese Society of Honolulu recruited volunteers for service in emergency medical units. Some 800 of them were gathered in the International Theater in Honolulu early Sunday morning to receive certificates of graduation from training courses when the Pearl Harbor attack got under way. Nearly all went directly from the ceremonies to emergency stations. In addition to nearly 4,000 military casualties, more than 300 civilians—most of them of Japanese ancestry—were killed or wounded by bombs and shells. Japanese Americans manned guns to repel the enemy, staffed

medical stations and operated on the wounded in hospitals, fought
fires, directed traffic, patrolled the beaches, transported sailors and
soldiers from the city back to their battle stations. Thousands of
Issei and *Nisei* stood in line to donate blood. When it was rumored
(falsely, it turned out) that two regiments of Japanese paratroops
had landed in the hills, the University of Hawaii R.O.T.C. battalion
—most of whom were *Nisei*—were deployed to engage them and
delay their advance into Honolulu. In this emergency no one hesi-
tated about sending them out to oppose the enemy. The Japanese
Americans distinguished themselves in Hawaii that black day, but
in the confusion and hysteria of the attack and its aftermath, dispatches to the mainland created a totally false impression of sabotage and disloyalty.

While the FBI and military intelligence had been compiling thor-
ough dossiers on individuals considered potentially dangerous, no
opportunity was lost before the outbreak of war to assure the Japanese American population that it had nothing to fear if it remained
loyal. Lt. Gen. Delos C. Emmons, the military governor of Hawaii
repeated this pledge on December 21, two weeks after the attack,
when it had become apparent that the Japanese Americans had behaved magnificently on and after December 7.

There is only one authenticated story of *Nisei* disloyalty, despite
all the rumors, and it is a weird tale. On Pearl Harbor Day a disabled Japanese plane crash-landed on Niihau, a small privately
owned island at the western end of the Hawaiian chain. Hawaiian
villagers, noticing the markings on the plane and suspecting something was amiss, took the pilot captive. There were only two Japanese on the island, an elderly *Issei* named Shintani and a thirty-year-
old *Nisei*, Harada. The pilot somehow talked Harada into freeing
him and helping him in a bizarre plot to seize the island. But when
a big Hawaiian picked up the pilot and crushed his head against a
stone wall, Harada panicked and blew out his brains.

All Hawaii united to repel the Japanese attack on December 7.
But once the danger was over, many whites began to look with
fear and apprehension at neighbors in whose veins coursed the same
blood as that of the enemy. *Nisei* members of the Hawaiian National Guard were disarmed and relieved of their duties, as were
members of the R.O.T.C. battalion. (Some of them organized into
the Varsity Victory Volunteers who under the direction of Army

engineers built roads and bridges, erected barracks, operated repair shops and in many other ways helped the war effort.)

In Washington, meanwhile, top officials were weighing steps that might be taken as a precaution against trouble from the Japanese Americans. About the time General Emmons was trying to reassure them, President Roosevelt's Cabinet agreed in principle that all Japanese aliens should be interned on an island other than Oahu. Secretary of the Navy Frank Knox, who had told the press of widespread "espionage and sabotage" in Hawaii, was the foremost advocate of strong action, and in this he had the support of the President. The responsibility for carrying out such action, however, was the Army's, and General Emmons was acutely aware of the tremendous problems involved.

Emmons had declared martial law in Hawaii, so there would be no legal complications. But he pointed out to his superiors in Washington that large amounts of construction materials would be needed to build shelters for the evacuees, shipping would have to be diverted to transport them and keep them supplied, and troops would be required to guard them. He was already lacking in construction materials, ships and troops. Emmons also declared that the adults among the Japanese American population on Oahu— 98,000 citizens and 20,000 aliens—provided the bulk of Hawaii's skilled labor. If they were moved out, it would be necessary to bring in a comparable amount of help from the mainland.

From Emmons' point of view, the Japanese in the islands were not causing trouble, and they were an important asset to the war effort. He had many things to do, and he was not particularly anxious to become bogged down with the task of moving out a group of civilians en masse. Nonetheless, the issue of removing Japanese from Oahu came up in Roosevelt's Cabinet meetings in late January, 1942, and again in February with Knox urging that they be concentrated on the island of Molokai. The Army countered with a proposal that 100,000 aliens and citizens be taken to the mainland "for internment or resettlement"—but only after the 20,000 dependents of servicemen were brought home. Stimson's notes record that "the President was staggered by this," and no decision was reached.

Obviously the problem was far larger and more complex than the men in Washington had realized. Roosevelt also understood the tremendous political furore he would create if he authorized the relocation of any substantial number of Japanese on the mainland. The Joint Chiefs of Staff then came up with a proposal to move 20,000 of "the most dangerous" aliens and citizens to the mainland. Emmons countered with an estimate that only 1,550 should be evacuated and interned, and so the numbers game with human beings went on. On March 13, the President approved the Joint Chiefs' proposal "to get rid of about 20,000 potentially dangerous Japanese" by sending them to the mainland.

Two weeks later Assistant Secretary of War McCloy went to Hawaii where, despite the Presidential decision, both Army and Navy officers told him they opposed large-scale evacuation to the mainland. They proposed, instead, that the Japanese in Hawaii be treated "as citizens of an occupied foreign country." McCloy seemed to side with this view, and Hawaii officials assumed evacuation would be confined to the 1,550 or so that General Emmons had mentioned.

Knox, however, with the President's backing continued to press for the movement of Japanese from Oahu, and the War Department instructed General Emmons to work out some extensive evacuation proposal to satisfy Roosevelt. Emmons' answer was to suggest a voluntary movement to the mainland of some 5,000 persons of low income who were a drain rather than an asset to the war effort. Later he changed the proposal to make evacuation compulsory for 3,000 low income individuals. Somewhere along the line the objective of evacuating "dangerous" persons had been replaced by an economic factor.

At this late date it is difficult to pinpoint the reason Emmons succeeded in blocking Secretary of the Navy Knox who, with President Roosevelt's support, wanted a drastic evacuation. Emmons was the general in charge of Hawaii. He was doing a good job, and in the end his superiors in Washington must have concluded that he knew what he was up to. And presently, as the war reached deeper and deeper into the western Pacific, any threat of enemy attack on Hawaii vanished and the evacuation issue was permitted to die a quiet death. War Relocation Authority figures show that during the entire war period only 1,875 persons of Japanese ancestry (including the 981 mentioned early in the war by the FBI) were moved from Hawaii to mainland relocation and internment camps.

The fact the Japanese Americans in Hawaii were not evacuated en masse had little to do with their loyalty or lack of it. It was a matter of manpower and logistics, pure and simple. Their skills and energies were needed in Hawaii, particularly on Oahu. The United States did not have the ships necessary to move 100,000 or more of them—plus 20,000 military dependents—to the mainland and bring back an equal number to take their places. Eventually, as so often happens, the problem solved itself while the government debated and procrastinated, and there was no reason to continue the demand for evacuation. Of course, if Hawaii's Japanese Americans had not been loyal, the Army would have moved swiftly and ruthlessly. But given an opportunity to prove their true colors, the Japanese Americans in Hawaii demonstrated that nothing needed to be done to restrict them. On the mainland, where danger of attack was exceedingly remote, the *Issei* and *Nisei* were never given that opportunity.

Meanwhile, as military service was reopened to *Nisei*, those from Hawaii served shoulder to shoulder with mainlanders in Europe and the far Pacific. At home, aliens and citizens alike pitched into the task of transforming Hawaii into a bustling support base for the Pacific war—a staging area for the Army, a repair and refitting base for the Navy, a stepping stone for air units, a bit of home in mid-Pacific for the wounded and weary. Japanese Americans redoubled their efforts to produce sugar, grow vegetables, build ever-expanding military installations, drive the buses, operate the laundries, cook in the restaurants, roll bandages in Red Cross classes and even entertain servicemen on leave. Fishermen who were forbidden to go to sea found jobs in a tuna cannery which was transformed into an aircraft parts assembly and repair plant. *Issei* women met in former Buddhist temples to sew and knit for the Red Cross.

On Memorial Day, 1945, with the war ended in Europe and victory within sight in the Pacific, Hawaii's Governor Ingram A. Stainback dedicated a temporary War Memorial in Honolulu with a speech that included these words:

"Over a test of time Hawaii has proved to the nation and to the world that people of every race and every creed can dwell in harmony in peaceful pursuits. Now, under the strain and stress of war, the question has arisen whether those of alien parents, or alien cultures, of many nations, many races, white, black, brown, yellow, red, can really and truly be knit by a common idealism into a nation, whether they have entered into and really become a part of the warp and woof of the pattern of our national life or whether they are merely a heterogeneous mass of clashing colors. You, William Anderson, Lawrence Murphy, William Kamaka, Shiro Togo, William Goo, George Bergstrom, Ernest Damkroger, Douglas McNair, Kyotoshi Watanabe, Alvin Wong, Ralph Yang, Howard Vierra, and all others listed on this monument have answered that question. Your deaths should silence for all time those preaching racial intolerance—should forever still the tongues of discord that would divide our people."

It was into this atmosphere that the *Nisei* servicemen returned to Hawaii. They had seen a great deal of the world, much of the United States, and experienced a large segment of life in the years they had been away. And some, like Dan Inouye, had come home determined that the old order would be changed. In his book Inouye traces his concern with Hawaii's political future to a talk he had one night in a military hospital with his friend Capt. Sakae Takahashi.

"We ought to have every single right that every single other American has!" Takahashi had exclaimed. "Man, we shed a lot of blood in this war. What was that all about? Was it all wasted?"

And Inouye writes: "What Sakae was saying, and what I came to believe with all my heart and soul, was that the time had come for us to step forward. We had fought for that right with all the furious patriotism in our bodies and now we didn't want to go back to the plantation. Times were changing. The old patterns were breaking down. We wanted to take our full place in society, to make the greatest contribution of which we were capable, not for Hawaii's Japanese Americans, but for Hawaii."

Inouye used his veteran's benefits to study law, as did many other *Nisei* vets. They talked to their friends and wartime buddies to persuade them that the good things they aspired to could be available through political action. And the party they chose was the Democrats. Inouye explains why:

"Before the war, the Republican grip on the territorial legislature had been ironclad. Economic power was still hard-held by the few

Three-fourths of Hawaii's delegation to Congress: From left, Senator Dan Inouye, Representatives Patsy Takemoto Mink and Spark M. Matsunaga.

dominant Caucasian families descended from the missionaries and traders who had organized the Islands' commerce 100 years before and created moneyed empires in banking, wholesaling and ship-ping—the Castles, Cookes, Baldwins, Damons, Athertons, Robin-sons and, most pervasively powerful of all, the Dillinghams. Their economic interests were best defended by the Republican party and their newspapers diligently preached the Republican message and their plantation supervisors hustled the Republican vote."

So the young veterans, idealistic, hopeful, educated through the GI Bill, embraced the Democratic party and set out to make their own kind of Hawaii, working diligently at the grass roots from whence they had sprung. By 1954 the Democrats were firmly in control of the territorial legislature. By 1959 Congress overrode token opposition repeating the old arguments against statehood and voted Hawaii into the union as the fiftieth state. It was a day of celebration. The people of Hawaii in a plebiscite confirmed the step by a vote of 132,773 to 7,971. Dan Inouye was elected first Representative from Hawaii by an overwhelming margin.

Inouye was reelected in 1960. When he ran for and was elected to the Senate in 1962, a comrade in arms from the 442nd, Spark Masayuki Matsunaga, succeeded him in the House. And when Hawaii was given a second seat in the House of Representatives in 1964, Mrs. Patsy Takemoto Mink, the state's first *Nisei* woman attorney, was elected. As this is written, the state of Hawaii has a congressional delegation made up of three men and one woman of Oriental extraction—Senators Daniel K. Inouye, Democrat, and Hiram L. Fong, a Republican of Chinese origin; and Representatives Matsunaga and Mrs. Mink. Although a feeble effort was made to dredge up the racial issue in the 1968 campaign when all three *Nisei* were running—"Hawaii should have an ethnically balanced delegation," some of their opponents said—no one has ever suggested that they represent less than the entire state of Hawaii.

All three served a lengthy political apprenticeship before moving on to Washington. Inouye was the majority leader in the territorial House from 1954 to 1958 and served in the territorial Senate in 1958–59. As a freshman Congressman from the newest state, Inouye quickly came to the attention of Speaker Sam Rayburn and moved up rapidly in Democratic councils. He seconded Lyndon Johnson's nomination in 1964 and made the keynote speech in the Democratic National Convention in 1968. Inouye is a member of the Senate's prestigious Armed Services Committee and the Commerce Committee.

Matsunaga, born in 1916, was commissioned as a second lieutenant in the U.S. Army Reserve after his graduation from the University of Hawaii in June, 1941. He volunteered for active duty in July, served with the 100th Battalion and the 442nd Regimental Combat Team, was wounded twice, and released as a captain with a Bronze Star and various other decorations. He won his law degree at Harvard, served in the territorial legislature from 1954 to 1959 and was candidate for lieutenant governor of Hawaii in 1959. Elected to Congress in 1962, he was named president of the 88th Congress Club and secretary of the House Democratic Steering Committee. He is a member of the Rules Committee which plays a key role in determining what business Congress shall take up.

Mrs. Mink attended Wilson College in Chambersburg, Pa., the University of Nebraska and the University of Hawaii before receiving her law degree from the University of Chicago in 1951. She is married to John Francis Mink and has one daughter. She was elected to the territorial House in 1956, to the Hawaii Senate for the 1958–59 and 1962–64 terms. Mrs. Mink was vice-president of the Young Democrats of America 1957–59. Elected to Congress in 1964, she was chosen secretary of the 89th Congress Club. She was reelected to Congress in 1966 and 1968 and is a member of the Education and Labor Committee and the Interior and Insular Affairs Committee.

The accomplishments of Hawaii *Nisei* in fields other than politics are too numerous to be detailed here. Flourishing in the benevolent postwar climate, they have attained key positions in business, finance and industry, as labor leaders, doctors of medicine, attorneys and horticulturists. In fact, there is hardly a field of endeavor in which they have not distinguished themselves, but two educators require special mention.

The first is Ralph Kiyosaki, state superintendent of schools. When the position opened a few years ago, a committee of educators studied the qualifications of scores of applicants, most of them prominent school administrators from the mainland. Kiyosaki was then superintendent of schools in Hilo, Hawaii's second largest city. A graduate of the University of Hawaii, he had been too busy teaching to complete work on his advanced degrees. Nonetheless, his qualifications rated him at the top. And so Kiyosaki, son of Japanese immigrants, was named to direct the education of Hawaii's future citizens. He since has resigned to enter politics.

The other is Y. (for Yasuo) Baron Goto, vice-chancellor of the Center for Cultural and Technical Interchange Between East and West (better known as the East-West Center) at the University of Hawaii. Goto was seven months old when his father, a rice farmer, moved to Hawaii from Japan with his family in 1902, and became a plantation laborer. Yasuo's first-grade teacher found it difficult to pronounce his name. There was a Baron Goto from Japan in the news about that time. "Your name," the teacher said, pointing to Yasuo, "will now be Baron," and eventually he had it legalized. Goto received his bachelor's degree from the University of Hawaii in 1924 and joined its faculty four years later. Through Army service in World War II—he was forty years old when the war started—he earned the right to become a naturalized citizen. In 1955 he was named director of the extension service of the University of Hawaii's college of tropical agriculture, and vice-chancellor in 1962. Through his work for the Agency of International Development, as a member of the United States Commission on the South Pacific and of the Pacific Science Board of the National

Academy of Science, Goto travels frequently deep into Southeast Asia and the Pacific Trust Territories. He is as much at home in a native village, practicing a unique kind of "chopsticks diplomacy" by sharing local foods and observing local customs, as he is in his book-lined campus office. In the finest sense he is helping to bring together the peoples and cultures of East and West through Hawaii.

On the occasion of the centennial of Japanese immigration to Hawaii, Representative Mink issued a statement that is particularly appropriate as an ending for this chapter. She said:

"The fact which these celebrations must highlight is not the hardships of plantation life nor the ordeal of adapting to a new land, but the astounding acceptance of the notion of freedom, of liberty and of equality, which once enjoyed required that they (the *Issei*) remain in America in order that they might bequeath this heritage to their children.

"We can herald their sacrifices, we can extol the achievements of their descendants and we can take real pride in the accomplishments of these past 100 years; but the thing which stands highest above all these proclamations is the tribute which must be paid to our democracy which made possible every measure of these successes we acknowledge today.

"Exclusion Acts, Yellow Peril laws, miscegenation laws, World War II relocation camps, hate campaigns, arbitrary firings from jobs, housing and employment discrimination; all these were suffered by the Japanese, alien or citizen, during our recent memory.

"Yet the astounding truth is that despite all this, this persecuted minority—classified as 'enemy' during the war—refused to believe that America did not offer them the best opportunities to be free, to be secure, to be prosperous, and to be happy! And so with deliberateness they sought to regain the confidence and trust of a suspicious nation.

"I believe this struggle for acceptance as Americans has been won; and this victory is not ours but belongs to white America for having found that those of the 'yellow' race have the same capacity as they to love their country, to honor and revere its heroes, to fight and die for its honor, and to cherish the blessings of liberty.

"May all of us who have flourished in this land become an emissary of brotherhood and love so that all who still suffer the indignities of the unequal shall have the chance that was ours!"

27

WHEN OPPORTUNITY KNOCKED

ONE BY ONE the barriers vanished for the Japanese Americans—legal barriers, social barriers, barriers that blocked the way to job opportunities. Although it was seldom articulated in this manner, it was as though the nation had been sickened by the evacuation experience and hoped to purge itself.

In time *Nisei* found they could live in virtually any area they could afford in any city, and many of them could afford a great deal. The doors to jobs were not simply opening; *Nisei* were astonished and delighted to find themselves being wooed by employers seeking better engineers or more imaginative designers, more efficient secretaries and more reliable clerks, more knowledgeable buyers and more brilliant laboratory researchers.

It was in this period also that, as though conscience-stricken over past injustices, America became deeply preoccupied with the problems of all minorities. Its concern was focused on the most visible of all, the Negroes. In 1942 the evacuees who were sent to Arkansas had been astonished to find they were regarded as white by the whites and colored by the blacks. The whites insisted the Japanese Americans sit in the front of the bus, drink from the white man's fountain and use the white man's rest rooms even though suspecting their loyalty to the nation. And the blacks embarrassed many a *Nisei* when they urged: "Us colored folks has got to stick together." If there was no middle ground in the South's polarized society of black and white, in the rest of the country a *Nisei* could live as a yellow-skinned American without upsetting too many people, and he also discovered it was not particularly difficult to be accepted into the white man's world. Some *Nisei* wished to forget their Japanese heritage and accomplished it easily. Others made no calculated effort to reject their heritage, but by reason of occupation and environment, found it increasingly harder to cling to that heritage. East of the Rockies it was a rare *Sansei* child who could understand more than a few phrases of the Japanese language. By the same token, however, many *Nisei* women found themselves taking a lively interest in Japanese cultural arts without self-consciousness, an interest shared by many Caucasians. The *Nisei* could also count many more Caucasians among their friends, politically and socially, than ever before. Men like Harold Gordon, a Chicago attorney, became so interested in the *Nisei* after first encountering them during military service that they joined the JACL and served it in many ways.

A people who had been concentrated heavily on the West Coast —and were thus a highly visible target in 1942 without benefit of the economic power which the Japanese in Hawaii had—by 1970 were scattered throughout the United States. California, and Hawaii of course, were home for the greatest number of *Nisei*. But the decennial census showed 1,079 in Alabama, 587 in Arkansas, 359 in Delaware. 1,009 in Iowa, 1,095 in Kentucky, 1,123 in Louisiana, 348 in Maine, 461 in Mississippi, 221 in South Dakota, 134 in Vermont. The 1970 Federal census shows 373,067 persons of Japanese extraction in the 48 contiguous states—213,280 in California alone, plus 217,307 in Hawaii and 916 in Alaska, a total of 591,290.

In the self-centered prewar days the *Nisei* press was quick to note the fact of Japanese Americans living in other than the Pacific Coast States and working at other than the stereotyped *Nisei* occupations. This was considered news. Today there is hardly an occupation—with the exception of professional football and basketball, where a large premium is put on physical size—in which *Nisei* are not involved. A miniature *Who's Who* would be required to list their individual achievements. Every second year, however, the JACL at its conventions presents awards to *Nisei* who have distinguished themselves in a variety of ways, and a review of the accomplishments of these honorees provides a cross-sectional look at the kind of things they are doing. The list is also revealing for the upgrading that has taken place since 1950 (when the awards were first instituted) in the criteria that the *Nisei* apply in selecting their honorees. The first awards were made largely for wartime JACL service. Those in later years have far broader implications. At any rate, here they are by year and site of the convention at which the award was made.

1950, Chicago

MIKE MASAOKA was named *Nisei* of the Biennium for distinguished leadership. His citation reads: "Rarely can a history of one decade of a people be identified with a single individual. But uniquely and unmistakably the history of American citizens of Japanese ancestry during the ten most crucial and tumultuous years of their existence is the story of Mike M. Masaoka. Appointed national secretary of the Japanese American Citizens League in 1941, his statesmanship, courage and vision during the evacuation, relocation and resettlement not only helped guide the organizations and persons of Japanese ancestry through their most difficult years, but also brought him recognition as their outstanding spokesman. Following his discharge from the Army, in which he served with the famed 442nd Regimental Combat Team, he became the national legislative director of the JACL Anti-Discrimination Committee in Washington, D.C. Largely through his vigorous efforts the vast reservoir of goodwill which the *Nisei* veterans won for persons of Japanese ancestry was translated into positive legislation for their common good . . ."

It should be noted parenthetically that some of Masaoka's most effective work—citizenship for the *Issei*, for example, and the change in immigration laws—came after he received his award.

Others recognized for distinguished achievement in 1950 were:

SABURO KIDO: For more than 25 years' service to the JACL. As national president during the war, "his inspiration, his leadership and his personal courage at a time when to be courageous meant facing the cold brutality of personal danger, guided the JACL through its most turbulent hours."

SETSUKO NISHI: In Chicago she "helped set the stage for the acceptance of all persons of Japanese ancestry." Mrs. Nishi served on the Chicago Resettlers Committee, the Welfare Council of Greater Chicago and the Community Fund. She was a director of the People's Forum of Parkway Interracial Community House, organizational secretary of the Chicago Council Against Religious and Racial Discrimination, and "Chicago Mother of the Year" in the field of community service.

Graying and thoughtful, Mike Masaoka is a veteran of Washington campaigns. (Toyo Miyatake Studio)

HITO OKADA: Recognized for leadership as postwar JACL president during which it became a national organization, and for raising funds to keep JACL operating during the war.

LARRY TAJIRI: He built the JACL's weekly organ, *The Pacific Citizen*, into "a newspaper among the most creditable in the realm of the minority press . . . *The Pacific Citizen* has come to be recognized as a distinguished spokesman not only for Japanese Americans, but all minorities . . ."

1952, San Francisco

MINORU YASUI, *Nisei* of the Biennium: "The continuing fight to insure the freedom of man's mind and heart is not always in the darkness of the battlefield; the struggle must sometimes be reaffirmed in the classroom, the home, on the street, and sometimes in the confines of prisons . . ." Yasui was recognized for the sacrifice he made in challenging the legality of the Army's curfew order in 1942, and for his service to JACL as the Denver regional director.

Recognized for distinguished achievement were:

TOMI KANAZAWA: California native living in New York, first *Nisei* singer to appear in a leading role with the Metropolitan Opera

Company and widely recognized nationally and in Europe as a concert performer.

FORD HIROSHI KONNO: Recognized as America's greatest swimmer of his day. He broke numerous records while swimming at Ohio State University, in National AAU and National Collegiate Athletic Association championships, and won the 1,500 meter free-style in the Olympic Games in Helsinki. Konno was born in Hawaii.

K. PATRICK OKURA: Staff psychologist since 1942 at Boys' Town, Nebraska, and president of the Nebraska Welfare Society. In 1959 Okura was appointed chief probation officer of the Douglas County (Omaha) Juvenile Court. Currently he is executive assistant to the director of the National Institute for Mental Health.

BILL HOSOKAWA: Sunday magazine editor of the Denver *Post*. As that newspaper's first foreign correspondent, he covered the Korean war, then appeared before scores of Colorado audiences to tell the story of America's fighting men.

CARL SATO: Mesa, Arizona, farmer and produce dealer named state president of the Arizona Junior Chamber of Commerce.

1954, Los Angeles

HIROSHI HERSHEY MIYAMURA, *Nisei* of the Biennium: The story of how he won the Medal of Honor in Korea is told in an earlier chapter. Miyamura returned to his home in Gallup, New Mexico, after 28 months in a North Korea prison camp and was cited by the United States Junior Chamber of Commerce as one of the "Ten Outstanding Young Men in the United States in 1953."

JOHN F. AISO: First mainland *Nisei* to be named to a judicial post when he was appointed to the Municipal Court in Los Angeles by then Gov. Earl Warren on September 25, 1953. He had served as commissioner in the Superior Court of California for a year previous to the appointment. After serving as a Superior Court judge for ten years, he was named a Justice in the California Court of Appeal in 1968.

DR. MINOL OTA: Veterinarian in Lovell, Wyoming, serving the needs of farmers and ranchers in vast areas of his sparsely populated state.

THE REVEREND JITSUO MORIKAWA: Pastor of an integrated Chicago church.

THOMAS YEGO: Veteran farm and civic leader in Newcastle, California.

Associate Justice John F. Aiso, California Court of Appeals, is highest ranking *Nisei* jurist on the mainland, retired from the U.S. Army Reserve as a colonel. (Toyo Miyatake Studio)

Special recognition awards in the fields of science and industry were also presented to Dr. Harvey A. Itano of Bethesda, Maryland, and George Iwashita of Bloomfield, New Jersey.

1956, San Francisco

George J. Inagaki, *Nisei* of the Biennium: National JACL president during the transition years, 1952–56, president of the Southern California Flower Market, member of the Los Angeles Welfare Council, Southern California Japanese Children's Home, Adoption Bureau, business and community leader.

Jack Murata: Agricultural chemist with the Department of Interior in Washington, D.C., cited for his research in geophysical and spectrographical analyses, fellow in various scientific societies in the United States and Great Britain, director of an agricultural research project for the Brazilian government.

Minoru Yamasaki: Architect from Detroit, Michigan, winner of numerous architectural awards, named by *Time* magazine as among the top ten American architects.

ROBERT SAKATA: Farmer from Brighton, Colorado. Chosen by the United States Junior Chamber of Commerce as "one of America's four outstanding young farmers in 1955," soil conservationist, chairman of the Brighton Agricultural Conference, adviser to Future Farmers of America, officer in the Brighton Junior Chamber of Commerce.

SHIGEO WAKAMATSU: Chemist with the Lever Brothers Co. in Chicago and the company's "Man of the Month" in March, 1955. Wakamatsu was national JACL president in 1959–60.

1958, Salt Lake City

BILL HOSOKAWA, *Nisei* of the Biennium: Assistant managing editor of the Denver *Post*, former president of the American Association of Sunday and Feature Editors.

HARRY AYAO OSAKI: Silversmith from Pasadena, California, whose creations are on display in more than sixty museums. His work was chosen six times by the State Department for display in Europe.

TOMMY KONO: Weightlifter from San Jose, California, holder of Amateur Athletic Union records in 4 divisions and of 22 world and 6 Olympic Games records. He won Olympic gold medals in 1952 and 1956.

TOM SHIMASAKI: Rancher from Lindsay, California, credited with being the one person most responsible for the high status and acceptance of Japanese Americans in Tulare County. Recipient of the Lindsay Community Citizen Award, president of the Y's Men's Club, officer in the Lindsay Chamber of Commerce, Lindsay Farm Bureau, president of Kiwanis, moderator of the First Baptist Church of Lindsay, District Commissioner of the Boy Scouts.

DR. IWAO MILTON MORIYAMA: Chief of the Mortality Analysis Section of the National Office of Vital Statistics in Washington, D.C., consultant to the United Nations, U.S. delegate to conferences in Egypt, Japan, Rome, Switzerland, France and Venezuela.

1960, Sacramento

CONGRESSMAN DANIEL K. INOUYE, *Nisei* of the Biennium: First Congressman from Hawaii, first *Nisei* in Congress.

PAT SUZUKI: Musical comedy star in the Broadway production of *Flower Drum Song*, nightclub and recording artist.

JACL leaders visited Vice President Richard M. Nixon in 1953. Left to right: Mike Masaoka; George Inagaki, then national president; Shig Wakamatsu; Abe Hagiwara; Masao Satow, national director. (Harris & Ewing)

STEPHEN K. TAMURA: County Counsel for Orange County, California, and formerly on the legal staff of the Federal Securities and Exchange Commission in Washington. Subsequently he was named to the California Superior Court bench.

DAVID M. TATSUNO: First *Nisei* on the National Board of the YMCA, chairman of the Pacific Southwest Area Council of YMCAs encompassing five states. Named "Man of the Year" by the Optimists of his home city, San Jose.

THE REVEREND DONALD K. TORIUMI: Moderator of the Los Angeles Presbytery with a membership of 200 churches and 150,-000 communicants in southern California. Also vice-president of the Pasadena Council of Churches, chairman of the Committee on Christian Education of the Los Angeles Presbytery, and a member of the National Committee of the Presbyterian General Assembly on Segregated Presbyteries and Synods.

1962, Seattle

MINORU YAMASAKI, *Nisei* of the Biennium: "By artfully blending his understanding of Japanese art and culture with that of Western architecture, he has attained in his profession a philosophy of humanism which seeks to elevate the dignity of man in his environment, a philosophy dedicated to and consistent with the highest ideals of democracy. His contributions to American and world architecture . . . serve to highlight the distinguished contributions of Japanese Americans to the contemporary American scene." Yamasaki was architect of the Federal Science Pavilion at Seattle's Century 21 Exposition and is creator of the Port of New York Authority's vast World Trade Center on Manhattan's Lower West Side.

DR. KIYO TOMIYASU: Technical director of General Electric's laser laboratory in Schenectady, New York, he is also an authority on radio microwaves and has had 12 patents issued for his original discoveries.

TOM KITAYAMA: Mayor of Union City, California, and owner with his brothers of a nursery that is the largest producer of carnations in the United States.

CAESAR UYESAKA: President of the nonprofit corporation that operates the Santa Barbara Rancheros, a professional baseball farm team of the New York Mets, Santa Barbara's "Father of the Year," commissioner of city recreation, Boy Scout commissioner.

JOHN YOSHINO: On the staff of the Committee on Equal Opportunity, he was loaned by his agency to a special White House task force charged with the difficult mission of eliminating discrimination in places of public accommodation along Route 40 between Washington and New York City.

1964, Detroit

HENRY Y. KASAI, *Nisei* of the Biennium: Technically an *Issei*, he was naturalized in 1952 in Salt Lake City. He is credited with persuading the Utah legislature to erase a number of racially discriminatory laws, notably the ban on miscegenation. He was chosen for the Junior Chamber of Commerce Americanism Award. The Anti-Defamation League of B'nai B'rith cited him "for his dedication to translating democratic ideals into a way of life for all Americans."

DR. THOMAS T. OMORI: "The first United States rocket to the moon will bear the personal imprint of his long years of dedicated service in the field of missiles and high energy propellants." Formerly European manager of Aero Jet General Corp., he was Far Eastern Manager of International Operations at the time of the award. A resident of Pasadena, he is considered one of the nation's top men in the field of lunar probes, rocket propulsion, nuclear energy and ballistic missiles.

REPRESENTATIVE SPARK M. MATSUNAGA: United States Congressman from Hawaii and war hero.

1966, San Diego

CONGRESSWOMAN PATSY TAKEMOTO MINK, *Nisei* of the Biennium: First woman of Asian ancestry to be elected to the United States House of Representatives, first woman in the state legislature of Hawaii, first woman of Oriental extraction to be admitted to the practice of law in Hawaii.

KENJI FUJII: A Hayward, California, flower grower, he was elected president of the American Carnation Society, the first *Nisei* named to that post in the 72-year history of this national trade association. Three-term president of the Northern California Carnation Growers Association, he contributed greatly to the growth of the flower industry in the San Francisco area.

DR. KAZUMI KASUGA: Deputy chief of the Division of Indian Health in the U.S. Public Health Service, he is one of the nation's foremost specialists in tuberculosis control. He has served in various phases of Indian and Alaska native health since 1946 and was awarded the Public Health Service's Meritorious Service Medal.

YOSHIHIRO UCHIDA: Manager-coach of the United States Olympic Judo Team at the Olympic Games held in Tokyo in 1964, chairman of the U.S. Olympic Judo Committee, organizer of the National Collegiate Judo Association, coach of the San Jose State College judo team.

HENRY T. USHIJIMA: Chicago movie producer known for his prizewinning documentary and educational films, member of the board of governors of the Academy of Television Arts and Sciences.

1968, San Jose

NORMAN MINETA, *Nisei* of the Biennium: San Jose city councilman and vice-mayor, Human Relations Commissioner and Housing Commissioner for San Jose. A native of San Jose, he is the first non-Caucasian to serve on the 117-year-old council. Named by the city council to fill a vacancy, he successfully ran for a full term in 1969. In 1971 he defeated 15 rivals to be elected mayor.

GEORGE K. TOGASAKI: A native of San Francisco, he made his home in Tokyo where he became president of the *Japan Times*, English language daily. He was also first chairman of the board of International Christian University in Japan, president of Rotary International with its 600,000 members in 1968–69, a Fellow of the University of California.

DAVID H. FURUKAWA: Research engineer in the desalinization of brackish water for the U.S. Bureau of Reclamation in Denver, and United Nations adviser on a demineralization project in Israel. Since receiving the award he moved to San Diego to become director of research and development for an international firm specializing in membrane filtration processes.

DR. CHIHIRO KIKUCHI: Mathematician, physicist, atomic engineer, he is on the faculty of the University of Michigan at Ann Arbor. His research uncovered the synthetic pink ruby as the ideal material for maser action, making possible current studies in space communication.

DR. JIN H. KINOSHITA: An ophthalmologist who was evacuated from California to Boston, he pioneered research into the formation of "sugar" cataracts and has paved the way toward prevention and treatment of the disease.

1970, Chicago

DR. PAUL I. TERASAKI, *Nisei* of the Biennium: Professor of surgery at the University of California in Los Angeles. His tests for tissue compatibility, to determine whether the recipient's body has a chance of accepting a transplanted organ, played a key role in the first heart transplant operations.

DR. SAMUEL ICHIYE (DON) HAYAKAWA: Canadian-born semanticist, an outspoken champion of Negro rights long before the cause became popular, president of San Francisco State College, author and lecturer on the relationships among psychology, sociology and language, jazz historian.

SHIRO KASHIWA: A Hawaii-born attorney, he served as assistant attorney general in the Department of Justice's Land and Natural Resources Division. Any litigation concerning Federal lands and resources, including environmental problems, came under his jurisdiction. In 1971 Kashiwa was named a justice in the U.S. Court of Claims.

1972, Washington, D.C.

CONGRESSMAN SPARK M. MATSUNAGA, *Nisei* of the Biennium: The award was made chiefly for his role in the repeal of the Emergency Detention Act of 1950, the so-called concentration camp law.

CHARLES C. KUBOKAWA: A scientist and aquanaut, he was cited for his research with NASA's Project Tektite II, studying relationships between man and environment.

DR. MAKIO MURAYAMA: A biological chemist with the National Institute of Health, his research led to great advances in the fight against sickle cell anemia.

These are the men and women who have been recognized with awards. For each of them, there are many others who have done noteworthy things deserving of kudos. It is not possible to mention more than a few, but this volume would not be complete without acknowledging the following:

WILLIAM M. MARUTANI of Philadelphia was the only attorney, outside of counsel for the principals, invited to speak when the Supreme Court of the United States heard the so-called Loving case. Richard P. Loving, a white man, challenged the anti-miscegenation laws of Virginia which refused to recognize the validity of his marriage to a part-Negro, part-Indian woman. Marutani, representing the Japanese American Citizens League, appeared as a "friend of the court" and argued against the law. The Court ruled unanimously that states cannot outlaw marriages between whites and nonwhites.

Another Canadian-born *Nisei* who has made his mark is the REVEREND KENRYU T. TSUJI, bishop of the Buddhist Churches of America with jurisdiction over 59 churches and 49 branches. A naturalized American citizen, he is the first English-speaking priest to hold the top position in the American Buddhist Church.

DR. NEWTON WESLEY of Chicago has played a big part in perfecting plastic contact lenses and popularizing their use. He was a young optometrist, freshly evacuated to the Midwest from Portland, Oregon, when he discovered he was going blind from keratoconus, a mysterious condition in which the cornea grows out like a cone. Ordinary glasses could not help. He reasoned that a contact lens, resting over the cornea and exerting a gentle pressure on it, might arrest the condition and restore normal sight. Contact lenses in 1943 were large, crude and too uncomfortable to wear for more than a few hours at a time. Wesley and his partner, Dr. George Jessen, eventually learned to make a small plastic lens that could be worn comfortably. It not only stopped the deterioration of Wesley's sight but the techniques learned in manufacturing the lens were applied to making lenses for patients with more common eye troubles. Today their lenses are worn all over the world, and much of their earnings have been plowed back into their nonprofit Eye Research Foundation. Born Uyesugi, Wesley changed his name legally when his patients complained they couldn't find him in the directory under the W's.

S. JOHN NITTA of Allentown, Pennsylvania, probably has done as much as anyone to change chicken from a Sunday luxury to an inexpensive source of protein. Utilizing techniques he studied in Japan, Nitta founded the American Chick Sexing School where hundreds of men were taught the demanding science of determining the sex of newborn chicks. An expert can examine from 900 to 1,400 baby chicks per hour and separate males from females with 99 percent accuracy. Female chicks are raised to become egg-layers. Cockerels are sold cheaply to broiler men who put them on special diets and grow them for meat.

In Federal government service, William H. Marumoto is staff assistant to President Nixon, concerned chiefly with recruiting among racial minorities for top-level appointments. Reared among Chicanos in California, Marumoto speaks Spanish fluently ("better than Japanese," he says) and has worked closely with Hispano groups. Perhaps the highest departmental appointee, since Shiro Kashiwa left the Department of Justice, is Dr. Robert Naka, Deputy Undersecretary of the Air Force. These two are among approximately 20 Asian Americans at the decision-making level of Federal service.

The next two are mentioned together because both are artists and they live in Seattle. GEORGE TSUTAKAWA is a sculptor. PAUL HORIUCHI is a painter. Tsutakawa's fountains grace the plazas of countless public buildings and parks. Horiuchi's yearning to create beauty survived years of back-breaking labor with a section gang on the Union Pacific near Green River, Wyoming. After a day's work he used to talk about painting pictures with a young boy who grew up to become Dr. Kayo Sunada, now director of Ridge Home near Denver, Colorado's principal institution for the mentally retarded which is looked on as a model.

Farming continues to attract many *Nisei*. But whereas their

fathers struggled to make a living on five or ten acres, a *Nisei* farm
extending over thousands of acres is no longer unusual. In Glendale, Arizona, nine of the twelve sons of Naomasa Tanita work
together to grow garden vegetables on some 2,200 acres of irrigated
land, harvest it and ship it under the "ta-NEET-ta" label. Shig, the
oldest, was leader of the clan until his death in 1969. Fukutaro
Mizokami went broke in Colorado's Arkansas Valley in the early
days of the century, moved westward to the San Luis Valley and
started over again as a sharecropper. Fukutaro is long dead but his
sons Mike, Sam and Tom, building on the foundations their father
established, are the biggest growers of summer spinach in the nation. At their peak a few years ago they worked 3,500 acres—
nearly six square miles—of vegetables and also have a winter operation in Mexico. James Imatani, another farmer's son, makes a
specialty of providing cucumbers for most of the nation's pickle
packers, dividing his time between Colorado and Texas. James
Kanemoto of Longmont, Colorado, is typical of *Nisei* whose farmland, painstakingly developed by their parents, has been made
fabulously valuable by expanding urban centers. Kanemoto has a
240-acre housing subdivision, another 100 acres zoned for commercial use, apartment houses, a restaurant, a manufacturing plant for
irrigation controls and other interests.

Nisei are making names for themselves in fields that seemed impossible only a few years ago. Thomas T. Yamauchi is the Viking
program manager for the Boeing Company which is working together with General Electric and Hughes Aircraft on a project to
land scientific payloads on Mars by 1973. Yamauchi was chief of
systems engineering and technology on the highly successful Lunar
Orbitor program. Y. Phillip Hayasaka is executive secretary of the
Human Rights Commission in Seattle. Bill Kajikawa, grand old
man of the athletic staff at the University of Arizona, has coached
varsity baseball, basketball and football teams. Yuriko Amemiya,
formerly a dancer with Martha Graham, has a modern dance group
of her own. Hank Shiroma is an airline pilot. Toge Fujihira is a
documentary cinematographer. Francis Takemoto, an educator in
Hawaii, was retired in 1968 as a brigadier general in the U.S. Army
Reserve. Sam Nakagama is a senior economist with the First National City Bank in New York, and few in the arts have not heard
of Isamu Noguchi the sculptor, or George Nakashima the furniture
designer.

Although lagging behind Hawaii *Nisei* in politics, the mainlanders have begun to move in the last few years. They have come a long way since Clarence Arai, the Seattle attorney, made token races for the Washington state legislature in the early 1930's just to show it could be done. The first and only *Nisei* so far to be elected to a state legislature on the mainland is Seiji Horiuchi of Brighton, Colorado. He ran for the 1962–64 term as a Republican in a Democratic district and won comfortably after a vigorous door-to-door campaign. Horiuchi established an excellent record but retired after the one term to go back to his business as an agricultural consultant. On the municipal level, Ken Nakaoka, real estate broker, is mayor of Gardena, a community of some 45,000 in Los Angeles County. Frank Ogawa, wholesale nurseryman, after five years on the Park Commission, was named councilman for the city of Oakland. Several other *Nisei* have been elected mayors of small rural communities, including Harry H. Iseki in Parlier, California, and Ted Hikida in Teton City, Idaho.

In the 1968 election, Grayson Taketa, a 33-year-old *Nisei* Democrat making his first political race polled nearly 74,000 votes to the eight-term Republican incumbent's 156,000 in the race for Congress in California's 10th District (San Benito and part of Santa Clara Counties). Taketa, an attorney, probably will run again. *Nisei* political neophytes also ran for the state legislature in Utah and New York. Raymond S. Uno, a Salt Lake City Democrat, lost his bid for the state senate to the incumbent, 10,105 to 9,958—a margin of just 147 votes. In New York City, Moonray Kojima, Republican, lost 14,571 to 4,171 in the race for a state assembly seat in a strongly Democratic district.

We must mention at least one *Issei*. Virtually all of them, unfortunately, were long past their most vigorous years at the end of World War II, and were satisfied to see the *Nisei* take over the reins. Not so with James Goro Otagiri who came to the United States from Yamanashi Prefecture as a teen-ager in 1917, attended high school in San Francisco and the University of California. At the time the war began, he was employed by the Nippon Dry Goods Company, a San Francisco importing firm. Evacuated to Topaz, Utah, he volunteered and was accepted as an instructor in the Navy's Japanese language school at Boulder, Colorado. At war's end, Otagiri wanted to return to California but lacked capital. He moved to Denver and bought a tiny restaurant for $7,000— with $2,000 representing his entire personal savings and the balance of $5,000 borrowed from friends. Otagiri and his wife worked from 5 A.M. to 11 P.M. every day, learning the business as they went along. They repaid their debt in one year. The second year they cleared $10,000, sold the restaurant and returned to San Francisco. Otagiri went into the business of shipping relief packages to Japan for *Issei* who wanted to help relatives and friends. For five years he assembled packages of clothing, sugar, salt, canned food, medicines—anything needed by the Japanese who were hungry and ragged in defeat. At the end of that time the Japanese economy was on its way back, and Otagiri began to import—china, lacquer, bamboo items, wood block prints, folk art. Today, fifteen years later, Otagiri Mercantile Co., importers and exporters, has offices in San Francisco, Los Angeles, New York, Chicago and Dallas.

"Only in America," says James Otagiri, a tiny man with smiling eyes, "can you make a comeback just by hard work."

It is a sentiment many *Nisei* would echo. Given a chance to prove their capabilities after their humiliating, disillusioning war experience, the *Nisei* quickly demonstrated their mettle. They worked hard, perhaps just a little harder than the next fellow, because they had something to prove, and they not only came back but moved swiftly ahead.

One other thought might be added to James Otagiri's observation. When opportunity knocked, the *Nisei* were ready. At the insistence of their *Issei* parents, they had gone to school for an education—usually at great family sacrifice—even when discrimination had seemed to make such effort pointless. From their parents they also had learned diligence and a sense of responsibility.

When their break came, the *Nisei* had the tools to do the job.

EPILOGUE

"WHAT AM I?" the *Nisei* had asked. *"What is my destiny? What can I do to claim my rightful place in this, my beloved native land?"*

Time has answered some of those questions. Time also has made other answers unnecessary, for the passage of years has a way of healing wounds and righting wrongs.

Item: In the spring of 1942, Buddy Tsuneo Iwata, a graduate of Stanford University, was among some 4,500 Japanese Americans herded into a concentration camp hurriedly hammered together at the fairgrounds in Merced, California. In America, there must be self-government even within a concentration camp. So on May 23, 1942, Buddy Iwata was chosen chairman of a governing body chartered to perform the futile pantomime of self-determination behind barbed wire. Exactly twenty years later Buddy Iwata, by then manager of the Farmers Association in nearby Livingston and secretary of the Allied Grape Growers, the largest wine cooperative in the world, returned to Merced Fairgrounds for a particularly poignant event. That night the citizens of the area installed him as chairman of the board of trustees of the brand new Merced Junior College.

Item: In the fall of 1943 young Paul Hagiya was elected president of the student body of Southwestern College in Winfield, Kansas, where he was studying on a Methodist scholarship. A group of local American Legionnaires considered this outrageous and announced they would correct the situation, by force if necessary. University officials spirited Hagiya out of town for a week as though he were a black suspected of rape and being hidden from a lynch mob. When the Legionnaires' patriotic fervor returned to more reasonable levels, Hagiya was brought back, allowed to resign his student office and resume his studies. Hagiya enlisted in the Army after graduation and served in Europe with the 442nd Regimental Combat Team. Today the Reverend Paul Hagiya is pastor of the Simpson Methodist Church in Denver. Not long ago he served a term as chaplain of the Colorado district of the American Legion.

Such stories are not rare. In San Jose, where once a civic organization called Knights of the Round Table had unchivalrously demanded the ouster of all Japanese from the Santa Clara Valley, a native son named Norman Mineta is the mayor. In Gardena, where the names of seventeen *Nisei* servicemen were removed from the community honor roll, a decorated veteran named Ken Nakaoka is mayor. In Hood River, Oregon, where the American Legion similarly censored the honor roll, Ray Yasui is prominent enough a citizen to have been named to the Oregon State Board of Education.

In Rexburg, a town in southeastern Idaho, the Army Reserve Building is named in honor of a local boy, Pvt. Ichiro Miyasaki who was awarded the Distinguished Service Cross posthumously for extraordinary valor in Korea. As Congressman Ralph R. Harding observed, the people around Rexburg think highly of the Miyasaki family, and not because of Ichiro alone. Four of his brothers, one of whom was permanently blinded, fought for the United States in World War II or Korea. Congressman Compton I. White, also of Idaho, remarked: "Perhaps the greatest single reason that the voters of my state in 1962 went to the polls and overwhelmingly repealed a constitutional prohibition against 'Mongolians not born in this country'—and especially the Japanese parents of our World War II servicemen—voting, serving on juries, or holding public offices, is the outstanding record compiled by the sons of these then ineligible Japanese on overseas battlefields."

The *Nisei*, except for officers who have achieved field grade, are now too old for combat, but their *Sansei* sons are carrying on the tradition of military service. Now, instead of being segregated in the Army, they find a welcome in the Navy, Marines, Air Force and Coast Guard. Many have graduated from the service schools. One of them, Capt. William T. Sakahara, graduate of the Air

Takeshi Yoshihara became the first *Nisei* graduate of the U.S. Naval Academy when he was commissioned a midshipman in 1953. He has risen through the ranks to commander. (U.S. Navy Photo)

Force Academy, can laugh now about a grim incident that proved that a uniform alone still is not a guarantee that a *Nisei* or *Sansei* always will be treated like an American. Captain Sakahara's supersonic fighter-bomber was disabled by enemy fire over Vietnam but he managed to ditch out at sea. The helicopter team that came to his rescue saw his Oriental features and veered away, fearing a fantastic Vietcong trap. Captain Sakahara was pulled up into the helicopter only after he cut loose with a stream of profanity that unmistakably established his American nationality.

Time causes men to change their opinions. General DeWitt, for example, retired to Washington, D.C., where he joined the Japan America Society. When the decorations committee needed help for a social function, this onetime three-star general would volunteer to come down and help string up Japanese lanterns. Perhaps that was a proud man's way of making amends. Fletcher Bowron, who as mayor of Los Angeles was a vigorous advocate of evacuation, was more forthright. At an evacuation claims hearing in 1954, Congressman Usher L. Burdick of North Dakota asked Bowron: "Is it admitted now quite generally that this order of evacuation was the wrong thing to do?" Mayor Bowron replied from the witness stand: "Well, personally, I thought it was the right thing to do at the time; in the light of after events, I think it was wrong, now."

Even the California State Legislature, perennial spawning ground of anti-Japanese legislation, had a change of heart. In February, 1967, the twenty-fifth anniversary of the beginning of evacuation, eight senators joined to present Senate Resolution No. 101. Some of its "whereases" recognized that the Japanese Americans "prevailed over adversity and proved their loyalty and worth by rebuilding their lives after the war," that the *Nisei* "are remarkably successful in all fields of business and the professions," that their accomplishments are "impressive testimony of their home-taught virtues of hard work, thrift, honesty and respect for the law," and that they "have conclusively demonstrated their loyalty and devotion to their country." On the basis of these florid commendations, the Senate resolved that the members take the opportunity "to express their sincere friendship and good will toward the Japanese Americans of California and of the United States, and to wish them continuing prosperity and closer ties with the many nationalities which populate this country, the 'melting pot' of the new world." The resolution was adopted unanimously.

Still, one of California's most powerful advocates of evacuation has yet to be heard from. He is Earl Warren, attorney general of California in 1942, later governor, and appointed Chief Justice of the Supreme Court by President Eisenhower. In a fateful meeting in 1942 Warren, Bowron and Tom Clark strongly urged the necessity of evacuation on General DeWitt. Later, Warren said he had "methods that will test the loyalty" of persons of German or Italian extraction, "but when we deal with the Japanese, we are in an entirely different field . . ." Chief Justice Warren has refused to comment on that segment of his career. At this juncture, perhaps,

THE WHITE HOUSE

WASHINGTON

May 28, 1969

It is an honor and a privilege for me to mark the
one hundredth anniversary of Japanese immigration
to the United States by sending warm greetings to all
who take part in its observance. Beginning with the
early days when emigration of its subjects was made
a capital offense by the Japanese Government, the
history of the development of Japanese emigration to
this country has indeed been encumbered by difficulties — doubtless portrayals of the unfortunate temper
of times now happily long past.

The immigrants from Japan who settled in this country raised civic-minded, law-abiding families, and
became doers and leaders in our communities. They
have enriched our way of life more than any of us can
ever say.

Their industry and integrity, their desire to further
their education and develop their talents; their celebrated bravery aptly reflected in the feats of the 442nd
Infantry Regimental Combat Team which served so
gloriously in the Second World War, their continuing
contributions to science and the arts — for all these,
and many more reasons, Americans of all races,
creeds and walks of life join in saluting our fellow
citizens of Japanese descent.

We sincerely appreciate the great good you have
brought to our shores, and we are proud to acknowledge the many benefits we derive from your continuing national service.

Richard Nixon

the *Nisei* can afford to respect his reluctance and display a little magnanimity. Justice Aiso, the first *Nisei* judge on the mainland, urges such a course. Warren appointed Aiso to the bench as one of his last acts as governor. Aiso feels that Warren's recognition that a *Nisei* was worthy of serving in the judicial system of his beloved state of California was his signal, and it would serve no purpose to press him further.

Time is also responsible for heartwarming changes. Mike Masaoka, who had been warned he would be the first *Nisei* to be hanged when the Japanese won World War II, was summoned to Tokyo in 1968. In special ceremonies at his official residence, Premier Eisaku Sato presented Masaoka with the Order of the Rising Sun, Third Class, one of the highest honors Japan can bestow on a foreigner and a decoration traditionally reserved for septuagenarians in a land where age is revered. Masaoka was fifty-three years old at the time.

That same month the Reverend Jonathan Fujita, Methodist minister and a naturalized American, led eleven elderly *Issei*, wrinkled and bowed with the years, into the offices of the American consulate in the city of Fukuoka. Fujita and his party were on a round-the-world tour. They had visited London and Paris, had been honored with a private audience with the Pope, toured the Holy Land and finally in Japan the mail they had been waiting for caught up with them. In private rooms in the consulate each of the *Issei* completed an absentee ballot, voting for either Richard Nixon or Hubert Humphrey as he desired, sealed the ballot and had it notarized by a consular official. This duty of citizenship fulfilled, they proceeded with their tour of the ancestral land.

The story of Americans with Japanese faces might be ended happily at this point, but there is a bit more to be said. There is another question to be answered: *"What is there about my cultural heritage that sustained me in the time of trial?"*

It is a question that has been given great pertinency by the often unproductive struggles of other minorities to win social respect and economic security. Looking on the extremes of apathy and militancy among Negroes and Hispanos, some *Nisei* from the comfort of their upper middle class homes have been led to ask: "Why can't they pull themselves up by their own bootstraps the way we did?"

To answer adequately would require another book the size of this one, but the key may be found by turning the earlier question into a statement: Something about my cultural heritage sustained me in the time of trial.

Defining that "something" is difficult for a *Nisei*. He is too close to the picture; to try would be like attempting self-psychoanalysis. So we shall turn to others for help. William Petersen, professor of sociology at the University of California at Berkeley, by reason of occupation and race, has been able to make some perceptive observations. Writing in the *New York Times Magazine* in 1966, he noted that every attempt to hamper the progress of Japanese Americans "resulted only in enhancing their determination to succeed." He went on to say that the *Issei* sprang from a culture in which "diligence in work, combined with simple frugality, had an almost religious imperative, similar to what has been called 'the Protestant ethic' in Western culture," and psychologically, they have an "achievement orientation."

Such values, Petersen said, were transmitted from one generation to the next by family and religion. The wishes of any individual counted for less than the good reputation of the family name, and *Nisei* were taught: "Honor your obligations to parents and avoid bringing them shame." This instilled respect of authority and pride of family and culture. Professor Petersen continued:

"A Negro who knows no other homeland, who is thoroughly American as any Daughter of the American Revolution, has no refuge when the United States rejects him. Placed at the bottom of this country's scale, he finds it difficult to salvage his ego by measuring his worth in another currency. The Japanese, on the contrary, could climb over the highest barriers our racists were able to fashion, in part because of their meaningful links with an alien culture. Pride in their heritage and shame for any reduction in its only partly legendary glory—these were sufficient to carry the group through its travail."

Was it, then, an element found deep in the *Nisei's* "Japaneseness" that enabled him to make good in America?

If this is so, then the *Nisei* was not as free of the influence of his heritage as he had believed after making an all-out effort to become American. And this, as it turned out, was not necessarily bad.

WAKAMATSU TEA AND SILK FARM COLONY

SITE OF THE ONLY TEA AND SILK FARM ESTABLISHED IN CALIFORNIA. FIRST AGRICULTURAL SETTLEMENT OF PIONEER JAPANESE IMMIGRANTS WHO ARRIVED AT GOLD HILL ON JUNE 8, 1869. DESPITE THE INITIAL SUCCESS, IT FAILED TO PROSPER. IT MARKED THE BEGINNING OF JAPANESE INFLUENCE ON THE AGRICULTURAL ECONOMY OF CALIFORNIA.

CALIFORNIA REGISTERED HISTORICAL LANDMARK NO. 815

PLAQUE PLACED BY THE STATE DEPARTMENT OF PARKS AND RECREATION IN COOPERATION WITH THE JAPANESE AMERICAN CITIZENS LEAGUE, EL DORADO COUNTY HISTORICAL SOCIETY, AND FRIENDS OF THE CENTENNIAL OBSERVANCE, JUNE 7, 1969.

More pertinent in the overall picture than the *Nisei's* own efforts is white America's attitude toward him. As late as 1967 a public opinion survey conducted in California at the instigation of the Japanese American Research Project revealed that there is still a strong relationship between the image of Japan and the acceptance of Japanese Americans. (The survey also showed that 80 percent of Californians approved evacuation in 1942, and a quarter century later, 48 percent still did!) If this survey is valid, it would mean that the *Nisei* might well suffer a new round of prejudice and discrimination as a result of all-out economic competition between the United States and an increasingly aggressive Japan. Indeed, *Nisei* find that despite their efforts some segments of the American public still are unable to identify them as Americans. Must it be inevitable that when some irritant from Tokyo causes Washington to sneeze, the *Nisei* will run a fever?

There is a futile and fatalistic outlook inherent in this thesis. It holds that the destiny of the *Nisei,* whatever his desires and whatever his efforts, is tied in perpetuity to the land of his ancestors because of white America's racism.

Many *Nisei* are unwilling to accept this thesis. They have sacrificed too greatly, moved too far, accomplished too much not to feel they have a large measure of control over their own destiny, and that although racism continues to exist in America, they are not likely to be susceptible to the more virulent forms. This is no reason for complacency. They know that when the rights of one minority are threatened, the rights of all are endangered.

Wiser and more sophisticated, many Americans now have abandoned the old concept of a national melting pot in which all elements must lose their identity and have adopted the idea of an all-American stew in which each of the ingredients remains identifiable. Under this concept, no minority need be considered an unassimilable clot. Retaining its identity, it nonetheless contributes its particular flavor to the enriching of a more desirable society.

What is there about my heritage that sustained me? What have I and my people contributed to this, my country?

This, then, has been an effort to provide an understanding.

GUIDE TO PRONUNCIATION
OF JAPANESE NAMES

PRONUNCIATION of Japanese words and names is not difficult. There are only three general rules:

Sound each syllable.

Give each syllable equal emphasis.

All vowels take the short sound.

Examples: The author's name, Hosokawa, is pronounced *Hoh-soh-kah-wah*. Hiroshima would be *Hih-roh-shih-mah*. Wakamatsu would be *Wah-kah-mah-tsu*. Masaoka is *Mah-sah-oh-kah*.

The words *Issei* and *Nisei* appear frequently in the text. *Issei* (*Ih-say*) is literally "first generation" but generally is applied to Japanese who immigrated to the United States prior to the Exclusion Act of 1924. *Nisei* (*Nih-say*), literally "second generation," is applied generally to the American-born offspring of Japanese immigrants. The children of the *Nisei* are *Sansei* (*Sahn-say*), literally "third generation."

INDEX